# BASIC LEGAL RESEARCH

# Basic Legal Research

## TOOLS AND STRATEGIES

### SECOND EDITION

## Amy E. Sloan

*Associate Professor of Law*
*Co-director, Legal Skills Program*
*University of Baltimore School of Law*

1185 Avenue of the Americas, New York, NY 10036
www.aspenpublishers.com

Permissions
Aspen Publishers
1185 Avenue of the Americas
New York, NY 10036

Printed in the United States of America

ISBN 0-7355-2779-2

1 2 3 4 5 6 7 8 9 0

**Library of Congress Cataloging-in-Publication Data**

Sloan, Amy E., 1964-
    Basic legal research : tools and strategies / Amy E. Sloan.—2nd ed.
      p. cm.
    Includes index.
    ISBN 0-7355-2779-2
      1. Legal research—United States.   I. Title.
    KF240.S66 2003
    340′.07′2073—dc21

                                                          2002034483

# About Aspen Publishers

Aspen Publishers, headquartered in New York City, is a leading information provider for attorneys, business professionals, and law students. Written by preeminent authorities, our products consist of analytical and practical information covering both U.S. and international topics. We publish in the full range of formats, including updated manuals, books, periodicals, CDs, and online products.

Our proprietary content is complemented by 2,500 legal databases, containing over 11 million documents, available through our Loislaw division. Aspen Publishers also offers a wide range of topical legal and business databases linked to Loislaw's primary material. Our mission is to provide accurate, timely, and authoritative content in easily accessible formats, supported by unmatched customer care.

To order any Aspen Publishers title, go to *www.aspenpublishers.com* or call 1-800-638-8437.

To reinstate your manual update service, call 1-800-638-8437.

For more information on Loislaw products, go to *www.loislaw.com* or call 1-800-364-2512.

For Customer Care issues, e-mail CustomerCare@aspenpublishers.com; call 1-800-234-1660; or fax 1-800-901-9075.

**Aspen Publishers**
**A Wolters Kluwer Company**

*For Bebe*

# Summary of Contents

# Contents

# PREFACE

The second edition of *Basic Legal Research: Tools and Strategies* contains new information on the following topics:

- Citation—The coverage of citation now includes both the *ALWD Citation Manual* (2d ed. 2003) and the *Bluebook* (17th ed. 2000).
- Procedural rules—Chapter 6, on Statutory Research, and Chapter 11, on Developing a Research Plan, now include coverage of court rules of procedure.
- State statutes—Chapter 6, on Statutory Research, also now includes a section of sample pages illustrating the process of state statutory research.
- Electronic research—Chapter 10, on Electronic Legal Research, and the discussions of electronic research in the other chapters have been updated to reflect new developments in electronic research, including electronic subject searching and table of contents searching.

The philosophy and the format of the second edition, however, remain the same as those of the first edition. The genesis of this book was a conversation I had with Todd Petit, a student in my Lawyering Skills class at Catholic University, in the fall of 1994. Todd was working on a research project, and he came to me in frustration and bewilderment over the research process. Over the course of the year, Todd ultimately mastered the skill of legal research. Nevertheless, our conversation that fall caused me to start thinking about how I could teach research more effectively, a process that ultimately culminated in this book.

I do not believe Todd's experience was unique. Mastering a skill is a form of experiential learning—learning that can only be done by doing. And the "doing" aspect necessarily involves periods of trial and error until a person grasps the skill. It is not surprising that this can be frustrating and even bewildering at times.

Having said that, however, even experiential learning has to be built on a base of information. My goal with this book is to provide two kinds of information necessary for students to learn the process of legal research: basic information about a range of research sources and a framework for approaching research projects.

This text provides instruction in a variety of legal research sources, including secondary sources, cases and digests, citators, statutes, federal legislative history, federal administrative regulations, and subject-matter ("looseleaf") services. Each of these sources is described in a separate chapter that includes the following components:

- background information on the source
- step-by-step instructions for print research, including textual explanations, charts, and annotated examples highlighting key features of the source
- an explanation of electronic research tools available for the source
- an explanation of citation rules for the source
- an annotated set of sample pages illustrating the research process for the source
- a checklist summarizing both the research process and the key features of the source.

The range of material in each of these chapters is intended to accommodate a variety of teaching and learning styles. The textual explanations, charts, and checklists can be used for in-class discussions and for out-of-class reference as students are working in the library. In addition, the sample pages illustrating the research process provide both instructional material and a useful summary synthesizing the information on the source from the rest of the chapter.

This text does more, however, than simply explain the bibliographic features of various research sources. It also provides instruction in research as a process, and it does this in two ways. First, Chapter 1 provides an overview of research sources and the research process. By providing a framework for understanding the relationships among different types of legal authority, this chapter sets the stage for a process-oriented introduction to research instruction. Second, Chapter 11 provides a framework for creating a research plan. By setting out a process based on a series of questions students can ask to define the contours of any type of research project, it provides a flexible approach that can be adapted to a variety of assignments. Although Chapter 11 is the last chapter in the text, it can be used whenever students are required to develop a strategy for approaching a research project.

Of course, a comprehensive understanding of legal research requires students to be familiar with both print and electronic research sources. This text explains electronic research in a way that will allow students to develop their computer research skills regardless of whether they learn about electronic research along with print research or as a separate component of the curriculum. Each chapter devoted to an individual research source includes information on the types of electronic research options available for that source. Techniques for conducting computer research, however, appear in a separate chapter, Chapter 10. Chapter 10 can be used in conjunction with other chapters at any point in the course when students begin learning about electronic legal research.

Moreover, the text provides instruction in a wide range of electronic research sources. It discusses research using commercial services such as Westlaw and LexisNexis that are available at most law libraries. But it also covers a range of other electronic research options, including subscription services and material available for free via the Internet. As part of this instruction, the text discusses cost considerations in a way not addressed in other texts so that students can learn to make informed decisions about when to use electronic sources and how to select the best electronic source for any research project.

The following quote from the 1998 film *Zero Effect* aptly summarizes the philosophy of this text. In that film, the main character, a private investigator named Daryl Zero, had this to say about research:

> I can't possibly overstate the importance of good research. Everyone goes through life dropping crumbs. If you can recognize the crumbs, you can trace a path all the way back from your death certificate to the dinner and a movie that resulted in you in the first place. But research is an art—not a science—because anyone who knows what they're doing can find the crumbs: the wheres, whats, and whos. The art is in the whys: the ability to read between the crumbs, not to mix metaphors.[1]

This text seeks to provide students with the skills to find the "wheres, whats, and whos" of legal research—the legal authorities necessary to resolve a research issue—as well as the "whys"—an understanding of research process that is an integral component of students' training in problem-solving skills. I hope this text will prove to be a useful guide to students as they undertake this intellectual challenge.

Amy E. Sloan

January 2003

---

[1]Many thanks to Gonzalo E. Mon, GW Class of 2000, for bringing this quote to my attention.

# Acknowledgments

Many people contributed to the second edition of this book. My thanks here will not be adequate for the assistance they provided. I extend special thanks to Susan B. Koonin for her efforts in obtaining the copyright permissions necessary for the sample pages in the text. John Maclean also provided research assistance. Scott Pagel, Robert Pool, Will Tress, and the other reference librarians at both GW Law School's Jacob Burns Law Library and the University of Baltimore Law Library deserve recognition for their assistance. Lynn Farnan's assistance with a variety of tasks both large and small is gratefully acknowledged. A number of my colleagues at other schools contributed to this project by sharing their experiences in teaching with the first edition, both by communicating with me directly and through anonymous reviews. I am indebted to them for their suggestions. In particular, I would like to thank Maria Perez Crist for her suggestions on researching procedural rules. In addition, I want to thank Dean Gilbert Holmes at the University of Baltimore School of Law for generous financial support.

The people at Aspen Publishers have been incredibly generous with their time and talents. Melody Davies, Elizabeth Kenny, Carol McGeehan, Margaret Rehberger, and their colleagues provided everything from moral support to editorial advice to production assistance. Their guidance and expertise contributed greatly to the content, organization, and layout of the text, and I am grateful for their assistance.

I want to thank my family and friends for their support. My parents, Matt and Sharon Sloan, and my brother, Dr. Thomas W. Sloan, were constant sources of encouragement. A community of good friends and kindred spirits supported this project on an energetic level. And most of all, thanks go to Peggy Metzger, my strength and inspiration in all I do.

I would be remiss if I limited my acknowledgments to those who assisted with the second edition of the text because much of what appears here originated in the first edition. In particular, I would like to acknowledge Susan Dunham, Carli Masia, Herb Somers, Robert Walkowiak III, and Michelle Wu for their work on the first edition of the text.

I would also like to acknowledge the publishers who permitted me to reprint copyrighted material in this text:

**For computer screen shots retrieved using Netscape**     Netscape browser window © 2002 Netscape Communications Corporation. Used with permission. Netscape Communications has not authorized, sponsored, endorsed, or approved this publication and is not responsible for its content.

**For computer screen shots retrieved using Internet Explorer™**     Screen shots reprinted by permission from Microsoft Corporation.

**Figure 3.1**     Index to Am. Jur. 2d
Reprinted with permission from Lawyers Cooperative Publishing, *American Jurisprudence,* 2d Ed., General Index (1999), p. 8.

**Figure 3.2**     Am. Jur. 2d main volume entry under False Imprisonment
Reprinted with permission from Lawyers Cooperative Publishing, *American Jurisprudence,* 2d Ed., Vol. 32 (1995), p. 46.

**Figure 3.3**     Am. Jur. 2d pocket part entry for False Imprisonment
Reprinted with permission from Lawyers Cooperative Publishing, *American Jurisprudence,* 2d Ed., Vol. 32 (1998), p. 7.

**Figure 3.4**     Treatise main volume entry for False Imprisonment
Reprinted with permission from Oscar S. Gray. Fowler V. Harper, Fleming James, Jr., & Oscar S. Gray, *The Law of Torts,* 2d Ed., Vol. 1 (1986), pp. 284–85. © 1986 Oscar S. Gray. Special thanks to Professor Gray for his forebearance and assistance.

**Figure 3.5**     ILP index entry
Reprinted with permission from The H.W. Wilson Company, *Index to Legal Periodicals,* Vol. 31 (1992), p. 269. © 1992 The H.W. Wilson Company.

**Figure 3.6**     CLI index entry
Cumulative Subject Index, Vol. 2 (1991–1995), p. 1858, from *Current Law Index,* by Gale Group, © 1999 Gale Group. Reprinted by permission of the Gale Group.

**Figure 3.7**     LegalTrac citation list
From *LegalTrac,* by Gale Group. Reprinted by permission of the Gale Group.

**Figure 3.8**     Starting page of an A.L.R. Annotation
Reprinted with permission from Lawyers Cooperative Publishing, *American Law Reports,* 3d Ser., Vol. 97 (1980), p. 688.

**Figure 3.9**   Later page of an A.L.R. Annotation
Reprinted with permission from Lawyers Cooperative Publishing, *American Law Reports,* 3d Ser., Vol. 97 (1980), p. 693.

**Figure 3.10**   Section 35 of the *Restatement (Second) of Torts*
© 1965 by The American Law Institute. Reprinted with permission, *Restatement (Second) of the Law of Torts,* 2d Ed., Vol. 1, § 35 (1965), p. 52.

**Figure 3.11**   Entry under § 35 in the Appendix to the *Restatement (Second) of Torts*
© 1995 by The American Law Institute. Reprinted with permission, *Restatement (Second) of the Law of Torts,* 2d Ed., Appendix through June 1994, §§ 1–309 (1995), p. 132.

**Figure 3.12**   ULA entry for the Uniform Absence as Evidence of Death and Absentees' Property Act
Reprinted with permission from West Group and National Conference of Commissioners on Uniform State Laws (NCCUSL), *Uniform Laws Annotated,* Vol. 8A (1993), pp. 5–6. The text of the Act and any comments are © 1939 by NCCUSL.

**Figure 3.14**   A.L.R. Index
Reprinted with permission from Lawyers Cooperative Publishing, *American Law Reports,* Index E–H (1992), p. 320.

**Figure 3.15**   A.L.R. Annotation
Reprinted with permission from Lawyers Cooperative Publishing, *American Law Reports,* 3d Ser., Vol. 97 (1980), pp. 688–89.

**Figure 3.16**   A.L.R. Annotation
Reprinted with permission from Lawyers Cooperative Publishing, *American Law Reports,* 3d Ser., Vol. 97 (1980), pp. 690–92.

**Figure 3.17**   A.L.R. Annotation
Reprinted with permission from Lawyers Cooperative Publishing, *American Law Reports,* 3d Ser., Vol. 97 (1980), p. 693.

**Figure 3.18**   Pocket part accompanying an A.L.R. volume
Reprinted with permission from Lawyers Cooperative Publishing, *American Law Reports Supplement,* 3d Ser., Insert in Back of Vol. 97 (Aug. 1997), p. 101.

**Figure 3.19**   Table of Contents, *Restatement (Second) of Torts*
© 1965 by The American Law Institute. Reprinted with permission, *Restatement (Second) of the Law of Torts,* 2d Ed., Vol. 1, §§ 1–280 (1965), p. XII.

**Figure 3.20**   *Restatement (Second) of Torts* § 35
© 1965 by The American Law Institute. Reprinted with permission, *Restatement (Second) of the Law of Torts,* 2d Ed., Vol. 1, §§ 1–280 (1965), pp. 52–53.

**Figure 3.21**   Appendix volume, *Restatement (Second) of Torts*
© 1995 by The American Law Institute. Reprinted with permission, *Restatement (Second) of the Law of Torts*, 2d Ed., Appendix Volume through June 1994, §§ 1–309 (1995), title page.

**Figure 3.22**   Appendix volume, *Restatement (Second) of Torts*
© 1995 by The American Law Institute. Reprinted with permission, *Restatement (Second) of the Law of Torts*, 2d Ed., Appendix through June 1994, §§ 1–309 (1995), p. 132.

**Figure 3.23**   Appendix volume, *Restatement (Second) of Torts*, pocket part
© 1998 by The American Law Institute. Reprinted with permission, *Case Citations to the Restatement of the Law*, Cumulative Annual Pocket Part for Use in 1998, §§ 1–309 (1998), p. 44.

**Figure 4.2**   Geographic boundaries of the federal courts of appeals
Reprinted with permission from West Group, West's *Federal Reporter*, 3d Ser., Vol. 124 (1997), inside cover.

**Figure 4.5**   Excerpt from *Popkin v. New York State*
Reprinted with permission from West Group, West's *Federal Reporter*, 2d Ser., *Popkin v. New York State*, 547 F.2d 18–19 (2d Cir. 1976).

**Figure 4.6**   Beginning of the West topic for Innkeepers
Reprinted with permission from West Group, West's *Federal Practice Digest*, 4th Ser., Vol. 63 (1991), p. 1.

**Figure 4.7**   Case summary under the Innkeepers topic, key number 10.1
Reprinted with permission from West Group, West's *Federal Practice Digest*, 4th Ser., Vol. 63 (1991), p. 4.

**Figure 4.12**   Excerpt from the Descriptive-Word Index
Reprinted with permission from West Group, West's *Federal Practice Digest*, 4th Ser., Descriptive-Word Index, Vol. 98 (1992), p. 202.

**Figure 4.13**   Interim pamphlet closing table
Reprinted with permission from West Group, West's *Federal Practice Digest*, 4th Ser., Pamphlet Part 2 (1997), inside cover.

**Figure 4.14**   Excerpt from the Table of Cases
Reprinted with permission from West Group, West's *Federal Practice Digest*, 4th Ser., Cumulative Pamphlet, Vol. 102 (2002), p. 291.

**Figure 4.15**   Words and Phrases
Reprinted with permission from West Group, West's *Federal Practice Digest*, 4th Ser., Vol. 105 (1992), p. 436.

**Figure 4.16**   Example of a case in Westlaw
Reprinted with permission of West Group, from Westlaw, 124 F.3d 47.

**Figure 4.17**   Example of a case in LexisNexis
Reprinted with permission of LexisNexis, from LexisNexis, 124 F.3d 47.

**Figure 4.19**   Descriptive-Word Index
Reprinted with permission from West Group, West's *Federal Practice Digest*, 4th Ser., Vol. 98 (1992), p. 132.

**Figure 4.20**   Descriptive-Word Index
Reprinted with permission from West Group, West's *Federal Practice Digest*, 4th Ser., Vol. 98 (1992), p. 202.

**Figure 4.21**   Descriptive-Word Index, pocket part
Reprinted with permission from West Group, West's *Federal Practice Digest*, 4th Ser., Cumulative Annual Pocket Part, Vol. 98 (1997), p. 8.

**Figure 4.22**   Key number outline, "Innkeepers" topic
Reprinted with permission from West Group, West's *Federal Practice Digest*, 4th Ser., Vol. 63 (1991), pp. 1–2.

**Figure 4.23**   Case summaries under "Innkeepers" topic
Reprinted with permission from West Group, West's *Federal Practice Digest*, 4th Ser., Vol. 63 (1991), p. 4.

**Figure 4.24**   Digest volume, pocket part
Reprinted with permission from West Group, West's *Federal Practice Digest*, 4th Ser., Pocket Part, Vol. 63 (1997), p. 1.

**Figure 4.25**   Noncumulative interim pamphlet
Reprinted with permission from West Group, West's *Federal Practice Digest*, 4th Ser., Pamphlet Part 2 (Aug. 1997), p. 236.

**Figure 4.26**   Noncumulative interim pamphlet, closing table
Reprinted with permission from West Group, West's *Federal Practice Digest*, 4th Ser., Pamphlet Part 2 (Aug. 1997), inside cover.

**Figure 4.27**   124 F.3d, mini-digest
Reprinted with permission from West Group, West's *Federal Reporter*, 3d Ser., Vol. 124 (1997), p. 93 (key number digest).

**Figure 4.28**   *Woods-Leber v. Hyatt Hotels of Puerto Rico, Inc.*, 124 F.3d 47 (1st Cir. 1997)
Reprinted with permission from West Group, West's *Federal Reporter*, 3d Ser., Vol. 124 (1997), pp. 47–52.

**Figure 5.2**   "What Your Library Should Contain"
Reproduced by permission of LexisNexis. Further reproduction of any kind is strictly prohibited.
From *Shepard's Atlantic Reporter Citations*, Vol. 87, No. 8 (August 2002), cover page.

**Figure 5.3**   Excerpt from *Shepard's Atlantic Reporter Citations*
Reproduced by permission of LexisNexis. Further reproduction of any kind is strictly prohibited.
From *Shepard's Atlantic Reporter Citations*, 1994 Bound Volume, Part 8, p. 108.

**Figure 5.4**   SHEPARD'S® entry for *Kenney v. Scientific, Inc.*
Reproduced by permission of LexisNexis. Further reproduction of any kind is strictly prohibited.
From *Shepard's Atlantic Reporter Citations*, 1994 Bound Volume, Part 8, p. 108.

**Figure 5.6**   SHEPARD'S® entry for *Kenney v. Scientific, Inc.*
Reproduced by permission of LexisNexis. Further reproduction of any kind is strictly prohibited.
From *Shepard's Atlantic Reporter Citations*, 1994 Bound Volume, Part 8, p. 108.

**Figure 5.8**   SHEPARD'S® entry for *Kenney v. Scientific, Inc.*
Reproduced by permission of LexisNexis. Further reproduction of any kind is strictly prohibited.
From *Shepard's Atlantic Reporter Citations*, 1994 Bound Volume, Part 8, p. 108.

**Figure 5.9**   Headnote 13 from the original case, *Kenney v. Scientific, Inc.*
Reprinted with permission from West Group, West's *Atlantic Reporter*, 2d Ser., Vol. 497, *Kenney v. Scientific, Inc.*, 497 A.2d 1310, 1311 (N.J. Super. L. Div. 1985).

**Figure 5.10**   SHEPARD'S® entry for *Kenney v. Scientific, Inc.*
Reproduced by permission of LexisNexis. Further reproduction of any kind is strictly prohibited.
From *Shepard's Atlantic Reporter Citations*, 1994 Bound Volume, Part 8, p. 108.

**Figure 5.11**   *Servis v. State*, citing *Kenney v. Scientific, Inc.*
Reprinted with permission from West Group, West's *Atlantic Reporter*, 2d Ser., Vol. 511, *Servis v. State*, 511 A.2d 1299, 1301 (N.J. Super. L. Div. 1986).

**Figure 5.14**   SHEPARD'S® entry excerpt in LexisNexis for 552 A.2d 258
Reprinted with permission of LexisNexis.
SHEPARD'S® entry for 552 A.2d 258.

**Figure 5.17**  KeyCite entry excerpt for 552 A.3d 258
Reprinted with permission from West Group, from Westlaw, KeyCite entry
for 552 A.2d 258.

**Figure 5.18**  "What Your Library Should Contain"
Reproduced by permission of LexisNexis. Further reproduction of any kind
is strictly prohibited.
From *Shepard's Atlantic Reporter Citations*, Vol. 87, No. 8 (August 2002), cover
page.

**Figure 5.19**  August 2002 Cumulative Supplement entry for 615 A.2d 321
Reproduced by permission of LexisNexis. Further reproduction of any kind
is strictly prohibited.
From *Shepard's Atlantic Reporter Citations*, Vol. 87, No. 8 (August 2002),
p. 156.

**Figure 5.20**  April 2002 Semi-Annual Cumulative Supplement entry for 615
A.2d 321
Reproduced by permission of LexisNexis. Further reproduction of any kind
is strictly prohibited.
From *Shepard's Atlantic Reporter Citations*, Vol. 87, No. 4 (April 2002), p. 625.

**Figure 5.21**  1996–1999 Bound Supplement entry for 615 A.2d 321
Reproduced by permission of LexisNexis. Further reproduction of any kind
is strictly prohibited.
From *Shepard's Atlantic Reporter Citations*, 1996–1999 Bound Supplement,
p. 600.

**Figure 5.22**  1994–1996 Bound Supplement entry for 615 A.2d 321
Reproduced by permission of LexisNexis. Further reproduction of any kind
is strictly prohibited.
From *Shepard's Atlantic Reporter Citations*, 1994–1996 Bound Supplement,
p. 533.

**Figure 5.23**  1994 Bound Volume entry for 615 A.2d 321
Reproduced by permission of LexisNexis. Further reproduction of any kind
is strictly prohibited.
From *Shepard's Atlantic Reporter Citations*, 1994 Bound Volume, Part 8,
p. 1535.

**Figure 6.2**  8 U.S.C.A. § 1423
Reprinted with permission from West Group, *United States Code Annotated*,
Title 8 (1970), p. 501.

**Figure 6.4**  Excerpt from the U.S.C.A. General Index
Reprinted with permission from West Group, *United States Code Annotated*,
1998 General Index, p. 722.

**Figure 6.6**   Annotations accompanying 8 U.S.C.A. § 1423
Reprinted with permission from West Group, *United States Code Annotated*,
Title 8 (1970), p. 502.

**Figure 6.7**   Pocket part update for 8 U.S.C.A. § 1423
Reprinted with permission from West Group, *United States Code Annotated*,
1997 Cumulative Pocket Part, Title 8, pp. 391–92.

**Figure 6.8**   Noncumulative pamphlet entry for 8 U.S.C.A. § 1423
Reprinted with permission from West Group, *United States Code Annotated*,
Pamphlet Number 2 (July 1997), p. 87.

**Figure 6.9**   FACE Act entry, popular name table
Reprinted with permission from West Group, *United States Code Annotated*,
General Index, 1998, p. 1195.

**Figure 6.10**   Conversion table entry for Pub. L. No. 103-259, the FACE Act
Reprinted with permission from West Group, Tables Vol. II, *United States
Code Annotated*, 1999, p. 933.

**Figure 6.11**   SHEPARD'S® entry for a statute
Reproduced by permission of LexisNexis. Further reproduction of any kind
is strictly prohibited.
From *Shepard's Federal Statute Citations*, Vol. 3, 1996, p. 240.

**Figure 6.12**   Two screens showing portions of 8 U.S.C.A. § 1423 in Westlaw
Reprinted with permission from West Group, from Westlaw, 8 U.S.C.A. § 1423.

**Figure 6.13**   Three screens showing portions of 8 U.S.C.S. § 1423 in LexisNexis
Reprinted with permission of LexisNexis, from LexisNexis, 8 U.S.C.S. § 1423.

**Figure 6.14**   Excerpt from the U.S.C.A. General Index
Reprinted with permission from West Group, *United States Code Annotated*,
1998 General Index, p. 722.

**Figure 6.15**   Excerpt from chapter outline, Title 8, U.S.C.A.
Reprinted with permission from West Group, *United States Code Annotated*,
Title 8, 1970, p. 11.

**Figure 6.16**   8 U.S.C.A. § 1423
Reprinted with permission from West Group, *United States Code Annotated*,
Title 8, 1970, p. 501.

**Figure 6.17**   Annotations accompanying 8 U.S.C.A. § 1423
Reprinted with permission from West Group, *United States Code Annotated*,
Title 8, 1970, p. 502.

**Figure 6.18**  Pocket part entry for 8 U.S.C.A. § 1423
Reprinted with permission from West Group, *United States Code Annotated*, 1997 Cumulative Pocket Part, Title 8, pp. 391–92.

**Figure 6.19**  Pocket part entry for 8 U.S.C.A. § 1423
Reprinted with permission from West Group, *United States Code Annotated*, 1997 Cumulative Pocket Part, Title 8, p. 393.

**Figure 6.20**  Noncumulative supplement entry for 8 U.S.C.A. § 1423
Reprinted with permission from West Group, *United States Code Annotated*, Pamphlet Number 1 (May 1997), p. 354.

**Figure 6.21**  Noncumulative supplement entry for 8 U.S.C.A. § 1423
Reprinted with permission from West Group, *United States Code Annotated*, Pamphlet Number 2 (July 1997), p. 87.

**Figure 6.22**  *Vernon's Texas Statutes and Codes Annotated* General Index
Reprinted with permission from West Group, *Vernon's Texas Statutes and Codes Annotated*, 2002 General Index A–E, p. 230.

**Figure 6.23**  Texas Civil Practice and Remedies Code § 93.001
Reprinted with permission from West Group, Vol. 4 *Vernon's Texas Codes Annotated* § 93.001, p. 142 (1997).

**Figure 6.24**  Pocket part entry for Texas Civil Practice and Remedies Code § 93.001
Reprinted with permission from West Group, Vol. 4 *Vernon's Texas Codes Annotated* Cumulative Annual Pocket Part, p. 54 (2002).

**Figure 7.1**  How a Bill Becomes a Law
Reprinted with permission from Congressional Quarterly Inc., *Congressional Quarterly's Guide to Congress*, 5th Ed. (2000), p. 1093.

**Figure 7.2**  Excerpt from annotations accompanying 18 U.S.C.A. § 2441
Reprinted with permission from West Group, *United States Code Annotated*, Vol. 18, 1999 Cumulative Annual Pocket Part, p. 146.

**Figure 7.3**  Starting page, House Judiciary Committee Report on the War Crimes Act of 1996
Reprinted with permission from West Group, *United States Code Congressional and Administrative News*, 104th Congress-Second Session 1996, Vol. 5 (1997), p. 2166.

**Figure 7.4**  CIS Legislative Histories entry for Pub. L. No. 104-192
Reprinted with permission of LexisNexis, *CIS/Annual 1996*, Legislative Histories of U.S. Public Laws (1997), p. 315.

**Figure 7.5**   CIS Index entry
Reprinted with permission of LexisNexis, *CIS/Annual 1996*, Index to Congressional Publications and Legislative Histories (1997), p. 531.

**Figure 7.6**   CIS Abstracts entry
Reprinted with permission of LexisNexis, *CIS/Annual 1996*, Abstracts from Congressional Publications (1997), p. 207.

**Figure 7.10**   Introductory screen for LexisNexis Congressional
Reprinted with permission of LexisNexis, LexisNexis Congressional introductory screen.

**Figure 7.11**   Search options for Congressional publications in LexisNexis Congressional
Reprinted with permission of LexisNexis, LexisNexis Congressional search options.

**Figure 7.12**   18 U.S.C.A. § 2441 and accompanying annotations
Reprinted with permission from West Group, *United States Code Annotated*, Vol. 18, 1999 Cumulative Annual Pocket Part, pp. 145–46.

**Figure 7.13**   House Judiciary Committee report reprinted in U.S.C.C.A.N.
Reprinted with permission from West Group, *United States Code Congressional and Administrative News*, 104th Congress-Second Session 1996, Vol. 5 (1997), p. 2166.

**Figure 7.17**   Search options, LexisNexis Congressional
Reprinted with permission of LexisNexis, LexisNexis Congressional search options.

**Figure 7.18**   Search options, LexisNexis Congressional
Reprinted with permission of LexisNexis, LexisNexis Congressional search options.

**Figure 7.19**   Search screen, LexisNexis Congressional
Reprinted with permission of LexisNexis, LexisNexis Congressional search screen.

**Figure 7.20**   Search results, LexisNexis Congressional
Reprinted with permission of LexisNexis, LexisNexis Congressional search results.

**Figure 7.21**   Abstracts entries from LexisNexis Congressional
Reprinted with permission of LexisNexis, LexisNexis Congressional abstracts entry.

**Figure 7.22**   House Judiciary Committee report retrieved from LexisNexis Congressional
Reprinted with permission of LexisNexis, LexisNexis Congressional house report.

**Figure 8.2** Annotations to 15 U.S.C.S. § 1476
Reprinted with permission from LexisNexis, *United States Code Service*, Title 15 Commerce and Trade §§ 1151–1600 (1993), p. 391.

**Figure 8.10** SHEPARD'S® entry for 16 C.F.R. § 1700.15
Reproduced by permission of LexisNexis. Further reproduction of any kind is strictly prohibited.
From *Shepard's Code of Federal Regulations Citations*, Titles 1–27; 1994, Part 1, p. 397.

**Figure 9.1** Sample entry from *Legal Looseleafs in Print*
Reprinted with permission from Arlene L. Eis, *Legal Looseleafs in Print 2002*, Title List (Infosources Publ'g 2002), p. 37.

**Figure 9.2** Sample entry from *Directory of Law-Related CD-ROMs*
Reprinted with permission from Arlene L. Eis, *Directory of Law-Related CD-ROMs 2002*, CD-ROM Product List (Infosources Publ'g 2002), p. 9.

**Figure 9.3** Premise search screen
Reprinted with permission from West Group, from Westlaw, Premise-based product—California Digest, 2002.

**Figure 9.5** Folio search screen
Reprinted with permission from West Group, from Americans With Disabilities LawDesk, Search All Cases screen, 1998.

**Figure 9.6** Introductory screen, American Bankruptcy Institute web site
Reprinted from ABI World (www.abiworld.org) with the permission of the American Bankruptcy Institute, 2002.

**Figure 9.7** Search results for abiworld.org showing the domain name registrant
© 2002 VeriSign, Inc. Reprinted with permission from VeriSign, Inc.

**Figure 9.8** Excerpt from the Overview, *BNA's Americans with Disabilities Act Manual*
Reproduced with permission from *BNA's Americans with Disabilities Act Manual*, pp. 10:0003–0004. Copyright 2001 by The Bureau of National Affairs, Inc. (800-372-1033) http://www.bna.com.

**Figure 9.9** Excerpt from the Master Index, *BNA's Americans with Disabilities Act Manual*
Reproduced with permission from *BNA's Americans with Disabilities Act Manual*, p. Index-1. Copyright 2002 by The Bureau of National Affairs, Inc. (800-372-1033) http://www.bna.com.

**Figure 9.10** Excerpt from Public Accommodations, *BNA's Americans with Disabilities Act Manual*
Reproduced with permission from *BNA's Americans with Disabilities Act Manual*, p. 30:0001. Copyright 2001 by The Bureau of National Affairs, Inc. (800-372-1033) http://www.bna.com.

**Figure 9.11**    28 C.F.R. Pt. 36, reprinted in *BNA's Americans with Disabilities Act Manual*
Reproduced with permission from *BNA's Americans with Disabilities Act Manual*, p. 70:0185. Copyright 1999 by The Bureau of National Affairs, Inc. (800-372-1033) http://www.bna.com.

**Figure 9.12**    Cumulative Digest and Index, BNA's A.D. Cases
Reproduced with permission from *Americans with Disabilities Cases Cumulative Digest and Index*, Table of Cases, Vol. 1–6 (1974–1997), pp. v–vi. Copyright 2002 by The Bureau of National Affairs, Inc. (800-372-1033) http://www.bna .com.

**Figure 9.13**    A.D. Cases Topic Finder
Reproduced with permission from *Americans with Disabilities Cases Cumulative Digest and Index*, Table of Cases, Vol. 1–6 (1974–1997), p. 51. Copyright 2002 by The Bureau of National Affairs, Inc. (800-372-1033) http://www.bna .com.

**Figure 9.14**    Case summaries, A.D. Cases Cumulative Digest and Index
Reproduced with permission from *Americans with Disabilities Cases Cumulative Digest and Index*, Table of Cases, Vol. 1–6 (1974–1997), p. 1527. Copyright 2002 by The Bureau of National Affairs, Inc. (800-372-1033) http://www.bna .com.

**Figure 9.15**    *Arnold v. United Artists Theatre Circuit*
Reproduced with permission from 5 A.D. Cases 685–86. Copyright 1996 by The Bureau of National Affairs, Inc. (800-372-1033) http://www.bna.com.

**Figure 10.1**    Westlaw search screen
Reprinted with permission from West Group, from Westlaw, search screen.

**Figure 10.2**    LexisNexis search screen
Reprinted with permission of LexisNexis, from LexisNexis, search screen.

**Figure 10.5**    Westlaw search results screen
Reprinted with permission from West Group, from Westlaw, search results display.

**Figure 10.6**    LexisNexis search results screen
Reprinted with permission of LexisNexis, from LexisNexis, search results display.

**Figure 10.7**    Introductory screen for FindLaw
Reprinted with permission © 2002 FindLaw, Inc., from http://www.findlaw .com.

**Figure 10.8**    Search options in FindLaw
Reprinted with permission © 2002 FindLaw, Inc., from http://www.findlaw .com/casecode.

**Figure 10.9**   Introductory screen, Legal Information Institute
Reprinted with permission © 2002 Cornell Law School, from http://www.law
.cornell.edu.

**Figure 10.10**   Search option in Legal Information Institute
Reprinted with permission © 2002 Cornell Law School, from http://www.law
.cornell.edu.

# BASIC LEGAL RESEARCH

# CHAPTER 1

# INTRODUCTION TO LEGAL RESEARCH

A. Sources of law

B. Types of authority

C. Introduction to the process of legal research

D. Overview of print and electronic sources of legal authority

E. Introduction to legal citation

F. Overview of this text

What is legal research and why do you need to learn about it? Researching the law means finding the rules that govern conduct in our society. To be a successful lawyer, you need to know how to research the law. Lawyers are often called upon to solve problems and give advice, and to do that accurately, you must know the rules applicable to the different situations you and your clients will face. Clients may come to you after an event has occurred and ask you to pursue a remedy for a bad outcome, or perhaps defend them against charges that they have acted wrongfully. You may be asked to help a client accomplish a goal like starting a business or buying a piece of property. In these situations and many others, you will need to know your clients' rights and responsibilities, as defined by legal rules. Consequently, being proficient in legal research is essential to your success in legal practice.

As a starting point for learning about how to research the law, it is important to understand some of the different sources of legal rules. This chapter discusses what these sources are and where they originate within our legal system. It also provides an introduction to the process of legal research, an overview of some of the research tools you will learn to use, and an introduction to legal citation. Later chapters explain how to locate legal rules using a variety of resources.

## A. SOURCES OF LAW

There are four main sources of law, which exist at both the state and federal levels:

- constitutions
- statutes
- court opinions (also called cases)
- administrative regulations.

A constitution establishes a system of government and defines the boundaries of authority granted to the government. The United States Constitution is the preeminent source of law in our legal system, and all other rules, whether promulgated by a state or the federal government, must comply with its requirements. Each state also has its own constitution. A state's constitution may grant greater rights than those secured by the federal constitution, but because a state constitution is subordinate to the federal constitution, it cannot provide lesser rights than the federal constitution does. All of a state's legal rules must comport with both the state and federal constitutions.

Since grade school, you have been taught that the United States Constitution created three branches of government: the legislative branch, which makes the laws; the judicial branch, which interprets the laws; and the executive branch, which enforces the laws. State governments are also divided into these three branches. Although this is elementary civics, this structure truly does define the way government authority is divided in our system of government.

The legislative branch of government creates statutes, which must be approved by the executive branch (the president, for federal statutes; the governor, for state statutes) to go into effect. The executive branch also makes rules. Administrative agencies, such as the federal Food and Drug Administration or a state's department of motor vehicles, are part of the executive branch. They execute the laws passed by the legislature and create their own regulations to carry out the mandates established by statute.

The judicial branch is the source of court opinions. Courts interpret rules created by the legislative and executive branches of government. If a court determines that a rule does not meet constitutional requirements, it can invalidate the rule. Otherwise, however, the court must apply the rule to the case before it. Court opinions can also be an independent source of legal rules. Legal rules made by courts are called "common-law" rules. Although courts are empowered to make these rules, legislatures can adopt legislation that changes or abolishes a common-law rule, as long as the legislation is constitutional.

**FIGURE 1.1**  BRANCHES OF GOVERNMENT AND LEGAL RULES

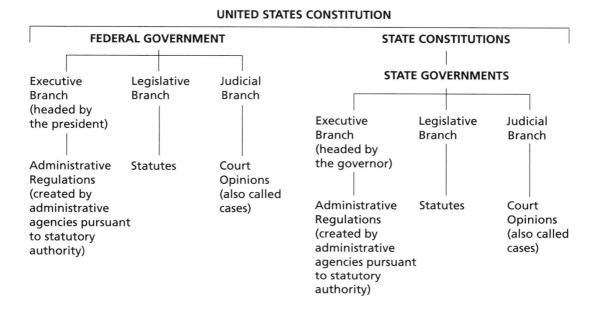

Figure 1.1 shows the relationships among the branches of government and the types of legal rules they create.

An example may be useful to illustrate the relationships among the rules created by the three branches of the federal government. As you know, the United States Constitution, through the First Amendment, guarantees the right to free expression. Congress could pass legislation requiring television stations to provide educational programming for children. The Federal Communications Commission (FCC) is the administrative agency within the executive branch that would have responsibility for carrying out Congress's will. If the statute were not specific about what constitutes educational programming or how much educational programming must be provided, the FCC would have to create administrative regulations to enforce the law. The regulations would provide the information not detailed in the statute, such as the definition of educational programming. A television station could challenge the statute and regulations by arguing to a court that prescribing the content of material that the station must broadcast violates the First Amendment. The court would then have to interpret the statute and regulations and decide whether they comply with the Constitution.

Another example illustrates the relationship between courts and legislatures in the area of common-law rules. The rules of negligence have been largely created by the courts. Therefore, liability for negligence is usually determined by common-law rules. A state supreme court could decide that a plaintiff who sues a defendant for negligence cannot recover any damages if the plaintiff herself was negligent and contributed to her own injuries. This decision would create a common-law rule governing future cases of negligence within that state. The state legislature could step in and pass a statute that changes the rule. For example, the legislature could enact a statute providing that juries are to determine the percentage of negligence attributable to either party and to apportion damages accordingly, instead of completely denying recovery to the plaintiff. Courts in that state would then be obligated to apply the rule from the statute, not the former common-law rule.

Although these examples are simplified, they demonstrate the basic roles of each of the branches of government in enunciating the legal rules governing the conduct of society. They also demonstrate that researching a legal issue may require you to research several different types of legal authority. The answer to a research question may not be found exclusively in statutes or court opinions or administrative regulations. Often, these sources must be researched together to determine all of the rules applicable to a factual scenario.

## B. TYPES OF AUTHORITY

One term used to describe the rules that govern conduct in society is "legal authority." Rules, however, are only one type of legal authority, and some types of legal authority are more authoritative than others. To understand how legal authority is categorized, you must be able to differentiate "primary" authority from "secondary" authority and "mandatory" authority from "persuasive" authority.

### 1. PRIMARY VS. SECONDARY AUTHORITY

Primary authority is the term used to describe rules of law. Primary authority includes all of the types of rules discussed so far in this chapter. Constitutional provisions, statutes, court opinions, and administrative regulations contain legal rules, and as a consequence, are primary authority. Because "the law" consists of legal rules, primary authority is sometimes described as "the law."

Secondary authority, by contrast, refers to commentary on the law or analysis of the law, but not "the law" itself. An opinion from the United States Supreme Court is primary authority, but an article written by a private party explaining and analyzing the opinion is secondary authority. Secondary authority is often quite useful in legal research because its analysis can help you understand complex legal issues and refer you to primary authority. Nevertheless, secondary authority is not "the law" and therefore is distinguished from primary authority.

## 2. MANDATORY VS. PERSUASIVE AUTHORITY

Mandatory and persuasive authority are terms courts use to categorize the different sources of law they use in making their decisions. Mandatory authority, which can also be called binding authority, refers to authority that the court is obligated to follow. For example, lower courts are required to follow decisions from higher courts in the same jurisdiction. A lower court would not be permitted to ignore the rulings from a higher court in making a decision. Accordingly, higher court opinions would constitute mandatory authority for a lower court.

Persuasive authority, which can also be called nonbinding authority, refers to authority that the court may follow if it is persuaded to do so, but is not required to follow. The highest court in a state, for instance, is not required to follow a decision of a lower court, nor is it obligated to comply with a ruling from a court in another state. If the issue before the court has not been clearly resolved by mandatory authority, the court may choose to follow a nonbinding rule that it finds persuasive, hence the term persuasive authority.

## 3. DISTINGUISHING AMONG TYPES OF AUTHORITY

It is important to be able to understand which categories a legal authority falls into because the categories help determine the weight a court will attach to the authority. Mandatory authority carries more weight than persuasive authority, and primary authority generally has more weight than secondary authority.

For the most part, a legal authority's status as a primary or secondary authority is fixed. An authority is either part of "the law," or it is not. Sometimes a rule proposed in a secondary authority is adopted as a legal rule, which in a sense converts the secondary authority into primary authority. Ordinarily, however, an authority's character as primary or secondary cannot change.

In addition to identifying primary and secondary authority, you must also be able to distinguish between mandatory and persuasive authority. Secondary authority is virtually always persuasive authority. Because a secondary authority is not a legal rule, a court generally would not be obligated to follow it. By contrast, a primary authority's status as mandatory or persuasive depends on the circumstances. Within the jurisdiction in which it was created, a primary authority such as a court opinion or statute is usually mandatory; a court would be required to follow it in deciding cases. Courts are not, however, obligated to follow primary authority in all circumstances. For example, primary authority that is mandatory in the jurisdiction where it was created would only be considered persuasive authority in another jurisdiction.

**FIGURE 1.2**   TYPES OF AUTHORITY

| TYPE OF AUTHORITY | MANDATORY (BINDING) | PERSUASIVE (NONBINDING) |
|---|---|---|
| **PRIMARY** (legal rules) | Constitutional provisions, statutes, and regulations in force within a jurisdiction are mandatory authority for courts within the same jurisdiction. Decisions from higher courts within a jurisdiction are mandatory authority for lower courts within the same jurisdiction. | Decisions from courts in one jurisdiction are persuasive authority for courts within another jurisdiction. Decisions from lower courts within a jurisdiction are persuasive authority for higher courts within the same jurisdiction. |
| **SECONDARY** (anything that is not primary authority; usually commentary on the law) | Secondary authority is *not* mandatory authority. | Secondary authority is persuasive authority. |

Figure 1.2 illustrates the relationships among these various types of authority.

## C. INTRODUCTION TO THE PROCESS OF LEGAL RESEARCH

Legal research is not a linear process. Most research projects do not have an established series of steps that must be followed sequentially until the answer to your question is uncovered. Although there are certain steps that you will ordinarily take with any research project, the starting, middle, and ending points will vary. When you know little or nothing about the issue you are researching, you will begin your research differently than if you were working on an issue about which you already had substantial background knowledge. One of the goals of this book is to help you learn to assess the appropriate starting, middle, and ending points for your research.

With most research projects, there are two preliminary steps that you will want to take before heading out on your search for authority: defining the scope of your project and generating search terms. In the first step, you will want to think about what you are being asked to do. Are you being asked to spend three weeks locating all information from every jurisdiction on a particular subject, or do you have a day to find out how courts in one state have ruled on an issue? Will you write an extensive analysis of your research, or will you summarize the results orally to the person who made the assignment? Evaluating the type of work product you are expected to produce, the amount of time you have, and the scope of the project will help you determine the best way to proceed. The second step is generating search terms to use to search for information in various research tools. Chapter 2 discusses different ways to do this. In general, however, you will need to construct a list of words or concepts to look up in an index, table of contents, or computer database to locate information relevant to your issue.

Once you have accomplished these preliminary steps, you need to decide which research tool to use as the starting point for your research. You will also need to think about other probable sources of information and the sequence in which you plan to research those sources. The more you know about your research issue going in, the easier it will be to plan the steps. The less you know, the more flexible you will need to be in your approach. If you do not find any information, or find too much information, you may need to backtrack or rethink your approach.

To plan your research path, it may be useful for you to think about three categories of authority: secondary authority, primary mandatory authority, and primary persuasive authority. Your goal in most research projects will be to locate primary mandatory authority, if it exists, on your research issue. If primary mandatory authority is not available or does not directly answer your research question, persuasive authority (either primary or secondary) may help you analyze the issue. For any given research project, you will need to determine the order in which you will research these three types of authority.

Because your goal will usually be to locate primary mandatory authority, you might think that you should begin your research with those sources. In fact, sometimes you will begin by researching primary mandatory authority, but that is not always the case. Secondary authorities that cite, analyze, and explain the law can provide a very efficient way to obtain background information and references to primary authority. Although they are not controlling in your analysis, they are invaluable research tools and can be a good starting point for your project. Persuasive primary authority will rarely provide a good starting place because it provides neither the controlling rules nor analysis explaining the law. Figure 1.3 shows the relationships among these three categories of authority.

Once you determine which category of authority to begin with, you need to decide which individual sources within the category to consult. In making this decision, it is important to bear in mind that many research sources are linked together. Once you find information in one

**FIGURE 1.3**   WHERE TO BEGIN YOUR RESEARCH PROJECT

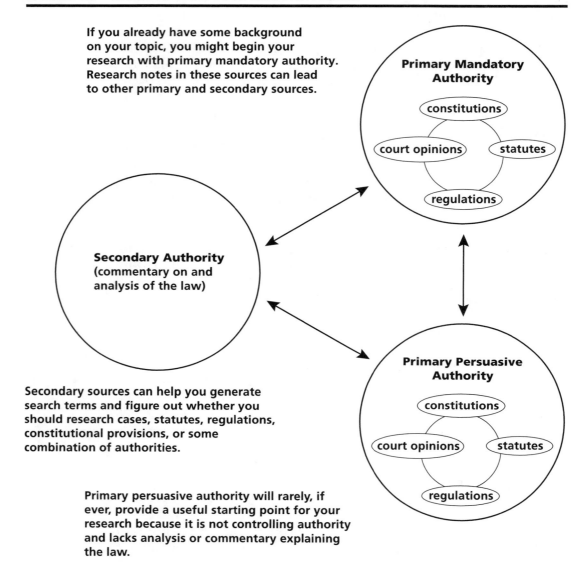

If you already have some background on your topic, you might begin your research with primary mandatory authority. Research notes in these sources can lead to other primary and secondary sources.

**Primary Mandatory Authority**

- constitutions
- court opinions
- statutes
- regulations

**Secondary Authority** (commentary on and analysis of the law)

Secondary sources can help you generate search terms and figure out whether you should research cases, statutes, regulations, constitutional provisions, or some combination of authorities.

Primary persuasive authority will rarely, if ever, provide a useful starting point for your research because it is not controlling authority and lacks analysis or commentary explaining the law.

**Primary Persuasive Authority**

- constitutions
- court opinions
- statutes
- regulations

source, research notes within that source may refer you to other relevant sources. Thus, there may be more than one source that would be an appropriate starting point for your research. The trick is to be able to determine for any given research project which source is most likely to lead you in the right direction the most quickly. This book will explain the features of a wide range of research sources so you can learn to make this assessment for different types of research projects.

## D. OVERVIEW OF PRINT AND ELECTRONIC SOURCES OF LEGAL AUTHORITY

Many of the primary and secondary authorities you will learn to research are available from a variety of sources. They may be published in one or more books. Many are now also available in electronic form. Electronic research services may include commercial databases that charge each user a fee for access; Internet and CD-ROM subscription services that libraries pay to access, but that are free to library patrons; and Internet sources available to anyone with a modem and a web browser. As noted earlier, legal research often requires research into several different types of legal authority. Therefore, you will need to learn how to use a variety of tools to be able to research effectively.

The chapters that follow explain how to use both print and electronic research tools to locate various types of legal authority. Sometimes print sources will provide the easiest and most efficient means of accessing the information you need. In other circumstances, electronic sources may provide a better avenue for research. The tools you use will depend on a number of factors, including the resources available in your library, the amount of time you have for your project, the depth of research you need to do, and the amount of money your client can spend. Often, you will find that the best way to accomplish your research is to use some combination of print and electronic tools.

Print research tools are generally organized by type of authority and jurisdiction. Thus, court opinions from Maryland will be in one set of books (called "reporters"), and those from Massachusetts will be in another set of reporters. The same holds true for print collections of statutes and other types of legal authority. Within each set of books, individual authorities, such as a case or statutory provision, can be located in one of two ways: by citation or by subject.

Each authority within a book will have a citation assigned to it. Once you know the citation, you can go directly to the appropriate book and locate the authority. For example, each court opinion is identified by a citation containing the volume number of the reporter in which it is published, the name of the reporter, and the starting page of the opinion. If you had the citation for a case, you could go to the library and locate it within a matter of minutes.

Of course, with most research projects, you will not know the citations to the authorities you need to find. You will have been sent to the library to find out which legal authorities, if any, pertain to the subject of your research project. In those situations, you will need to research information by subject, using either the index or table of contents accompanying each research tool to see what information you can find.

One challenge in researching with print sources is making sure the information is current. Most print research sources consist of hardcover books that can be difficult to update when the law changes. Some print tools are published in chronological order. For those tools, new books are published periodically as new material is compiled. Many, however, are organized by subject. For those tools, publishers cannot print new books every time the law changes. This would be prohibitively expensive, and because the law can change at any time, the new books would likely be out of date as soon as they were printed. To keep the books up to date, therefore, many print sources are updated with softcover pamphlets containing new information that became available after the hardcover book was published. These supplementary pamphlets are often called "pocket parts" because many of them fit into a "pocket" in the inside back cover of the hardcover book. You will see pocket parts mentioned throughout this text in reference to print research tools.

Electronic research tools are organized somewhat differently. Not all electronic resources are divided by jurisdiction and type of authority. Some provide access to only one type of authority, while others provide access to multiple types of authority from many different jurisdictions. In addition, most electronic resources fall into one of two general categories: index services and services containing the full text of various legal authorities (full-text services). Both index and full-text services will allow you to conduct "word searches" that locate documents containing words you specify. The results of the search, however, will differ depending on which type of service you are using. An index service will generate a list of citations to legal authorities containing the words in your search, but you would need to go to print or other electronic sources to obtain the full text of the documents. In a full-text service, you have the choice of viewing either a list of citations or the full text of the documents retrieved from your word search. Full-text services will also allow you to retrieve a document from its citation, much as you would in a print resource.

The two most commonly used commercial databases are Westlaw and LexisNexis. These are full-text services with databases that allow you to access all of the types of legal authority discussed in this chapter. They charge subscribers for use of their services, although your law school probably subsidizes the cost of student research while you are in school. Other commercial and government-operated research services also provide access to legal authority. LexisNexis, Westlaw, and other electronic research services are discussed throughout this text.

## E. INTRODUCTION TO LEGAL CITATION

When you present the results of your research in written form, you will need to include citations to the legal authorities you have found. One place to find the rules for citing legal authority is *The Bluebook: A Uniform System of Citation* (17th ed. 2000). Another source for rules on citation is the *ALWD Citation Manual: A Professional System of Citation* (2d ed. 2003). The citation rules in these two sources overlap to a large degree, but they are not identical. Although the *Bluebook* has been around longer, many people find the *ALWD Manual* to be better organized, more consistent, and easier to follow. You should use whichever citation manual your professor directs you to use.

This text provides information on citations in both *Bluebook* and *ALWD Manual* format. This section provides a brief overview of the organization of both citation manuals and will make the most sense if you have your citation manual in front of you as you read. Later chapters contain instructions for citing individual sources of legal authority. In many cases, the citation rules in the *Bluebook* and the *ALWD Manual* will be identical. Where there are differences, this text will alert you to that fact.

## 1. THE *BLUEBOOK*

The first part of the *Bluebook* that you should review is the Introduction. This section explains how the *Bluebook* is organized. It also explains some general principles of citation and provides some examples of typical citations.

As you will see when you review the Introduction, learning to cite authority in *Bluebook* format requires you to become familiar with five items:

- the Table of Contents and Index
- the text of the citation rules
- the Tables
- the Practitioners' Notes
- the Quick Reference examples on the inside front and back covers.

**THE TABLE OF CONTENTS AND INDEX.** To locate individual citation rules, you can use the Table of Contents at the beginning of the *Bluebook* or the Index at the end. The Index references in ordinary type refer to the pages with relevant rules. Those in italics refer to examples of citations.

**THE TEXT OF THE CITATION RULES.** Most of the *Bluebook* is devoted to explaining the rules for citing different types of authority. These rules appear in the white pages in the middle of the *Bluebook* and can be divided into five categories:

1. Rules 1 through 9 are general rules applicable to a citation to any type of authority. For example, Rule 5 discusses the proper format for quotations.
2. Rules 10 through 17 contain rules for citing various primary and secondary authorities. For example, Rule 10 explains how to cite a court opinion, and Rule 12 explains how to cite a statute.
3. Rule 18 contains rules for citing authorities published in electronic format.
4. Rule 19 contains rules for citing authorities published in subject-matter services. Subject-matter services are explained in Chapter 9 of this text.
5. Rules 20 and 21 contain rules for citing foreign and international materials. This text does not discuss foreign or international materials.

Most of the rules for citing individual authorities begin with a description of the elements necessary for a full citation. You should read this part of the rule first. The remainder of the rule will explain each component in greater detail.

Frequently, the rule will be accompanied by examples. Although this might seem like it would simplify things, in fact, sometimes it just complicates the citation. This is because the examples in the white pages are in the format required for the footnotes that appear in law review articles. A law review is a type of secondary source explained in more detail in Chapter 3. Suffice it to say at this point that the work you will do in your legal research class is unlikely to be in law review format. Therefore, although the examples in the white pages of the *Bluebook* will be somewhat useful to you in understanding how to cite legal authority, you cannot rely on them exclusively.

In the margins next to the rules, you will find cross-references to the relevant Tables and Practitioners' Notes that you may need for a complete citation. Explanations of the Tables and Practitioners' Notes follow.

**THE TABLES.** The Tables appear in the blue pages at the back of the *Bluebook.* The citation rules in the white pages explain the general requirements for different types of citations. Most of these rules require that certain words be abbreviated. The Tables contain abbreviations necessary for proper citations.[1] For example, Table T.1 lists each jurisdiction in the United States, and under each jurisdiction, it shows the proper abbreviations for citations to that jurisdiction's cases and statutes.

---

[1]Citations in *ALWD Manual* format also require abbreviations. The *Bluebook* and the *ALWD Manual* use identical abbreviations for many words. Some abbreviations vary, however, depending on which format you use.

Whenever you have a citation that includes an abbreviation, you will need to check the appropriate Table to find the precise abbreviation required for a proper citation. You should note, however, that the type styles of some of the abbreviations in the Tables apply to law review footnotes and may need to be modified for the work you will produce in your first year of law school.

**THE PRACTITIONERS' NOTES.** The Practitioners' Notes appear in the blue pages near the beginning of the *Bluebook*. They tell you how to convert the examples in the white pages and the abbreviations in the Tables into the proper format for briefs and legal memoranda, which are the types of documents most students write in their first year of law school. For instance, in the examples accompanying Rule 10, the rule on citing cases, the case names appear in regular type. Practitioners' Note P.1(a), however, indicates that case names should be underlined or italicized. Similarly, in Table T.1 under New York, the abbreviations for the statutory compilations appear in large and small capital letters. Practitioners' Note P.1(h) indicates that citations to statutory compilations should appear in ordinary type, not large and small capitals. Unless your citations will appear in law review footnotes, you will need to refer to the Practitioners' Notes to cite authority correctly.

**THE QUICK REFERENCE EXAMPLES ON THE INSIDE FRONT AND BACK COVERS.** On the inside front and back covers of the *Bluebook* you will find Quick Reference examples of different types of citations. The examples on the inside front cover are in the format for law review footnotes and will be of little or no use to you in your first year of law school. The examples on the inside back cover are in the proper format for the types of documents you are likely to draft in your first year.

All of the pieces of the *Bluebook* work together to help you determine the proper citation format for a legal authority:

1. Use the Table of Contents or Index to find the rule governing the authority you want to cite.
2. Read the rule in the white pages, beginning with the components of a full citation at the beginning of the rule.
3. Use the Tables and Practitioners' Notes to find additional information necessary for a correct citation.
4. Use the Quick Reference guide on the inside back cover for additional examples of citations.

As you read the remaining chapters in this book, you will find more specific information about citing individual legal authorities. In general, however, you will be able to figure out how to cite almost any type of authority in *Bluebook* format by following these four steps.

## 2. THE *ALWD MANUAL*

The first part of the *ALWD Manual* that you should review is Part 1, Introductory Material. This section explains what citations are and how to use them, how to use the *ALWD Manual*, how local citation rules can affect citation format, and how your word processor's settings may affect citations. It explains the *ALWD Manual*'s organization clearly, so it would be redundant to repeat all of that information here. Nevertheless, a few comments on the *ALWD Manual* may be useful as you begin learning about it.

Perhaps the biggest difference between the *ALWD Manual* and the *Bluebook* is that the *ALWD Manual* uses the same citation format for all documents. The *Bluebook*, by contrast, uses one format for citations in law review footnotes and another for practice documents like briefs and memoranda. When you are using the *ALWD Manual*, you do not need to convert any of the citations into different formats for different documents.

As you will see when you review Part 1, learning to cite authority in *ALWD Manual* format requires you to become familiar with five items:

- the Table of Contents and Index
- the text of the citation rules
- the Appendices
- the "Fast Formats"
- the ALWD web site.

**THE TABLE OF CONTENTS AND INDEX.** To locate individual citation rules, you can use the Table of Contents at the beginning of the *ALWD Manual* or the Index at the end. Unless otherwise indicated, the references in the Index are to rule numbers, not page numbers or specific examples.

**THE TEXT OF THE CITATION RULES.** Most of the *ALWD Manual* is devoted to explaining the rules for citing different types of authority. The rules are divided into the following Parts:

1. Part 2 (with Rules 1 through 11) contains general rules applicable to a citation to any type of authority. For example, Rule 3 discusses spelling and capitalization.
2. Part 3 (with Rules 12 through 37) contains rules for citing various primary and secondary authorities. For example, Rule 12 governs citations to court opinions, and Rule 14 governs citations to statutes.

3. Part 4 (with Rules 38 through 42) contains rules for citing authorities published in electronic format.
4. Part 5 (with Rules 43 through 46) contains rules for incorporating citations into documents.
5. Part 6 (with Rules 47 through 49) contains rules regarding quotations.

At the beginning of each citation rule in Parts 3 and 4, you will find a description of the elements necessary for a full citation, followed by an annotated example showing how all of the elements fit together to create a complete citation. You should read this part of the rule first. The remainder of the rule will explain each component in greater detail.

Within the text of each rule in the *ALWD Manual*, you will find cross-references to other citation rules and to Appendices containing additional information that you may need for a complete citation. An explanation of the Appendices appears below.

You will also find "Sidebars" in some rules. The "Sidebars" are literally asides on citation. They provide information about sources of legal authority, help you avoid common citation errors, and offer citation tips.

**THE APPENDICES.** The *ALWD Manual* contains seven Appendices that follow the Parts containing the citation rules. The citation rules in Parts 3 and 4 explain the general requirements for citations to different types of authority. Most of these rules require that certain words be abbreviated. Appendices 1, 3, 4, and 5 contain abbreviations necessary for proper citations. For example, Appendix 1 lists Primary Sources by Jurisdiction. It lists each jurisdiction in the United States, and under each jurisdiction, it shows the proper abbreviations for citations to that jurisdiction's cases and statutes. Whenever you have a citation that includes an abbreviation, you will need to check the appropriate Appendix to find the precise abbreviation required for a proper citation.[2]

Appendix 2 contains local court citation rules. Some courts require special citation formats for authorities cited in documents filed with those courts. The *ALWD Manual* includes these rules in Appendix 2, so you do not have to look them up in another source if you need to use them.

Appendix 6 contains an example of a memorandum with citations included. This example can help you see how citations are integrated into a document.

Appendix 7 contains information on citations to federal taxation materials.

---

[2]Citations in *Bluebook* format also require abbreviations. The *ALWD Manual* and the *Bluebook* use identical abbreviations for many words. Some abbreviations differ, however, depending on which format you use.

**THE FAST FORMATS.** Before the text of each citation rule in Parts 3 and 4, you will find a section called "Fast Formats." The "Fast Formats" provide citation examples for each rule, in addition to the examples interwoven with the text of the rule. A "Fast Formats Locator" appears on the inside front cover of the *ALWD Manual*. You can use this alphabetical list to find "Fast Formats" pages without going to the Table of Contents or Index.

**THE ALWD WEB SITE.** Updates to the *ALWD Manual* are posted on the Internet. The Internet address is listed in Appendix A at the end of this text, as well as in Part 1 of the *ALWD Manual*.

All of the pieces of the *ALWD Manual* work together to help you determine the proper citation format for a legal authority:

1. Use the Table of Contents or Index to find the rule governing the authority you want to cite.
2. Read the rule, beginning with the components of a full citation at the beginning of the rule.
3. Use the Appendices to find additional information necessary for a correct citation.
4. Use the "Fast Formats" preceding the rule for additional examples of citations.
5. If necessary, check the web site for any updates.

As you read the remaining chapters in this book, you will find more specific information about citing individual legal authorities. In general, however, you will be able to figure out how to cite almost any type of authority in *ALWD Manual* format by following these five steps.

## F. OVERVIEW OF THIS TEXT

Because different research projects have different starting and ending points, it is not necessary that you follow the chapters in this book in order. The sequence of assignments in your legal research class will determine the order in which you need to cover the material in this book.

Although you may not cover the chapters in order, a brief overview of the organization of this text may provide useful context for the material that follows. As noted earlier, Chapter 2 discusses how to generate search terms, one of the first steps in any research project. Secondary sources are covered next in Chapter 3. Chapters 4 through 8 explain how to research different types of primary authority, and

Chapter 9 discusses how to use specialized research tools to locate both secondary and primary authority in specific subject areas of the law.

Chapters 3 through 9 are organized in a similar way. They all begin with an overview of the type of authority discussed. Then you will find an explanation of the print research process, followed by a description of electronic research sources. The material on print and electronic research will include excerpts from various research tools to highlight some of their key features. After the discussion of the research process, you will find information on citation format. The next item in each of these chapters is a section of sample pages. The sample pages contain step-by-step illustrations of the research process described earlier in the chapter. As you read through the text, you may find it helpful to review both the excerpts within the chapter and the sample pages section to get a sense of the research process for each type of authority. These chapters conclude with research checklists that summarize the research process and may be helpful to you as you work in the library.

Chapter 10 discusses general techniques for electronic research. The process of using print research sources varies according to the type of authority you are researching, which is why the preceding chapters largely focus on individual types of authority. With electronic research, however, there are certain common search techniques that can be used to research many types of authority. As a consequence, the discussion of electronic research in Chapters 3 through 9 focuses on where to locate legal authority using electronic resources, leaving most of the "how" of electronic research to Chapter 10. If you are learning about print and electronic research simultaneously, you should read Chapter 10 early in your studies. If you are learning about print research first, save Chapter 10 until you begin instruction in electronic research. When you begin learning about electronic research, you may also want to review Appendix A at the end of the text, which lists a number of Internet research sites.

The final chapter, Chapter 11, discusses research strategy and explains how to create a research plan. You do not need to read all of the preceding chapters before reading Chapter 11, although you may find Chapter 11 easier to follow after you have some background on a few research sources. Learning about research involves more than simply learning how to locate individual types of authority. You must also be able to plan a research strategy that will lead to accurate research results, and you must be able to execute your research strategy efficiently and economically. Chapter 11 sets out a process that will help you achieve these goals in any research project, whether in your legal research class or in legal practice.

# GENERATING SEARCH TERMS

All research sources, whether print or electronic, are indexed in some way. With print resources, you might use a subject index or a table of contents to locate information. With electronic resources, you might use word searches to find documents containing particular terms. No matter where you begin your search for authority, one of the first steps in the research process is generating a list of words that are likely to lead you through each resource's indexing system. This chapter discusses how to generate a useful list of search terms.

## A. GENERATING SEARCH TERMS BASED ON CATEGORIES OF INFORMATION

When presented with a set of facts, you could generate a list of search terms by constructing a random list of words that seem relevant to the issue. But a more structured approach—working from a set of categories, instead of random terms that sound relevant—will help ensure that you are covering all of your bases in conducting your research.

There are a number of ways that you could categorize the information in your research issue to create a list of search terms. Some people prefer to use the six questions journalists ask when covering a story: who, what, when, where, why, and how. Another way to generate search terms is to categorize the information presented by the facts as follows.

■ **THE *PARTIES* INVOLVED IN THE PROBLEM, DESCRIBED ACCORDING TO THEIR RELATIONSHIPS TO EACH OTHER.**
Here, you might be concerned not only with parties who are in direct conflict with each other, but also any other individuals, entities, or groups involved. These might include fact witnesses who can testify as to what

happened, expert witnesses if appropriate to the situation, other potential plaintiffs (in civil cases), or other potential defendants (in criminal or civil cases).

In describing the parties, proper names will not ordinarily be useful search terms, although if one party is a public entity or corporation, you might be able to locate other cases in which the entity or corporation was a party. Instead, you will usually want to describe the parties in terms of their legal status or relationships to each other, such as landlords and tenants, parents and children, employers and employees, or doctors and patients.

### ■ THE *PLACES AND THINGS* INVOLVED IN THE PROBLEM.

In thinking about place, both geographical locale and type of location can be important. For example, the conduct at issue might have taken place in Pennsylvania, which would help you determine which jurisdiction's law applies. It might also have taken place at a school or in a church, which could be important for determining which legal rules apply to the situation.

"Things" can involve tangible objects or intangible concepts. In a problem involving a car accident, tangible things could include automobiles or stop signs. In other types of situations, intangible "things," such as a vacation or someone's reputation, could be useful search terms.

### ■ THE *POTENTIAL CLAIMS AND DEFENSES* THAT COULD BE RAISED.

As you become more familiar with the law, you may be able to identify claims or defenses that a research problem potentially raises. The facts could indicate to you that the problem potentially involves particular claims (such as breach of contract, defamation, or bribery) or particular defenses (such as consent, assumption of the risk, or self-defense). When that is the case, you can often use claims and defenses effectively as search terms.

If you are dealing with an unfamiliar area of law, however, you might not know of any claims or defenses potentially at issue. In that situation, you can generate search terms by thinking about the conduct and mental states of the parties, as well as the injury suffered by the complaining party. Claims and defenses often flow from these considerations, and as a result, these types of terms can appear in a research tool's indexing system. When considering conduct, consider what was not done, as well as what was done. The failure to do an act might also give rise to a claim or defense.

For example, you could be asked to research a situation in which one person published an article falsely asserting that another person was guilty of tax evasion, knowing that the accusation was not true. You might recognize this as a potential claim for the tort of defamation, which occurs when one person publishes false information that is damaging to another person's reputation. Even if you were unfamiliar with this tort, however, you could still generate search terms relevant to the claim by considering the defendant's conduct (publication) or mental state (intentional actions), or the plaintiff's injury (to reputation). These search terms would likely lead you to authority on defamation.

■ **THE *RELIEF* SOUGHT BY THE COMPLAINING PARTY.**
Indexing systems often categorize information according to the relief a party is seeking. Damages, injunction, specific performance, restitution, attorneys' fees, and other terms relating to the relief sought can lead you to pertinent information.

As an example of how you might go about using these categories to generate search terms, assume you have been asked to research the following situation: Your client recently went to Puerto Rico on vacation. While on the premises of the hotel where she was staying, she was bitten by a parrot she was feeding with birdseed provided by the hotel. No signs warned that the parrot might bite. Your client was hospitalized with a serious infection.

- ■ **PARTIES:** hotel, guest, parrot.
- ■ **PLACES AND THINGS:** hotel, vacation, Puerto Rico (parrot could also fit here).
- ■ **POTENTIAL CLAIMS AND DEFENSES:** negligence, strict liability, assumption of the risk, contributory negligence. Additional terms could be generated according to conduct ("failure to warn"), mental state ("knowledge," relating to the parrot's propensity to bite), or injury ("bite wound").
- ■ **RELIEF:** damages, restitution for expenses, physical pain and suffering, mental or emotional distress.

This is not an exhaustive list of search terms for this problem, but it illustrates how you can use these categories of information to develop useful search terms.

## B. EXPANDING THE INITIAL SEARCH

Once you have developed an initial set of search terms for your issue, the next task is to try to expand that list. The terms you originally generated may not appear in a print index or electronic database. Therefore, once you have developed your initial set of search terms, you should try to increase both the breadth and the depth of the list. You

**FIGURE 2.1**   EXPANDING THE BREADTH OF SEARCH TERMS

Increasing breadth with synonyms and related terms:    motel ↔ hotel ↔ inn

can increase the breadth of the list by identifying synonyms and terms related to the initial search terms, and you can increase the depth by expressing the concepts in your search terms both more abstractly and more concretely.

Increasing the breadth of your list with synonyms and related terms is essential to your research strategy. This is especially true for word searches in computer research. In a print index, if you get close to the correct term, a cross-reference might refer you to an entry with relevant information. In computer word searching, however, the computer searches only for the specific terms you identify. Therefore, to make sure you locate all of the pertinent information on your issue, you need to have a number of synonyms for the words and concepts in your search. In the research scenario described above, there are a number of synonyms and related terms for one of the initial search terms: hotel. As Figure 2.1 illustrates, you might also search for terms such as motel or inn.

You are also more likely to find useful research material if you increase the depth of your list by varying the level of abstraction at which you express the terms you have included. For example, while the research scenario above involves a parrot, an index or computer database might not contain that term. Instead, you would be more likely to find relevant information if you expressed the term more abstractly: bird or animal. *See* Figure 2.2. In the same vein, if you were researching a problem involving "transportation equipment," you would want to consider search terms that are more concrete: automobile, train, airplane, etc.

**FIGURE 2.2**   INCREASING THE DEPTH OF SEARCH TERMS

Increasing depth with varying levels of abstraction:    parrot
↕
bird
↕
animal

Once you have developed a list of search terms, you are ready to begin looking for authority in print or electronic legal research tools. The chapters that follow explain the indexing tools in a variety of legal research sources. Regardless of where you begin your research, you will be able to use the techniques described in this chapter to access information using the indexing tools in each resource you use.

# SECONDARY SOURCE RESEARCH

A. What are secondary sources and why use them?

B. How to use secondary sources

C. Electronic research of secondary sources

D. Citing secondary sources

E. Sample pages for secondary source research

F. Checklist for secondary source research

## A. WHAT ARE SECONDARY SOURCES AND WHY USE THEM?

As you read in Chapter 1, primary authority refers to sources of legal rules, such as cases, statutes, and administrative regulations. Secondary sources, by contrast, provide commentary on the law. Although they are not binding on courts and are not cited as frequently as primary sources, secondary sources are excellent research tools. Because they often summarize or collect authorities from a variety of jurisdictions, they can help you find mandatory or persuasive primary authority on a subject. They also often provide narrative explanations of complex concepts that would be difficult for a beginning researcher to grasp thoroughly simply from reading primary sources. Equipped with a solid understanding of the background of an area of law, you will be better able to locate and evaluate primary authority on your research issue.

Secondary sources will be most useful to you in the following situations:

**(1) WHEN YOU ARE RESEARCHING AN AREA OF LAW WITH WHICH YOU ARE UNFAMILIAR.** Secondary sources can give you the necessary background to generate search terms. They can also lead you directly to primary authorities.

**(2) WHEN YOU ARE LOOKING FOR PRIMARY PERSUASIVE AUTHORITY BUT DO NOT KNOW HOW TO NARROW THE JURISDICTIONS THAT ARE LIKELY TO HAVE USEFUL INFORMATION.** If you need to find primary persuasive authority on a subject, conducting a nationwide survey of the law on the topic is not likely to be an efficient research strategy. Secondary sources can help you locate persuasive authority relevant to your research issue.

**(3) WHEN YOU ARE RESEARCHING AN UNDEVELOPED AREA OF THE LAW.** When you are researching a question of first impression, commentators may have analyzed how courts should rule on the issue.

**(4) WHEN AN INITIAL SEARCH OF PRIMARY SOURCES YIELDS EITHER NO AUTHORITY OR TOO MUCH AUTHORITY.** If you are unable to find any authority at all on a topic, you may not be looking in the right places. Secondary sources can educate you on the subject in a way that may allow you to expand or refocus your research efforts. When your search yields an unmanageable amount of information, secondary sources can do two things. First, their citations to primary authority can help you identify the most important authorities pertaining to the research issue. Second, they can provide you with information that may help you narrow your search or weed out irrelevant sources.

Knowing when *not* to use secondary sources is also important. As noted above, secondary sources are not binding on courts. Therefore, you will not ordinarily cite them in briefs or memoranda. This is especially true if you use secondary sources to lead you to primary authority. It is important never to rely exclusively on a discussion of a primary authority that appears in a secondary source. If you are discussing a primary authority in a legal analysis, you must read that authority yourself and update your research to make sure it is current.

This is true for two reasons. First, a summary of a primary authority might not include all of the information necessary to your analysis. It is important to read the primary authority for yourself to make sure you represent it correctly and thoroughly in your analysis.

Second, the information in the secondary source might not be completely current. Although most secondary sources are updated on a regular basis, the law can change at any time. The source may contain incomplete information simply because of the inevitable time lag between changes to the law and the publication of a supplement. One mistake some beginning researchers make is citing a secondary source for the text of a case or statute without checking to make sure that the case has not been overturned or that the statute has not been changed. Another potential error is citing a secondary source for a proposition about the state of the law generally, such as, "Forty-two states now recognize a cause of action for invasion of privacy based on disclosure of private facts." While statements of that nature were probably true when the secondary source was written, other states may have acted, or some of those noted may have changed their law, in the intervening time period. Accordingly, secondary sources should only be used as a starting point for locating primary authority, not an ending point.

## B. HOW TO USE SECONDARY SOURCES ∎

This section discusses the following commonly used secondary sources: legal encyclopedias, treatises, legal periodicals, *American Law Reports*, Restatements of the law, and uniform laws and model acts. Locating material within each of these sources generally involves three steps: (1) using an index or table of contents to find references to material on the topic you are researching; (2) locating the material in the main text of the source; and (3) updating your research.

The first step is using an index or table of contents to find out where information on a topic is located within the secondary source. As with the index or table of contents in any other book, those in a secondary source will refer you to volumes, chapters, pages, or sections where you will find text explaining the topic you are researching. Some secondary sources consist only of a single volume. In those situations, you need simply to look up the table of contents or index references within the text. Often, however, the information in a secondary source is too comprehensive to fit within a single volume. In those cases, the source will consist of a multivolume set of books, which may be organized alphabetically by topic or numerically by volume number. The references in the index or table of contents will contain sufficient information for you to identify the appropriate book within the set, as well as the page or section number specifically relating to the topic you are researching. Locating material in the main text of the source is the second step in the process.

The final step in your research is updating the information you have located. Most secondary sources are updated with pocket parts, as described in Chapter 1. The pocket part will be organized the same way as the main volume of the source. Thus, to update your research, you need to look up the same provisions in the pocket part that you read in the main text to find any additional information on the topic. If you do not find any reference to your topic in the pocket part, there is no new information to supplement the main text.

As you will see later in this chapter, there are some variations on this technique that apply to some secondary sources. For the most part, however, you will be able to use this three-step process to research a variety of secondary sources.

## 1. LEGAL ENCYCLOPEDIAS

Legal encyclopedias are just like the general subject encyclopedias you have used in the past, except they are limited in scope to legal subjects. Legal encyclopedias provide a general overview of the law on a variety of topics. They do not provide analysis or suggest solutions to conflicts in the law. Instead, they simply report on the general state of the law. Because encyclopedias cover the law in such a general way, you will usually use them to get background information on your research topic and, to a lesser extent, to locate citations to primary authority. You will rarely, if ever, cite directly to a legal encyclopedia.

There are two general legal encyclopedias, *American Jurisprudence, Second Edition* (Am. Jur. 2d) and *Corpus Juris Secundum* (C.J.S.). Each is a multivolume set organized alphabetically by topic. These sources can be researched using the three-step process described above. The indices for these encyclopedias are contained in separate softcover volumes that are usually shelved at the end of the set. The index volumes are published annually, so be sure to use the most current set. You can also find information by scanning the table of contents at the beginning of each topic. Am. Jur. 2d and C.J.S. cover material in such a general way that they are useful primarily for background information. Many of the citations to primary authority are relatively old and, as a consequence, may not provide you with much useful information.

In addition to Am. Jur. 2d and C.J.S., your library may also have encyclopedias for individual states. For example, state encyclopedias are published for California, Maryland, New York, and Ohio, among other states. State encyclopedias can be researched using the same process you would use with Am. Jur. 2d or C.J.S. When you are researching a question of state law, state encyclopedias are often more helpful than the general encyclopedias for two reasons. First, the summary of the law will be tailored to the rules and court decisions within that state, and therefore is likely to be more helpful. Second, the citations to primary authority will usually be more up to date and will, of course, be from the controlling jurisdiction. Consequently, state encyclopedias can be more useful for leading you to primary sources.

The examples in Figures 3.1 through 3.3 are taken from Am. Jur. 2d.

**FIGURE 3.1** INDEX TO AM. JUR. 2d

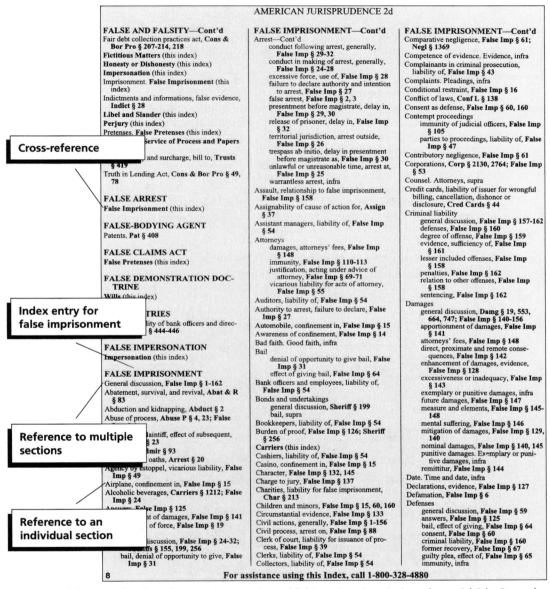

Reprinted with permission from Lawyers Cooperative Publishing, *American Jurisprudence*, 2d Ed., General Index (1999), p. 8.

**FIGURE 3.2**   AM. JUR. 2d MAIN VOLUME ENTRY UNDER FALSE IMPRISONMENT

§ 1                         FALSE IMPRISONMENT                    32 Am Jur 2d

**Sections on false imprisonment**

tives[6] the tort of false arrest or false imprisonment exists to protect and [an in]dividual's interest in freedom from unwarranted interference [with one]'s personal liberty.[7]

**§ 2.   False arrest; generally**

False arrest, a name sometimes given to the tort more generally known as false imprisonment,[8] has also been defined as the unlawful restraint by one person of the physical liberty of another, by acting to cause a false arrest, that is, an arrest made without legal authority,[9] or without sufficient legal authority,[10] resulting in damages.[11] However, the tort of false arrest does not require a formal arrest, but rather a manifest intent to take someone into custody and subject that person to the defendant's control.[12] For false arrest, there is no requirement that the arrest be formal, that the detention be for the purpose of arraignment or that the detention continue until presentation to a judicial officer in order for the arrest to be actionable.[13]

**§ 3.   Distinction between false imprisonment and false arrest**

Some courts have described false arrest and false imprisonment as causes of action which are distinguishable only in terminology.[14] The two have been called virtually indistinguishable,[15] and identical.[16] However, the difference between them lies in the manner in which they arise.[17] In order to commit false imprisonment, it is not necessary either to intend to make an arrest[18] or actu-

To constitute false imprisonment, restraint must be unreasonable and unwarranted under the circumstances. Kanner v First Nat'l Bank (Fla App D3) 287 So 2d 715.

The restraint must be "false," that is, without right or authority to do so. Tumbarella v Kroger Co., 85 Mich App 482, 271 NW2d 284.

**6.** Fermino v Fedco, Inc., 7 Cal 4th 701, 30 Cal Rptr 2d 18, 872 P2d 559, 59 Cal Comp Cas 296, 94 CDOS 3399, 94 Daily Journal DAR 6423, 9 BNA IER Cas 1132.

**7.** Phillips v District of Columbia (Dist Col App) 458 A2d 722.

**8.** Headrick v Wal-Mart Stores, Inc., 293 Ark 433, 738 SW2d 418.

**9.** Stern v Thompson & Coates, 185 Wis 2d 221, 517 NW2d 658, reconsideration den (Wis) 525 NW2d 736.

**10.** Limited Stores v Wilson-Robinson, 317 Ark 80, 876 SW2d 248.

**11.** Ting v United States (CA9 Cal) 927 F2d 1504, 91 CDOS 1794, 91 Daily Journal DAR 2996; Trenouth v United States (CA9 Cal) 764 F2d 1305, 119 BNA LRRM 3615.

**12.** Cooper v Dyke (CA4 Md) 814 F2d 941.

**13.** Day v Wells Fargo Guard Service Co. (Mo) 711 SW2d 503.

**46**

**14.** Johnson v Weiner, 155 Fla 169, 19 So 2d 699; Fox v McCurnin, 205 Iowa 752, 218 NW 499; Holland v Lutz, 194 Kan 712, 401 P2d 1015.

Although the distinctions are not always clearly set out by the authorities, false arrest, or unlawful arrest, is a species of the common-law action for false imprisonment. Bonkowski v Arlan's Dep't Store, 12 Mich App 88, 162 NW2d 347, revd on other grounds 383 Mich 90, 174 NW2d 765.

*Forms:* Instructions to jury defining false arrest. 10 Am Jur Pl & Pr [... False] Imprisonment, Form 4.

**References to primary authority from multiple jurisdictions**

**15.** Kraft v Bettendorf (Io[wa ...])

**16.** Fermino v Fedco, Inc[., 7 Cal 4th 701, 30] Cal Rptr 2d 18, 872 P2d 55[9, 59 Cal Comp Cas] 296, 94 CDOS 3399, 94 Daily Journal DAR 6423, 9 BNA IER Cas 1132.

**17.** Harrer v Montgomery Ward & Co., 124 Mont 295, 221 P2d 428; Houghtaling v State, 11 Misc 2d 1049, 175 NYS2d 659; Alter v Paul (Franklin Co) 101 Ohio App 139, 1 Ohio Ops 2d 80, 72 Ohio L Abs 332, 135 NE2d 73; Alsup v Skaggs Drug Center, 203 Okla 525, 223 P2d 530; Bender v Seattle, 99 Wash 2d 582, 664 P2d 492, 9 Media L R 2101.

**18.** Harrer v Montgomery Ward & Co., 124 Mont 295, 221 P2d 428; Hepworth v Covey Bros. Amusement Co., 97 Utah 205, 91 P2d 507.

Reprinted with permission from Lawyers Cooperative Publishing, *American Jurisprudence*, 2d Ed., Vol. 32 (1995), p. 46.

**FIGURE 3.3** AM. JUR. 2d POCKET PART ENTRY FOR FALSE IMPRISONMENT

# FALSE IMPRISONMENT

**KeyCite™/Insta-Cite®:** Cases referred to herein can be further researched through the KeyCite™ and Insta-Cite® computer-assisted services. Use KeyCite or Insta-Cite to check citations for form, parallel references, and prior and later history. For comprehensive citator information, including citations to other decisions and secondary materials that have mentioned or discussed the cases cited, use KeyCite. ALR and ALR Fed Annotations referred to herein can be further researched through the WESTLAW® Find service.

> If the pocket part contained any new information on § 2, it would appear here.

> New research references for § 3

### § 1 Definition of false imprisonment

**Research References**

Instruction to jury—False imprisonment defined. 10A Am Jur Pleading and Practice Forms, Annotated (Revised), False Imprisonment § 14.

### § 3 Distinction between false imprisonment and false arrest

**Research References**

Instruction to jury—False arrest defined. 10A Am Jur Pleading and Practice Forms, Annotated (Revised), False Imprisonment § 5.

### Generally

**Research References**

Instruction to jury—Elements of false imprisonment. 10A Am Jur Pleading and Practice Forms, Annotated (Revised), False Imprisonment § 193.

### § 9 Malice or motive; good faith

**Research References**

Instruction to jury—Good faith no justification. 10A Am Jur Pleading and Practice Forms, Annotated (Revised), False Imprisonment § 18.

### § 18 Use of force; threats

**Research References**

Complaint, petition, or declaration—False imprisonment imposed by private individual—Attempted extortion by means of threats of violence. 10A Am Jur Pleading and Practice Forms, Annotated (Revised), False Imprisonment § 34.

Complaint, petition, or declaration—Allegation—Assault during detention—Aggravation of damages. 10A Am Jur Pleading and Practice Forms, Annotated (Revised), False Imprisonment § 51.

### § 19 Necessity of apprehension of force

**Research References**

Instruction to jury—Recovery not barred where consent to restraint induced by

threatened and reasonably apprehended use of force. 10A Am Jur Pleading and Practice Forms, Annotated (Revised), False Imprisonment § 17.

### § 29 Delay in presentment before magistrate

**Research References**

Complaint, petition, or declaration—Confinement without charge after arrest without warrant—Against city and jailer. 10A Am Jur Pleading and Practice Forms, Annotated (Revised), False Imprisonment § 162.

Complaint, petition, or declaration—Unreasonable delay in taking prisoner before magistrate after arrest without warrant—Aggravation of damages by subjection of prisoner to public disgrace and humiliation—Against city and police officer. 10A Am Jur Pleading and Practice Forms, Annotated (Revised), False Imprisonment § 163.

### § 33 Generally; commitment pursuant to valid legal proceeding

**Research References**

Complaint, petition, or declaration—Instigation of arrest and imprisonment without warrant on insanity charge. 10A Am Jur Pleading and Practice Forms, Annotated (Revised), False Imprisonment § 86.

### § 38 Generally

**Research References**

Complaint, petition, or declaration—Allegation—False imprisonment by causing customer's arrest. 10A Am Jur Pleading and Practice Forms, Annotated (Revised), False Imprisonment § 50.

Complaint, petition, or declaration—Arrest and imprisonment of employee under arrest warrant—Against former employer, co-employee, and private investigator—Attempt to coerce plaintiff to abandon workers' compensation claim and contest of wrongful discharge. 10A Am Jur Pleading and Practice Forms, Annotated (Revised), False Imprisonment § 85.

Pub. 5/98

Page 7

Reprinted with permission from Lawyers Cooperative Publishing, *American Jurisprudence*, 2d Ed., Vol. 32 (1998), p. 7.

## 2. TREATISES

Treatises have a narrower focus than legal encyclopedias. Where legal encyclopedias provide a general overview of a broad range of topics, treatises generally provide in-depth treatment of a single subject, such as torts or constitutional law. A treatise may consist of a single volume.[1] Many, however, consist of multiple volumes. Most treatises provide both an overview of the topic and some analysis or commentary. They also usually contain citations to many primary and secondary authorities.

Using a treatise once you have located it ordinarily is not difficult. With most treatises, you can use the three-step process described at the beginning of this section. The more difficult aspect of using treatises is finding one on your research topic. The on-line catalog in your library is the first place to look. Treatises will be listed there by call number with all other library holdings. Because treatises do not usually have titles identifying them as treatises, however, sometimes it can be difficult figuring out which listings refer to treatises. The reference librarians in your library are a great asset in this area; they should be able to recommend treatises on your subject.

Figure 3.4 is an example from a treatise on torts.

## 3. LEGAL PERIODICALS

Articles in legal periodicals can be very useful research tools. You may hear periodical articles referred to as "law review" or "journal" articles. Many law schools publish periodicals known as law reviews or journals that collect articles on a wide range of topics. Many other types of legal periodicals also exist, however, including commercially published journals, legal newspapers, and magazines.

Articles published in law reviews or journals are thorough, thoughtful treatments of legal issues by law professors, practitioners, judges, and even students. The articles are usually focused fairly narrowly on a specific issue, although they often include background or introductory sections that provide a general overview of the topic. They are generally well researched and contain citations to many primary and secondary authorities. In addition, they often address undeveloped areas in the law and propose solutions for resolving problems in the law. As a result, periodical articles can be useful for obtaining an overview of an area of law, finding references to primary and secondary authority, and developing ideas for analyzing a question of first impression or resolving a conflict in the law.

---

[1]One type of single-volume source with which you may already be familiar is a "hornbook." A hornbook provides a clear and straightforward statement of the law on a topic. Because a hornbook is a single volume, however, it usually is not an exhaustive source of information.

**FIGURE 3.4**    TREATISE MAIN VOLUME ENTRY FOR FALSE IMPRISONMENT

§3.5          INTERFERENCE WITH THE PERSON

in holding that the defendant had committed an assault, "The act was not only apparently a most dangerous assault, but accompanied with a present purpose to do great bodily harm; and the only declaration by which its character is attempted to be changed, is, that the assailant was not determined to execute his savage purpose unconditionally and without a moment's delay. He had commenced the attack and raised the deadly weapon and was in the attitude to strike, but suspended the blow to afford the object of his vengeance an opportunity to buy his safety, by compliance with the defendant's terms. To hold such an act, under such circumstances, was not an offer of violence — not an attempt to commit violence — would be, we think, to outrage principle and manifest an utter want of that solicitude for the preservation of peace which characterizes our law."[16]

It is no defense that the defendant mistakes the identity of the person assaulted. This is the same principle as is involved in the case of a battery. If defendant intentionally puts the plaintiff in apprehension of a battery by a show or offer of violence, the mistaken belief that the plaintiff is some other person, or that the circumstances justify the action by creation of a privilege to do so, will make no difference. On the other hand, if the plaintiff suffered an invasion of his interest in freedom from apprehension of a battery by accident, the defendant obviously has a complete defense, because an essential element in the defendant's conduct is wanting, namely, the intention to invade the plaintiff's interest.[17]

**Textual explanation of false imprisonment**

## TOPIC C.    FALSE IMPRISONMENT

**§3.6    The interests protected.** False imprisonment was one of the earliest torts known to the common law.[1] Like assault and battery, it was the type of wrong most calculated to lead to a breach of the peace and, like assault and battery, was regarded as a trespass to the person. Indeed the usual imprisonment in the early law, says Street, was undoubtedly brought about by a

[16]See Restatement (Second) of Torts §30. Comment *b* (1965).
[17]Whittier, Mistake in the Law of Torts, 15 Harv. L. Rev. 335, 339 (1901).
**§3.6**  [1]2 Brac., Note Book, pl. 314 (1229).

284

**FIGURE 3.4** TREATISE MAIN VOLUME ENTRY FOR FALSE IMPRISONMENT *(Continued)*

INTERFERENCE WITH THE PERSON        §3.6

battery. "Just as assault represents an extension of the conception of harm involved in the battery in one direction, so the wrong of imprisonment represents the extension of that conception in another direction."[2]

The law of false imprisonment protects that interest in personality described as the interest in freedom from confinement. The nature of the interest appears in a general way from the early descriptions of the wrong by writers and courts. "False imprisonment," it is said, "consists in imposing an unlawful restraint upon one's freedom of locomotion or action."[3] "The essential thing," says the New Jersey court, "is the constraint of the person."[4] Again, it is described as "the total restraint of the liberty of the person,"[5] or "the placing of a person against his will in a position where he cannot exercise it in going where he may lawfully go, and detaining him at the will of another without lawful authority."[6] While these statements are on the whole inexact as definitions, they indicate the nature of the interest to be protected. A more nearly complete description is [given by] the American Law Institute in the Restatement (Second) [of Torts]: "An actor is subject to liability to another for false imprisonment if . . . he acts intending to confine the other or another person within boundaries fixed by the actor, and . . . his act directly or indirectly results in such a confinement."[7]

**References to other secondary sources**

**References to primary authority from multiple jurisdictions**

[2]1 Foundations of Legal Liability 12 (1906).

[3]Efroymson v. Smith, 29 Ind. App. 451, 455, 63 N.E. 328 (1902).

[4]Hebrew v. Pulis, 73 N.J.L. 621, 624, 64 A. 121, 7 L.R.A. (N.S.), Am. St. Rep. 716 (1906).

[5]Patteson, J., in Bird v. Jones, 7 A. & E.N.S. 742, 68 Rev. Rep. [561, 571,] 7 Q.B. 742, 115 Eng. Rep. 668 (1845). Cf. R. Dias and B. Markesidis, Tort Law 175 (1984).

[6]Robinson & Co. v. Greene, 148 Ala. 434, 440, 43 So. 797 (1906). See similarly Marshall v. District of Columbia, 391 A.2d 1374, 1380 (D.C. 1978) (gist of action "is an unlawful detention. . . . An unlawful deprivation of freedom of locomotion for any amount of time, by actual force or a threat of force, is sufficient"); Broughton v. State of New York, 37 N.Y.2d 451, 456, 373 N.Y.S.2d 87, 93, 335 N.E.2d 310, 314 (1975) (action "protects the personal interest in freedom from restraint of movement"); Herbst v. Wuennenberg, 83 Wis. 2d 768, 774, 266 N.W.2d 391, 394 (1978) (same); Dupler v. Seubert, 69 Wis. 2d 373, 381, 230 N.W.2d 626, 631 (1975) ("The essence . . . is the intentional, unlawful and unconsented restraint by one person of the physical liberty of another").

[7]Restatement (Second) of Torts §35 (1965).

285

Reprinted with permission from Oscar S. Gray. Fowler V. Harper, Fleming James, Jr., & Oscar S. Gray, *The Law of Torts,* 2d Ed., Vol. 1 (1986), pp. 284–285. © 1986 Oscar S. Gray.

Researching legal periodicals is somewhat different from researching the other secondary sources discussed in this chapter. Thousands of articles in hundreds of periodicals are published each year. Because each periodical is an independent publication, trying to find articles through the indices or tables of contents within individual publications would be impossible. Instead, you need to use an indexing service that collects references to a wide range of legal periodicals. Two print indices, the *Index to Legal Periodicals and Books* (ILP) and the *Current Law Index* (CLI), will lead you to periodical articles. Electronic indexing services can also be used to locate articles. ILP is available in electronic form at many law libraries. LegalTrac is another popular electronic indexing service.

ILP and CLI do not have identical coverage, but they index largely the same universe of publications. They both consist of noncumulative volumes covering specific periods of time. Because the volumes are noncumulative, they are not updated with pocket parts. Instead, subsequent volumes cover later time periods. This means that you must use multiple volumes to look for articles over a period of time. Both indices publish annual hardbound volumes and monthly softcover updates. Both indices organize articles by subject. Thus, to find citations to articles on a subject, you simply look up the subject within ILP or CLI. You can also find articles indexed in ways other than by subject. For example, CLI contains a separate index of authors and titles. In ILP, author names are included in the general subject index. Both ILP and CLI also contain features called the table of cases and table of statutes. You can use these tables to locate citations to articles discussing specific cases or statutes. Figures 3.5 and 3.6 illustrate index entries from ILP and CLI.

LegalTrac or the electronic version of ILP may also be available on your library's computer network. These services allow you to search for legal periodicals in a variety of ways, including by keyword and by author. When you execute the search, you will retrieve a list of citations to articles that fit the specifications of your search. You can then print a list of citations and locate the articles on the shelves in your library. Figure 3.7 shows a portion of the results of a subject search for false imprisonment on LegalTrac.

Equipped with a list of citations, you are ready to head to the shelves. The citations in ILP, CLI, and LegalTrac will contain the abbreviated name of the periodical, the number of the volume containing the article, and the starting page of the article, e.g., 25 Val. U. L. Rev. 407. This citation tells you to locate the *Valparaiso University Law Review* on the shelves, locate volume 25, and turn to page 407. You can locate the periodical on the shelves by checking the on-line catalog for the call number of the publication.

With most legal research tools, the next step in the process would be to update your research. Periodical articles are one exception to this

**FIGURE 3.5** ILP INDEX ENTRY

**SUBJECT AND AUTHOR INDEX** 269

**Index entry for false imprisonment**

**Article on false imprisonment**

...ran J.

...f strength or source of weakness?: A critique ...“source-of-strength” doctrine in banking reform. 66 *N.Y.U. L. Rev.* 1344-403 N '91

**Fallon, Richard H., Jr.**
Claims Court at the crossroads. 40 *Cath. U. L. Rev.* 517-32 Spr '91
Common law court or council of revision? 101 *Yale L.J.* 949-68 Ja '92
Reflections on Dworkin and the two faces of law. 67 *Notre Dame L. Rev.* 553-85 '92

**False imprisonment**
Detention in a police station and false imprisonment. J. Mackenzie. 142 *New L.J.* 534-6 Ap 17 '92
He who controls the mind controls the body: false imprisonment, religious cults, and the destruction of volitional capacity. 25 *Val. U. L. Rev.* 407-54 Spr '91

**Falvey, Joseph L., Jr.**
Health care professionals and rights warning requirements. ...*rmy Law.* 21-31 O '91
...re professionals and rights warnings. 40 *Naval* ... 173-91 '92
...rts
...e also
...Juvenile courts

**Family law** *See* Domestic relations
**Family planning** *See* Birth control
**Family violence** *See* Domestic violence

**Fanter, William F.**
Attacking safety belt limitations: unconstitutional restraint of defendants; by W. F. Fanter, B. A. Hering. 42 *Fed'n Ins. & Corp. Couns. Q.* 181-90 Wint '92

**Farber, Daniel A.**
Economic analysis and just compensation. 12 *Int'l Rev. L. & Econ.* 125-38 Je '92
Free speech without romance: public choice and the first amendment. 105 *Harv. L. Rev.* 554-83 D '91
The inevitability of practical reason: statutes, formalism, and the rule of law. 45 *Vand. L. Rev.* 533-59 Ap '92
The jurisprudential cab ride: a Socratic dialogue. 1992 *B.Y.U. L. Rev.* 363-70 '92
Risk regulation in perspective: Reserve Mining [Reserve Mining Co. v. EPA, 514 F.2d 492] revisited. 21 *Envtl. L.* 1321-57 '91
“Terminator 2?”: the Constitution in an alternate world. 9 *Const. Commentary* 59-73 Wint '92

**Farina, Cynthia R.**
Getting from here to there. 1991 *Duke L.J.* 689-710 Je '91

**Farley, E. Milton, III**
Experts are everywhere! 12 *E. Min. L. Inst.* 5.1-.82 '91

**Farley, John J., III**
The new kid on the block of veterans' law: the United States Court of Veterans Appeals. 38 *Fed. B. News & J.* 488-92 N/D '91
Robin Hood jurisprudence: the triumph of equity in American tort law. 65 *St. John's L. Rev.* 997-1021 Aut '91

**Farm bankruptcy**
Recent developments in Chapter 12 bankruptcy. S. A. Schneider. 24 *Ind. L. Rev.* 1357-78 '91
The search for the proper interest rate under Chapter 12 (Family Farmer Bankruptcy Act). T. O. Depperschmidt, N. H. Kratzke. 67 *N.D. L. Rev.* 455-68 '91
Selected issues of federal farm program payments in bankruptcy. C. R. Kelley, S. A. Schneider. 14 *J. Agric. Tax'n & L.* 99-139 Summ '92

**Farm tenancy**
The mystical art of valuing agricultural tenancies. 1991 *Brit. Tax Rev.* 181-7 '91

**Farmer, Larry**
Feminist theory, professional ethics, and gender-related distinctions in attorney negotiating styles; by L. Burton, L. Farmer, E. D. Gee, L. Johnson, G. R. Williams. 1991 *J. Disp. Resol.* 199-257 '91

**Farmer, Lindsay**
'The genius of our law...': criminal law and the Scottish legal tradition. 55 *Mod. L. Rev.* 25-43 Ja '92

**Farmer, Susan Beth**
Market power and the National Association of Attorneys General Horizontal Merger Guidelines. 60 *Antitrust L.J.* 839-48 '91/'92

**Farming** *See* Agriculture

**Farnham, David**
The marital privilege. 18 *Litig.* 34-7 Wint '92

**Farnsworth, E. Allan (Edward Allan), 1928-**
Comments on Professor Waddams' “Precontractual duties of disclosure”. 19 *Can. Bus. L.J.* 351-6 '91
Punitive damages in arbitration. 20 *Stetson L. Rev.* 395-418 Spr '91

**Farnsworth, Edward Allan** *See* Farnsworth, E. Allan (Edward Allan), 1928-

**Farrar, John H.**
Cross frontier mergers. 4 *Canterbury L. Rev.* 429-46 '91

**Farrell, L. M.**
Financial guidelines for investing in motion picture limited partnerships. 12 *Loy. L.A. Ent. L.J.* 127-51 '92

**Farrier, David**
Vegetation conservation: the planning system as a vehicle for the regulation of broadacre agricultural land clearing. 18 *Melb. U. L. Rev.* 26-59 Je '91

**Farrington, David P.**
Advancing knowledge about co-offending: results from a prospective longitudinal survey of London males; by A. J. Reiss, Jr., D. P. Farrington. 82 *J. Crim. L. & Criminology* 360-95 Summ '91

**Farris, Juli E.**
Grassroots impact litigation: mass filing of small claims; by A. D. Freeman, J. E. Farris. 26 *U.S.F. L. Rev.* 261-81 Wint '92

**Farris, Martin T.**
Antitrust irrelevance in air transportation and the redefining of price discrimination; by L. E. Gesell, M. T. Farris. 57 *J. Air L. & Com.* 173-97 Fall '91

**Fatum, Stephen M.**
A review of the Illinois Health Care Surrogate Act; by S. M. Fatum, R. J. Kane, T. R. LeBlang. 80 *Ill. B.J.* 124-9+ Mr '92

**Faulk, Richard O.**
Epidemiology in the courtroom: a problem of statistical significance. 59 *Def. Couns. J.* 25-30 Ja '92

**Faulkner, Ellen**
Lesbian abuse: the social and legal realities. 16 *Queen's L.J.* 261-86 Summ '91

**Faulkner, James**
Mens rea in rape: Morgan [R. v. Morgan, [1976] A.C. 182] and the inadequacy of subjectivism or why no should not mean yes in the eyes of the law. 18 *Melb. U. L. Rev.* 60-82 Je '91

**Faull, Jonathan**
The enforcement of competition policy in the European Community: a mature system. 15 *Fordham Int'l L.J.* 219-47 '91/'92

**Faure, Michael**
Self-regulation of the professions in Belgium; by R. Van Den Bergh, M. Faure. 11 *Int'l Rev. L. & Econ.* 165-82 S '91

**Faust, Richard**
The great writ in action: empirical light on the federal habeas corpus debate; by R. Faust, T. J. Rubenstein, L. W. Yackle. 18 *N.Y.U. Rev. L. & Soc. Change* 637-710 '90/'91

**Fauteux, Paul**
Sources d'énergie nucléaire dans l'espace: Bilan réglementaire et incertitudes américaines. 16 *Annals Air & Space L.* 267-306 '91

**Favoreu, Louis**
The principle of equality in the jurisprudence of the Conseil constitutionnel. 21 *Cap. U. L. Rev.* 165-97 Wint '92

**Fawcett, James**
The interrelationships of jurisdiction and choice of law in private international law. 44 *Current Legal Probs.* 39-62 '91

**FIGURE 3.6**　CLI INDEX ENTRY

FALSE ADVERTISING　　　　　　　SUBJECT INDEX

An empirical study of the weight of survey evidence in deceptive advertising litigation. (New Zealand) by Robert Langton and Lindsay Trotman
*5 Canterbury Law Review 147-170 Annual '92*

Recovery for false advertising under the revised Lanham Act; a methodology for the computation of damages. by Paul D. Frederickson
*29 American Business Law Journal 585-624 Wntr '92*

**-Reports**
Drug ads in medical journals often misleading, study finds. by Georgia Sargeant　*28 Trial 84(3) August '92*

**-Surveys**
The battle against claims of presale misrepresentations and allegations of guaranteed success. by Kim A. Lambert　*11 Franchise Law Journal 95(4) Wntr '92*

**FALSE certification**
Name games: signing blank documents is a shortcut to trouble. by Joanne Pelton Pitulla
*80 ABA Journal 102(1) Dec '94*

A little learning. (forged medical diploma and training certificates may haved led to the death of an elderly patient) (United Kingdom) by Jonathan Goodman
*61 Medico-Legal Journal 216-218 Fall '93*

[...]ce of a signature requirement in Mississippi [...] fraud waiting to happen. (Symposium on [...]aw) by David W. Marcase
*13 Mississippi College Law Review 371-384 Spring '93*

[...]e; Agriculture Act 1970, s. 29(5) - making a [...] statement depends upon receipt of statement. (United Kingdom) by Lynne Knapman and J.C. Smith
*Criminal Law Review 874-875 Dec '92*

**FALSE claims** (Insurance) *see*
Insurance fraud

**FALSE imprisonment**

> Index entry for false imprisonment

**-Analysis**
[...]es en matiere d'allegations d'abus sexuels: [...]n a la prudence. (Quebec) (Les Journees de [...] Pluridisciplinaire Charles-Coderre) by Luc
*23 Revue de Droit Universite de Sherbrooke 415-436 Wntr '93*

[...]f proceedings as a remedy in criminal cases: [...] abuse of process concept. (Great Britain) by David M. Paciocco
*15 Criminal Law Journal 315-350 Oct '91*

> Article on false imprisonment

**-Cases**
Putting the Foreign Sovereign Immunity Act's commercial activities exception in context.(Case Note) Cicippio v. Islamic Republic of Iran 30 F.3d 164 (D.C. Cir. 1994) by Kevin Leung
*17 Loyola of Los Angeles International and Comparative Law Journal 701-736 April '95*

The Fifth Circuit extends qualified immunity to police officers who arrest anti-abortion protestors.(Case Note) Mangieri v. Clifton 29 F.3d 1012 (5th Cir. 1994) by Ugo Colella　*69 Tulane Law Review 833-846 Feb '95*

Death Row Briton 'could have been me.' (executed British murderer Nicholas Ingram; Kevin Callan, released from prison after proving his innocence) by Sarah Strickland　*v6 Colorado Journal of International Environmental Law and Policy p3(1) Wntr '95*

The constitutional ramifications of calling a police officer an 'asshole.' (Case Note) Buffkins v. City of Omaha 922 F.2d 465 (8th Cir. 1990) by Allen T. McGlynn　*16 Southern Illinois University Law Journal 741-761 Spring '92*

**-International aspects**
Saudi Arabia v. Nelson: the Foreign Sovereign Immunities Act in perspective. by Everett C. Johnson Jr.
*16 Houston Journal of International Law 291-309 Winter '93*

**-Laws, regulations, etc.**
Detention in a police station and false imprisonment. (Great Britain) by John Mackenzie
*142 New Law Journal 534(3) April 17 '92*

Innocent until proven guilty: shallow words for the falsely accused in a criminal prosecution for child sexual abuse. by Terese L. Fitzpatrick
*12 University of Bridgeport Law Review 175-208 Winter '91*

Release of the guilty to protect the innocent. by Robert Sommer, Barbara A. Sommer and Mati Heidmets
*18 Criminal Justice and Behavior 480-490 Dec '91*

**-Litigation**
No interference with Scottish warrants. (United Kingdom) by J.A. Coutts
*59 Journal of Criminal Law 321-323 Nov '95*

1858

Arrest, false imprisonment and malicious prosecution.(United Kingdom) by J.A. Coutts
*59 Journal of Criminal Law 48-50 Feb '95*

Freedom to denounce your fellow citizens to the police. (United Kingdom) by J.R. Spencer
*53 Cambridge Law Journal 433-435 Nov '94*

Claims of innocence; court to define evidence standard for prisoners alleging wrongful conviction. (U.S. Supreme Court) (includes a preview of two other cases on the court's 1994-95 docket) by L. Anita Richardson
*80 ABA Journal 38(2) Oct '94*

Rape - indecent assault - unlawful imprisonment - consent - intention - Crimes Act 1958 (Vic.) by Robyn Leggett　*18 Criminal Law Journal 293-296 Oct '94*

Longer than normal sentence - false imprisonment. (United Kingdom)
*Criminal Law Review 462-463 June '94*

David Milgaard, the Supreme Court and section 690: a wrongful conviction revisited. (Canada) by Neil Boyd and Kim Rossmo　*18 Canadian Lawyer 28(3) Feb '94*

Mandated affidavit required in false imprisonment case against hospital. (Missouri) (Case Note)
*26 Journal of Health and Hospital Law 253(1) August '93*

The murder case that unravelled; after almost six years behind bars, wrongly convicted man goes free. (Walter McMillian) (Alabama) by Mark Hansen
*79 ABA Journal 30(2) June '93*

Extradition - delay - abuse of process - Extradition Act 1988 (Cth). (Australia) by Ned Aughterson
*17 Criminal Law Journal 206-208 June '93*

Crime reporter. (wrongful arrest, suspended sentences, parole) (United Kingdom) by C.A. Hopkins
*137 Solicitors Journal 450(2) May 14 '93*

Evidence - Criminal Justice Act 1988, s. 23(3)(b), s. 26 - witness giving no material evidence through fear - admissibility of written statement. (United Kingdom) by Lynne Knapman and D.J. Birch
*Criminal Law Review 879-880 Dec '92*

The trial that failed; only a civil suit can hold a confessed murderer accountable. (murderer Russell Swart confesses and wrongfully accused murderer Keith Bullock goes free in slaying of Julie Everson) (Minnesota) by Mark Hansen
*78 ABA Journal 24(1) August '92*

Bright lights, big pity. (murder convictions overturned after 17 years for Benny Powell and Clarence Chance) by Amy Singer　*14 American Lawyer 72(6) June '92*

Tort and the treatment of prisoners. by C.A. Hopkins
*51 Cambridge Law Journal 12-15 March '92*

Abuse of process - failure to make available or reveal to the defence the existence of unused material - principles to be applied - whether matter for judge. (Great Britain) by Owen Davies and J.C. Smith
*Criminal Law Review 117-119 Feb '92*

Custody time expiring - D released by justices and re-arrested on new charge - whether abuse of process. (Great Britain) by Veronica Cowan and J.C. Smith
*Criminal Law Review 116-117 Feb '92*

Convicted prisoner's rights to sue. (Great Britain)
*56 Journal of Criminal Law 66-68 Feb '92*

Charging the wrong person - the competency of amendment out of time. (Scotland)
*36 Journal of the Law Society of Scotland 482-483 Dec '91*

Guilty until proven innocent. (Canada) by Jim Middlemiss　*15 Canadian Lawyer 20(6) Nov '91*

Compensation for arrest. (Great Britain) by Ruth Harrison　*55 Journal of Criminal Law 300(1) August '91*

Is conviction proof of lawfulness of arrest? (Great Britain) by J.A. Coutts
*55 Journal of Criminal Law 76-78 Feb '91*

**-Psychological aspects**
The psychological and legal aftermath of false arrest and imprisonment. by Robert T. Simon
*21 The Bulletin of the American Academy of Psychiatry and the Law 523-528 Dec '93*

**-Religious aspects**
He who controls the mind controls the body: false imprisonment, religious cults, and the destruction of volitional capacity. by Laura B. Brown
*25 Valparaiso University Law Review 407-454 Spring '91*

**-Remedies**
Malicious prosecution: invasion of Charter interests; remedies; Nelles v. Ontario; R. v. Jedynack; R. v. Simpson. (Canada) by John Sopinka
*74 Canadian Bar Review 366-374 June '95*

Injury by justice: inadequacy of ex-gratia compensation for wrongful conviction. (New South Wales) (Cover Story) by Greg Walsh
*32 Law Society Journal 32(5) June '94*

Remedies for miscarriage of justice: wrongful imprisonment. (New South Wales) by George Zdenkowski　*5 Current Issues in Criminal Justice 105-110 July '93*

**FALSE light invasion of privacy** *see*
Privacy, Right of

**FALSE memory** (Psychology) *see*
Recovered memory (Psychology)

**FALSE Memory Syndrome Foundation**
Fact or fantasy? The debate over 'repressed memory syndrome' enters the courtroom. (includes related material) by Holly Metz
*24 Student Lawyer 20(10) Dec '95*

**FALSE personation**
Postal inspectors barred from posing as journalists: some federal agencies still allow media impersonation.
*19 News Media & the Law 27(1) Fall '95*

A little learning. (forged medical diploma and training certificates may haved led to the death of an elderly patient) (United Kingdom) by Jonathan Goodman
*61 Medico-Legal Journal 216-218 Fall '93*

Crimes of mobility. by Lawrence M. Friedman
*43 Stanford Law Review 637-658 Feb '91*

**FALSE swearing** *see*
Perjury

**FALSE teeth** *see*
Dentures

**FALSE testimony** *see*
Perjury

**FALSE witness** *see*
Perjury

**FALSEHOOD** *see*
Truthfulness and falsehood

**FALWELL, Jerry**
NCAA is no match for Jerry Falwell and his lawyers. (prayer in the end zone) by Bill Haltom
*31 Tennessee Bar Journal 37(2) Sept-Oct '95*

**FAMA publica** *see*
Reputation (Law)

**FAMILIAL diseases**
Whose genes are these anyway? Familial conflicts over access to genetic information. by Sonia M. Suter
*91 Michigan Law Review 1854-1908 June '93*

**FAMILIES**, Dual-career *see*
Dual-career families

**FAMILIES of military personnel** *see*
Military dependents

**FAMILIES with problems** *see*
Problem families

**FAMILY** *see also*
Adult children
Birth order
Broken homes
Brothers and sisters
Children
Clans
Divorce
Domestic relations
Dual-career families
Eugenics
Fathers
Grandparent and child
Grandparents
Heredity, Human
Home
Households
Kinship
Marriage
Matriarchy
Mothers
Parent and child
Parenthood
Parents
Patriarchy
Prisoners' families
Problem families
Rural families
Single-parent family
Stepfamilies
Tribes
Twins
Unmarried couples
Widows

**-Analysis**
The family in transition: from Griswold to Eisenstadt and beyond. by Janet L. Dolgin
*82 Georgetown Law Journal 1519-1571 April '94*

La complementarite des institutions dans le domaine de la protection. (Quebec) (Les Journees de Formation Pluridisciplinaire Charles-Coderre) by Oscar d'Amours
*23 Revue de Droit Universite de Sherbrooke 289-304 Wntr '93*

Genetic narratives: biology, stories, and the definition of the family. by James Lindemann Nelson
*2 Health Matrix 71-83 Spring '92*

Let the legislatures define the family: why default statutes should be used to eliminate potential confusion. by Hubert J. Barnhardt III
*40 Emory Law Journal 571-609 Spring '91*

Cumulative Subject Index, Vol. 2 (1991–1995), p. 1858, from *Current Law Index,* by Gale Group, © 1999 Gale Group. Reprinted by permission of the Gale Group.

**FIGURE 3.7**   LEGALTRAC CITATION LIST

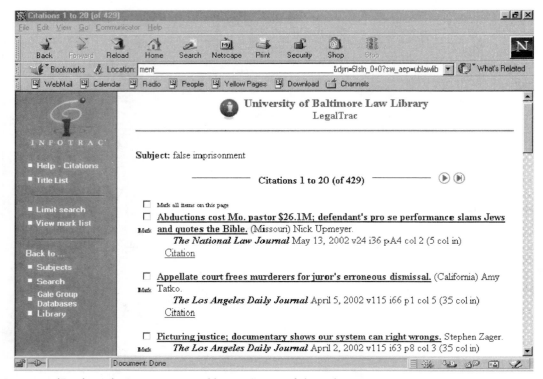

From *LegalTrac* by Gale Group. Reprinted by permission of the Gale Group.

rule. As noted above, ILP and CLI are updated with new, noncumulative volumes published periodically. There is no way to update an individual periodical article, however, short of locating later articles that add to or criticize an earlier article. As a consequence, it is important to note the date of any periodical article you use. If the article is more than a few years old, you may want to supplement your research with more current material. In addition, as noted earlier, if you use the article to lead you to primary authority, you will need to update your research using the updating tools available for those primary sources to make sure your research is completely current.

## 4. AMERICAN LAW REPORTS

*American Law Reports*, or A.L.R., contains articles called "Annotations." Annotations collect summaries of cases from a variety of jurisdictions to provide an overview of the law on a topic. A.L.R. combines the breadth of topic coverage found in an encyclopedia with the depth of discussion in a treatise or legal periodical. Nevertheless, A.L.R. is different from these other secondary sources in significant ways. Because A.L.R. Annotations provide summaries of individual cases, they are more detailed than encyclopedias. Unlike treatises or legal periodicals, however, they mostly report the results of the cases without much analysis or commentary. A.L.R. Annotations are especially helpful at the beginning of your research to give you an overview of a topic. Because Annotations collect summaries of cases from many jurisdictions, they can also be helpful in directing you toward mandatory or persuasive primary authority. More recent Annotations also contain references to other research sources, such as other secondary sources and tools for conducting additional case research. Although A.L.R. is a useful research tool, you will rarely, if ever, cite directly to an A.L.R. Annotation.

There are six series of A.L.R.: A.L.R., A.L.R.2d, A.L.R.3d, A.L.R.4th, A.L.R.5th, and A.L.R. Fed. Each series contains multiple volumes organized by volume number. A.L.R. Fed. covers issues of federal law. The remaining series usually cover issues of state law, although they do bring in federal law as appropriate to the topic. A.L.R. and A.L.R.2d are, for the most part, out of date and will not be useful to you. They are also updated using special tools not applicable to any of the other A.L.R. series. Generally, you will find A.L.R.3d, 4th, 5th, and Fed. to be the most useful.

A.L.R. Annotations can be researched using the three-step process described earlier in this chapter. Annotations can be located using the A.L.R. Index.[2] The A.L.R. Index is a separate set of index volumes usually shelved near the A.L.R. sets. It contains references to Annotations in A.L.R.2d, 3d, 4th, 5th, and Fed. The A.L.R. Index and the individual volumes in A.L.R.3d, 4th, 5th, and Fed. are updated with pocket parts.

Figures 3.8 and 3.9 illustrate some of the features of an A.L.R. Annotation.

## 5. RESTATEMENTS

The American Law Institute publishes what are called Restatements of the law in a variety of fields. You may already be familiar with the Restatements for contracts or torts from your other classes. Restatements essentially "restate" the common-law rules on a subject. Restatements have been published in the following fields:

- Agency
- Conflicts of Laws
- Contracts
- Foreign Relations

---

[2] A.L.R. also publishes "digests," which are separate finding tools from the A.L.R. Index. You do not need to use the A.L.R. digests to locate Annotations. Annotations can be located directly from the A.L.R. Index.

**FIGURE 3.8**    STARTING PAGE OF AN A.L.R. ANNOTATION

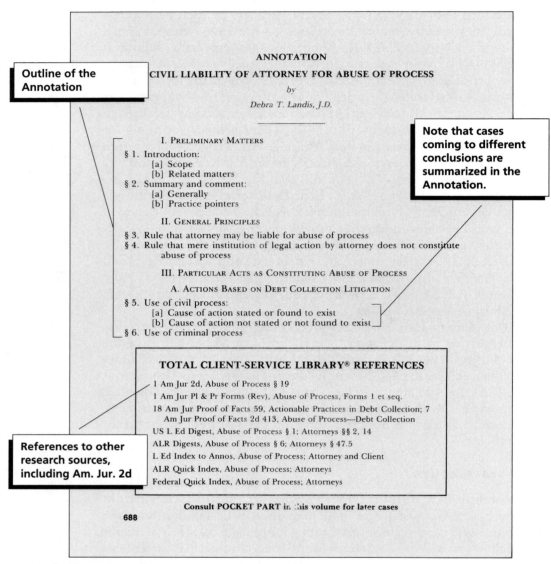

Reprinted with permission from Lawyers Cooperative Publishing, *American Law Reports*, 3d Ser., Vol. 97 (1980), p. 688.

**FIGURE 3.9**   LATER PAGE OF AN A.L.R. ANNOTATION

97 ALR3d   LIABILITY OF ATTORNEY FOR ABUSE OF PROCESS   § 3
97 ALR3d 688

and another statute governed "injuries to the rights of others," the court held that an action for abuse of process was controlled by the latter statute.[16]

**II. General principles**

**§ 3. Rule that attorney may be liable for abuse of process**

[Citations to cases from multiple jurisdictions]

The following cases support the rule that an attorney may be held liable in a civil action for abuse of process where the acts complained of are his own personal acts, or the acts of others instigated and carried on by him.

US—For federal cases involving state law, see state headings infra.

Ga—Walker v Kyser (1967) 115 Ga App 314, 154 SE2d 457 (by implication).

Kan—Little v Sowers (1949) 167 Kan 72, 204 P2d 605.

Me—Lambert v Breton (1929) 127 Me 510, 144 A 864 (recognizing rule).

Minn—Hoppe v Klapperich (1937) 224 Minn 224, 28 NW2d 780, 173 ALR 819.

NJ—Ash v Cohen (1937) 119 NJL 54, 194 A 174.

Voytko v Ramada Inn of Atlantic City (1978, DC NJ) 445 F Supp 315 (by implication; applying New Jersey law).

NY—Board of Education v Farmingdale Classroom Teachers Asso. (1975) 38 NY2d 397, 380 NYS2d 635, 343 NE2d 278 (by implication).

Dishaw v Wadleigh (1897) 15 App Div 205, 44 NYS 207.

Cote v Knickerbocker Ice Co. (1936) 160 Misc 658, 290 NYS 483 (recognizing rule); Rothbard v Ringler (1947, Sup) 77 NYS2d 351 (by

implication); Weiss v Hunna (1963, CA2 NY) 312 F2d 711, cert den 374 US 853, 10 L Ed 2d 1073, 83 S Ct 1920, reh den 375 US 874, 11 L Ed 2d 104, 84 S Ct 37 (by implication; applying New York law).

Pa—Haggerty v Moyerman (1936) 321 Pa 555, 184 A 654 (by implication).

Adelman v Rosenbaum (1938) 133 Pa Super 386, 3 A2d 15; Sachs v (1963, ED Pa) 216 F Supp 4 implication; applying Pennsy law).

Wash—Fite v Lee (1974) 11 App 21, 521 P2d 964, 97 ALR3d 678, (by implication).

[Discussion of the law with a more detailed case summary]

An attorney is personally liable to a third party if he maliciously participates with others in an abuse of process, or if he maliciously encourages and induces another to act as his instrumentality in committing an act constituting an abuse of process, the court held in Hoppe v Klapperich (1947) 224 **Minn** 224, 28 NW2d 780, 173 ALR 819. The court reversed the order of the trial court which had sustained the demurrers of an attorney and other defendants in a proceeding for abuse of process and malicious prosecution. The plaintiff had alleged, as to the cause of action for abuse of process, that it was the intent of the defendants, an attorney, his client, a sheriff, and a municipal judge, to force her to part with certain bonds, negotiable instruments, and other valuable papers by threatening her with arrest and prosecution on a criminal charge of theft of a watch. The plaintiff's subsequent arrest and confinement on the charge of theft were alleged to constitute a continuing abuse of process. The court noted that in the performance

16. See 7 Am Jur Proof of Facts 2d, Abuse of Process—Debt Collection § 4.

693

Reprinted with permission from Lawyers Cooperative Publishing, *American Law Reports*, 3d Ser., Vol. 97 (1980), p. 693.

- Judgments
- Law Governing Lawyers
- Property
- Restitution
- Security
- Suretyship and Guaranty
- Torts
- Trusts
- Unfair Competition

In determining what the common-law rules are, the Restatements often look to the rules in the majority of United States jurisdictions. Sometimes, however, the Restatements will also state emerging rules where the rules seem to be changing, or proposed rules in areas where the authors believe a change in the law would be appropriate. Although the Restatements are limited to common-law doctrines, the rules in the Restatements are set out almost like statutes, breaking different doctrines down into their component parts. In addition to setting out the common-law rules for a subject, the Restatements also provide commentary on the proper interpretations of the rules, illustrations demonstrating how the rules should apply in certain situations, and summaries of cases applying and interpreting the Restatement.

Although a Restatement is a secondary source, it is one with substantial weight. Courts can decide to adopt a Restatement's view of an issue, which then makes the comments and illustrations especially persuasive in that jurisdiction. If you are researching the law of a jurisdiction that has adopted a Restatement, you can use the Restatement volumes effectively to locate persuasive authority from other Restatement jurisdictions. As a result, a Restatement is an especially valuable secondary source.

Figures 3.10 and 3.11 show some of the features of one Restatement, the *Restatement (Second) of Torts*. There are two components to the *Restatement (Second) of Torts*: the Restatement volumes, which contain the Restatement rules, comments, and illustrations; and the Appendix volumes, which contain case summaries. To research the *Restatement (Second) of Torts*, you must follow two steps: (1) find relevant sections of the Restatement in the Restatement volumes; and (2) find case summaries interpreting the Restatement in the Appendix volumes.

In the first step, the subject index or table of contents in the Restatement volumes will direct you to individual rules within the Restatement. After the formal statement of the rule, the comments and illustrations will follow.

In the second step, you need to go to the separate Appendix volumes. The Appendix volumes are organized numerically by Restatement section number. By looking up the appropriate section number, you will

**FIGURE 3.10** SECTION 35 OF THE *RESTATEMENT (SECOND) OF TORTS*

§ **35**                 TORTS, SECOND                 Ch. 2

TOPIC 4.   THE INTEREST IN FREEDOM FROM
CONFINEMENT

§ **35.** False Imprisonment

**Rule from the Restatement**

(1) An actor is subject to liability to another for false imprisonment if

(a) he acts intending to confine the other or a third person within boundaries fixed by the actor, and

(b) his act directly or indirectly results in such a confinement of the other, and

(c) the other is conscious of the confinement or is harmed by it.

(2) An act which is not done with the intention stated in Subsection (1, a) does not make the actor liable to the other for a merely transitory or otherwise harmless confinement, although the act involves an unreasonable risk of imposing it and therefore would be negligent or reckless if the risk threatened bodily harm.

See Reporter's Notes.

Caveat:

The Institute expresses no opinion as to whether the actor may not be subject to liability for conduct which involves an unreasonable risk of causing a confinement of such duration or character as to make the other's loss of freedom a matter of material value.

**Comment**

**Comment on Subsection (1):**

*a. Common-law action of trespass for false imprisonment.* At common law, the appropriate form of action for imposing a confinement was trespass for false imprisonment except where the confinement was by arrest under a valid process issued by a court having jurisdiction, in which case the damages for the confinement were recoverable, if at all, as part of the damages in an action of trespass on the case for malicious prosecution or abuse of process. Therefore, an act which makes the actor liable under this Section for a confinement otherwise than by arrest under a valid process is customarily called a false imprisonment.

*b.* As to the meaning of the words "subject to liability," see § 5.

See Appendix for Reporter's Notes, Court Citations, and Cross References

52

© 1965 by The American Law Institute. Reprinted with permission, *Restatement (Second) of the Law of Torts*, 2d Ed., Vol. 1, § 35 (1965), p. 52.

**FIGURE 3.11**     ENTRY UNDER § 35 IN THE APPENDIX TO THE *RESTATEMENT (SECOND) OF TORTS*

---

§ **34**                              **TORTS**                              **Ch. 2**

complaint. Affirming in part, this court held that the plaintiff's allegations of duress and undue influence in that the defendant had forced her to submit her final class paper, thus depriving her of free exercise of her will and her constitutional rights, did not state a cognizable claim. The specially concurring opinion argued that it was not prepared at this time to adopt the Restatement sections as the law of the state for civil assault and civil battery. Jung–Leonczynska v. Steup, 782 P.2d 578, 583, 584, appeal after remand 803 P.2d 1358 (1990).

### TOPIC 4.   THE INTEREST IN FREEDOM FROM CONFINEMENT

**Ariz.App.**1987.  Cit. in disc. §§ 35–45A, comprising all of Ch. 2, Topic 4. A bank customer sued a bank for false arrest and false imprisonment after he was arrested and detained by police as a result of bank employees' allegations that the plaintiff was fraudulently using a credit card. The trial court denied the bank's motion for a directed verdict and granted the plaintiff's motion for a directed verdict on the ground that there was insufficient probable cause to believe that the plaintiff committed a felony. This court reversed the grant of the plaintiff's motion and remanded for a jury trial of his claims. The court also affirmed the denial of the bank's motion, stating that, based on the evidence, a jury could reasonably conclude that the bank instigated or participated in the arrest. Deadman v. Valley Nat. Bank of Arizona, 154 Ariz. 452, 743 P.2d 961, 966.

**Miss.**1987. Cit. in disc. §§ 35–45A, comprising all of Ch. 2, Topic 4. Two police officers who responded to a report of gunshots detained a belligerent and intoxicated individual for 15 minutes of interrogation and investigation. The individual who had been detained sued the police officers, an alderman, and the city for false imprisonment. The trial court entered judgment in favor of the defendants. Affirming, this court held that the 15-minute detention of the plaintiff by the police was not unreasonable in terms of purpose, duration, or extent under the circumstances. The court reasoned that the law affords as a defense to one sued for false imprisonment that the plaintiff was temporarily detained for reasonable investigative purposes. Thornhill v. Wilson, 504 So.2d 1205, 1207.

**Cases interpreting § 35**

### § 35.   False Imprisonment

**C.A.1,** 1991. Subsec. (1) cit. in disc. A debtor in bankruptcy, jailed for contempt in state court proceedings brought by a judgment creditor without notice of the bankruptcy filing to collect on its judgment debt, sued the judgment creditor for false imprisonment, inter alia. The district court entered judgment on a jury verdict for the defendant. This court affirmed, holding that the district court correctly stated the law of false imprisonment regarding the element of willful detention of the plaintiff by requiring the jury to find that the defendant knew that there was no right to pick the plaintiff up and have him put in jail, or to ask a judge to do that, yet went ahead in reckless disregard of that fact. The court said that the instruction was the correct approach to defining the willfulness requirement where the defendant had not physically confined the plaintiff but had effected the plaintiff's confinement through the police acting pursuant to a warrant valid on its face. Under these circumstances, the court concluded that the defendant could have acted "willfully" only if it knew that the warrant had been maliciously or wrongfully obtained—that is, the defendant knew that the process was for some reason void. Vahlsing v. Commercial Union Ins. Co., Inc., 928 F.2d 486, 492.

**C.A.2,** 1986. Cit. in disc. After a man was convicted of first-degree criminal possession of stolen property, he sued the arresting officers for damages, claiming that they had lacked probable cause to arrest him. The trial court granted the defendants' motion for summary judgment. Affirming, this court held that regardless of whether the action was characterized as one for false imprisonment or malicious prosecution, the fact that the person against whom criminal proceedings were instituted was found guilty of the crime charged against him was a complete defense against liability. The court reasoned that in either case a plaintiff could not challenge probable cause in the face of a judgment of conviction unless the conviction was obtained by improper means. Cameron v. Fogarty, 806 F.2d 380, 387, cert. denied 481

See also cases under division, chapter, topic, title, and subtitle that include section under examination. For earlier citations see the Restatement of the Law, Second, Torts 2d Appendix Volumes covering §§ 1–309 through 1963, through 1975, and through 1984.

132

find cases from a variety of jurisdictions interpreting that section. The Appendix volumes are not cumulative; each volume covers only a specific period of time. Therefore, to find all of the cases interpreting a section, you would need to look it up in each Appendix volume. The latest Appendix volume will have a pocket part with the most recent references.

Figure 3.11 shows the Appendix entry under § 35, which lists several cases involving this section of the Restatement.

## 6. UNIFORM LAWS AND MODEL ACTS

Uniform laws and model acts are proposed statutes that can be adopted by legislatures. Two examples with which you may already be familiar are the Uniform Commercial Code and the Model Penal Code. Uniform laws and model acts are similar to Restatements in that they set out proposed rules, followed by commentary, research notes, and summaries of cases interpreting the rules. Unlike Restatements, which are limited to common-law doctrines, uniform laws and model acts exist in areas governed by statutory law.

Although uniform laws and model acts look like statutes, they are secondary sources. Their provisions do not take on the force of law unless they are adopted by a legislature. When that happens, however, the commentary, research references, and case summaries become very useful research tools. They can help you interpret the law and direct you to persuasive authority from other jurisdictions that have adopted the law.

One of the best ways to locate uniform laws and model acts is through a publication entitled *Uniform Laws Annotated, Master Edition* (ULA). This is a multivolume set of books containing the text of a number of uniform laws and model acts. You can locate it through the on-line catalog in your library.

Once you have located the ULA set, you have several research options. To determine the best research option for your project, you should review the *Directory of Uniform Acts and Codes: Tables and Index*. This softcover booklet is published annually and explains the finding tools available in this resource. You can research uniform laws and model acts by subject, by the name of the law, or by adopting jurisdiction. Once you have located relevant information, use the pocket part to update your research.

You are most likely to research uniform laws and model acts when your project involves research into state statutes, and generally speaking, researching in the ULA set is similar to statutory research. As a consequence, if you decide to use this resource, you may also want to review Chapter 6, which discusses statutory research.

Figure 3.12 shows a uniform law as it appears in the ULA set.

**FIGURE 3.12** ULA ENTRY FOR THE UNIFORM ABSENCE AS EVIDENCE OF DEATH AND ABSENTEES' PROPERTY ACT

# UNIFORM ABSENCE AS EVIDENCE OF DEATH AND ABSENTEES' PROPERTY ACT

## 1939 ACT

**Outline of the uniform law**

**Section**

1. Death not Presumed from Absence; Exposure to Peril to be Considered.
2. Insurance Policy Provisions Invalid.
3. Receiver May Be Appointed When.
4. Notice.
5. Search for Absentee.
6. Final Hearing and Finding.
7. Claim of Absentee Barred.
8. Termination of Receivership and Disposition of the Property of the Absentee.
9. Distribution of Property of Absentee.
10. Insurance Policies.
11. Absentee Insurance Fund.
12. Uniformity of Interpretation.
13. Short Title.
14. Repeal.
15. Severability.
16. Time of Taking Effect and Not Retroactive.

**WESTLAW Computer Assisted Legal Research**

WESTLAW supplements your legal research in many ways. WESTLAW allows you to

- update your research with the most current information
- expand your library with additional resources
- retrieve direct history, precedential history and parallel citations with the Insta-Cite service

...nore information on using WESTLAW to supplement your research, see the ...LAW Electronic Research Guide, which follows the Explanation.

**Text of the law that could be adopted by a legislature**

## § 1. Death not Presumed from Absence; Exposure to Peril to be Considered.

(1) Death Not to be Presumed from Mere Absence. In any proceeding under this Act where the death of a person and the date thereof, or either, is in issue, the fact that he has been absent from his place of residence, unheard of for seven years, or for any other period, creates no presumption requiring the Court or the jury to find that he is now deceased. The issue shall go to the Court or jury as one of fact to be determined upon the evidence.

(2) Exposure to Specific Peril to be Considered in Every Case. If during such absence the person has been exposed to a specific peril of death, this fact shall be considered by the Court; or if there be a jury, shall be sufficient evidence for submission to the jury.

5

**FIGURE 3.12** ULA ENTRY FOR THE UNIFORM ABSENCE AS EVIDENCE OF DEATH
AND ABSENTEES' PROPERTY ACT *(Continued)*

Explanation of any
changes to the
uniform law in
adopting jurisdictions

Summary of a case
interpreting the
uniform law

References to other
research sources

## ABSENCE AS EVIDENCE OF DEATH

### Action in Adopting Jurisdictions

**Variations from Official Text:**

**Tennessee.** Adds a subsection which reads: "If the clerks of the respective courts of record and/or the personal representatives have any funds belonging to such absentee who, upon the order of the court, is determined to be dead, such funds shall be distributed according to law as of the date of death of the absentee as determined by the court. The validity and effect of the distribution of the property shall be determined by the court having probate jurisdiction administering the estate."

**Wisconsin.** Omits this section.

### Library References

**American Digest System**

Evidence of death and of survivorship, see Death ⚏1 to 6.

**Encyclopedias**

Evidence of death and of survivorship, see C.J.S. Death §§ 5 to 12(2).

### WESTLAW Electronic Research

Death cases: 117k[add key number].
See, also, WESTLAW Electronic Research Guide following the Explanation.

### Notes of Decisions

Burden of proof   3
Time for presuming death   2
Time of death   1

**1. Time of death**

Although there is a presumption of death of an absence of seven years there is no presumption as to the seven-year period the subject actually died. Hubbard v. Equitable Life Assur. Soc. of U.S., 1946, 21 N.W.2d 665, 248 Wis. 340.

**2. Time for presuming death**

Unless the facts and circumstances shown in any particular case are such as to warrant a reasonable inference that death took place at some particular time within the seven-year period of unexplained absence, death is not presumed before the end of the period. Hubbard v. Equitable Life Assur. Soc. of U.S., 1946, 21 N.W.2d 665, 248 Wis. 340. See, also, Hogaboam v. Metropolitan Life Ins. Co., 1946, 21 N.W.2d 268, 248 Wis. 146.

Permitting the rebuttable presumption of death to remain in effect for purposes of distributing the funds and other personalty of the absentee, and into the hands of the court clerks, administrators and executors after the person has been missing for seven years does not mean that the Uniform Absence as Evidence of Death and Absentees' Property Law retains the rebuttable presumption of death for all purposes given the clear distinction therein between the absentee's personalty on the one hand and the

proceeds of a life insurance policy on the other. Armstrong v. Pilot Life Ins. Co., Tenn.App.1983, 656 S.W.2d 18.

Provisions of the Uniform Absence as Evidence of Death and Absentees' Property Law expressly modified the common-law rule by abolishing the seven-year presumption of death while permitting a period of absence, for seven or any other number of years, to be considered with all other circumstantial evidence to determine whether by a preponderance of the evidence the absentee is deceased. Armstrong v. Pilot Life Ins. Co., Tenn.App.1983, 656 S.W.2d 18.

**3. Burden of proof**

A beneficiary suing on policy on life of husband who had been absent and unheard from for more than seven years had burden of proving that presumption of death from seven years' absence prevailed, and that death occurred before lapse of policy some eight months after husband's disappearance. Hubbard v. Equitable Life Assur. Soc. of U.S., 1946, 21 N.W.2d 665, 248 Wis. 340.

The party who would benefit from the absentee's death is the party with the burden of proof of death under the Uniform Absence as Evidence of Death and Absentees' Property Law permitting a period of absence, for seven or any other number of years, to be considered with all other circumstantial evidence to determine whether by a preponderance of the evidence the absentee is deceased. Armstrong v. Pilot Life Ins. Co., Tenn.App.1983, 656 S.W.2d 18.

6

## C. ELECTRONIC RESEARCH OF SECONDARY SOURCES

### 1. LEXISNEXIS AND WESTLAW

LexisNexis and Westlaw can be useful in locating secondary sources, especially if you are looking for material that is not available in print in your law library. As of this writing, Am. Jur. 2d is available in both LexisNexis and Westlaw, and C.J.S. is available in Westlaw. A.L.R. Annotations are available in both services, as are a number of uniform laws, model acts, and most Restatements of the law. Many legal periodicals are available, but not all of them. Of those publications that are available, LexisNexis and Westlaw may not list every issue or every article in every issue, and the holdings go back only until the early 1980s. In addition, only a limited number of treatises can be accessed through these services. Thus, while LexisNexis and Westlaw are very good sources of secondary material, they are not exhaustive. You may find that computer searches do not yield all of the information you need and must be supplemented with book research.

In general, if you know which type of secondary authority you want to research, you can execute a word search in the database for that type of authority, e.g., the database for A.L.R. Annotations. LexisNexis and Westlaw also offer combined databases containing multiple secondary sources. Furthermore, you can limit your research to secondary sources covering a particular jurisdiction or subject area by searching in jurisdictional or subject area databases.

You can also view the table of contents for some secondary sources electronically. This will allow you to retrieve sections of the publication by selecting them from the table of contents without having to execute a word search. In Westlaw, click on the Table of Contents link near the top of the screen to review the publications for which tables of contents are available. In LexisNexis, if you select a source for which the table of contents is available, you will have a choice of accessing the table of contents or continuing with a word search.

The process of researching in LexisNexis and Westlaw is explained in more detail in Chapter 10.

### 2. INTERNET SOURCES

Although most secondary sources are not available via the Internet, some legal periodicals are. An increasing number of law reviews, journals, and other legal periodicals are beginning to publish their articles on the Internet.

To locate periodical articles on the Internet,[3] you must first identify

---

[3]This is different from using LegalTrac or the electronic version of ILP on the Internet. They are commercial services that generate lists of citations, and they are available only to

publications that have made their contents available on the web. General legal research web sites will often contain links to legal periodicals. You can also go to individual law school web sites to see if their publications are accessible on the Internet. Appendix A lists a number of Internet sites that may be useful in locating periodical articles. Some of these sites will allow you to execute word or subject searches. Others will list the tables of contents for periodicals available electronically.

If you have the citation or title of an article available on the Internet, this can be a quick and economical way to obtain it. Nevertheless, the number of periodicals accessible on the Internet is still small relative to the total number of publications available, and limitations on searching capabilities can make it difficult to locate pertinent material. Although this will no doubt change over time, at this point you would not want to rely on the Internet as the sole or starting point for periodical research. Moreover, it is important to remember that any person with a message and the appropriate equipment can publish material on the Internet. Therefore, you must evaluate the source of any secondary information you find this way. The Internet version of an established periodical is likely to be authoritative, but other sources may not be.

## D. CITING SECONDARY SOURCES

The chart in Figure 3.13 lists the rules in the *ALWD Manual* and the *Bluebook* governing citations to secondary sources. Citations to each of these sources are discussed in turn.

One general comment about citing secondary sources is in order at this point. If you are using the *Bluebook*, you will notice that many of the examples of citations to secondary sources appear in large and small capital letters. Secondary sources cited in briefs and memoranda, however, should not appear in large and small capital letters. Instead, you need to use the Practitioners' Notes to convert the typeface used in the examples. According to Practitioners' Notes P.1(b) and P.1(h), secondary source citations should either appear in ordinary type or be underlined or italicized, depending on the source. If you are using the *ALWD Manual*, you do not need to convert the typeface used in any of the examples. You can follow the examples exactly as they appear in the text, regardless of the type of document you are writing.

### 1. LEGAL ENCYCLOPEDIAS

Citations to legal encyclopedias are covered in *ALWD Manual* Rule 26 and *Bluebook* Rule 15.7 and are the same using either format. The citation

---

subscribers. The search methods described here allow you to retrieve the full text of a periodical article from a publicly available Internet site.

**FIGURE 3.13**   RULES FOR CITING SECONDARY SOURCES

| SECONDARY SOURCE | ALWD MANUAL | BLUEBOOK |
|---|---|---|
| Legal encyclopedias | Rule 26 | Rule 15.7 |
| Treatises | Rule 22 | Rule 15 |
| Legal periodicals | Rule 23 | Rule 16 |
| A.L.R. Annotations | Rule 24 | Rule 16.6.5 |
| Restatements | Rule 27 | Rule 12.8.5 |
| Uniform laws & Model acts | Rule 27 | Uniform laws—Rule 12.8.4<br>Model acts—Rule 12.8.5 |

consists of five elements: (1) the volume number; (2) the abbreviated name of the encyclopedia; (3) the name of the topic, underlined or italicized; (4) the section cited (with a space between the section symbol (§) and the section number); and (5) a parenthetical containing the date of the book, including, if appropriate, the date of the pocket part or supplement. Here is an example:

┌─→ abbreviated name of encyclopedia

**35 C.J.S.  <u>False Imprisonment</u> § 1 (1960).**

└─→ volume                  └─→ date of book
     number      └─→ name of topic   └─→ section number

Sometimes determining which date or dates to include in the parenthetical can be confusing. The answer is always a function of where a reader would have to look to find all of the text and footnote information on the section you are citing. If all of the information appears in the main volume of the encyclopedia, the date in the parenthetical should refer only to the main volume. If the section is a new section that appears only in the pocket part, the date should refer only to the pocket part. If the reader must refer both to the main volume and to the pocket part, the parenthetical should list both dates. Here are several examples:

**35 C.J.S. <u>False Imprisonment</u> § 1 (1960).**

In this example, the reference is only to the main volume.

**35 C.J.S. <u>False Imprisonment</u> § 1 (1960 & Supp. 1997).**

In this example, the reference is both to the main volume and to the pocket part.

**32 Am. Jur. 2d <u>False Imprisonment</u> § 1 (Supp. 1997).**

In this example, the reference is only to the pocket part. For purposes of *Bluebook* format, note that Am. Jur. 2d is in ordinary type, not large and small capital letters.

## 2. TREATISES

Citations to treatises contain roughly the same elements in both *ALWD Manual* and *Bluebook* formats. There are a few differences between them, however, and the order of the elements varies in minor respects.

In the *ALWD Manual*, citations to treatises are covered in Rule 22 and consist of four elements: (1) the author's full name (if the treatise has more than two authors, you may list the first, followed by et al.); (2) the title of the treatise, underlined or italicized; (3) a pinpoint reference containing the volume of the treatise (in a multivolume treatise), the section cited (with a space between the section symbol (§) and the section number), and the specific page or pages cited; and (4) a parenthetical containing the edition (if more than one edition has been published), the publisher, and the date, including, if appropriate, the date of the pocket part. Here is an example in *ALWD Manual* format:

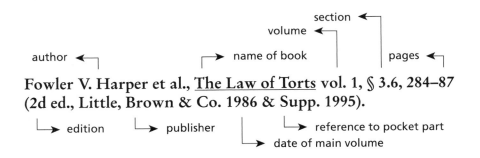

**Fowler V. Harper et al., <u>The Law of Torts</u> vol. 1, § 3.6, 284–87 (2d ed., Little, Brown & Co. 1986 & Supp. 1995).**

In the *Bluebook*, citations to treatises are covered in Rule 15 and consist of five elements: (1) the volume number of the treatise (in a multivolume set); (2) the author's full name (if the treatise has more than two authors, list the first, followed by et al.); (3) the title of the treatise, underlined or italicized; (4) the section cited (with a space between the section symbol (§) and the section number); and (5) a parenthetical containing the edition (if more than one edition has been published) and the date, including, if appropriate, the date of the pocket part. Here is an example in *Bluebook* format:

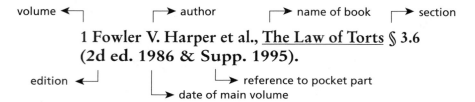

Note that in both citation formats, a comma separates the part of the citation identifying the author or authors from the title of the treatise. No other commas appear in a *Bluebook* citation. In an *ALWD Manual* citation, commas also separate the components of the pinpoint reference, as well as the edition and publisher's name in the parenthetical.

Both the *ALWD Manual* and the *Bluebook* have additional requirements for books with editors or translators.

## 3. LEGAL PERIODICALS

Legal periodicals are published in two formats. Some publications begin the first issue within each volume with page one and continue numbering the pages of subsequent issues within that volume consecutively. These are called consecutively paginated publications. Most law reviews and journals are consecutively paginated. Other publications, such as monthly magazines, begin each new issue with page one, regardless of where the issue falls within the volume. These are called nonconsecutively paginated publications.

There are some differences in the citations to articles published in consecutively and nonconsecutively paginated periodicals. The explanation in this section focuses on citations to articles published in consecutively paginated law reviews, which are covered in *ALWD Manual* Rule 23 and *Bluebook* Rule 16.

A citation to a law review article in both *ALWD Manual* and *Bluebook* formats consists of seven elements: (1) the author's full name; (2) the title of the article, underlined or italicized; (3) the volume number of the publication; (4) the abbreviated name of the publication; (5) the starting page of the article; (6) the pinpoint citation to the specific page or pages cited; and (7) a parenthetical containing the date of the publication. Here is an example:

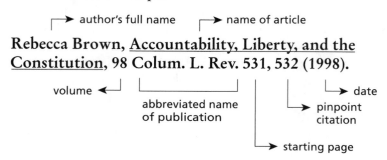

Note that the author's name, the name of the article, and the starting page of the article are followed by commas. The comma following the name of the article is not underlined or italicized.

Publication abbreviations can be found in *ALWD Manual* Appendix 5 and *Bluebook* Table T.14. Both the *ALWD Manual* and the *Bluebook* have additional rules for citing articles appearing in nonconsecutively paginated publications, articles written by students, and articles with more than one author.

### 4. A.L.R. ANNOTATIONS

Citations to A.L.R. Annotations are covered in *ALWD Manual* Rule 24 and *Bluebook* Rule 16.6.5. They are almost identical in both formats, with only one minor difference between them. A citation to an A.L.R. Annotation consists of seven elements: (1) the author's full name (in a *Bluebook* citation, the author's name is followed by the notation "Annotation"); (2) the title of the Annotation, underlined or italicized; (3) the volume number; (4) the A.L.R. series; (5) the starting page of the Annotation; (6) the pinpoint citation to the specific page or pages cited; and (7) a parenthetical containing the date, including, if appropriate, the date of the pocket part. Here is an example in *ALWD Manual* format:

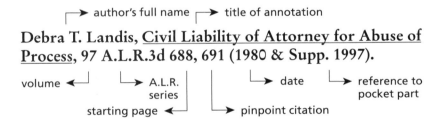

Here is an example in *Bluebook* format:

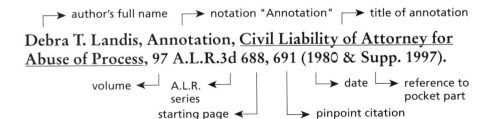

### 5. RESTATEMENTS

Citations to Restatements are covered in *ALWD Manual* Rule 27 and *Bluebook* Rule 12.8.5. They contain three elements using either format:

(1) the name of the Restatement; (2) the section cited (with a space between the section symbol (§) and the section number); and (3) a parenthetical containing the date. The only difference is that the name of the Restatement is underlined or italicized in *ALWD Manual* format, but not in *Bluebook* format. Here is an example in *ALWD Manual* format:

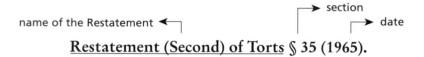

Here is an example in *Bluebook* format:

## 6. Uniform Laws and Model Acts

The citation format for a uniform law depends on whether the law has been adopted by a jurisdiction. If a jurisdiction adopts a uniform law, the law will be published with all of the other statutes for that jurisdiction. In that situation, cite directly to the jurisdiction's statute. The requirements for statutory citations are explained in Chapter 6.

Citations to uniform laws published in the ULA set are governed by *ALWD Manual* Rule 27 and *Bluebook* Rule 12.8.4. The citation is the same using either format and consists of six elements: (1) the title of the act; (2) the section cited (with a space between the section symbol (§) and section number); (3) the ULA volume number; (4) the abbreviation "U.L.A."; (5) the page of the ULA on which the section appears; and (6) a parenthetical containing the date of the ULA volume, including, if appropriate, the date of the pocket part. Here is an example:

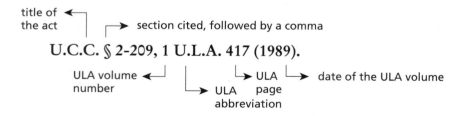

Citations to model acts are covered in *ALWD Manual* Rule 27 and *Bluebook* Rule 12.8.5. Model act citations are almost identical in both formats, with only one minor difference between them. The citation consists of three elements: (1) the name of the act; (2) the section cited (with a space between the section symbol (§) and the section number); and (3) a parenthetical.

In *ALWD Manual* citations, the parenthetical contains the name of the organization that issued the act, abbreviated according to Appendix 3, and the date. Here is an example in *ALWD Manual* format:

name of the act ← ┐    section ← ┐    ┌ → date

**Model Penal Code § 5.03 (ALI 1985).**

organization that issued the act ← ┘

The *Bluebook* requires that the parenthetical include the name of the organization that issued the act for some model acts, but not others. In all model act citations, however, the *Bluebook* requires the date in the parenthetical. Here is an example in *Bluebook* format:

name of the act ← ┐    section ← ┐

**Model Penal Code § 5.03 (1985).**

date ← ┘

# E. SAMPLE PAGES FOR SECONDARY SOURCE RESEARCH

Beginning on the next page, Figures 3.14 through 3.23 are sample pages from A.L.R. and the *Restatement (Second) of Torts* showing what you would see in the books if you had researched false imprisonment and the related topic of abuse of process.

**To locate an A.L.R. Annotation, begin by looking up your subject in the A.L.R. Index. The A.L.R. Index will refer you directly to applicable Annotations. The reference will tell you the volume number, series, and starting page of the Annotation.**

**FIGURE 3.14**   A.L.R. INDEX

---

### ALR INDEX

#### FALSE DEMONSTRATION DOCTRINE
**Wills** (this index)

#### FALSE IDENTIFICATION CRIME CONTROL ACT
Search and seizure, admissibility in criminal case of evidence obtained by law enforcement officer allegedly relying reasonably and in good faith on defective warrant, 82 L Ed 2d 1054, § 9

> Index entry for false imprisonment

#### FALSE IMPRISONMENT AND ARREST
For digest treatment, see title **False Imprisonment in ALR Digest**

Abduction and kidnapping
- authority of parent or one in loco parentis, taking under, 20 ALR4th 823
- foreign country, district court jurisdiction over criminal suspect who was abducted in foreign country and returned to United States for trial or sentencing, 64 ALR Fed 292
- ded offense within charge of kidnapping, 68 ALR3d 828
- prison official, seizure by inmates as kidnapping, 59 ALR3d 1306

Abuse of process

> Reference to an Annotation

- attorney, civil liability of attorney for abuse of process, 97 ALR3d 688
- private citizen calling on police for assistance after disturbance or trespass for false arrest by officer, liability of, 98 ALR3d 542
- threatening, instituting, or prosecuting legal action as invasion of right of privacy, 42 ALR3d 865, § 8

Actionability, under 42 USCS § 1983, of claims against persons other than police officers for false arrest or false imprisonment, 44 ALR Fed 225

Apparent authority of servant as rendering master liable for false imprisonment, 2 ALR2d 412

Appellate review of excessiveness or inadequacy of damages for false imprisonment or arrest, 35 ALR2d 276

#### FALSE IMPRISONMENT AND ARREST—Cont'd
Assault and battery, Federal Tort Claims Act, provision excepting from coverage claim arising out of assault, battery, false imprisonment, false arrest, malicious prosecution, etc., 23 ALR2d 574

Attorneys
- abuse of process, civil liability of attorney for abuse of process, 97 ALR3d 688
- fees of attorney as element of damages in action for false imprisonment or arrest, or for malicious prosecution, 21 ALR3d 1068
- prosecuting attorneys, immunity of prosecuting attorney or similar officer from action for false arrest or imprisonment, 79 ALR3d 882
- third persons, liability of attorney acting for client, for false imprisonment or malicious prosecution of third party, 27 ALR3d 1113

Attorneys' fees as element of damages in action for false imprisonment or arrest, or for malicious prosecution, 21 ALR3d 1068

Bad checks
- excessiveness or inadequacy of compensatory damages for false imprisonment or arrest, 48 ALR4th 165, § 17[a]
- mistake, liability for false arrest or imprisonment under warrant as affected by mistake as to identity of person arrested, 39 ALR4th 705, §§ 6[a], 8[a]
- postdated checks, application of bad check statute with respect to, 52 ALR3d 464, § 7[b]

Bankruptcy, claim of judgment based on malicious prosecution, false imprisonment, or other similar tort, as liability for wilful and malicious injury within § 17(2) of the Bankruptcy Act (11 USCS § 35(a)), barring discharge of such liability, 78 ALR2d 1226

Battery, Federal Tort Claims Act, provision excepting from coverage claim arising out of assault, battery, false imprisonment, false arrest, malicious prosecution, etc., 23 ALR2d 574

**320**     **Consult POCKET PART for Later Annotations**

---

Reprinted with permission from Lawyers Cooperative Publishing, *American Law Reports*, Index E–H (1992), p. 320.

**The Annotation will begin with an outline and references to related research sources. After the outline, an alphabetical index of topics within the Annotation will appear.**

**FIGURE 3.15**   A.L.R. ANNOTATION

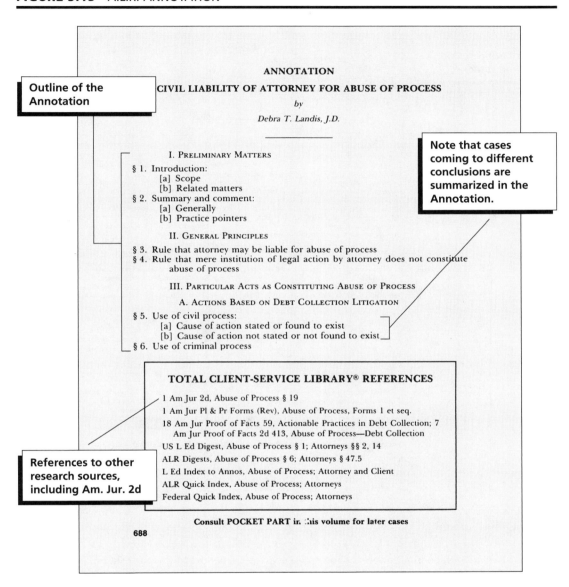

Outline of the Annotation

ANNOTATION

CIVIL LIABILITY OF ATTORNEY FOR ABUSE OF PROCESS

*by*

*Debra T. Landis, J.D.*

Note that cases coming to different conclusions are summarized in the Annotation.

I. PRELIMINARY MATTERS

§ 1. Introduction:
　　[a] Scope
　　[b] Related matters
§ 2. Summary and comment:
　　[a] Generally
　　[b] Practice pointers

II. GENERAL PRINCIPLES

§ 3. Rule that attorney may be liable for abuse of process
§ 4. Rule that mere institution of legal action by attorney does not constitute abuse of process

III. PARTICULAR ACTS AS CONSTITUTING ABUSE OF PROCESS

A. ACTIONS BASED ON DEBT COLLECTION LITIGATION

§ 5. Use of civil process:
　　[a] Cause of action stated or found to exist
　　[b] Cause of action not stated or not found to exist
§ 6. Use of criminal process

**TOTAL CLIENT-SERVICE LIBRARY® REFERENCES**

References to other research sources, including Am. Jur. 2d

1 Am Jur 2d, Abuse of Process § 19

1 Am Jur Pl & Pr Forms (Rev), Abuse of Process, Forms 1 et seq.

18 Am Jur Proof of Facts 59, Actionable Practices in Debt Collection; 7 Am Jur Proof of Facts 2d 413, Abuse of Process—Debt Collection

US L Ed Digest, Abuse of Process § 1; Attorneys §§ 2, 14

ALR Digests, Abuse of Process § 6; Attorneys § 47.5

L Ed Index to Annos, Abuse of Process; Attorney and Client

ALR Quick Index, Abuse of Process; Attorneys

Federal Quick Index, Abuse of Process; Attorneys

**Consult POCKET PART in this volume for later cases**

688

**FIGURE 3.15**   A.L.R. ANNOTATION *(Continued)*

After the outline, each Annotation has its own subject index to help you locate information within the Annotation.

97 ALR3d        LIABILITY OF ATTORNEY FOR ABUSE OF PROCESS
97 ALR3d 688

B. OTHER ACTIONS

§ 7. Filing of action alone or together with initial process or pleading:
    [a] At law for tort
    [b] In equity
    [c] For unspecified relief
§ 8. Use of subpoena
§ 9. Use of other process

**INDEX**

Affidavit, making oath to as abuse of process, § 5[a]
Alimony, attempt to force payment of by arrest and imprisonment, § 6
Arrest, matters concerning, §§ 4, 6
Attempted extortion, allegation of, § 5
Bank account, garnishment of, § 5[b]
Body process, necessity for in abuse of process action, § 7[a]
Bonds, attempt by attorney to force client to part with, §§ 3, 9
Chose in action, withholding of, § 5[b]
Civil process based on debt collection litigation as constituting abuse of process, § 5
Comment and summary, § 2
Conspiracy, allegations as to, §§ 3, 5[b], 7[a]
Criminal process based on debt collection litigation as constituting abuse of process, §§ 4, 6, 7[a]
Debt collection litigation, actions based on as abuse of process, §§ 3, 5, 6
Default judgment, entering of, § 5[b]
Disorderly persons charge, attempt to collect hotel bill by, § 6
Elements necessary to establish cause of action for abuse of process, § 4
Equitable proceedings, institution of as constituting abuse of process, § 7[b]
Equity, filing of action alone or together with initial process or pleading as abuse of process, § 7[b]
Execution sale of judgment debtors' assets, § 5[b]
Extortion of money, allegation of attempt, § 5
Filing of action alone or together with initial process or pleading, as abuse of process, § 7

Forgery of signature, request for admissions related to alleged forgery as abuse, § 9
Garnishment procedure, institution of, § 5
Harassment, issuance of process for purposes of as abuse, § 7[a]
Hotel bill, prosecution for failure to pay as abuse, § 6
Imprisonment, attempt to collect debt by as abuse, § 6
Income tax refund check, request for admissions related to cashing of as abuse, § 9
Institution of legal action by attorney as not constituting abuse of process, § 4
Interrogation at police station, issuance of grand jury subpoena for purposes of as abuse, § 8
Introduction, § 1
Judgment by confession, securing of, § 5[b]
Judgment debt, use of writ of execution to sell, § 5[b]
Lien as constituting abuse of process, §§ 5[a], 7[a]
Malice, disclosure of as affecting abuse of process action, § 5[a]
Medical malpractice suit, filing of against physician as abuse of process, § 7[a]
Money, alleged attempt to extort, § 5
Negotiable instruments, attempt by attorney to force plaintiff to part with as abuse, §§ 3, 9
Other actions constituting abuse of process, §§ 7-9
Other process as constituting abuse of process, § 9
Particular acts as constituting abuse of process, §§ 5-9
Physician, effect of filing medical malprac-

**689**

Reprinted with permission from Lawyers Cooperative Publishing, *American Law Reports,* 3d Ser., Vol. 97 (1980), pp. 688–689.

**Following the subject index, you will see a list of the jurisdictions from which authority is cited within the Annotation. The first part of the Annotation will set out the scope of coverage, list Annotations on related subjects, and summarize the law on the topic.**

**FIGURE 3.16** A.L.R. ANNOTATION

Jurisdictions from which authority is cited

Introduction to the Annotation

§ 1[a]    LIABILITY OF ATTORNEY FOR ABUSE OF PROCESS    97 ALR3d
97 ALR3d 688

tice suit against that resulted in no cause of action, § 7[a]
Power of attorney, use of against client's interest as abuse, § 7[b]
Practice pointers, § 2[b]
Preliminary matters, §§ 1, 2
Related matters, § 1[b]
Rent, filing suit for return of, § 5[b]
Scope of annotation, § 1[a]
Security deposit, filing suit for return of, § 5[b]
Seizure of property, necessity for in abuse of process action, § 4
Subpoena, use of as constituting abuse of process, § 8
Summary and comment, § 2
Teachers, issuance of subpoenas to force attendance at hearing as abuse, § 8

Temporary injunction, use of to delay delivery for monetary gain as abuse, § 7[b]
Theft, prosecution for to force plaintiff to part with bonds as abuse, §§ 3, 9
Tort, filing of action alone or together with initial process or pleading at law for, § 7[a]
Unspecified relief, filing of action alone or together with initial process or pleading for, § 7[c]
Void orders, procurance of as constituting abuse of process, § 5[a]
Writ, use of as constituting abuse of process, §§ 5, 6, 7[a]
Wrong parties, knowingly proceeding against as constituting abuse of process, § 5[a]

**TABLE OF JURISDICTIONS REPRESENTED**
Consult POCKET PART in this volume for later cases

**US:** §§ 3, 6, 7[b]
**Cal:** §§ 9
**DC:** §§ 5[b]
**Ga:** §§ 3, 5[a]
**Ill:** §§ 4, 5[b], 7[a]
**Kan:** §§ 3, 5[a]
**Me:** §§ 3

**Mass:** §§ 5[b]
**Mich:** §§ 4, 7[a]
**Minn:** §§ 3, 9
**NJ:** §§ 3, 6
**NY:** §§ 3, 4, 5[b], 6, 7[a-c], 8, 9
**Pa:** §§ 3, 5[a, b]
**Wash:** §§ 3, 4, 5[b]

**I. Preliminary matters**

**§ 1. Introduction**

**[a] Scope**

This annotation collects and analyzes those state and federal cases in which the courts have decided or discussed the question of the civil liability of an attorney for an abuse of civil or criminal process.

For the purposes of this annotation, the term "attorney," refers to the person being sued for an abuse of process arising out of, or apparently out of, an attorney-client relationship.

Therefore, cases in which the person being sued for an abuse of process happens to be an attorney but in which there is no indication that an attorney-client relationship was involved are beyond the scope of this annotation. Also beyond the scope of this annotation are cases involving the civil liability of a prosecuting attorney for an alleged abuse of process resulting from acts done in an official capacity.[1]

The cases considered herein are those which clearly specify that the cause of action is founded on abuse

1. As to the civil liability of a prosecuting attorney for acts done in an official **690**

capacity, see 63 Am Jur 2d, Prosecuting Attorneys § 34.

**FIGURE 3.16**   A.L.R. ANNOTATION *(Continued)*

> **Summary of the law on this topic**

> **Related A.L.R. Annotations**

97 ALR3d     Liability of Attorney for Abuse of Process
97 ALR3d 688

of process, as distinguished from those which, although involving alleged wrongful conduct similar to that found in an action for abuse of process, do not state that the action is based on that tort.

Thus, beyond the scope of this annotation is the liability of an attorney for wrongful execution or attachment of property unless the cause of action is specified to be that for an abuse of process.[2]

**[b] Related matters**

Institution of confessed judgment proceedings as ground of action for abuse of process or malicious prosecution. 87 ALR3d 554.

Action for breach of contract as basis of action for malicious prosecution or abuse of process. 87 ALR3d 580.

Civil liability of judicial officer for malicious prosecution or abuse of process. 64 ALR3d 1251.

What constitutes malice sufficient to justify an award of punitive damages in action for wrongful attachment or garnishment. 61 ALR3d 984.

Liability of attorney acting for client, for false imprisonment or malicious prosecution of third party. 27 ALR3d 1113.

Use of criminal process to collect debt as abuse of process. 27 ALR3d 1202.

What statute of limitations governs action for malicious use of process or abuse of process, in the absence of an express provision for such tort. 10 ALR3d 533.

When statute of limitations begins to run against action for abuse of process. 1 ALR3d 953.

**§ 2. Summary and comment**

**[a] Generally**

It has been generally stated that an abuse of legal process consists of the malicious misuse or misapplication of regularly issued civil or criminal process to accomplish some purpose not warranted or commanded by the writ.[3] The Restatement of Torts 2d § 682 similarly provides that one who uses legal process, either civil or criminal, against another person primarily to accomplish a purpose for which it was not designed is liable to the other for harm caused by the abuse of process.

The question whether an attorney, by virtue of the attorney-client relationship, enjoys exemption from civil liability for abuse of process, similar to that of a judicial officer, has arisen in some cases, and it has been held that an attorney may be held liable in an action for damages for abuse of process where the acts complained of are his own personal acts, or the acts of others wholly instigated and carried on by him.[4] However, courts have held that the mere institution of a legal action by an attorney does not constitute an abuse of process, absent other circumstances.[5]

Turning to particular allegations against attorneys in actions for abuse of process, courts have reached opposite results, under varying factual circumstances, in determining whether a cause of action was stated or existed

---

**2.** As to the liability of an attorney for wrongful attachment or execution, see 7 Am Jur 2d, Attorneys at Law § 197.

**3.** 1 Am Jur 2d, Abuse of Process § 1.
As to the distinction between an abuse of process and an action for malicious

prosecution, malicious use of process, or false imprisonment, see generally 1 Am Jur 2d, Abuse of Process §§ 2, 3.

**4.** § 3, infra.

**5.** § 4, infra.

**691**

**FIGURE 3.16** A.L.R. ANNOTATION *(Continued)*

§ 2[a]    LIABILITY OF ATTORNEY FOR ABUSE OF PROCESS    97 ALR3d
97 ALR3d 688

against an attorney by virtue of the use of civil process to collect a debt for a client.[6] Some courts have also held that where it was alleged that an attorney used criminal process as a means of collecting a debt due a client, a cause of action against the attorney for abuse of process was stated.[7]

In cases involving the filing of a tort action by an attorney, where no acts were alleged against the attorney involving the improper use of process, it has been held that a cause of action against the attorney was not stated.[8] Likewise, in a case in which no facts were stated in a complaint for abuse of process against an attorney showing that he was the active and procuring cause of the institution by his client of civil actions, whose nature was not specified in the court's opinion, or showing interference with the plaintiff's personal property, the court held that no cause of action for abuse of process was stated.[9] However, where a complaint alleged that an attorney did not act in a bona fide effort to protect the interest of a client in filing equitable actions, but rather acted in the interest of other clients to prevent the plaintiff from delivering shares of stock before a contractual deadline, the court held that a cause of action for abuse of process against the attorney was stated.[10]

It has been held or recognized that a cause of action was stated or found to exist against an attorney where the attorney was alleged to have used subpoenas for other than their legitimate purpose.[11] However, in cases involving the use of other types of process, the courts, under the particular facts, found that the complaints failed to state a cause of action against the attorney.[12]

**[b] Practice pointers**

Counsel representing a plaintiff in an action for abuse of process against an attorney should be aware that the same facts which give rise to the action may also establish an action for malicious prosecution, false arrest, or false imprisonment, and that the causes may be joined in the same action, but not in the same count.[13] The attorney should, however, keep in mind that an action for abuse of process is based on the improper use of the process after it has been issued, while malicious prosecution is based on the wrongful intent or malice that caused the process to be issued initially.[14]

Counsel should note that an action for abuse of process has generally been held to accrue, and the statute of limitations to commence to run, from the termination of the acts which constitute the abuse complained of and not from the completion of the action in which the process issued.[15] Actions for abuse of process are generally governed by the statute of limitations applicable to actions for injury to the person. However, in a jurisdiction in which one statute governed injury to the person

Practice pointers

6. § 5[a], [b], infra.

7. § 6, infra.

8. § 7[a], infra.

9. § 7[c], infra.

10. § 7[b], infra.

11. § 8, infra.

692

12. § 9, infra.

13. As to pleading in actions for abuse of process, see generally 1 Am Jur 2d, Abuse of Process § 21.

14. 1 Am Jur 2d, Abuse of Process § 2.

15. 1 Am Jur 2d, Abuse of Process § 24.

**After the introductory material, the Annotation will explain the law on the topic in greater detail, summarize key cases, and provide citations to additional cases on the topic.**

**FIGURE 3.17**   A.L.R. ANNOTATION

97 ALR3d      Liability of Attorney for Abuse of Process      § 3
97 ALR3d 688

and another statute governed "injuries to the rights of others," the court held that an action for abuse of process was controlled by the latter statute.[16]

**II. General principles**

**§ 3. Rule that attorney may be liable for abuse of process**

[following] cases support the [rule that] an attorney may be held [liable in] a civil action for abuse of [process, w]here the acts complained of [are his o]wn personal acts, or the acts of others instigated and carried on by him.

US—For federal cases involving state law, see state headings infra.

**Ga**—Walker v Kyser (1967) 115 Ga App 314, 154 SE2d 457 (by implication).

**Kan**—Little v Sowers (1949) 167 Kan 72, 204 P2d 605.

**Me**—Lambert v Breton (1929) 127 Me 510, 144 A 864 (recognizing rule).

**Minn**—Hoppe v Klapperich (1937) 224 Minn 224, 28 NW2d 780, 173 ALR 819.

**NJ**—Ash v Cohen (1937) 119 NJL 54, 194 A 174.

Voytko v Ramada Inn of Atlantic City (1978, DC NJ) 445 F Supp 315 (by implication; applying New Jersey law).

**NY**—Board of Education v Farmingdale Classroom Teachers Asso. (1975) 38 NY2d 397, 380 NYS2d 635, 343 NE2d 278 (by implication).

Dishaw v Wadleigh (1897) 15 App Div 205, 44 NYS 207.

Cote v Knickerbocker Ice Co. (1936) 160 Misc 658, 290 NYS 483 (recognizing rule); Rothbard v Ringler (1947, Sup) 77 NYS2d 351 (by

implication); Weiss v Hunna (1963, CA2 NY) 312 F2d 711, cert den 374 US 853, 10 L Ed 2d 1073, 83 S Ct 1920, reh den 375 US 874, 11 L Ed 2d 104, 84 S Ct 37 (by implication; applying New York law).

**Pa**—Haggerty v Moyerman (1936) 321 Pa 555, 184 A 654 (by implication).

Adelman v Rosenbaum (1938) 133 Pa Super 386, 3 A2d 15; Sachs v [...] (1963, ED Pa) 216 F Supp 4[...] implication; applying Pennsy[lvania] law).

**Wash**—Fite v Lee (1974) 11 [Wash] App 21, 521 P2d 964, 97 ALR3d 678, (by implication).

An attorney is personally liable to a third party if he maliciously participates with others in an abuse of process, or if he maliciously encourages and induces another to act as his instrumentality in committing an act constituting an abuse of process, the court held in Hoppe v Klapperich (1947) 224 **Minn** 224, 28 NW2d 780, 173 ALR 819. The court reversed the order of the trial court which had sustained the demurrers of an attorney and other defendants in a proceeding for abuse of process and malicious prosecution. The plaintiff had alleged, as to the cause of action for abuse of process, that it was the intent of the defendants, an attorney, his client, a sheriff, and a municipal judge, to force her to part with certain bonds, negotiable instruments, and other valuable papers by threatening her with arrest and prosecution on a criminal charge of theft of a watch. The plaintiff's subsequent arrest and confinement on the charge of theft were alleged to constitute a continuing abuse of process. The court noted that in the performance

16. See 7 Am Jur Proof of Facts 2d, Abuse of Process—Debt Collection § 4.

**693**

*Citations to cases from multiple jurisdictions*

*Discussion of the law with a more detailed case summary*

**To update, check the pocket part. The pocket part is organized by the page numbers of the Annotations, not by their titles.**

**FIGURE 3.18** POCKET PART ACCOMPANYING AN A.L.R. VOLUME

SUPPLEMENT                    **97 ALR3d 688-705**

**97 ALR3d 688-705**

**Research References**

35 Am Jur Trials 225, Physicians' c
suits.

> The pocket part is organized by page numbers.

ployer had any knowledge of dangerous condition of helicopter. Moreover, employee's previous acceptance of benefits on his workers' compensation claim against his employer precluded any right of recovery based upon theory of strict products liability since employee was working within scope of his employment when his injuries occurred and, therefore, dual capacity doctrine, pursuant to which acceptance of workers' compensation benefits will not necessarily preclude strict liability action against employer based upon allegations of defects in products manufactured by employer, was inapplicable to case. Kennedy v Helicopter Minit-Men, Inc. (1990, **Ohio App, Franklin Co**) 1990 Ohio App LEXIS 2084.

A motion by the plaintiff seeking a declaration that failure by the defendant manufacturer of a helicopter to comply with maintenance regulations constituted negligence per se was properly denied, since the purpose of such regulations was not to protect persons such as the plaintiff from loss of helicopters in crashes, but rather, was to ensure safety of persons both in the aircraft and on the ground. Erickson Air-Crane Co. v United Technologies Corp. (1987) 87 **Or App** 577, 743 P2d 747, review den 304 Or 680, 748 P2d 142.

In action brought by and on behalf of survivors of Army pilot who was killed in crash of Army Cobra AH-1 helicopter, in which it was alleged that civilian company which had at one time been responsible for maintenance of helicopter was negligent in using improper grease, using improper maintenance procedure, and failing to supply adequate information to Army of swashplate (bearing container) malfunction that occurred in helicopter prior to swashplate malfunction that occurred when helicopter crashed, judgment on jury verdict in favor of maintenance company was affirmed on appeal. Appellate court noted that Army report of accident made no final conclusions or recommendations regarding accident. Court further noted that in addition to developing evidence to rebut allegations of negligence, maintenance company presented evidence that product defect, and not improper maintenance, caused accident. Court stated that in its review of all evidence presented at trial, it could not find that verdict was so contrary to overwhelming weight of evidence as to be clearly wrong and unjust. Beavers v Northrop Worldwide Aircraft Services, Inc. (1991, **Tex App Amarillo**) 821 SW2d 669, reh overr (Tex App Amarillo) 1992 Tex App LEXIS 104 and writ den (Jun 24, 1992) and rehg of writ of error overr (Sep 9, 1992).

**§ 1. Introduction**
**[b] Related matters**
Necessity and permissibility of raising claim for abuse of process by reply or counterclaim in same proceeding in which abuse occurred—state cases. 82 ALR4th 1115.

Attorney's liability, to one other than immediate client, for negligence in connection with legal duties. 61 ALR4th 615.

Liability of attorney, acting for client, for malicious prosecution. 46 ALR4th 249.

Initiating, or threatening to initiate, criminal prosecution as ground for disciplining counsel. 42 ALR4th 1000.

Abuse of process action based on misuse of discovery or deposition procedures after commencement of civil action without seizure of person or property. 33 ALR4th 650.

Authority of United States District Court, under 28 USCS § 1651(a), to enjoin, sua sponte, a party from filing further papers in support of frivolous claim. 53 ALR Fed 651.

**§ 2. Summary and comment**
**[a] Generally**
Allegations that attorneys obtained default judgment based on error, and demanded payment of fee for services rendered prior to agreeing to enter satisfaction of judgment to correct error, did not state cause of action for abuse of process. Varela v Investors Ins. Holding Corp. (1992, 2d Dept) 185 App Div 2d 309, 586 **NYS2d** 272.

**§ 3. Rule that attorney may be liable for abuse of process**
See Mozzochi v Beck (1987) 204 **Conn** 490, 529 A2d 171, § 7[a].

See Tedards v Auty (1989) 232 **NJ Super** 541, 557 A2d 1030, § 5[a].

Attorney is liable if he or she causes irregular process to be issued which occasions loss to party against whom it is enforced. ERA Realty Co. v RBS Properties (1992, 2d Dept) 185 App Div 2d 871, 586 **NYS2d** 831.

**§ 4. Rule that mere institution of legal action by attorney does not constitute abuse of process**
See Tedards v Auty (1989) 232 **NJ Super** 541, 557 A2d 1030, § 5[a].

**101**

**For latest cases, call the toll free number appearing on the cover of this supplement.**

Reprinted with permission from Lawyers Cooperative Publishing, *American Law Reports Supplement*, 3d Ser., Insert in Back of Vol. 97 (Aug. 1997), p. 101.

To research in the *Restatement (Second) of Torts,* the first step is locating pertinent Restatement sections using either the subject index or the table of contents. This example shows a portion of the table of contents.

**FIGURE 3.19**   TABLE OF CONTENTS, *RESTATEMENT (SECOND) OF TORTS*

---

TABLE OF CONTENTS

XII

Table of contents entry for false imprisonment

**The Restatement sections are organized numerically. Comments follow the Restatement section. If Illustrations are provided, they will follow the appropriate Comment. The Illustrations demonstrate how the Restatement section is intended to apply to hypothetical situations.**

**FIGURE 3.20** *RESTATEMENT (SECOND) OF TORTS § 35*

§ **35**     TORTS, SECOND          Ch. 2

### TOPIC 4. THE INTEREST IN FREEDOM FROM CONFINEMENT

§ **35.** False Imprisonment

Rule from the Restatement

(1) An actor is subject to liability to another for false imprisonment if

(a) he acts intending to confine the other or a third person within boundaries fixed by the actor, and

(b) his act directly or indirectly results in such a confinement of the other, and

(c) the other is conscious of the confinement or is harmed by it.

(2) An act which is not done with the intention stated in Subsection (1, a) does not make the actor liable to the other for a merely transitory or otherwise harmless confinement, although the act involves an unreasonable risk of imposing it and therefore would be negligent or reckless if the risk threatened bodily harm.

See Reporter's Notes.

Caveat:

The Institute expresses no opinion as to whether the actor may not be subject to liability for conduct which involves an unreasonable risk of causing a confinement of such duration or character as to make the other's loss of freedom a matter of material value.

Comment

Comment on Subsection (1):

*a. Common-law action of trespass for false imprisonment.* At common law, the appropriate form of action for imposing a confinement was trespass for false imprisonment except where the confinement was by arrest under a valid process issued by a court having jurisdiction, in which case the damages for the confinement were recoverable, if at all, as part of the damages in an action of trespass on the case for malicious prosecution or abuse of process. Therefore, an act which makes the actor liable under this Section for a confinement otherwise than by arrest under a valid process is customarily called a false imprisonment.

*b.* As to the meaning of the words "subject to liability," see § 5.

See Appendix for Reporter's Notes, Court Citations, and Cross References

52

**FIGURE 3.20**   *RESTATEMENT (SECOND) OF TORTS* § 35 *(Continued)*

Ch. 2                    FALSE IMPRISONMENT                    **§ 35**

*c.* As to confinement caused indirectly by the institution of criminal proceedings against another, see § 37, Comment *b.*

**Comment on Clause (a) of Subsection (1):**

*d.* The actor is liable under this Section if his act was done for the purpose of imposing confinement upon the other or with knowledge that such confinement would, to a substantial certainty, result from it.  As to the effect of an intention to confine a third party, see § 43.

> **Illustration containing a hypothetical situation**

**Illustration:**

1. A, knowing that B, a customer, is in his shop, locks its only door in order to prevent a third person from entering. This is a confinement of B, and A is subject to liability to him unless, under the circumstances, he is privileged.

*e.* As to the necessity for the other's knowledge of his confinement, see § 42.

*f.* As to what constitutes consent to a confinement, see §§ 892–892 D.

*g.* As to the circumstances which create a privilege to confine another irrespective of the other's consent, see §§ 63–156.

**Comment on Subsection (2):**

*h. Extent of protection of interest in freedom from confinement.*  Under this Section the actor is not liable unless his act is done for the purpose of imposing confinement upon the other, or with knowledge that such a confinement will, to a substantial certainty, result from it.  It is not enough that the actor realizes or should realize that his actions involve a risk of causing a confinement, so long as the likelihood that it will do so falls short of a substantial certainty.

The mere dignitary interest in feeling free to choose one's own location and, therefore, in freedom from the realization that one's will to choose one's location is subordinated to the will of another is given legal protection only against invasion by acts done with the intention stated in Subsection (1, a).  It is not protected against acts which threaten to cause such an invasion even though the likelihood is so great that if a more perfectly protected interest, such as that in bodily security, were imperiled, the actor's conduct would be negligent or even reckless.

See Appendix for Reporter's Notes, Court Citations, and Cross References

53

**To locate cases interpreting the Restatement section, use the Appendix volume or volumes. Each volume is organized by section number and covers a specific period of time.**

**FIGURE 3.21** APPENDIX VOLUME, *RESTATEMENT (SECOND) OF TORTS*

RESTATEMENT OF THE LAW

SECOND

# TORTS 2d

*As Adopted and Promulgated*

BY

THE AMERICAN LAW INSTITUTE
AT WASHINGTON, D.C.

May 25, 1963 and May 22, 1964

APPENDIX

Volume Through June 1994

§§ 1–309

> **Time period covered by this Appendix volume**

Citations to the Restatement from July 1984 through June 1994

ST. PAUL, MINN.
AMERICAN LAW INSTITUTE PUBLISHERS
1995

© 1995 by The American Law Institute. Reprinted with permission, *Restatement (Second) of the Law of Torts*, 2d Ed., Appendix Volume through June 1994, §§ 1–309 (1995), title page.

**The Appendix will list cases interpreting the Restatement section.**

**FIGURE 3.22**   APPENDIX VOLUME, *RESTATEMENT (SECOND) OF TORTS*

§ 34                                    TORTS                                   Ch. 2

complaint. Affirming in part, this court held that the plaintiff's allegations of duress and undue influence in that the defendant had forced her to submit her final class paper, thus depriving her of free exercise of her will and her constitutional rights, did not state a cognizable claim. The specially concurring opinion argued that it was not prepared at this time to adopt the Restatement sections as the law of the state for civil assault and civil battery. Jung–Leonczynska v. Steup, 782 P.2d 578, 583, 584, appeal after remand 803 P.2d 1358 (1990).

### TOPIC 4.   THE INTEREST IN FREEDOM FROM CONFINEMENT

**Ariz.App.**1987.   Cit. in disc. §§ 35–45A, comprising all of Ch. 2, Topic 4. A bank customer sued a bank for false arrest and false imprisonment after he was arrested and detained by police as a result of bank employees' allegations that the plaintiff was fraudulently using a credit card. The trial court denied the bank's motion for a directed verdict and granted the plaintiff's motion for a directed verdict on the ground that there was insufficient probable cause to believe that the plaintiff committed a felony. This court reversed the grant of the plaintiff's motion and remanded for a jury trial of his claims. The court also affirmed the denial of the bank's motion, stating that, based on the evidence, a jury could reasonably conclude that the bank instigated or participated in the arrest. Deadman v. Valley Nat. Bank of Arizona, 154 Ariz. 452, 743 P.2d 961, 966.

**Miss.**1987.   Cit. in disc. §§ 35–45A, comprising all of Ch. 2, Topic 4. Two police officers who responded to a report of gunshots detained a belligerent and intoxicated individual for 15 minutes of interrogation and investigation. The individual who had been detained sued the police officers, an alderman, and the city for false imprisonment. The trial court entered judgment in favor of the defendants. Affirming, this court held that the 15-minute detention of the plaintiff by the police was not unreasonable in terms of purpose, duration, or extent under the circumstances. The court reasoned that the law affords as a defense to one sued for false imprisonment that the plaintiff was temporarily detained for reasonable investigative purposes. Thornhill v. Wilson, 504 So.2d 1205, 1207.

### § 35.   False Imprisonment

**C.A.1,** 1991.   Subsec. (1) cit. in disc. A debtor in bankruptcy, jailed for contempt in state court proceedings brought by a judgment creditor without notice of the bankrupt-

cy filing to collect on its judgment debt, sued the judgment creditor for false imprisonment, inter alia. The district court entered judgment on a jury verdict for the defendant. This court affirmed, holding that the district court correctly stated the law of false imprisonment regarding the element of willful detention of the plaintiff by requiring the jury to find that the defendant knew that there was no right to pick the plaintiff up and have him put in jail, or to ask a judge to do that, yet went ahead in reckless disregard of that fact. The court said that the instruction was the correct approach to defining the willfulness requirement where the defendant had not physically confined the plaintiff but had effected the plaintiff's confinement through the police acting pursuant to a warrant valid on its face. Under these circumstances, the court concluded that the defendant could have acted "willfully" only if it knew that the warrant had been maliciously or wrongfully obtained—that is, the defendant knew that the process was for some reason void. Vahlsing v. Commercial Union Ins. Co., Inc., 928 F.2d 486, 492.

**C.A.2,** 1986.   Cit. in disc. After a man was convicted of first-degree criminal possession of stolen property, he sued the arresting officers for damages, claiming that they had lacked probable cause to arrest him. The trial court granted the defendants' motion for summary judgment. Affirming, this court held that regardless of whether the action was characterized as one for false imprisonment or malicious prosecution, the fact that the person against whom criminal proceedings were instituted was found guilty of the crime charged against him was a complete defense against liability. The court reasoned that in either case a plaintiff could not challenge probable cause in the face of a judgment of conviction unless the conviction was obtained by improper means. Cameron v. Fogarty, 806 F.2d 380, 387, cert. denied 481

Cases interpreting § 35

See also cases under division, chapter, topic, title, and subtitle that include section under examination. For earlier citations see the Restatement of the Law, Second, Torts 2d Appendix Volumes covering §§ 1–309 through 1963, through 1975, and through 1984.

132

**The latest volume of the Appendix is updated with a pocket part containing references to the most current cases.**

**FIGURE 3.23** APPENDIX VOLUME, *RESTATEMENT (SECOND) OF TORTS*, POCKET PART

---

## RESTATEMENT CASE CITATIONS

### TOPIC 4. THE INTEREST IN FREEDOM FROM CONFINEMENT

C.A.1, 1995. §§ 35–45A, constituting all of Ch. 2, Topic 4, cit. in sup. and adopted. Puerto Rican resident was arrested by federal agents who mistakenly believed that she was the subject of a 1975 arrest warrant; following the dismissal of all proceedings against her, she sued the United States for false arrest. Affirming the district court's grant of summary judgment for the United States, this court held that the United States was not liable for the false arrest of plaintiff, since the name in the warrant, together with information contained in the arrest packet, provided ample basis for the arresting agents to form an objectively reasonable belief that plaintiff was the person named in the warrant. The court also held that the conduct of the federal agent responsible for instigating the errant arrest was conditionally privileged, since the [detai]nee was sufficiently named in the war[rant] and the agent reasonably believed that [plain]tiff was the subject of the warrant. Rod[rigu]ez v. U.S., 54 F.3d 41, 45.

> **Most recent cases interpreting § 35**

### § 35. False Imprisonment

C.A.1, 1995. Cit. in ftn. Two men who were arrested and acquitted of selling cocaine sued police officers of Puerto Rico and their confidential informants for constitutional violations, alleging that defendants falsely identified them as sellers. District court held that the false arrest claims were barred by the one-year statute of limitations and that the malicious prosecution claims were not actionable under 42 U.S.C. § 1983. This court vacated and remanded, holding that, for purposes of determining the appropriate accrual rule, both the Fourth and Fourteenth Amendment claims more closely resembled the common law tort of malicious prosecution. Consequently, plaintiffs' § 1983 claims did not accrue until their respective criminal prosecutions ended in acquittals. Calero–Colon v. Betancourt–Lebron, 68 F.3d 1, 3.

E.D.Ark.1995. Cit. in ftn. Owner of a store located in front of a county detention facility was raped by an unsupervised "trusty" pretrial detainee, who had been directed by the county deputy sheriff to unload groceries from a police car behind the store. Store owner brought a § 1983 civil rights claim, as well as pendent state-law tort claims, against the county, the deputy sheriff, and others. Granting in part defendants' motion to dismiss, the court held that defendants were not liable, as a matter of law, for the intentional torts of battery, assault, and false imprisonment committed by detainee against plaintiff; even though detainee could be viewed as defendants' agent insofar as he was enlisted to perform various services for them as a trusty detainee, plaintiff did not allege that the attack by detainee was in any way related to the performance of his duties or that it was motivated by his desire to benefit any of the defendants. Davis v. Fulton County, Ark., 884 F.Supp. 1245, 1262.

D.Mass.1995. Cit. in disc. Motorist who allegedly was beaten by town police officers during his arrest for driving under the influence of alcohol brought a civil rights action and asserted various state-law claims against the town, its police chief, and six police officers. The court denied summary judgment for the two arresting officers on plaintiff's false imprisonment claim, holding that a disputed issue of fact existed as to whether the police officers had had reasonable grounds for the arrest. Noel v. Town of Plymouth, Mass., 895 F.Supp. 346, 354.

M.D.N.C.1996. Cit. in headnotes, cit. in disc. Eighth-grade student who became disruptive on a school field trip to a local detention center and who was consequently placed in a holding cell for seven minutes sued sheriff, his employees, school board, and teacher for, inter alia, false imprisonment. Defendants moved for summary judgment. Granting the motion, the court held that student failed to state a cause of action for false imprisonment since her confinement, which was necessary for purposes of maintaining order and control and protecting the residents of the facility as well as the schoolchildren, was lawful. Additionally, student, who had consented to the deprivation of her freedom of movement when she agreed to participate in the field trip, was not restrained against her will. Harris by Tucker v. County of Forsyth, 921 F.Supp. 325, 327, 333.

Alaska, 1995. Cit. in headnote, cit. in ftn. Gentleman who was wrongfully arrested by

---

See also cases under division, chapter, topic, title, and subtitle that include section under examination. For earlier citations see the Restatement of the Law, Second, Torts 2d Appendix Volumes covering §§ 1–309.

44

# F. CHECKLIST FOR SECONDARY SOURCE RESEARCH

## 1. LEGAL ENCYCLOPEDIAS

❏ Use legal encyclopedias for very general background information and limited citations to primary authority, but not for in-depth analysis of a topic.

❏ Use Am. Jur. 2d or C.J.S. for a general overview; look for a state encyclopedia for an overview of the law in an individual state.

❏ Locate material in a print encyclopedia by (1) using the subject index or table of contents; (2) locating relevant sections in the main subject volumes; and (3) updating with the pocket part.

❏ Locate material in legal encyclopedias in LexisNexis and Westlaw by searching in the databases for individual publications or multiple secondary sources or by viewing the table of contents.

## 2. TREATISES

❏ Use treatises for an in-depth discussion and some analysis of an area of law and for citations to primary authority.

❏ Locate treatises in print through the on-line catalog or by asking a reference librarian for a recommendation; locate material within a treatise by (1) using the subject index or table of contents; (2) locating relevant sections within the main text; and (3) updating with the pocket part.

❏ Locate material in treatises in LexisNexis and Westlaw by executing word searches in the databases for individual publications, multiple secondary sources, specific subject areas, or individual jurisdictions. View the table of contents for individual publications if available.

## 3. LEGAL PERIODICALS

❏ Use legal periodicals for background information, citations to primary authority, in-depth analysis of a narrow topic, or information on a conflict in the law or an undeveloped area of the law.

❏ Locate citations to periodical articles using print resources with the *Index to Legal Periodicals and Books* or the *Current Law Index*; check as many noncumulative volumes as necessary to locate relevant citations.

❏ Locate citations to periodical articles electronically with LegalTrac or the electronic version of ILP; execute a search to obtain a list of citations.

❐ Locate citations to, or the full text of, legal periodicals in LexisNexis and Westlaw by searching in the databases for multiple or individual publications.

❐ Selected periodicals may be available on the Internet.

### 4. *AMERICAN LAW REPORTS*

❐ Use A.L.R. Annotations for an overview of an area of law and citations to primary authority (especially to locate persuasive authority from other jurisdictions), but not for in-depth analysis of a topic.

❐ Use A.L.R.3d, A.L.R.4th, A.L.R.5th, and A.L.R. Fed.; avoid A.L.R. and A.L.R.2d as generally out-of-date sources.

❐ Locate material within A.L.R. in print by (1) using the A.L.R. Index; (2) locating relevant Annotations in the main volumes; and (3) updating with the pocket part.

❐ Locate A.L.R. Annotations in LexisNexis and Westlaw by searching in the databases for A.L.R. or multiple secondary sources.

### 5. RESTATEMENTS

❐ Use Restatements for research into common-law subjects and to locate mandatory and persuasive authority from jurisdictions that have adopted a Restatement.

❐ Locate Restatements in print through the on-line catalog.

❐ Locate information within a print Restatement by (1) using the subject index or table of contents to identify relevant sections within the Restatement volumes; (2) using the noncumulative Appendix volumes to find pertinent case summaries; and (3) using the pocket part in the latest Appendix volume to locate the most recent cases.

❐ Locate selected Restatements in LexisNexis and Westlaw.

### 6. UNIFORM LAWS AND MODEL ACTS

❐ Use uniform laws and model acts to interpret a law adopted by a legislature and to locate persuasive authority from other jurisdictions that have adopted the law.

❐ Locate uniform laws and model acts in print using *Uniform Laws Annotated, Master Edition* (ULA).

❐ Locate information in the ULA set by (1) using the *Directory of Uniform Acts and Codes: Tables and Index* to search by subject, by the name of the law, or by adopting jurisdiction; (2) locating relevant provisions in the main volumes; and (3) updating with the pocket part.

❏ Locate selected uniform laws and model acts in LexisNexis and Westlaw.

# CASE RESEARCH

## A. COURT OPINIONS

### 1. THE STRUCTURE OF THE COURT SYSTEM

The United States has more than fifty separate court systems, including the federal system, the fifty state systems, and the District of Columbia system. As Figure 4.1 illustrates, there are three levels of courts in the federal system: the United States District Courts (the trial courts), the United States Courts of Appeals (the intermediate appellate courts), and the United States Supreme Court (the court of last resort). The geographic boundaries of each of the federal courts of appeals are shown in Figure 4.2. Most state court systems are structured the same way as the federal court system. See Figure 4.3.

Judges from any of these courts can issue written decisions, and their decisions are one of the sources of law, as discussed more generally in Chapter 1. This chapter focuses on where these decisions are published and how they are indexed.

### 2. CASE REPORTERS

Court opinions, or cases, are published in books called reporters. Reporters are sets of books collecting cases in chronological order. Many sets of reporters are limited to opinions from a single jurisdiction or level of court. Thus, for example, federal reporters contain opinions from federal courts, and state reporters contain opinions from state courts.

**FIGURE 4.1**   STRUCTURE OF THE FEDERAL COURT SYSTEM

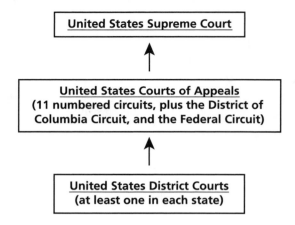

**FIGURE 4.2**   GEOGRAPHIC BOUNDARIES OF THE FEDERAL COURTS OF APPEALS

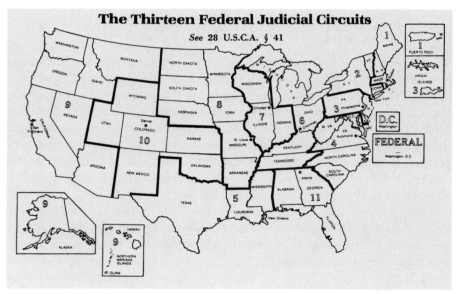

Reprinted with permission from West Group, West's *Federal Reporter,* 3d Ser., Vol. 124 (1997), inside cover.

**FIGURE 4.3** STRUCTURE OF MOST STATE COURT SYSTEMS

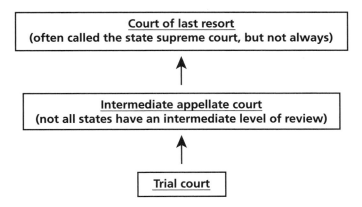

In addition, each set of reporters may be subdivided into different series covering different time periods.

A reporter published under government authority is known as an official reporter.[1] Reporters published by commercial publishers are called unofficial reporters. Because these two types of reporters exist, the same opinion may be published in more than one reporter. The text of the opinion should be exactly the same in an official and an unofficial reporter; the only difference is that the former is published by the government, and the latter is not. When a case appears in more than one reporter, it is described as having parallel citations. This is because each set of reporters will have its own citation for the case.

The only federal court opinions published by the government are those of the United States Supreme Court; these are published in a reporter called *United States Reports*. State governments usually publish the decisions of their highest courts, and most also publish decisions from some of their lower courts.

Perhaps the largest commercial publisher of cases is West Group, formerly West Publishing Company. West has created a network of unofficial reporters called the *National Reporter System*, which comprises reporters with decisions from almost every United States jurisdiction.

West publishes United States Supreme Court decisions in the *Supreme Court Reporter*. Decisions from the United States Courts of Appeals are published in the *Federal Reporter*, and those from United States District Courts are published in the *Federal Supplement*. West also publishes some specialized reporters that contain decisions from

---

[1]The government may publish the reporter itself, or it may arrange for the reporter to be published by a commercial publisher. As long as the government arranges for the publication, the reporter is official, even if it is physically produced by a commercial publisher.

the federal courts. For example, *Federal Rules Decisions* (F.R.D.) contains federal district court decisions interpreting the Federal Rules of Civil and Criminal Procedure, and *Federal Appendix* (F. Appx.) contains non-precedential decisions from some of the federal courts of appeals.

West publishes state court decisions in what are called regional reporters. West has divided the country into seven regions. The reporter for each region collects state court decisions from all of the states within that region.

Because West publishes reporters for almost every jurisdiction in a common format with common indexing features, this chapter will focus on research using West publications. The chart in Figure 4.4 shows where cases from the various state and federal courts can be found. Decisions for most states can be found in the state's official reporter, as well as in the reporters listed in Figure 4.4[2]

### 3. THE ANATOMY OF A COURT OPINION

A case published in a West reporter has five components:

1. The heading containing the parallel citation (if any) to an official reporter, the case name, the court that rendered the decision, and the date of the decision.
2. A synopsis of the decision written by case editors, not by the court.
3. One or more paragraphs summarizing the key points within the decision. These summary paragraphs are called headnotes, and they are written by case editors, not by the court.
4. The names of the attorneys who represented the parties and the judge or judges who decided the case.
5. The opinion of the court. If the decision has any concurring or dissenting opinions, these will follow immediately after the majority or plurality opinion.

Only the fifth item on this list, the opinion of the court, constitutes legal authority. All of the remaining items are editorial enhancements. These editorial enhancements are very useful for locating cases, but they are not part of the court's opinion. Therefore, you should never rely on any part of a case other than the text of the opinion itself.[3]

Figure 4.5 shows an excerpt from a case published in a West reporter.

---

[2]West also publishes separate unofficial state reporters for New York, California, and Illinois. Thus, New York, California, and Illinois cases may appear in three places: (1) an official state reporter; (2) a West regional reporter; and (3) a West unofficial state reporter. Some lower court opinions published in West's New York and California reporters are not published in the regional reporters covering those states. By contrast, all of the cases in West's *Illinois Decisions* are included in the regional reporter covering Illinois.

[3]There are limited exceptions to this rule. For example, in Ohio, the text of the opinion is preceded by a "syllabus," or summary of the opinion, which is written by the court and which contains the holding of the decision. Ordinarily, however, everything other than the opinion itself is an editorial enhancement. Unless you see a notation indicating otherwise, you should assume that only the text of the opinion is authoritative.

**FIGURE 4.4** REPORTERS

| COURT OR JURISDICTION | REPORTER (followed by reporter abbreviation; multiple abbreviations denote multiple series) |
|---|---|
| United States Supreme Court | *United States Reports* (U.S.)*<br><br>*Supreme Court Reporter* (S. Ct.)<br><br>*United States Supreme Court Reports, Lawyer's Edition* (L. Ed., L. Ed. 2d) |
| United States Courts of Appeals | *Federal Reporter* (F., F.2d, F.3d)<br><br>*Federal Appendix* (F. Appx.) |
| United States District Courts | *Federal Supplement* (F. Supp., F. Supp. 2d)<br><br>*Federal Rules Decisions* (F.R.D.) |
| Atlantic Region States (Connecticut, Delaware, District of Columbia, Maine, Maryland, New Hampshire, New Jersey, Pennsylvania, Rhode Island, Vermont) | *Atlantic Reporter* (A., A.2d) |
| North Eastern Region States (Illinois, Indiana, Massachusetts, New York, Ohio) | *North Eastern Reporter* (N.E., N.E.2d)<br><br>*New York: New York Supplement* (N.Y.S., N.Y.S.2d)<br><br>Illinois: *Illinois Decisions* (Ill. Dec.) |
| South Eastern Region States (Georgia, North Carolina, South Carolina, Virginia, West Virginia) | *South Eastern Reporter* (S.E., S.E.2d) |
| Southern Region States (Alabama, Florida, Louisiana, Mississippi) | *Southern Reporter* (So., So. 2d) |
| South Western Region States (Arkansas, Kentucky, Missouri, Tennessee, Texas) | *South Western Reporter* (S.W., S.W.2d, S.W.3d) |
| North Western Region States (Iowa, Michigan, Minnesota, Nebraska, North Dakota, South Dakota, Wisconsin) | *North Western Reporter* (N.W., N.W.2d) |
| Pacific Region States (Alaska, Arizona, California, Colorado, Hawaii, Idaho, Kansas, Montana, Nevada, New Mexico, Oklahoma, Oregon, Utah, Washington, Wyoming) | *Pacific Reporter* (P., P.2d, P.3d)<br><br>California: *California Reporter* (Cal. Rptr., Cal. Rptr. 2d) |

*Official reporter published by the federal government.

**FIGURE 4.5**   EXCERPT FROM *POPKIN v. NEW YORK STATE*

**Case name**

**Headnote**

18                    547 FEDERAL REPORTER, 2d SERIES

**2. States ⊕4.1**

In the absence of a plain indication to the contrary by Congress, the application of a federal act is not dependent on state law.

Mildred POPKIN, Plaintiff-Appellant,

v.

NEW YORK STATE HEALTH AND MENTAL HYGIENE FACILITIES IMPROVEMENT CORPORATION, Defendant-Appellee.

No. 80, Docket 76–7167.

United States Court of Appeals, Second Circuit.

Argued Oct. 20, 1976.

Decided Dec. 15, 1976.

**Court**

**3. Civil Rights ⊕41**

The Equal Employment Opportunity Act of 1972 was designed to broaden jurisdictional coverage of Title VII of the Civil Rights Act of 1964 by deleting the existing exemptions of state and local government employees and of certain employees of educational institutions. Civil Rights Act of 1964, §§ 701 et seq., 701(b) as amended 42 U.S.C.A. §§ 2000e et seq., 2000e(b).

**4. Civil Rights ⊕2**

The 1972 Amendments to Title VII of the Civil Rights Act of 1964 have no retroactive effect where they create new substantive rights. Civil Rights §§ 701 et seq., 701(b) as amended U.S.C.A. §§ 2000e et seq., 2000e(b).

**Attorneys**

Former employee of corporation which was created to provide improved state facilities for the care of the mentally disabled brought civil rights action charging sex discrimination in her discharge. The United States District Court for the Southern District of New York, Lloyd F. MacMahon, J., 409 F.Supp. 430, granted a defense motion to dismiss for failure to state a claim on which relief could be granted, and plaintiff appealed. The Court of Appeals, J. Joseph Smith, Circuit Judge, held that although the aforesaid corporation was classified under New York law as a public benefit corporation, not as a political subdivision, the corporation was nevertheless excluded before 1972 from coverage under Title VII of the Civil Rights Act of 1964.

Affirmed.

**Editorial summary**

⊕41

Although corporation, which was created by state to provide improved state facilities for the care of the mentally disabled, was classified under New York law as a public benefit corporation, not as a political subdivision, the corporation was nevertheless excluded before 1972 from coverage under Title VII of the Civil Rights Act of 1964, §§ 701(b), as amended 42 U.S.C.A. §§ 2000e(b), 2000e–1, McK.Unconsol.Laws N.Y. §§ 4402, 4404.

**The court's opinion**

Floyd S. Weil, New York City (Milton Kean, New York City, of counsel), for plaintiff-appellant.

Joan P. Scannell, Deputy Asst. Atty. Gen., New York City (Louis J. Lefkowitz, Atty. Gen., State of New York, Samuel A. Hirshowitz, First Asst. Atty. Gen., New York City, of counsel), for defendant-appellee.

Before SMITH, OAKES and TIMBERS, Circuit Judges.

J. JOSEPH SMITH, Circuit Judge:

**Judges**

Mildred Popkin appeals from the order of the United States District Court for the Southern District of New York, Lloyd F. MacMahon, *Judge*, dismissing her complaint, brought under Title VII of the Civil Rights Act of 1964, 42 U.S.C. § 2000e, *et seq.*, for failure to state a claim upon which relief can be granted, pursuant to Rule 12(b)(6) of the Federal Rules of Civil Procedure. We affirm.

Appellant was employed as an architect by the New York State Health and Mental Hygiene Facilities Improvement Corporation ("the Corporation"). In November,

**FIGURE 4.5** EXCERPT FROM *POPKIN v. NEW YORK STATE* (Continued)

POPKIN v. N. Y. ST. HEALTH & MENTAL HYGIENE, ETC.          19
Cite as 547 F.2d 18 (1976)

1970 she was notified that her employment would be terminated as of January 15, 1971. Appellant instituted this action under Title VII alleging that the termination was an act of discrimination based on her sex. Jurisdiction was based on 42 U.S.C. § 2000e et seq. and 28 U.S.C. § 1332. The district court dismissed the complaint on the ground that the Corporation was a "political subdivision" of New York State and was therefore excluded from coverage of 42 U.S.C. § 2000e et seq. prior to March 24, 1972.[1] The 1972 amendments to Title VII, extending coverage of the Act to political subdivisions, were held by the district court not to have retroactive effect.

[1, 2] The Corporation was created by the Health and Mental Hygiene Facilities Improvement Act as a "corporate governmental agency constituting a public benefit corporation." McKinney's Unconsol.Laws §§ 4402, 4404. Appellant contends that because under New York law her employer is classified as a public benefit corporation and not as a political subdivision, the Corporation was not excluded from Title VII coverage before 1972 under 42 U.S.C. § 2000e(b). We disagree. Title VII does not provide that the terms of the federal statute are to be construed according to state law. Title 42 U.S.C. § 2000e–7 merely provides that state laws prohibiting employment discrimination will remain in effect. In the absence of a plain indication to the contrary by Congress, the application of a federal act is not dependent on state law. *Jerome v. United States*, 318 U.S. 101, 104,

63 S.Ct. 483, 87 L.Ed. 640 (1943). Congressional intent concerning coverage of Title VII and the actual nature of appellee's relationship to the state determine whether or not the Corporation was covered by Title VII before 1972.

[3] The Equal Employment Opportunity Act of 1972 was designed to broaden jurisdictional coverage of Title VII by deleting the existing exemptions of state and local government employees and of certain employees of educational institutions. The bill amended the Civil Rights Act of 1964 to include state and local governments, governmental agencies, and political subdivisions within the definition of "employer" in 42 U.S.C. § 2000e(b). H.R.Rep.No.92–238, 92nd Cong., 2d Sess., *reprinted in* 1972 U.S. Code Cong. & Ad.News 2137, 2152. The conference report of the Senate Amendment to H.R. 1746, which was adopted by the conference, stated explicitly that the Senate Amendment "expanded coverage to include: (1) State and local governments, governmental agencies, political subdivisions . . . ." *Id.* at 2180. The 1964 House Report on the Civil Rights Act of 1964, on the other hand, refers to the exclusion from the term "employer" of "all Federal, State, and local government agencies. . . ." 1964 U.S.Code Cong. & Ad. News 2402. Until 1972, state agencies as well as political subdivisions were exempt from Title VII. Under the terms of the Mental Hygiene Facilities Development Corporation Act, "state agencies" include public benefit corporations.[2]

1. Section 701(b) of Title VII, the Civil Rights Act of 1964, P.L. 88–352 as enacted provided in relevant part:

(b) The term "employer" means a person engaged in an industry affecting commerce who has twenty-five or more employees for each working day in each of twenty or more calendar weeks in the current or preceding calendar year, and any agent of such a person, but such term does not include (1) the United States, a corporation wholly owned by the Government of the United States, an Indian tribe, or a State or political subdivision thereof. . . .

In 1972 § 701(b), 42 U.S.C. § 2000e(b) was amended as follows:

(b) The term "employer" means a person engaged in an industry affecting commerce who has fifteen or more employees for each working day in each of twenty or more calendar weeks in the current or preceding calendar year, and any agent of such a person, but such term does not include (1) the United States, a corporation wholly owned by the Government of the United States, an Indian tribe, or any department or agency of the District of Columbia subject by statute to procedures of the competitive service (as defined in section 2102 of Title 5). . . .

2. McKinney's Unconsol.Laws § 4403(17) contains the following definition:

"State agency" means any officer, department, board, commission, bureau division,

Bracketed numbers indicate the place in the opinion where material summarized in the headnotes appears.

## B. LOCATING CASES USING A DIGEST

### 1. WHAT IS A DIGEST?

Reporters are published in chronological order; they are not organized by subject. Trying to research cases in chronological order would be impossible. The research tool that organizes cases by subject is called a digest, and that is the finding tool you will ordinarily use to locate cases by topic.

The term "digest" literally means to arrange and summarize, and that is exactly what a digest does. In a digest, the law is arranged into different subject categories such as torts, contracts, or criminal law. Then, within each category, the digest provides summaries of cases that discuss the law on that subject. You can use the summaries to decide which cases you should read to find the answer to your research question.

The digest system created by West is the most commonly used digest in legal research. West has divided the law into more than 400 subject categories called topics. Under each topic, West provides summaries of cases relevant to the subject. Each topic is listed alphabetically in the digest. Because there are so many topics, a digest actually consists of a multivolume set of books. This is similar to a set of encyclopedias with multiple volumes covering topics in alphabetical order.

The West topics are quite broad. Subject areas such as torts or contracts generate thousands of cases. Therefore, the topics have been further subdivided into smaller categories. Each subdivision within a topic is assigned a number that West calls a key number. Thus, the case summaries within a West digest will appear under the relevant key number. Instead of requiring you to read summaries of all the cases on a very broad topic, the key number subdivisions allow you to focus more specifically on the precise issue you are researching.

The topic, key number, and case summary that you find in a West digest will correspond exactly to one of the headnotes at the beginning of an opinion published in a West reporter.

The following examples illustrate some of the features of a West digest. Figure 4.6 shows the beginning of the West topic for Innkeepers, including the outline of subtopics covered in each key number. Figure 4.7 shows a summary of a case under key number 10.1.

Digests, like many other research tools, are updated with pocket parts, which are explained in Chapter 1. If the pocket part gets too big to fit in the back of the book, you may find a separate softcover pamphlet on the shelf next to the hardcover volume. Whenever you use any hardcover book in digest research, it is especially important to check the pocket part for new information because hardcover digest volumes are not reprinted frequently.

**FIGURE 4.6** BEGINNING OF THE WEST TOPIC FOR INNKEEPERS

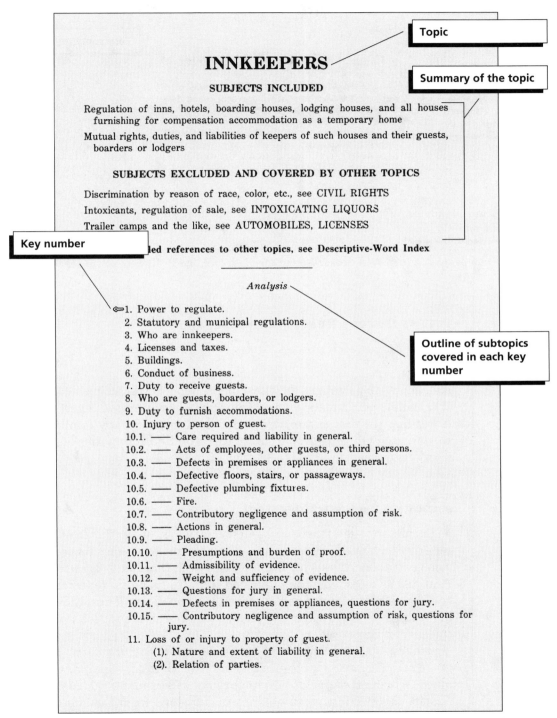

# INNKEEPERS

**Topic**

### SUBJECTS INCLUDED

**Summary of the topic**

Regulation of inns, hotels, boarding houses, lodging houses, and all houses furnishing for compensation accommodation as a temporary home

Mutual rights, duties, and liabilities of keepers of such houses and their guests, boarders or lodgers

### SUBJECTS EXCLUDED AND COVERED BY OTHER TOPICS

Discrimination by reason of race, color, etc., see CIVIL RIGHTS

Intoxicants, regulation of sale, see INTOXICATING LIQUORS

Trailer camps and the like, see AUTOMOBILES, LICENSES

**Key number**

led references to other topics, see Descriptive-Word Index

*Analysis*

1. Power to regulate.
2. Statutory and municipal regulations.
3. Who are innkeepers.
4. Licenses and taxes.
5. Buildings.
6. Conduct of business.
7. Duty to receive guests.
8. Who are guests, boarders, or lodgers.
9. Duty to furnish accommodations.
10. Injury to person of guest.

**Outline of subtopics covered in each key number**

10.1. —— Care required and liability in general.
10.2. —— Acts of employees, other guests, or third persons.
10.3. —— Defects in premises or appliances in general.
10.4. —— Defective floors, stairs, or passageways.
10.5. —— Defective plumbing fixtures.
10.6. —— Fire.
10.7. —— Contributory negligence and assumption of risk.
10.8. —— Actions in general.
10.9. —— Pleading.
10.10. —— Presumptions and burden of proof.
10.11. —— Admissibility of evidence.
10.12. —— Weight and sufficiency of evidence.
10.13. —— Questions for jury in general.
10.14. —— Defects in premises or appliances, questions for jury.
10.15. —— Contributory negligence and assumption of risk, questions for jury.
11. Loss of or injury to property of guest.
    (1). Nature and extent of liability in general.
    (2). Relation of parties.

Reprinted with permission from West Group, West's *Federal Practice Digest,* 4th Ser., Vol. 63 (1991), p. 1.

**FIGURE 4.7**   CASE SUMMARY UNDER THE INNKEEPERS TOPIC, KEY NUMBER 10.1

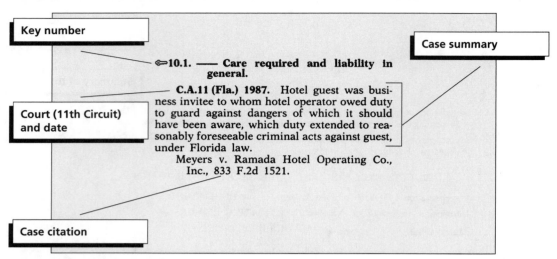

**Key number**

**Case summary**

🔑**10.1.** —— **Care required and liability in general.**

**C.A.11 (Fla.) 1987.**  Hotel guest was business invitee to whom hotel operator owed duty to guard against dangers of which it should have been aware, which duty extended to reasonably foreseeable criminal acts against guest, under Florida law.
  Meyers v. Ramada Hotel Operating Co., Inc., 833 F.2d 1521.

**Court (11th Circuit) and date**

**Case citation**

Reprinted with permission from West Group, West's *Federal Practice Digest,* 4th Ser., Vol. 63 (1991), p. 4.

## 2. THE DIGEST RESEARCH PROCESS

The digest research process consists of four steps:

a. locating the correct digest set for the type of research you are doing
b. locating relevant topics and key numbers within the digest
c. reading the case summaries under the topics and key numbers
d. updating your research to make sure you find summaries of the most recent cases.

### a. Locating the Correct Digest Set

Reporters and digests are similar in several ways. Just as there are different reporters containing cases from different jurisdictions, there are also different sets of digests for finding cases from these various jurisdictions. And just as a case may be published in more than one reporter, so also could a case be summarized in more than one digest. Thus, the first step in finding cases that will help you answer a research question is choosing the correct digest set.

   Digest sets are organized by jurisdiction and by date. The four jurisdictional categories for digests are federal, state, regional, and combined. A federal digest, as you might imagine, summarizes federal cases. A state digest contains summaries of decisions from that state as well as opinions from the federal courts located in that state. A regional digest summarizes state court decisions from the states within the region, but it does not contain summaries of any federal cases. West publishes regional digests for some, but not all, of its regional reporters. A combined digest summarizes cases from all state and federal jurisdictions.

Within each category, the digest set may be divided into different series covering different time periods. For example, West's *Federal Practice Digest*, one of the federal digests, is currently in its Fourth Series. The Fourth Series contains cases from the early 1980s to the present. Earlier cases, from 1975 through the early 1980s, can be found in the Third Series of the digest. Ordinarily, you will want to begin your research in the most current series. If you are unable to find information in the most current series, however, you could locate older cases by looking in the earlier series.

Figures 4.8 through 4.10 summarize some of the characteristics of West digests.

To decide which digest is the best choice for your research, you will need to consider the nature and scope of the project. Usually, you will want to choose the narrowest digest that still has enough information for you to find relevant legal authority. Sometimes you will need to use more than one digest to find all of the cases you need.

West's *Federal Practice Digest* is the best place to start looking for federal cases. If you are researching case law from an individual state, the digest from that state is usually the best starting place. If you do

**FIGURE 4.8**  FEDERAL DIGESTS

| DESCRIPTION | WEST'S FEDERAL PRACTICE DIGEST, FOURTH SERIES | WEST'S SUPREME COURT DIGEST |
| --- | --- | --- |
| What is included | Summaries of cases from all federal courts | Summaries of cases from the United States Supreme Court |
| What is excluded | Summaries of state cases | Summaries of cases from lower federal courts and all state courts |
| Coverage | Includes summaries of cases from the early 1980s–present. Older cases are summarized in prior series of this set (e.g., West's *Federal Practice Digest*, Third Series). | Includes summaries of all United States Supreme Court cases |

**FIGURE 4.9** STATE AND REGIONAL DIGESTS

| DESCRIPTION | STATE DIGESTS | REGIONAL DIGESTS |
|---|---|---|
| What is included | Summaries of cases from the state's courts *and* the federal courts within the state | Summaries of cases from the state courts within the region |
| What is excluded | Summaries of state and federal cases from courts outside the state | Summaries of state cases from states outside the region and all federal cases |
| Coverage | West publishes state digests for all states except Delaware, Nevada, and Utah. The *Virginia Digest* summarizes cases from both Virginia and West Virginia. The *Dakota Digest* summarizes cases from both North and South Dakota. Some state digests have multiple series. | West publishes Atlantic, North Western, Pacific, and South Eastern Digests. West *does not* publish North Eastern, Southern, or South Western Digests. All of the regional digests have multiple series. |

not have access to the state digest, the regional digest is another good place to look. It is also a good place to find persuasive authority from surrounding jurisdictions. Remember, however, that regional digests summarize only state court decisions, no federal decisions. Therefore, if you also want to find cases from the federal courts located within an individual state, you will need to supplement your regional digest research by using West's *Federal Practice Digest*.

The combined digests have the most comprehensive coverage, but they are also the most difficult to use. You would probably begin with the *General Digest*, which covers cases from 2001 to the present. West publishes a complete set of *General Digest* books for each year from 2001 to the present. Thus, you would need to begin by researching in the most recent set, and then repeat the research process in each of the previous annual sets. For cases before 2001, you would also need to use the *Eleventh Decennial Digest*, Part I, and as many previous sets as necessary to locate cases on your topic. Because this is a cumbersome process, the combined digests are usually only useful when you know the approximate time period you want to research or when you are conducting nationwide research.

**FIGURE 4.10** COMBINED DIGESTS

| DESCRIPTION | COMBINED DIGESTS |
|---|---|
| What is included | Summaries of state and federal cases from all jurisdictions across the United States |
| What is excluded | Nothing |
| Coverage | The combined digests are divided into the *General*, *Decennial*, and *Century Digests*, covering the following dates: |

| | |
|---|---|
| *General Digest*, 10th Series | 2001–present |
| (There is a separate set of the *General Digest* for each year from 2001 to the present, e.g., 2001 set, 2002 set, etc.) | |
| *Eleventh Decennial Digest*, Part I | 1996–2001 |
| *Tenth Decennial Digest*, Part II | 1991–1996 |
| *Tenth Decennial Digest*, Part I | 1986–1991 |
| *Ninth Decennial Digest*, Part II | 1981–1986 |
| *Ninth Decennial Digest*, Part I | 1976–1981 |
| *Eighth Decennial Digest* | 1966–1976 |
| *Seventh Decennial Digest* | 1956–1966 |
| *Sixth Decennial Digest* | 1946–1956 |
| *Fifth Decennial Digest* | 1936–1946 |
| *Fourth Decennial Digest* | 1926–1936 |
| *Third Decennial Digest* | 1916–1926 |
| *Second Decennial Digest* | 1907–1916 |
| *First Decennial Digest* | 1897–1906 |
| *Century Digest* | 1658–1896 |

Figure 4.11 summarizes when you might want to consider using each of these types of digests.

## b. Locating Topics and Key Numbers

Once you have decided which set or sets of the digest to use, the next step is locating topics and key numbers relevant to your research issue. You can do this in three ways:

**(1)** using the headnotes in a case on point
**(2)** using the index to the digest
**(3)** going directly to topics relevant to your research.

### (1) Using the headnotes in a case on point

The easiest way to find relevant topics and key numbers is to use the headnotes in a case that you have already determined is relevant to your

**FIGURE 4.11**   WHEN TO USE DIFFERENT DIGESTS

| FEDERAL DIGESTS | STATE DIGESTS | REGIONAL DIGESTS | COMBINED DIGESTS |
|---|---|---|---|
| To research federal cases | To research state and federal cases from an individual state | To research state cases from an individual state within the region (may require additional research with the federal digest) | To research federal cases or cases from an individual state if you know the approximate time period you wish to research |
| To supplement regional digest research by locating federal cases within an individual state | | To locate persuasive authority from surrounding jurisdictions | To research the law of all jurisdictions within the United States |

research. If you have read other chapters in this book, you already know that the digest is not the only way to locate cases. Many other research sources, including secondary sources (covered in Chapter 3) and statutes (covered in Chapter 6), can lead you to relevant cases. Therefore, when another source has led you to a relevant case that is published in a West reporter, you can use the headnotes to direct you to digest topics and key numbers.

*(2) Using the Descriptive-Word Index*

If you do not already have a case on point, you will need to use the index to find topics and key numbers in the digest. The index in a West digest is called the Descriptive-Word Index (DWI). The DWI actually consists of several volumes that may be located either at the beginning or at the end of the digest set, and it lists subjects in alphabetical order.

To use the DWI, all you need to do is look up the subjects you want to research. The subjects will be followed by abbreviations indicating the topics and key numbers relevant to each subject. A list of abbreviations appears at the beginning of the volume. You may also see cross-references to other index entries with additional information on the subject. An excerpt from a page in the DWI appears in Figure 4.12.

The DWI volumes, like all other hardcover volumes within the digest set, are updated with pocket parts. The next step in using the index is checking the pocket part. Because the hardcover DWI volumes are not reprinted frequently, many of the newer entries may be in the pocket part. Moreover, West sometimes uses information from specific cases to

**FIGURE 4.12** EXCERPT FROM THE DESCRIPTIVE-WORD INDEX

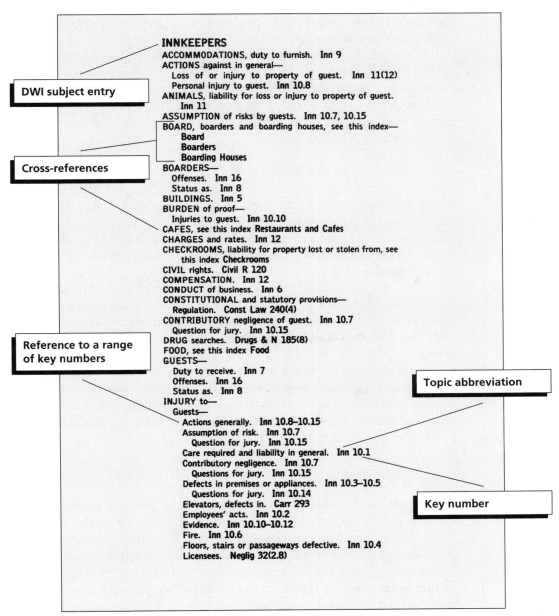

**INNKEEPERS**
ACCOMMODATIONS, duty to furnish. Inn 9
ACTIONS against in general—
    Loss of or injury to property of guest. Inn 11(12)
    Personal injury to guest. Inn 10.8
ANIMALS, liability for loss or injury to property of guest.
    Inn 11
ASSUMPTION of risks by guests. Inn 10.7, 10.15
BOARD, boarders and boarding houses, see this index—
    **Board**
    **Boarders**
    **Boarding Houses**
BOARDERS—
    Offenses. Inn 16
    Status as. Inn 8
BUILDINGS. Inn 5
BURDEN of proof—
    Injuries to guest. Inn 10.10
CAFES, see this index Restaurants and Cafes
CHARGES and rates. Inn 12
CHECKROOMS, liability for property lost or stolen from, see
    this index **Checkrooms**
CIVIL rights. Civil R 120
COMPENSATION. Inn 12
CONDUCT of business. Inn 6
CONSTITUTIONAL and statutory provisions—
    Regulation. Const Law 240(4)
CONTRIBUTORY negligence of guest. Inn 10.7
    Question for jury. Inn 10.15
DRUG searches. Drugs & N 185(8)
FOOD, see this index **Food**
GUESTS—
    Duty to receive. Inn 7
    Offenses. Inn 16
    Status as. Inn 8
INJURY to—
    Guests—
      Actions generally. Inn 10.8–10.15
      Assumption of risk. Inn 10.7
        Question for jury. Inn 10.15
      Care required and liability in general. Inn 10.1
      Contributory negligence. Inn 10.7
        Questions for jury. Inn 10.15
      Defects in premises or appliances. Inn 10.3–10.5
        Questions for jury. Inn 10.14
      Elevators, defects in. Carr 293
      Employees' acts. Inn 10.2
      Evidence. Inn 10.10–10.12
      Fire. Inn 10.6
      Floors, stairs or passageways defective. Inn 10.4
      Licensees. Neglig 32(2.8)

**DWI subject entry**

**Cross-references**

**Reference to a range of key numbers**

**Topic abbreviation**

**Key number**

Reprinted with permission from West Group, West's *Federal Practice Digest*, 4th Ser., Descriptive-Word Index, Vol. 98 (1992), p. 202.

generate index entries. Therefore, it is important to check the pocket part for new material that may be relevant to your research. If you do not find anything listed in the pocket part, no new index entries on that subject are available.

Once you have identified relevant topics and key numbers, the next step is looking them up within the digest volumes. Remember that digest volumes are organized alphabetically. Therefore, you will need to look on the spines of the books until you locate the volume covering your topic. When you look up the topic, you will see that the key numbers follow in numerical order.

### (3) *Going directly to relevant topics*

Because digest topics are arranged alphabetically, you can bypass the DWI and go directly to the topic you are interested in researching. At the beginning of each topic, West provides an overview section that lists the subjects included and excluded, as well as an outline of all the key numbers under the topic. Case summaries, of course, follow the overview in key number order.

This can be a difficult way to start your research unless you are already familiar with an area of law and know which topics are likely to be relevant. For example, cases regarding immigration are listed under the topic "Aliens," which might not be a topic you would have considered using.

Although you might not want to start your research by going directly to a digest topic, once you have identified useful topics through other means, you may want to review the overview section. The list of subjects included and excluded and outline of key numbers can provide additional helpful research leads.

### c. Reading Case Summaries

Once you have reviewed the topic overview, you are ready to begin reading case summaries. There is some inconsistency in the way West organizes its digest summaries, but in general, summaries are organized in descending order from highest to lowest court. If the digest contains summaries of both federal and state cases, federal cases will appear first. If the digest contains summaries of cases from multiple states, the states will be listed alphabetically. Summaries of multiple decisions from the same level of court and the same jurisdiction are listed in reverse chronological order.

One of the most difficult aspects of digest research is deciding which cases to read based on the summaries. The court and date abbreviations at the beginning of each entry will help you decide which cases to review. If you are using a digest with cases from more than one jurisdiction, paying attention to the abbreviations will help you stay focused on the summaries of cases from the appropriate jurisdiction. The abbreviations will also help you figure out which cases are from the highest court in the jurisdiction and which are the most recent decisions. In addition, many case summaries include not only a synopsis of the rule the court applied in the case, but also a concise description of the facts. You can use the factual summaries to narrow down the cases applicable to your issue.

Even a fact-specific summary, however, does not provide the full context of the case. Using the digest is only the first step in researching cases; all the digest can do is point you toward cases that may help answer your research question. Digest summaries, like headnotes, are editorial enhancements designed to assist you with your research. They are not authoritative, and you should never rely on one as a statement of the law. Always read the case in full before relying on it to answer a research question.

### d. Updating Digest Research

The final step in digest research is updating. The updating process involves three steps:

(1) checking the pocket part for the subject volume covering your topic
(2) checking a separate set of interim pamphlets at the end of the digest set
(3) updating beyond the digest set for cases published after the supplements were printed.

It is very important to update your research for new cases. Newer cases may reflect a change in the law, or cases more factually relevant to your problem may have been decided since the hardcover books were published. Obviously, in legal practice you must find these cases for your research to be complete. In law school, professors love to assign research problems for which the best material is in the updating sources. Therefore, you should get in the habit now of updating your research thoroughly.

### (1) Pocket parts

Each subject volume should have either a pocket part or a separate supplement on the shelf next to the hardcover book. This is the first place to look to update your research.

The pocket part is organized the same way as the main volume. The topics are arranged alphabetically, and the key numbers are arranged in numerical order within each topic. There are two pieces of information you will find in the pocket part. First, if any cases under the key number were decided after the main volume was published, you will find summaries of those cases in the pocket part. These case summaries will be organized in the same order as those in the main volume. If no reference to your topic and key number appears in the pocket part, no new decisions have been issued during the time period covered by the pocket part.

Second, you may find that West has created new key numbers or divided the key numbers from the main volume into a series of subsections. If that is the case, you will find a short outline of the new subsections at the beginning of the original key number, along with summaries of any cases categorized under the new subsections.

### (2) Interim pamphlets

The pocket part is not the only supplement you should check. Pocket parts are generally published only once a year. For some digest sets, West also publishes interim pamphlets to update for cases decided since the pocket part was published. These pamphlets are ordinarily softcover booklets, although occasionally you will see hardcover supplements. They are usually shelved at the end of the digest set. The pamphlets contain summaries of new decisions under all of the topics and key numbers within the digest set. Just as with pocket parts, the topics in the interim pamphlets are arranged alphabetically. And as with pocket parts, if no entry appears under your topic and key number, no new cases have been decided during the time period covered by the interim pamphlet.

Some interim pamphlets are cumulative, meaning you only need to look in the one book to update your research. Others, however, are noncumulative. If the pamphlets you are using are noncumulative, each one covers a specific time period, and you must check each one to update your research completely. To determine the dates covered by an interim pamphlet, check the dates on the spine or cover of the book.

### (3) Closing tables

Once you have checked the interim pamphlets accompanying the digest, you have updated your research as far as the digest will take you. The final step in the process is checking for cases decided after the last interim pamphlet was published.

To do this, you will need to refer to the chart on the inside front cover of the latest interim pamphlet. This chart is called a closing table. Figure 4.13 contains an example of a closing table. If the digest set you are using does not have interim pamphlets, you should check the closing table on the inside front cover of the pocket part for the subject volume.

The closing table lists the names of all of the reporters whose decisions are summarized within the digest set. For each of those reporters, the table lists the last volume with decisions summarized in the interim pamphlet. For example, the closing table in Figure 4.13

**FIGURE 4.13**   INTERIM PAMPHLET CLOSING TABLE

**Closing with Cases Reported in**

| | |
|---|---|
| Supreme Court Reporter | 117 S.Ct. 1864 |
| Federal Reporter, Third Series | 114 F.3d 205 |
| Federal Supplement | 962 F.Supp. 1520 |
| Federal Rules Decisions | 172 F.R.D. 549 |
| Bankruptcy Reporter | 209 B.R. 28 |
| Federal Claims Reporter | 37 Fed.Cl. 792 |
| Military Justice Reporter — U.S.Armed Forces | 46 M.J. 128 |
| Military Justice Reporter — A.F.Ct.Crim.App. | 46 M.J. 744 |
| Veterans Appeals Reporter | 10 Vet.App. 247 |

Reprinted with permission from West Group, West's *Federal Practice Digest*, 4th Ser., Pamphlet Part 2 (1997), inside cover.

lists the *Federal Reporter*, Third Series, closing with volume 114, page 205. That means that decisions up to volume 114 of F.3d appearing on or before page 205 are summarized within the interim pamphlet. Any cases reported in volume 114 on page 206 or higher, or any cases appearing in volume 115 and beyond, came out too late to be included in the interim pamphlet.

To find out if any relevant cases are reported after volume 114, page 205, therefore, you will need to check the reporters on the shelves. Within each reporter, you will find a mini-digest in the back of the book. The mini-digest summarizes all of the decisions within that volume. You need to look up your topic and key number in each of the reporter volumes after volume 114, page 205, through the end of the set to make sure no new relevant decisions were issued after the interim pamphlet was published. Again, if nothing is listed under the topic and key number, no new decisions were issued, and your updating is complete.

Students often ask whether this last updating step is truly necessary. The answer largely depends on the progress of your research. If you have not been able to locate a sufficient amount of authority, you might want to use the closing table and mini-digests to expand your research results. This is especially true if the digest set does not have interim pamphlets and a number of months have passed since the pocket part was printed. If you are satisfied that you have located the pertinent cases on your issue and only need to verify that they still state the law accurately, the closing table and mini-digests are not the best tools for you to use. Chapter 5 discusses resources you can use to verify case research. These resources will allow you to check your research more efficiently than the closing table and mini-digests. As Chapter 5 explains, they can also be used to expand your research results, although you may still find the case summaries in the mini-digests helpful.

## C. ADDITIONAL FEATURES OF DIGESTS

In addition to collecting case summaries under subject matter topics, digests have two other features you can use to locate cases: the Table of Cases and the Words and Phrases feature. All West digest sets have a Table of Cases, but not all have the Words and Phrases feature.

### 1. TABLE OF CASES

The Table of Cases lists cases alphabetically by the name of both the plaintiff and the defendant.[4] Thus, if you know either party's name, you can find the case in the Table of Cases. In the Table of Cases, you will find the following items of information:

1. the full name of the case
2. the court that decided the case
3. the complete citation to the case, including the parallel citation (if any) to an official reporter
4. a list of the topics and key numbers appearing in the headnotes to the case.

Figure 4.14 is an excerpt from the Table of Cases.

The Table of Cases usually appears at the end of the digest set. Often, it is contained in a separate volume or set of volumes, but in smaller digest sets, it may be included in a volume containing other material.

The Table of Cases is updated the same way as the subject volumes. The volumes containing the Table of Cases should have pocket parts. Some older digest sets also have hardcover supplements. If the digest set has interim pamphlets, one of those pamphlets will also contain a Table of Cases listing cases decided during the time period covered by the pamphlet.

---

[4]West used to divide the Table of Cases into two tables: the Table of Cases, which listed cases by the plaintiff's name, and the Defendant-Plaintiff Table, which listed cases by the defendant's name. West now consolidates these two tables into one, called the Table of Cases. In some older digest sets, however, you may still find a separate Defendant-Plaintiff Table.

**FIGURE 4.14** EXCERPT FROM THE TABLE OF CASES

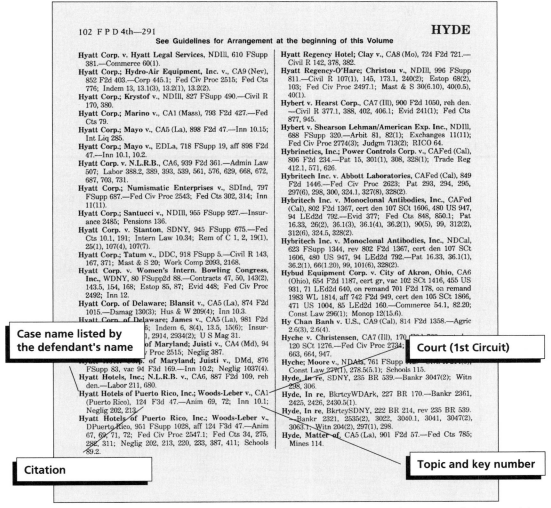

Reprinted with permission from West Group, West's *Federal Practice Digest*, 4th Ser., Cumulative Pamphlet, Vol. 102 (2002), p. 291.

## 2. WORDS AND PHRASES

The Words and Phrases feature provides citations to cases that have defined legal terms or phrases. Because dictionary definitions are not legally binding on courts, Words and Phrases can help you find legally binding definitions from cases that have interpreted or construed a term. Words and Phrases is organized much like a dictionary. To determine whether the courts have defined a term, you simply look up the term alphabetically. If the term is listed, you will find citations to cases construing it.

Words and Phrases is usually located near the Table of Cases within the digest set and is updated the same way as that table.

Figure 4.15 illustrates the Words and Phrases feature.

**FIGURE 4.15** WORDS AND PHRASES

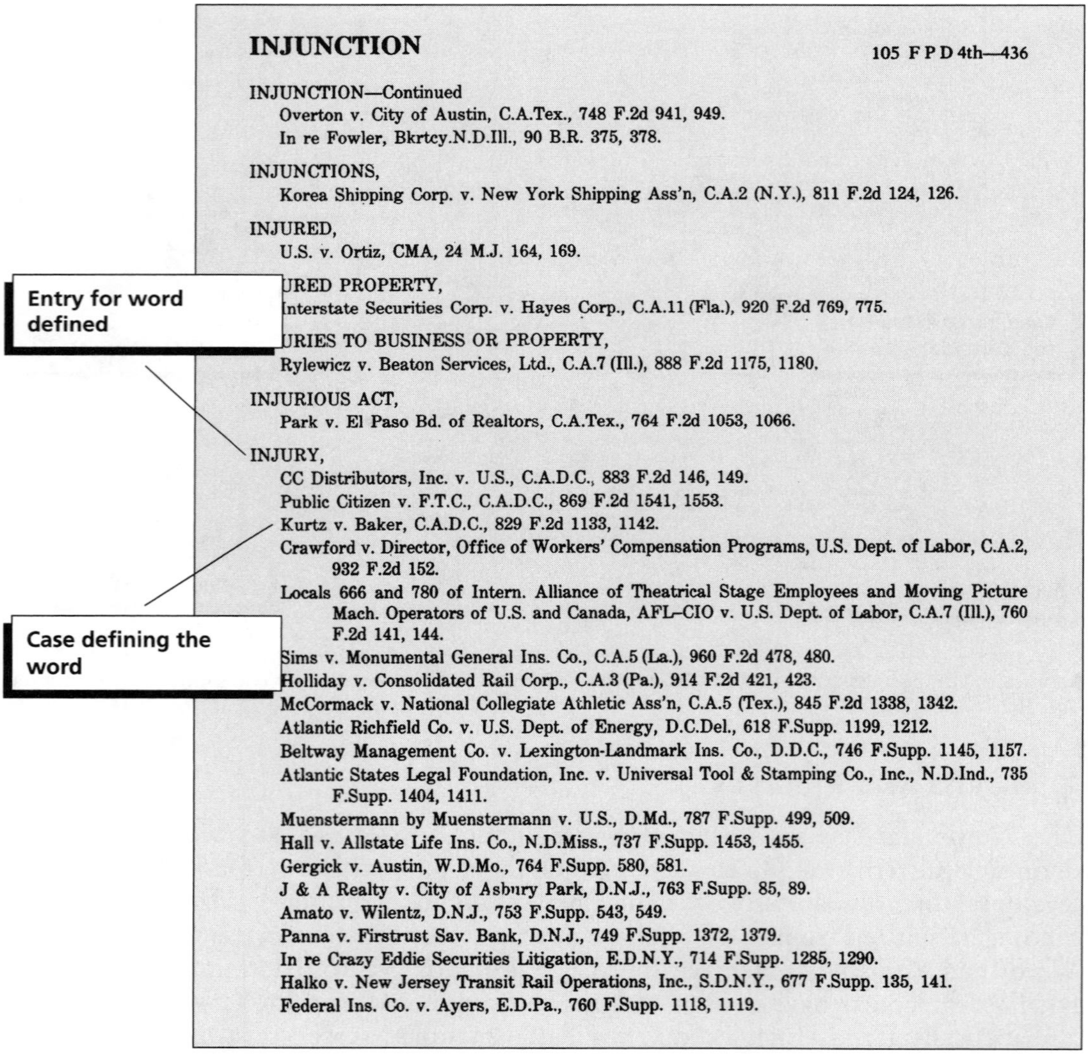

**INJUNCTION** 105 F P D 4th—436

INJUNCTION—Continued
Overton v. City of Austin, C.A.Tex., 748 F.2d 941, 949.
In re Fowler, Bkrtcy.N.D.Ill., 90 B.R. 375, 378.

INJUNCTIONS,
Korea Shipping Corp. v. New York Shipping Ass'n, C.A.2 (N.Y.), 811 F.2d 124, 126.

INJURED,
U.S. v. Ortiz, CMA, 24 M.J. 164, 169.

[Entry for word defined]

URED PROPERTY,
Interstate Securities Corp. v. Hayes Corp., C.A.11 (Fla.), 920 F.2d 769, 775.

URIES TO BUSINESS OR PROPERTY,
Rylewicz v. Beaton Services, Ltd., C.A.7 (Ill.), 888 F.2d 1175, 1180.

INJURIOUS ACT,
Park v. El Paso Bd. of Realtors, C.A.Tex., 764 F.2d 1053, 1066.

INJURY,
CC Distributors, Inc. v. U.S., C.A.D.C., 883 F.2d 146, 149.
Public Citizen v. F.T.C., C.A.D.C., 869 F.2d 1541, 1553.
Kurtz v. Baker, C.A.D.C., 829 F.2d 1133, 1142.
Crawford v. Director, Office of Workers' Compensation Programs, U.S. Dept. of Labor, C.A.2, 932 F.2d 152.

[Case defining the word]

Locals 666 and 780 of Intern. Alliance of Theatrical Stage Employees and Moving Picture Mach. Operators of U.S. and Canada, AFL–CIO v. U.S. Dept. of Labor, C.A.7 (Ill.), 760 F.2d 141, 144.
Sims v. Monumental General Ins. Co., C.A.5 (La.), 960 F.2d 478, 480.
Holliday v. Consolidated Rail Corp., C.A.3 (Pa.), 914 F.2d 421, 423.
McCormack v. National Collegiate Athletic Ass'n, C.A.5 (Tex.), 845 F.2d 1338, 1342.
Atlantic Richfield Co. v. U.S. Dept. of Energy, D.C.Del., 618 F.Supp. 1199, 1212.
Beltway Management Co. v. Lexington-Landmark Ins. Co., D.D.C., 746 F.Supp. 1145, 1157.
Atlantic States Legal Foundation, Inc. v. Universal Tool & Stamping Co., Inc., N.D.Ind., 735 F.Supp. 1404, 1411.
Muenstermann by Muenstermann v. U.S., D.Md., 787 F.Supp. 499, 509.
Hall v. Allstate Life Ins. Co., N.D.Miss., 737 F.Supp. 1453, 1455.
Gergick v. Austin, W.D.Mo., 764 F.Supp. 580, 581.
J & A Realty v. City of Asbury Park, D.N.J., 763 F.Supp. 85, 89.
Amato v. Wilentz, D.N.J., 753 F.Supp. 543, 549.
Panna v. Firstrust Sav. Bank, D.N.J., 749 F.Supp. 1372, 1379.
In re Crazy Eddie Securities Litigation, E.D.N.Y., 714 F.Supp. 1285, 1290.
Halko v. New Jersey Transit Rail Operations, Inc., S.D.N.Y., 677 F.Supp. 135, 141.
Federal Ins. Co. v. Ayers, E.D.Pa., 760 F.Supp. 1118, 1119.

Reprinted with permission from West Group, West's *Federal Practice Digest*, 4th Ser., Vol. 105 (1992), p. 436.

## D. ELECTRONIC CASE RESEARCH

### 1. WESTLAW AND LEXISNEXIS FORMATS

The format of a case varies slightly in Westlaw and LexisNexis. In both systems, you will see a caption with the name of the case and other identifying information. The caption will be followed by an editorial summary of the decision.

In Westlaw, the summary will be followed by one or more numbered headnotes and then the full text of the opinion. Just as in the print version of a case, the editorial summary and headnotes, if any, are not part of the decision and are not authoritative.

No key number headnotes appear in the LexisNexis version of a case because the key number system is an editorial feature unique to West. LexisNexis has a similar editorial feature, however, called Core Concepts. At the beginning of a case, you will find one or more summary paragraphs organized by subject and quoting passages from the case. Even though the Core Concepts summaries usually quote the opinion verbatim, they are not part of the decision and are not authoritative. The Core Concepts feature is relatively new, so although you will find the summary paragraphs at the beginning of many cases, you will not see them with all cases as of this writing. LexisNexis has been adding Core Concepts summaries to all cases decided since 1999 and is gradually adding them to the older cases in its database.

Figures 4.16 and 4.17 show what a case looks like in Westlaw and LexisNexis.

### 2. WORD SEARCHING IN WESTLAW AND LEXISNEXIS

In both Westlaw and LexisNexis, you can locate cases by executing word searches. Word searching differs from digest searching. Because the digest organizes case summaries by subject, you are conducting a subject search when you use a digest. Electronic word searches, by contrast, retrieve cases containing the precise terms and characteristics you specify. In a sense, this allows you to create your own "digest."

To locate cases using word searches, you must select a database in which to search. Selecting a database is similar to selecting a print digest. You should use the narrowest one that still has enough information to answer your research question. In general, both Westlaw and LexisNexis have databases with cases from federal courts or individual states, as well as combined databases with both federal and state decisions. In addition, both systems have subject-matter databases containing federal and state cases in specific subject areas such as products liability or family law.

**FIGURE 4.16**   EXAMPLE OF A CASE IN WESTLAW

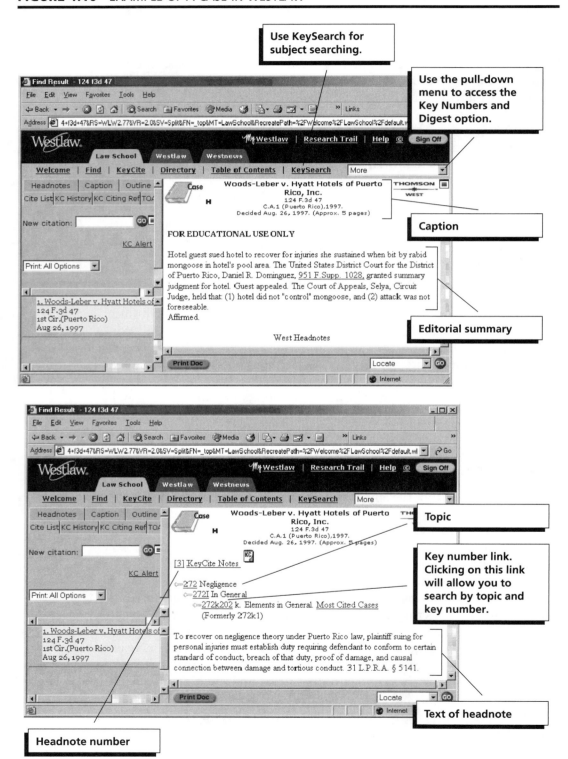

**FIGURE 4.16** EXAMPLE OF A CASE IN WESTLAW *(Continued)*

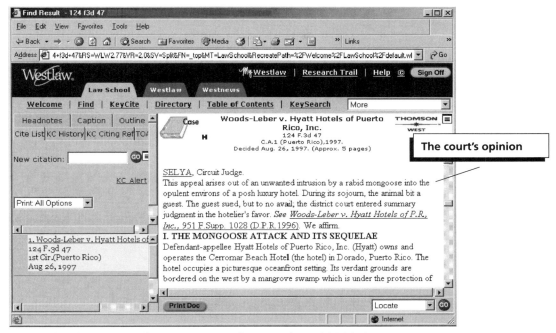

Reprinted with permission from West Group, from Westlaw, 124 F.3d 47.

Once you have selected a database, you are ready to construct and execute a word search. Chapter 10 contains more information on the process of word searching in Westlaw and LexisNexis.

### 3. ELECTRONIC SUBJECT SEARCHING IN WESTLAW AND LEXISNEXIS

Although the digests themselves are not accessible electronically in exactly the same way they are in print, you can still search for cases by subject in Westlaw and LexisNexis.

Westlaw has two functions that allow you to search by subject using the digest topics and key numbers. One is the Custom Digest function. You can access Custom Digest by choosing the Key Numbers and Digest option from the pull-down menu in the upper right corner. This will display a list of the digest topics. You can view individual key numbers by expanding the list under each topic, and you can select the topic(s) and key number(s) you want to search. If you locate a relevant case, you can also access the Custom Digest function by clicking on the key number link. Using either approach brings up a search screen that allows you to customize your search. For example, you can select the jurisdiction in which to execute the search and add your own terms to further refine the search.

**FIGURE 4.17**   EXAMPLE OF A CASE IN LEXISNEXIS

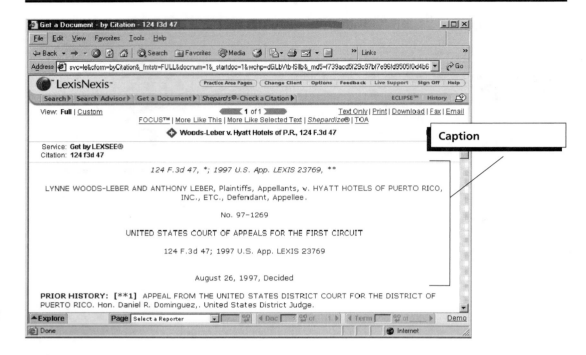

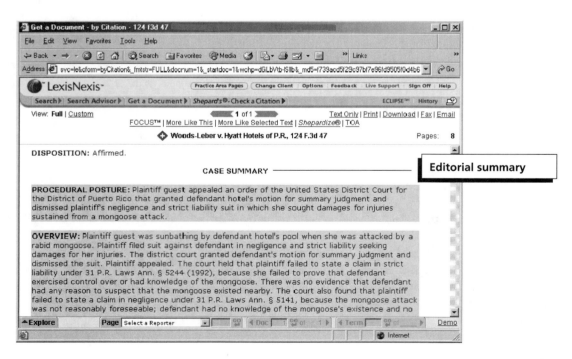

**FIGURE 4.17** EXAMPLE OF A CASE IN LEXISNEXIS *(Continued)*

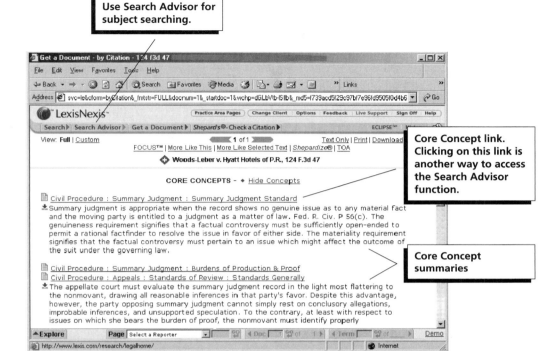

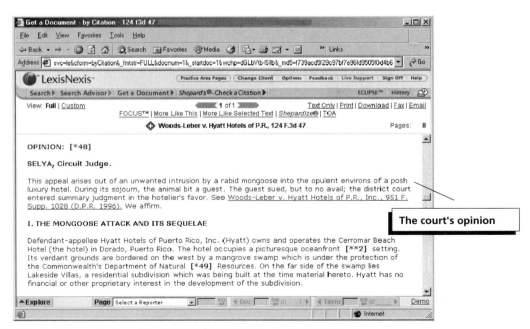

Reprinted with permission of LexisNexis, from LexisNexis, 124 F.3d 47.

Another way to search using the West digest topics and key numbers is with the KeySearch function. You can access this function by clicking on the KeySearch link near the top of the screen. This brings up an alphabetical list of search topics. Each topic contains multiple subtopics, and most subtopics are further subdivided into even narrower categories. You can find a subject to search by selecting a subject and browsing the subdivisions, or you can search for a subject using the search box on the left side of the screen.

The relationship between the KeySearch function and the West digest topics is not immediately apparent. Although KeySearch lists subjects alphabetically, the subject categories are not identical to the topics in a West digest. In a KeySearch search, the query consists of a combination of various topics and key numbers, plus additional search terms that West selects. Thus, although it is largely driven by the topic and key number system, it usually will not retrieve exactly the same results that a Custom Digest search will. From the KeySearch search screen, you can further customize the search by selecting the jurisdiction and sources you wish to search, as well as by adding your own search terms.

The topic and key number system is unique to West. Therefore, you can search by topic and key number only in Westlaw. LexisNexis, however, has its own subject searching capabilities through the Search Advisor function and Core Concepts. Clicking on the Search Advisor link near the top of the screen brings up an alphabetical list of search topics. Each topic contains multiple subtopics, and most subtopics are further subdivided into even narrower categories. You can find a subject to search in three ways: You can select a subject you have searched before by browsing the last twenty topics you have selected. You can search for a subject using the search box. Or you can explore a general subject by clicking on it and browsing the subtopics.

After you select a search topic, LexisNexis displays a search screen. At the top of the search screen, you will see a list of secondary sources that you can search. Clicking on one of the secondary sources will automatically generate a list of citations to information within the source you selected. Below the list of secondary sources, you will see a search screen that allows you to customize your search. For example, you can select the jurisdiction in which to execute the search and add search terms to further refine the search.

Search Advisor is linked to the Core Concepts summaries. Therefore, you can click on the link to a Core Concept at the beginning of a case to locate additional cases under the same Core Concept. This brings up a search screen from which you can customize your search.

Search Advisor is a relatively new feature, and as noted above, not all cases in the LexisNexis database contain Core Concepts summaries. Therefore, although the Search Advisor and Core Concepts searching options will search many cases in the LexisNexis database, they will not search all of them as of this writing.

### 4. RESEARCHING CASES ON THE INTERNET

Judicial opinions are increasingly available on the Internet. To locate cases on the Internet, you can try two approaches. The first is to review the web site for the court whose decisions you are trying to locate. Many courts and government organizations maintain web sites with the full text of court opinions. The second is to go to general legal research sites. Many of these sites either include links to sites with court opinions or index their own databases of cases. Appendix A lists the Internet addresses for a number of legal research web sites that may be useful for case research.

Once you have located a source containing cases, several searching options may be available. You may be able to search by date, docket number, case name, or key word, depending on how the web site is organized.

Because comprehensive digesting tools are not yet available on the Internet, it is not likely to be an effective resource unless you know the jurisdiction you want to research. In addition, a number of databases only contain decisions going back a few years, so comprehensive research over time may not be possible. Once you have located a case, you will usually only see the text of the court's opinion. Internet sources generally lack the editorial enhancements available with commercial research services, which may hinder your research efforts.

Despite these difficulties, the Internet can be effective for locating the most recent opinions, opinions from courts that maintain up-to-date web sites, and opinions from lower courts whose decisions are not published in any print reporters. For example, United States Supreme Court decisions are available on the Internet within hours after they are issued. Opinions of municipal courts or local agencies may only be available on the Internet. In addition, the Internet is a more cost-effective way to access cases otherwise available in LexisNexis, Westlaw, or other commercial services. Thus, although cases are not yet sufficiently accessible to make Internet research viable as your sole or beginning avenue for research, it may be a cost-effective way to supplement other research methods.

## E. CITING CASES

As Chapter 1 explains, any time you report the results of your research in written form, you must cite your sources properly. This is especially important for cases because the information in the citation can help the reader assess the weight of the authority you are citing.

A case citation has three basic components:

1. the case name
2. information on the reporter in which the case is published
3. a parenthetical containing the jurisdiction, the level of court that decided the case, and the year of decision.

You can find rules for each component in the *ALWD Manual* and the *Bluebook*. Using the *ALWD Manual*, you should read Rule 12 and use Appendices 1 and 3 for any necessary abbreviations. Using the *Bluebook*, you should begin with Rule 10. Then you should refer to the Practitioners' Notes to convert the requirements of Rule 10 into the proper format for briefs or memoranda. You will then need to use Tables T.1, T.6, and T.11 to find any necessary abbreviations. Figure 4.18 directs you to the citation rules for cases.

The remainder of this section uses an example citation to illustrate each of these components. The example citation is to a fictional 1983 decision of the Delaware Court of Chancery in the case of Patricia Ellis and Sam Anson versus Acme Manufacturing Company, published in volume 327 of the *Atlantic Reporter*, Second Series, beginning on page 457.

## 1. THE CASE NAME

The name of the case appears first and must be <u>underlined</u> or *italicized*. The case name consists of the name of the first party on either side of the "v." In other words, if more than one plaintiff or defendant is listed in the full case name, give only the name of the first named plaintiff or first named defendant. In the example citation, Sam Anson would not be listed. Do not include "et al." when a case has multiple parties; simply refer to the first named party on both sides. If a person is named as a party, use only the person's last name, but if a company or other entity is listed, use the entity's full name.

Often, the case name will be abbreviated. The abbreviation rules vary slightly in the *ALWD Manual* and the *Bluebook*. You will need to read the rules and refer to the appropriate appendix or table to determine when words should be abbreviated and what the proper abbreviations are. The case name should be followed by a comma, which is not underlined or italicized.

**FIGURE 4.18** *ALWD MANUAL* AND *BLUEBOOK* RULES GOVERNING CASE CITATIONS

| CITATION COMPONENT | *ALWD MANUAL*, RULE 12 | *BLUEBOOK*, RULE 10 |
|---|---|---|
| **Case name** | Rule 12.2 & Appendix 3 | Rule 10.2, Practitioners' Note P.1(a), & Tables T.6 & T.11 |
| **Reporter information** | Rules 12.3–12.5 & Appendix 1 | Rule 10.3 & Table T.1 |
| **Parenthetical** | Rules 12.6–12.7 & Appendix 1 | Rules 10.4–10.5 & Table T.1 |

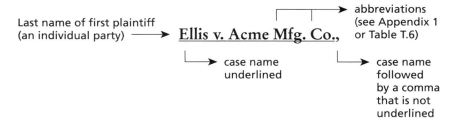

## 2. THE REPORTER

After the case name, the citation should list information on the reporter in which the case is published. If the case is published in more than one reporter, you will need to determine which reporter or reporters to cite, as explained in *ALWD Manual* Rule 12.4 and *Bluebook* Rule 10.3. In the citation, the name of the reporter will be abbreviated, so you must also determine the proper abbreviation. In the *ALWD Manual*, you can find this information in Appendix 1, which lists each jurisdiction in the United States alphabetically. For each jurisdiction, Appendix 1 lists reporter names and abbreviations. In the *Bluebook*, this same information appears in Table T.1.

Ordinarily, you will list the volume of the reporter, the reporter abbreviation, and the starting page of the case. If you are citing a specific page within the case, you will also usually cite to that page as well, using what is called a pinpoint citation. A comma should appear between the starting page and the pinpoint citation, but the pinpoint citation should not be followed by a comma.

reporter abbreviation (see Appendix 1 or Table T.1)

volume number ⟶ 327 A.2d 475, 460

starting page of the case ⟵ | | ⟶ pinpoint citation
followed by a comma

## 3. THE PARENTHETICAL

Following the information on the reporter, the case citation should include a parenthetical containing the abbreviated name of the jurisdiction, the abbreviated name of the level of court that decided the case, and the year the court issued its decision. This information is important because it can help the reader assess the weight of the authority you are citing.

The place to find the proper abbreviation for the jurisdiction and level of court is Appendix 1 in the *ALWD Manual* or Table T.1 in the

*Bluebook.* Appendix 1 and Table T.1 list the levels of courts under each jurisdiction. Next to the name of each court, an abbreviation will appear in parentheses. This is the abbreviation for both the jurisdiction and the level of court, and this is what should appear in your parenthetical. You will notice that for the highest court in each state, the jurisdiction abbreviation is all that is necessary. This alerts the reader that the decision came from the highest court in the state; no additional court name abbreviation is necessary.

The last item to appear in the parenthetical is the year of the decision. The date when the court heard the case is not necessary in the citation; only the year of decision is required. No comma should appear before the year. After the year, the parenthetical should be closed.

year of decision

**(Del. Ch. 1983).**

abbreviation for the
jurisdiction and level of court
(see Appendix 1 or Table T.1)

When all of the pieces are put together, the citation should look like this:

**<u>Ellis v. Acme Mfg. Co.</u>, 327 A.2d 457, 460 (Del. Ch. 1983).**

## F. SAMPLE PAGES FOR RESEARCHING CASES USING A PRINT DIGEST

On the following pages, you will find sample pages illustrating the process of print digest research. If you have read Chapter 2 on generating search terms, you may recall that the hypothetical fact pattern used in that chapter involved a hotel guest injured in Puerto Rico by a parrot living on the hotel grounds. If you were researching this issue, you might want to see if any federal cases were relevant. Figures 4.19 through 4.26 show what you would see in West's *Federal Practice Digest*, Fourth Series. Figures 4.27 and 4.28 are sample pages from West's *Federal Reporter*, Third Series.

**The first step is using the Descriptive-Word Index to lead you to relevant topics and key numbers. One search term you might have used is "Hotels." This entry directs you to another term: "Innkeepers." Because digests are organized by subject, other terms in the DWI could have referred you to "Innkeepers" as well.**

**FIGURE 4.19** DESCRIPTIVE-WORD INDEX

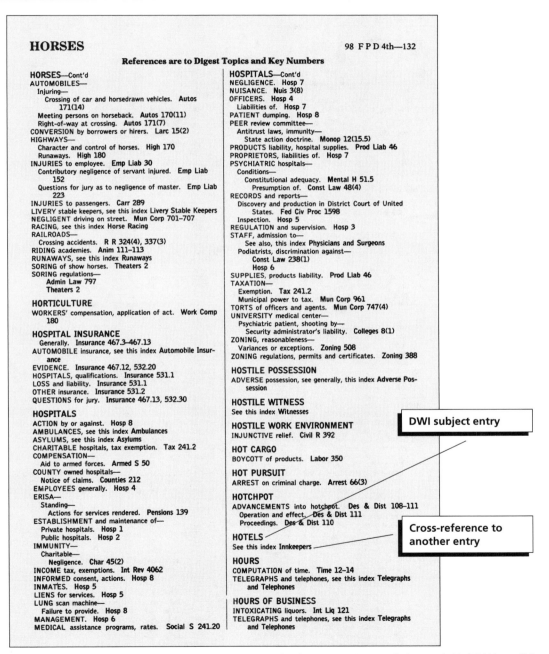

Reprinted with permission from West Group, West's *Federal Practice Digest*, 4th Ser., Vol. 98 (1992), p. 132.

Under "Innkeepers," the entry for "injury to guests" refers to relevant topics and key numbers. The abbreviation "Inn" refers to the "Innkeepers" topic, and the numbers refer to key numbers under that topic. "Care required and liability in general" refers you to key number 10.1.

**FIGURE 4.20** DESCRIPTIVE-WORD INDEX

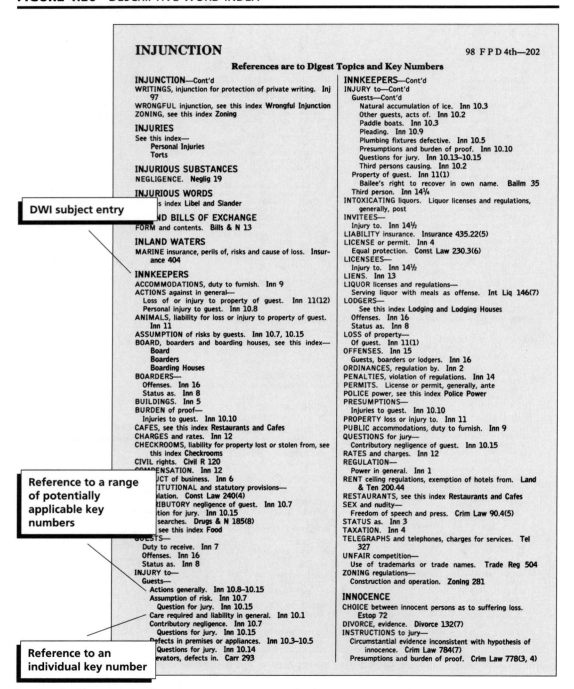

Reprinted with permission from West Group, West's *Federal Practice Digest*, 4th Ser., Vol. 98 (1992), p. 202.

**The index, as a hardcover volume, is updated with a pocket part. The pocket part entry under "Innkeepers" does not provide any additional topic and key number references relevant to this issue.**

**FIGURE 4.21** DESCRIPTIVE-WORD INDEX, POCKET PART

---

# INDICTMENT

98 F P D 4th—8

### References are to Digest Topics and Key Numbers

**INDICTMENT AND INFORMATION**
AMENDMENT—
  Double jeopardy, effect on.  Double J 85
COPY—
  Service, see Service, post
HABEAS CORPUS to review defects.  Hab Corp 474
  Existence or exhaustion of remedy by appeal or other direct review.  Hab Corp 292
  Federal court review of petitions by state prisoners.  Hab Corp 336
  Weight and sufficiency of evidence.  Hab Corp 717(1)
RACKETEERING—
  Federal cases.  RICO 91
  State cases.  RICO 120
SERVICE.  Crim Law 627

**INDIVIDUAL DEBT ADJUSTMENT**
BANKRUPTCY cases, see this index Individual Repayment Plans

**INEFFECTIVE ASSISTANCE OF COUNSEL**
PREJUDICE.  Crim Law 641.13(1)

**INFANTS**
ABDUCTION—
  Hague Convention.  Parent & C 18
ABUSE—
  Expert testimony.  Crim Law 474.4(4)
CONSORTIUM—
  Children's consortium, loss of.  Parent & C 7(1–14)
  Parents' consortium, loss of.  Parent & C 7.5
CORPORAL punishment.  Parent & C 2(1)
CREDIBILITY as witness—
  Expert testimony.  Crim Law 474.3(3)
CUSTODY and control—
  Habeas corpus—
    Determination and disposition.  Hab Corp 798
    Existence and exhaustion of other remedies.  Hab Corp 280
    Grounds for relief.  Hab Corp 531–536
    Hearing.  Hab Corp 744
    Jurisdiction.  Hab Corp 614(1, 2), 624
    Mootness and prematurity of application.  Hab Corp 232
    Petition, sufficiency.  Hab Corp 670(10)
    Venue and personal jurisdiction.  Hab Corp 636
    Weight and sufficiency of evidence.  Hab Corp 731
  Interference.  Parent & C 18
  Relinquishment of custody.  Infants 19.4
  Tender years doctrine—
    Infants 19.2(4)
    Parent & C 2(3.2)
  Threats—
    Removal of children.  Const Law 274(5)
FAMILY purpose doctrine, see generally, this index Family Purpose Doctrine
NEGLECT—
  Failure to support, see generally, Parent and child, post
OBVIOUS danger—
  Appreciation of.  Neglig 85(4)
PARENT and child—
  Negligent entrustment.  Parent & C 13(1)
  Negligent supervision.  Parent & C 13(1)
PRECONCEPTION negligence—
  Rights of action.  Infants 72(2)
TENDER years doctrine, see Custody and control, ante

**INFRINGEMENT**
COPYRIGHTS—
  Encouragement of infringer.  Copyr 75

**INHERITANCE AND TRANSFER TAXES**
REFUNDING—
  Equitable tolling.  Int Rev 4960

**INJUNCTION**
ARBITRATION.  Arbit 10.10
BASELESS lawsuits—
  Unfair labor practices.  Labor 612
BUILDING and loan associations—
  Resolution Trust Corporation.  B & L Assoc 42(16)
CABLE television systems.  Tel 449.10(2)
CIVIL rights—
  See this index Civil Rights
CIVIL rights actions, see this index Civil Rights
COMMODITY futures trading regulation.  Com Fut 91–95
CRIMINAL law—
  Criminal acts generally.  Inj 102–104
    Preliminary injunctions—
      Grounds and objections.  Inj 138.78
      Proceedings.  Inj 139–159.5
  Prosecutions, restraining.  Inj 105
    Preliminary injunctions—
      Grounds and objections.  Inj 138.78
      Proceedings.  Inj 139–159.5
ELEVENTH Amendment immunity—
  What are suits against states.  Fed Cts 272
ENFORCEMENT of statutes.  Bankr 2371(1)
HANDICAPPED children—
  Proceedings to enforce right to instruction.  Schools 155.5(5)
LIMITATION of actions—
  Period applicable—
    Generally.  Inj 113
PERSONAL rights and duties—
  Evidence—
    Sufficiency.  Inj 128(9)
  Preliminary injunctions—
    Grounds and objections.  Inj 138.75
    Proceedings.  Inj 139–159.5
PUBLIC—
  Rights, protection of.  Inj 89–93
    Preliminary injunctions—
      Grounds and objections.  Inj 138.72
      Proceedings.  Inj 139–159.5
UNITED States magistrates, jurisdiction and proc
  S Mag 16

**INJURIOUS FALSEHOOD**
ELEMENTS.  Libel 1

**INNKEEPERS**
CIVIL rights.  Civil R 120
DRUG searches.  Drugs & N 185(8)
INVASION of privacy.  Inn 10.1
SEX and nudity—
  Freedom of speech and press.  Const Law 90.4(5)

**INSIDERS**
BANKRUPTCY, see this index Bankruptcy
PREFERENCES.  Bankr 2608(2)
REORGANIZATION in bankruptcy, see this index Reincorporation and Reorganization

> No new relevant entries are listed.

---

Reprinted with permission from West Group, West's *Federal Practice Digest*, 4th Ser., Cumulative Annual Pocket Part, Vol. 98 (1997), p. 8.

**The next step is looking up the topic "Innkeepers" in the subject volumes. The outline at the beginning of the topic identifies other key numbers that may be relevant.**

**FIGURE 4.22**    KEY NUMBER OUTLINE, "INNKEEPERS" TOPIC

# INNKEEPERS

## SUBJECTS INCLUDED

Regulation of inns, hotels, boarding houses, lodging houses, and all houses furnishing for compensation accommodation as a temporary home

Mutual rights, duties, and liabilities of keepers of such houses and their guests, boarders or lodgers

## SUBJECTS EXCLUDED AND COVERED BY OTHER TOPICS

Discrimination by reason of race, color, etc., see CIVIL RIGHTS

Intoxicants, regulation of sale, see INTOXICATING LIQUORS

Trailer camps and the like, see AUTOMOBILES, LICENSES

**For detailed references to other topics, see Descriptive-Word Index**

---

*Analysis*

&#9756;1. Power to regulate.
2. Statutory and municipal regulations.
3. Who are innkeepers.
4. Licenses and taxes.
5. Buildings.
6. Conduct of business.
7. Duty to receive guests.
8. Who are guests, boarders, or lodgers.
9. Duty to furnish accommodations.
10. Injury to person of guest.
10.1. —— Care required and liability in general.
10.2. —— Acts of employees, other guests, or third persons.
10.3. —— Defects in premises or appliances in general.
10.4. —— Defective floors, stairs, or passageways.
10.5. —— Defective plumbing fixtures.
10.6. —— Fire.
10.7. —— Contributory negligence and assumption of risk.
10.8. —— Actions in general.
10.9. —— Pleading.
10.10. —— Presumptions and burden of proof.
10.11. —— Admissibility of evidence.
10.12. —— Weight and sufficiency of evidence.
10.13. —— Questions for jury in general.
10.14. —— Defects in premises or appliances, questions for jury.
10.15. —— Contributory negligence and assumption of risk, questions for jury.
11. Loss of or injury to property of guest.
    (1). Nature and extent of liability in general.
    (2). Relation of parties.

> Range of relevant key numbers

**FIGURE 4.22** KEY NUMBER OUTLINE, "INNKEEPERS" TOPIC *(Continued)*

**INNKEEPERS**
63 F P D 4th—2

&#8477;11. Loss of or injury to property of guest.—Continued.
(3). Care required of innkeeper.
(4). Loss of or injury to property by servants.
(5). Loss of or injuries to animals.
(6). Property for which innkeeper is liable.
(7). Rules and regulations.
(8). Property transported to and from depot.
(9). Place of leaving property.
(10). Contributory negligence.
(11). Statutes limiting liability.
(12). Actions.
12. Compensation.
13. Lien.
14. Penalties for violations of regulations.
14¼. Injuries to third persons.
14½. Liabilities of guests for injuries.
15. Offenses by innkeepers.
16. Offenses by guests, boarders, or lodgers.

**For detailed references to other topics, see Descriptive-Word Index**

Reprinted with permission from West Group, West's *Federal Practice Digest*, 4th Ser., Vol. 63 (1991), pp. 1–2.

**The case summaries under key number 10.1 include one potentially relevant case from Puerto Rico.**

**FIGURE 4.23**   CASE SUMMARIES UNDER "INNKEEPERS" TOPIC

⟲9   **INNKEEPERS**                                                          63 F P D 4th—4

**For later cases see same Topic and Key Number in Pocket Part**

| Key number 10.1 |

...but agency was awarded damages... to goodwill.
Rainbow Travel Service, Inc. v. Hilton Hotels Corp., 896 F.2d 1233.

⟲**10. Injury to person of guest.**

**Library references**
C.J.S. Inns, Hotels, and Eating Places § 20.

⟲**10.1.** —— **Care required and liability in general.**

**C.A.11 (Fla.) 1987.** Hotel guest was business invitee to whom hotel operator owed duty to guard against dangers of which it should have been aware, which duty extended to reasonably foreseeable criminal acts against guest, under Florida law.
Meyers v. Ramada Hotel Operating Co., Inc., 833 F.2d 1521.

**C.A.7 (Ill.) 1989.** Any loss of business sustained by innkeeper from telling truth as to dangers to which guests might be exposed is not social loss, but social gain.
Wassell v. Adams, 865 F.2d 849.

**C.A.5 (La.) 1987.** Innkeeper's position vis-a-vis his guests under Louisiana law is similar to that of common carrier toward its passengers.
Murray v. Ramada Inn, Inc., 821 F.2d 272, certification of question granted 514 So.2d 21, certified question answered 521 So.2d 1123, certified question adhered to 843 F.2d 831.

Under Louisiana law, innkeeper is obligated to take reasonable steps to minimize dangers to his guests from risks within his control.
Murray v. Ramada Inn, Inc., 821 F.2d 272, certification of question granted 514 So.2d 21, certified question answered 521 So.2d 1123, certified question adhered to 843 F.2d 831.

**E.D.La. 1989.** Hotel did not breach any duty to patron under Louisiana law and was not liable for injuries sustained by patron, who had significant amounts of alcohol and cocaine in his system and who chose to use hotel stairs rather than elevator suggested by security guard and who fell downstairs; actions of hotel security officer in assisting patron down stairs were only passive, and hotel did not take any affirmative action to increase patron's peril.
Mayo v. Hyatt Corp., 718 F.Supp. 19, affirmed 898 F.2d 47.

**D.N.J. 1989.** Owner or operator of an inn is under a duty to exercise ordinary care to render its premises reasonably safe for the use of its guests.
Nebel v. Avichal Enterprises, Inc., 704 F.Supp. 570.

Degree of care which an... exercise for the safety, conve... fort of its guests may vary with... quality of the accommodation...
Nebel v. Avichal Enterp... F.Supp. 570.

| Summary of a potentially relevant case |

**D.Puerto Rico 1989.** Hotel had only duty under Puerto Rico law to exercise reasonable care for protection of its guests and was not negligent in failing to warn against possibility of power outages and failing to equip bathrooms with emergency lighting in case of blackout and, thus, could not be held liable for injuries sustained by guest who was taking shower at time of power outage and fell when bathroom went dark.
Ottimo v. Posadas de Puerto Rico Associates, Inc., 721 F.Supp. 1499.

⟲**10.2.** —— **Acts of employees, other guests, or third persons.**

**C.A.11 (Fla.) 1987.** Hotel guest was business invitee to whom hotel operator owed duty to guard against dangers of which it should have been aware, which duty extended to reasonably foreseeable criminal acts against guest, under Florida law.
Meyers v. Ramada Hotel Operating Co., Inc., 833 F.2d 1521.

**C.A.7 (Ill.) 1989.** As general rule, Illinois does not impose duty to protect others from criminal attacks by third parties; however, exception is recognized where criminal attack was reasonably foreseeable and parties had special relationship such as carrier-passenger, innkeeper-guest, business invitor-invitee, or voluntary custodian-protectee.
Figueroa v. Evangelical Covenant Church, 879 F.2d 1427, rehearing denied.

**C.A.7 (Ill.) 1989.** Negligence of motel owners in connection with intruder's early-morning assault of guest in her room was at most "simple" under Illinois law, rather than "willful and wanton," in context of guest's claim that her own negligence was irrelevant; although motel was located near high-crime area and owners failed to specifically warn guest of neighborhood's dangers or of previous crimes involving guests, no rational jury could find that owners consciously disregarded high probability of serious physical harm.
Wassell v. Adams, 865 F.2d 849.

As innkeepers, motel owners had duty to exercise high degree of care under Illinois law to protect guests from assaults on motel premises.
Wassell v. Adams, 865 F.2d 849.

Under Illinois law, motel owners were not required to tell guest not to open her door in middle of night under any circumstances without carefully ascertaining who was trying to

**For cited U.S.C.A. sections and legislative history, see United States Code Annotated**

**The next step is checking the pocket part for this volume. The entry under key number 10.1 in the pocket part includes two potentially relevant cases from Puerto Rico.**

**FIGURE 4.24** DIGEST VOLUME, POCKET PART

63 F P D 4th—1

**INNKEEPERS** ☞10.1

## INNKEEPERS

**Library references**
C.J.S. Inns, Hotels, and Eating Places § 2 et seq.

☞**2. Statutory and municipal regulations.**
**C.A.9 (Cal.) 1996.** Motel owners' equal protection rights were not violated by city's inspection program, which resulted in closure of owners' motel as nuisance; owners conceded that program was devised for inspection of all motels, including their own, and similarly situated property owners, i.e., those who owned motels within city's boundaries, were inspected. U.S.C.A. Const.Amend. 14; San Bernardino, Cal., Municipal Code Chapter 15.28.—Patel v. Penman, 103 F.3d 868, certiorari denied 117 S.Ct. 1845, 137 L.Ed.2d 1048.

☞**4. Licenses and taxes.**
**C.A.9 (Cal.) 1996.** Federal credit union employees who were attending credit union seminar in city were constituent parts of credit union and, thus, were exempt from city's transient occupancy tax under Federal Credit Union Act section exempting credit unions from taxation. Federal Credit Union Act, § 122, 12 U.S.C.A. § 1768; Anaheim, California, Municipal Code Chapter 2.12.—California Credit Union League v. City of Anaheim, 95 F.3d 30, certiorari granted, vacated 117 S.Ct. 2429, 138 L.Ed.2d 191.
**Bkrtcy.N.D.Ill. 1993.** Illinois Hotel Operators' Occupation Tax Act did not create trust in favor of state with respect to taxes collected by Chapter 11 trustee in operation of debtor's hotel and restaurant, absent any language in statute purporting to impose such trust. S.H.A. 35 ILCS 145/1, 1–10, 3, 3(e).—In re Markos Gurnee Partnership, 163 B.R. 124.
Illinois Hotel Operators' Occupation Tax Act was imposed directly on hotel operators, not on their customers, and tax was plainly obligation of operator, and thus, Act did not create trust in favor of state in taxes collected by Chapter 11 trustee in operation of debtor's hotel and restaurant. S.H.A. 35 ILCS 145/1, 3(a, b, e).—Id.

☞**5. Buildings.**
**C.A.9 (Cal.) 1996.** Fifth Amendment takings clause preempted motel owners' substantive due process claim against city, based on owners' allegations that city closed motel for code violations and refused to issue building permits necessary for owners to bring motel into compliance, all in order to drive motel out of business; if allegations were true, such actions would be "taking" of owners' property, and takings clause provided explicit textual source of constitutional protection against type of conduct challenged by owners. U.S.C.A. Const. Amends. 5, 14; San Bernardino, Cal., Municipal Code Chapter 15.28.—Patel v. Penman, 103 F.3d 868, certiorari denied 117 S.Ct. 1845, 137 L.Ed.2d 1048.
Plaintiff motel owners failed to show that defendant city's closure of downtown motels for code violations was based on irrational distinction in violation of equal protection; there was no evidence that nondowntown motels with code violations similar to theirs were not closed. U.S.C.A. Const. Amend. 14; San Bernardino, Cal., Municipal Code Chapter 15.28.—Id.
Owners of motel that city closed as nuisance due to various code violations failed to show that city violated their equal protection rights by refusing to issue permits that they needed to remedy code violations; evidence did not indicate that city used its code enforcement process as pretext to drive downtown motels out of business, and there was no evidence that other motel owners whose buildings were summarily abated applied for and were granted permits to carry out repairs, and no evidence of

owners of other residential properties that had been summarily abated applying for and receiving such permits. U.S.C.A. Const.Amend. 14; San Bernardino, Cal., Municipal Code Chapter 15.28.—Id.

☞**6. Conduct of business.**
**D.D.C. 1995.** Under District of Columbia law, former gubernatorial candidate failed to prove existence of implied contract with hotel under which hotel was obligated not to disclose receipt indicating that candidate had stayed there; candidate never made nondisclosure of receipts condition of his stay at hotel, fact that hotel had previously informed candidate that it was hotel's policy to require written request from guests prior to furnishing such records did not manifest intent by either party to be bound or to provide candidate with contractual right, and there was no suggestion that candidate was even aware of hotel's legal manual stating that information about registration of guests was to be kept confidential.—Grunseth v. Marriott Corp., 872 F.Supp. 1069, affirmed 79 F.3d 169, 316 U.S.App.D.C. 367.
**Bkrtcy.D.Me. 1993.** Under Maine law, hotel guests are licensees, holding revocable right to use the premises, subject to owner's retained control and possession.—In re Green Corp., 154 B.R. 819.

☞**8. Who are guests, boarders, or lodgers.**
**N.D.Ohio 1994.** Under Ohio law, persons staying in hotels acquire no greater rights than those acquired by guest; they are mere guests, who acquire no proprietary interest in hotel property.—Great-West Life & Annuity Assur. Co. v. Parke Imperial Canton, Ltd., 177 B.R. 843.
**Bkrtcy.S.D.Tex. 1991.** Under Texas law, guest at hotel is mere licensee, not tenant; guests have only personal contract and acquire no interest in realty.—In re Corpus Christi Hotel Partners, Ltd., 133 B.R. 850.

☞**9. Duty to furnish accommodations.**
**N.D.Tex. 1996.** Under Texas law, guest in hotel acquires no interest in the realty.—Patel v. Nofield Ins. Co., 940 F.Supp. 995.
**Bkrtcy.N.D.Ga. 1993.** Interest which hotel guest acquires is not "usufruct," under Georgia law, but, rather, hotel guest pays for "license" to use room.—In re Tollman-Hundley Dalton, L.P., 162 B.R. 26, affirmed Financial Sec. Assur., Inc. v. Tollman-Hundley Dalton, L.P., 165 B.R. 698, reversed 74 F.3d 1120.
**Bkrtcy.S.D.Tex. 1991.** Under Texas law, general rule is that tenant is vested with estate in property while hotel guest is not.—In re Corpus Christi Hotel Partners, Ltd., 133 B.R. 850.

☞**10. Injury to person of guest.**
See ☞10.1.

☞**10.1. —— In general.**
**C.A.5 (La.) 1987.** Murray v. Ramada Inn, 821 F.2d 272, certified question accepted So.2d 21, certified question answered 521 S 1123, answer to certified question conformed to 843 F.2d 831.
**C.A.1 (Puerto Rico) 1997.** Under Puerto Rico law, hotels are held to stringent standard of care with respect to their guests, which requires hotels to respond to various risks of harm with security measures, and which thus effectively exposes hotels in certain circumstances to liability for injuries inflicted on guests by third parties.—Mejias-Quiros v. Maxxam Property Corp., 108 F.3d 425.
**C.A.1 (Puerto Rico) 1995.** Under Puerto Rico law, Civil Code imposes liability upon certain establishments, such as hotels, schools, and hospitals, that fail to provide security commensurate with circumstances attendant to their operations; duty to furnish heightened security is thought to stem form character of enterprise in which defendant

**Pocket part entry for key number 10.1**

**Summaries of potentially relevant cases**

Reprinted with permission from West Group, West's *Federal Practice Digest*, 4th Ser., Pocket Part, Vol. 63 (1997), p. 1.

**At the end of West's *Federal Practice Digest*, Fourth Series, are a series of noncumulative interim pamphlets with cases decided after the pocket part was published. Under the topic "Innkeepers" in this example, one case from Arizona is summarized under key number 10.1.**

**FIGURE 4.25**   NONCUMULATIVE INTERIM PAMPHLET

---

## ⟜150  INJUNCTION                                                    236

**S.D.Ohio 1997.** Temporary restraining order (TRO) preventing electronic mail (e-mail) advertising company from using commercial online compute service's accounts, equipment, or support services, from inserting any false reference to service's accounts or equipment in messages, and from falsely representing that any e-mail sent by company originated from service or service's accounts would be extended in duration until final judgment was entered in litigation brought by service, even though company no longer had account with service; fact that company no longer had account with service did not vitiate need which service demonstrated for injunction proscribing acts set forth in TRO subsections.—CompuServe Inc. v. Cyber Promotions, Inc., 962 F.Supp. 1015.

**(B) CONTINUING, MODIFYING, VACATING, OR DISSOLVING.**

**⟜176. —— Order.**
**C.A.3 (N.J.) 1997.** District court's order denying motion to vacate and thus continuing temporary restraining order had same effect as preliminary injunction, but was entered without required development of preliminary injunction record and findings of fact by court.—Nutrasweet Co. v. Vit-Mar Enterprises, Inc., 112 F.3d 689.

**V. PERMANENT INJUNCTION AND OTHER RELIEF.**

**⟜189. Nature and scope of relief.**
**W.D.Mich. 1997.** Broad permanent injunction is unavailable absent most extraordinary circumstances.—Spruytte v. Govorchin, 961 F.Supp. 1094.

**S.D.N.Y. 1997.** Although Eleventh Amendment bars damage claims against state officials acting in their official capacity, federal courts can enjoin state officials acting in their official capacity, as long as injunction governs only the officer's future conduct and no retroactive remedy is provided; rule extends to declaratory judgments also. U.S.C.A. Const.Amend. 11.—Ippolito v. Meisel, 958 F.Supp. 155.

**VII. VIOLATION AND PUNISHMENT.**

**⟜231. Review.**
**C.A.D.C. 1997.** Remand was required for Medicare provider, who sought contempt order for violation of preliminary injunction prohibiting United States from disseminating publicly any information that suggested that provider had been excluded from Medicare and Medicaid programs, to prove whether he suffered losses due to Medicare carrier's violation of injunction and whether United States caused these losses.—U.S. v. Waksberg, 112 F.3d 1225.

**INNKEEPERS**

**⟜10. Injury to person of guest.**
See ⟜10.1.
**⟜10.1. —— In general.**
**D.Ariz. 1997.** Under New Jersey law, "good samaritan" statute does not apply to provide immunity for any actions which violate higher duty of care owed by innkeepers and common carriers, as established under Restatement (Second) of Torts. Restatement (Second) of Torts § 314A.—Gingeleskie v. Westin Hotel Co., 961 F.Supp. 1310.

Under New Jersey law, innkeeper owes duty to guests to take reasonable action to protect them against unreasonable risk of physical harm, and to give them first aid after it knows or has reason to

know that they are ill or injured and care for them until they can be cared for by others. Restatement (Second) of Torts § 314A.—Id.

Under New Jersey law, hotel at which guest was staying when he sought ride to hospital, which owed guest heightened duty as innkeeper, did not breach duty owed to guest to give first aid after hotel staff knew or had reason to know guest was injured, and was not liable for fatal heart attack suffered by guest while on his way to hospital; guest did not appear severely ill or indicate that he was anything more than merely sick, and had been able to think for himself and move without assistance. Restatement (Second) of Torts § 314A.—Id.

**⟜10.8. —— Actions in general.**
**D.Ariz. 1997.** No conflict of law issue was presented in tort action against hotel and shuttle service which had been brought in New Jersey based on events occurring in Arizona, because both Arizona and New Jersey law follow Restatement (Second) of Torts in relation to creation of duties, and thus, federal district court in Arizona, to which action had been transferred, would apply New Jersey case law in interpreting Restatement.—Gingeleskie v. Westin Hotel Co., 961 F.Supp. 1310.

Under New Jersey choice of law principles, New Jersey law applied to tort action against hotel and shuttle service arising from death of New Jersey resident while he was staying as guest at Arizona hotel; while all relevant factual contacts were with Arizona, those factors did not outweigh interest of New Jersey in protecting its domiciliary, and Arizona's interests were not qualitatively superior to those of New Jersey.—Id.

**INSURANCE**

*The headings and/or sub-headings of this topic have been changed to read as follows:*

I. NATURE, CONTROL, AND REGULATION, ⟜1–31.

II. INSURANCE ORGANIZATIONS, ⟜31.1–72.13.

  (A) IN GENERAL, ⟜31.1–31.4.

  (B) STOCK COMPANIES, ⟜32–51.

  (C) MUTUAL COMPANIES, ⟜52–59.

  (D) REHABILITATION, INSOLVENCY, AND DISSOLUTION, ⟜72.1–72.13.

III. INSURANCE AGENTS AND BROKERS, ⟜73–113.

  (A) NATURE OF AGENCY, ⟜73–73.5.

  (B) AGENCY FOR INSURER, ⟜74–95.

  (C) AGENCY FOR APPLICANT OR INSURED, ⟜96–113.

IV. INSURABLE INTEREST, ⟜114–123.1.

V. CONTRACT AND POLICY, ⟜124–179.1.

  (A) NATURE, REQUISITES, AND VALIDITY, ⟜124–145.2.

  (B) CONSTRUCTION AND OPERATION, ⟜146–179.1.

VI. PREMIUMS, DUES, AND ASSESSMENTS, ⟜180–198.

VII. ASSIGNMENT OR OTHER TRANSFER OF POLICY, ⟜199–225.1.

VIII. CANCELLATION OR OTHER REVOCATION OF POLICY, ⟜226–249.1.

*Interim pamphlet entry for key number 10.1*

*Case summary*

Reprinted with permission from West Group, West's *Federal Practice Digest*, 4th Ser., Pamphlet Part 2 (Aug. 1997), p. 236.

**On the inside front cover of the August 1997 pamphlet is the closing table indicating the last volumes of the reporters with cases summarized in this pamphlet.** *The Federal Reporter,* **Third Series, closes with volume 114, page 205.**

**FIGURE 4.26**   NONCUMULATIVE INTERIM PAMPHLET, CLOSING TABLE

---

**Closing with Cases Reported in**

Supreme Court Reporter ------------------------------------------------ 117 S.Ct. 1864
Federal Reporter, Third Series ------------------------------------- 114 F.3d 205
Federal Supplement ----------------------------------------------- 962 F.Supp. 1520
Federal Rules Decisions ------------------------------------------- 172 F.R.D. 549
Bankruptcy Reporter ----------------------------------------------- 209 B.R. 28
Federal Claims Reporter ------------------------------------------- 37 Fed.Cl. 792
Military Justice Reporter — U.S.Armed Forces ---------------------- 46 M.J. 128
Military Justice Reporter — A.F.Ct.Crim.App. ---------------------- 46 M.J. 744
Veterans Appeals Reporter ----------------------------------------- 10 Vet.App. 247

COPYRIGHT © 1997
By
WEST GROUP

The above symbol, INSTA-CITE, WESTLAW, WEST's, and Federal Practice Digest are registered
trademarks of West Publishing Co. Registered in U.S. Patent and Trademark Office.

---

Reprinted with permission from West Group, West's *Federal Practice Digest*, 4th Ser., Pamphlet Part 2 (Aug. 1997), inside cover.

**To find cases decided after the interim pamphlet closed, the next step is checking the mini-digest in the back of each individual volume of F.3d after volume 114, page 205. Most of them do not include any entries under "Innkeepers." The example below comes from 124 F.3d, which lists one case under this topic and key number.**

**FIGURE 4.27** 124 F.3d, MINI-DIGEST

INSURANCE ☞146.1(1)

which indicated that inmate calls were subject to monitoring and had opportunity to withhold consent to monitoring procedures. M.G.L.A. c. 272, § 99, subd. B.—Gilday v. Dubois, 124 F.3d 277.

Regulatory requirement that prison inmates consent to monitoring, recording, and detailing of their telephone calls before they were permitted to use system did not violate injunction prohibiting prison officials from unlawfully intercepting or attempting to intercept inmate's calls, despite inmate's claim that consent requirement was coercive endeavor to intercept inmate's calls.—Id.

System which recorded, monitored, and detailed [pris]on inmates' telephone calls did not clearly [viola]te Federal Wiretap Act, and thus did not [viol]ate injunction prohibiting prison officials from [unla]wfully intercepting or attempting to intercept [parti]cular inmate's calls, since answering party [dem]onstrated implied consent to such procedures by accepting call after hearing prerecorded message disclosing such procedures. 18 U.S.C.A. § 2510 et seq.—Id.

> **Mini-digest entry for key number 10.1**

### INNKEEPERS

☞**10.1. —— In general.**
**C.A.1 (Puerto Rico) 1997.** Under Puerto Rico law, hotel-keeper owes its guests heightened duty of care and protection. 31 L.P.R.A. § 5141.—Woods–Leber v. Hyatt Hotels of Puerto Rico, Inc., 124 F.3d 47.

Under Puerto Rico law, hotel-keeper is not insurer of its guests' well-being. 31 L.P.R.A. § 5141.—Id.

Notwithstanding heightened duty of care and protection that hotel-keeper owes its guests under Puerto Rico law, hotel-keeper is not liable for harm unless harm is reasonably foreseeable. 31 L.P.R.A. § 5141.—Id.

### INSURANCE

> **Case summary**

[I. N]ATURE, CONTROL, AND REGULATION.

☞**4(2). Validity of statutes.**
**C.A.7 (Ill.) 1997.** Illinois law limiting preexisting condition limitations in health benefit plans for small employers and requiring that certain coverage be portable was not preempted by ERISA Employee Retirement Income Security Act of 1974, § 514(b)(2)(A), 29 U.S.C.A. § 1144(b)(2)(A); S.H.A. 215 ILCS 95/20.—Plumb v. Fluid Pump Service, Inc., 124 F.3d 849.

### III. INSURANCE AGENTS AND BROKERS.

(C) AGENCY FOR APPLICANT OR INSURED.

☞**103. Authority and duties as to principal.**
**C.A.7 (Ill.) 1997.** Under Illinois law, insurance broker must exercise competence and skill when rendering service of procuring insurance.—Plumb v. Fluid Pump Service, Inc., 124 F.3d 849.

Under Illinois law, relationship between insured and insurance broker is fiduciary one.—Id.

Under Illinois law, basic duties of insurance broker are to procure insurance in timely manner and to procure insurance in accordance with client's special circumstances after being informed about client's needs.—Id.

Under Illinois law, insurance broker is obligated not to mislead insured.—Id.

Under Illinois law, primary function of agent or broker acting in agency relationship for insured is faithfully to negotiate and procure insurance policy according to wishes and requirements of insured.—Id.

Under Illinois law, insurance brokers are not required to sell only full coverage to insureds.—Id.

Under Illinois law, insureds have primary responsibility to determine their own insurance needs.—Id.

Under Illinois law, broker is not liable if he acts in good faith and with reasonable care, skill, and diligence to place insurance in compliance with principal's instructions.—Id.

☞**103.1(1). In general.**
**C.A.7 (Ill.) 1997.** Under Illinois law as predicted by court of appeals, employer's allegation that company that assisted employer in getting new ERISA insurance coverage failed to inform employer that its medical insurance coverage for employees would lapse if it did not pay premiums did not state claim for breach of fiduciary duty, absent allegation that company failed to procure insurance according to their wishes, that employer requested policy without preexisting condition restriction, or that company knew of any employee's preexisting condition or that they had basis to suspect that restriction on coverage of preexisting conditions would be of concern to employer. Employee Retirement Income Security Act of 1974, § 2 et seq., 29 U.S.C.A. § 1001 et seq.—Plumb v. Fluid Pump Service, Inc., 124 F.3d 849.

Under Illinois law, broker is not liable if he acts in good faith and with reasonable care, skill, and diligence to place insurance in compliance with principal's instructions.—Id.

### V. CONTRACT AND POLICY.

(A) NATURE, REQUISITES, AND VALIDITY.

☞**138(3). Violation of statute.**
**C.A.7 (Ill.) 1997.** Under Illinois law, insurance policy terms that are in conflict with statutory provisions are invalid.—Plumb v. Fluid Pump Service, Inc., 124 F.3d 849.

☞**141(4). Estoppel of insured.**
**C.A.7 (Ill.) 1997.** Under Illinois law, insureds have burden of knowing contents of their insurance policies.—Plumb v. Fluid Pump Service, Inc., 124 F.3d 849.

☞**144(4). Oral modification; endorsement on or attachment to policy.**
**C.A.7 (Ill.) 1997.** If written terms of ERISA plan do not entitle claimant to coverage sought, benefits will not be forthcoming on the basis of oral representations to the contrary. Employee Retirement Income Security Act of 1974, § 2 et seq., 29 U.S.C.A. § 1001 et seq.—Plumb v. Fluid Pump Service, Inc., 124 F.3d 849.

One of ERISA's purposes is to protect the financial integrity of pension and welfare plans by confining benefits to terms of plans as written, thus ruling out oral modifications. Employee Retirement Income Security Act of 1974, § 2 et seq., 29 U.S.C.A. § 1001 et seq.—Id.

(B) CONSTRUCTION AND OPERATION.

☞**146.1(1). In general.**
**C.A.3 (N.J.) 1997.** Under New Jersey law, when terms of insurance contract are clear, it is function of court to enforce it as written and not make a
(93)

Reprinted with permission from West Group, West's *Federal Reporter*, 3d Ser., Vol. 124 (1997), p. 93 (key number digest).

**This is the opinion in *Woods-Leber v. Hyatt Hotels of Puerto Rico*, the case summarized in the mini-digest in the back of 124 F.3d. You would want to review this case, as well as the others identified in the digest subject volume and pocket part, in conducting your research.**

**FIGURE 4.28**   *WOODS-LEBER v. HYATT HOTELS OF PUERTO RICO, INC.*, 124 F.3d 47 (1ST CIR. 1997)

---

### WOODS–LEBER v. HYATT HOTELS OF PUERTO RICO, INC.          47
Cite as 124 F.3d 47 (1st Cir. 1997)

ment delay lacks substance. A criminal defendant who asserts such a claim bears the heavy burden of showing not only that the preindictment delay caused him actual, substantial prejudice, but also that the prosecution orchestrated the delay to gain a tactical advantage over him. *See Marion,* 404 U.S. at 324, 92 S.Ct. at 465; *United States v. Henson,* 945 F.2d 430, 439 (1st Cir.1991). The appellee shows neither.

[20] Stokes argues that he satisfied the first prong of the test because, had the federal government promptly indicted him, he would have continued searching for a potential defense witness, Sherry Parkman, who disappeared between the date of the offense and the date of the state court trial. Since the appellee was unable to locate the witness at the time of his state trial, there is no credible reason to believe that the delay on the federal side placed him in a position less advantageous than he would have occupied had the indictments been contemporaneous.[5]

The appellee's fallback position is that the delay prejudiced him by denying him the benefit of running his state and federal sentences concurrently. This is pure speculation and, hence, inadequate to the task. *See McCoy,* 977 F.2d at 711.

[21] At the expense of carting coal to Newcastle, we add that Stokes also fails on the second prong of the test. By all accounts, the government temporized until it knew the result of the state court prosecution. Even then, the government deferred an indictment because it gave priority to the prosecution of offenders who, unlike Stokes, were not already in custody.

The government's explanation is plausible and unimpeached; it should, therefore, be accepted. *See United States v. Marler,* 756 F.2d 206, 215 n. 6 (1st Cir.1985). It indicates that the government acted out of proper motives and achieved no undue tactical advantage. For these reasons, Stokes fails to persuade us that the district court erred in refusing to dismiss the case based on inordinate preindictment delay.

5.   In all events Parkman's statements are ambiguous. *See Commonwealth v. Stokes,* 653 N.E.2d at 185. Because proof of actual prejudice must be

### III.  CONCLUSION

We need go no further. It is evident to us that the district court erred as a matter of law in dismissing the case prior to trial. Having obtained a valid indictment within the limitations period, the government is entitled to try the defendant on the merits. Moreover, we think it best that the case be transferred to a new trier on remand, and we so direct. *See, e.g, United States v. Muniz,* 49 F.3d 36, 42–43 (1st Cir.1995); *Cia. Petrolera Caribe, Inc. v. Arco Caribbean, Inc.,* 754 F.2d 404, 430 (1st Cir.1985).

*Reversed.*

Lynne WOODS–LEBER and Anthony Leber, Plaintiffs, Appellants,

v.

HYATT HOTELS OF PUERTO RICO, INC., Etc., Defendant, Appellee.

No. 97–1269.

United States Court of Appeals, First Circuit.

Heard July 30, 1997.

Decided Aug. 26, 1997.

Hotel guest sued hotel to recover for injuries she sustained when bit by rabid mongoose in hotel's pool area. The United States District Court for the District of Puerto Rico, Daniel R. Dominguez, 951 F.Supp. 1028, granted summary judgment for hotel. Guest appealed. The Court of Appeals, Selya, Circuit Judge, held that: (1) hotel did not "control" mongoose, and (2) attack was not foreseeable.

Affirmed.

definite and not speculative, *see Acha,* 910 F.2d at 32, this fact, without more, would sink the appellee's argument.

**FIGURE 4.28**    *WOODS-LEBER v. HYATT HOTELS OF PUERTO RICO, INC.*, 124 F.3d 47 (1ST CIR. 1997) *(Continued)*

48    124 FEDERAL REPORTER, 3d SERIES

**1. Animals ⬤—69, 72**

To prevail on claim under Puerto Rico statute that imposes strict liability on possessor or user of animal for any damages which animal causes, plaintiff must show, at bare minimum, that defendant owned, possessed, or used wild animal. 31 L.P.R.A. § 5144.

**2. Animals ⬤—72**

Hotel did not "control" rabid mongoose that emerged from nearby swamp and bit hotel guest in hotel's pool area, thus precluding hotel's liability to guest under Puerto Rico statute that imposes strict liability on possessor or user of animal for any damages which animal causes; there was no evidence that hotel even knew of mongoose's existence, and no evidence to support plaintiff's claim that hotel must have benefitted from mongooses' natural affinity for devouring snakes and rodents. 31 L.P.R.A. § 5144.

> See publication Words and Phrases for other judicial constructions and definitions.

**3. Negligence ⬤—1**

To recover on negligence theory under Puerto Rico law, plaintiff suing for personal injuries must establish duty requiring defendant to conform to certain standard of conduct, breach of that duty, proof of damage, and causal connection between damage and tortious conduct. 31 L.P.R.A. § 5141.

**4. Negligence ⬤—10**

Personal injury plaintiff asserting negligence claim under Puerto Rico law must prove, inter alia, that injury was reasonably foreseeable and, thus, could have been avoided had defendant acted with due care. 31 L.P.R.A. § 5141.

**5. Innkeepers ⬤—10.1**

Under Puerto Rico law, hotel-keeper owes its guests heightened duty of care and protection. 31 L.P.R.A. § 5141.

**6. Innkeepers ⬤—10.1**

Under Puerto Rico law, hotel-keeper is not insurer of its guests' well-being. 31 L.P.R.A. § 5141.

\* Hon. John R. Gibson, of the Eighth Circuit, sit-

**7. Innkeepers ⬤—10.1**

Notwithstanding heightened duty of care and protection that hotel-keeper owes its guests under Puerto Rico law, hotel-keeper is not liable for harm unless harm is reasonably foreseeable. 31 L.P.R.A. § 5141.

**8. Animals ⬤—69**

It was not reasonably foreseeable to hotel that rabid mongoose from nearby swamp would emerge and attack hotel guest in hotel's pool area, thus precluding hotel's liability to guest on negligence claim under Puerto Rico law; hotel had no knowledge, actual or constructive, either of mongooses' existence or of incipient danger that they presented, at any time before attack. 31 L.P.R.A. § 5141.

---

Iván Díaz–López and Gerardo A. Quirós–López, with whom Law Offices of Gerardo A. Quirós–López, P.S.C., Santurce, PR, were on brief, for appellants.

Hector F. Oliveras, with whom Luis Ramón Ortiz–Segura was on brief, for appellee.

Before SELYA, Circuit Judge, GIBSON,\* Senior Circuit Judge, and LYNCH, Circuit Judge.

SELYA, Circuit Judge.

This appeal arises out of an unwanted intrusion by a rabid mongoose into the opulent environs of a posh luxury hotel. During its sojourn, the animal bit a guest. The guest sued, but to no avail; the district court entered summary judgment in the hotelier's favor. *See Woods–Leber v. Hyatt Hotels of P.R., Inc.,* 951 F.Supp. 1028 (D.P.R.1996). We affirm.

**I.  THE MONGOOSE ATTACK AND ITS SEQUELAE**

Defendant-appellee Hyatt Hotels of Puerto Rico, Inc. (Hyatt) owns and operates the Cerromar Beach Hotel (the hotel) in Dorado, Puerto Rico. The hotel occupies a picturesque oceanfront setting. Its verdant grounds are bordered on the west by a mangrove swamp which is under the protection of the Commonwealth's Department of Natural

ting by designation.

**FIGURE 4.28** *WOODS-LEBER v. HYATT HOTELS OF PUERTO RICO, INC.*, 124 F.3d 47 (1ST CIR. 1997) *(Continued)*

---

### WOODS–LEBER v. HYATT HOTELS OF PUERTO RICO, INC. 49

Cite as 124 F.3d 47 (1st Cir. 1997)

Resources. On the far side of the swamp lies Lakeside Villas, a residential subdivision which was being built at the time material hereto. Hyatt has no financial or other proprietary interest in the development of the subdivision.

On April 10, 1995, at approximately 5:00 p.m., plaintiff-appellant Lynne Woods–Leber, a guest, was sunbathing near the hotel's pool. Suddenly (and without any apparent provocation) a wild mongoose scurried into the pool area and bit her. Because the mongoose carried rabies, Woods–Leber underwent a series of painful inoculations.

A few days after the attack, the hotel hired an exterminator, Pest Management International (PMI), to implement a mongoose control program. PMI set several baited traps and captured fifteen mongooses in a week's time.[1] PMI concluded that the most likely explanation for the infestation was that mongooses living in the mangrove swamp had been disturbed by the construction activity at Lakeside Villas and had migrated eastward onto the hotel's grounds. The traps were left in place on the premises.

In due season, Woods–Leber invoked diversity jurisdiction, 28 U.S.C. § 1332(a) (1994), and sued Hyatt in Puerto Rico's federal district court.[2] Her suit sought damages for personal injuries under local law. Hyatt denied responsibility and, following a period of discovery, moved for *brevis* disposition, supporting its motion with a number of affidavits and declarations. The plaintiff opposed the motion but made only one evidentiary proffer: her husband's conclusory recitation of his suspicion that a temporary food preparation and storage area which had been installed near the pool functioned as a mongoose magnet.[3]

On December 30, 1996, the district court granted Hyatt's motion. The court conclud-

ed, in substance, that Hyatt could not be held strictly liable because it had not exerted any control over the mongoose, and that it could not be held liable in negligence because it could not reasonably have been expected to foresee the mongoose attack. *See Woods–Leber*, 951 F.Supp. at 1039. This appeal followed.

### II. THE SUMMARY JUDGMENT STANDARD

Summary judgment is appropriate when the record shows "no genuine issue as to any material fact and ... the moving party is entitled to a judgment as a matter of law." Fed. R. Civ. P 56(c); *see also Anderson v. Liberty Lobby, Inc.*, 477 U.S. 242, 247, 106 S.Ct. 2505, 2509–10, 91 L.Ed.2d 202 (1986). The genuineness requirement signifies that a factual controversy "must be sufficiently open-ended to permit a rational factfinder to resolve the issue in favor of either side." *National Amusements, Inc. v. Town of Dedham*, 43 F.3d 731, 735 (1st Cir.1995). The materiality requirement signifies that the factual controversy must pertain to an issue which "might affect the outcome of the suit under the governing law." *Morris v. Government Dev. Bank*, 27 F.3d 746, 748 (1st Cir.1994).

Like the nisi prius court, we must evaluate the summary judgment record in the light most flattering to the nonmovant, drawing all reasonable inferences in that party's favor. *See Coyne v. Taber Partners I*, 53 F.3d 454, 457 (1st Cir.1995). Despite this advantage, however, the party opposing summary judgment cannot simply rest on "conclusory allegations, improbable inferences, and unsupported speculation." *Medina–Munoz v. R.J. Reynolds Tobacco Co.*, 896 F.2d 5, 8 (1st Cir.1990). To the contrary, at least with respect to issues on which she bears the

---

1. The plural of "mongoose" is a matter of some debate in lexicographic circles. *See, e.g., Webster's Ninth New Collegiate Dictionary* 767 (1989) ("mongoose ... *n, pl* mongooses *also* mongeese...."). Having noted the debate, however, we choose not to enter it. Thus, while we use the term "mongooses" throughout, we express no opinion on which plural noun is linguistically preferable.

2. Woods-Leber's husband, Anthony Leber, joined as a co-plaintiff. Inasmuch as his claim is derivative, we treat the appeal as if Woods-Leber were the sole plaintiff and appellant. Of course, our decision disposes of Anthony Leber's claim as well.

3. The gist of Leber's statement is reprinted in the district court's opinion. *See Woods–Leber*, 951 F.Supp. at 1033.

**FIGURE 4.28**   *WOODS-LEBER v. HYATT HOTELS OF PUERTO RICO, INC.*, 124 F.3d
47 (1ST CIR. 1997) (*Continued*)

burden of proof, the nonmovant must identify properly substantiated facts sufficient to establish a trialworthy issue. *See Morris,* 27 F.3d at 748; *Kelly v. United States,* 924 F.2d 355, 358 (1st Cir.1991).

Appellate review of an order granting summary judgment is plenary. *See Coyne,* 53 F.3d at 457; *Morris,* 27 F.3d at 748.

### III.  ANALYSIS

The substantive law of Puerto Rico governs the liability question in this diversity action. *See Erie R.R. Co. v. Tompkins,* 304 U.S. 64, 78, 58 S.Ct. 817, 822, 82 L.Ed. 1188 (1938); *Daigle v. Maine Med. Ctr., Inc.* 14 F.3d 684, 689 (1st Cir.1994). The plaintiff makes two claims under that law. We consider them sequentially.

### A.  *The Article 1805 Claim.*

[1]  Article 1805 of the Civil Code, P.R. Laws Ann. tit. 31, § 5144 (1992), imposes strict liability on the possessor or user of an animal for any damages which the animal causes. *See Serrano v. Lopez,* 79 P.R.R. 922, 927 (1957). In order to prevail on an Article 1805 claim, a plaintiff must show, at a bare minimum, that the defendant owned, possessed, or used the wild animal. *See Ferrer v. Rivera,* 56 P.R.R. 480, 482 (1940); *Redinger v. Crespo,* 18 P.R.R. 106, 111 (1912). This customarily involves a showing that the defendant exercised control over the animal. *See* P.R. Laws Ann. tit. 31, § 1480 (1993).

[2]  The district court ordered summary judgment on this count, holding that Woods–Leber failed to present any evidence tending to show that Hyatt controlled the rabid mongoose. *See Woods–Leber,* 951 F.Supp. at 1035. We agree. A person cannot control an animal of which he is completely unaware. Here, the uncontradicted evidence indicates that Hyatt had no inkling of the mongoose's existence, had no reason to suspect that mongooses were lurking nearby, and received as jolting a surprise as Woods–Leber when the

mongoose struck. In the utter absence of any evidence of either knowledge or control, the district court properly entered summary judgment on the Article 1805 claim.

The plaintiff endeavors to avoid this predictable result by arguing that a symbiotic relationship existed between Hyatt and the mongoose population in the mangrove swamp. She pins this rather exotic theory to a suggestion that Hyatt must have benefitted from the mongooses' natural affinity for devouring snakes and rodents, and that this benefit is legally tantamount to control. This argument is woven entirely from the gossamer strands of speculation and surmise. The record is devoid of any evidence that mongooses patrolled the perimeters of the hotel's grounds, performing pest control functions. And, moreover, the argument is unaccompanied by any meaningful citation to applicable legal authority.[4] In sum, this argument is factually barren, legally bankrupt, and altogether insufficient to breathe life into the plaintiff's Article 1805 claim.

### B.  *The Article 1802 Claim.*

[3, 4]  Article 1802 of the Civil Code, P.R. Laws Ann. tit. 31, § 5141, imposes liability on any person or entity which, by his, her, or its negligent acts or omissions, causes harm or damage. In broad perspective, Puerto Rico law defines negligence as the failure to exercise due diligence to avoid foreseeable risks. *See Coyne,* 53 F.3d at 459; *Malave–Felix v. Volvo Car Corp.,* 946 F.2d 967, 971–72 (1st Cir.1991).[5] To recover on a negligence theory, a plaintiff suing for personal injuries under Article 1802 must establish (1) a duty requiring the defendant to conform to a certain standard of conduct, (2) a breach of that duty, (3) proof of damage, and (4) a causal connection between the damage and the tortious conduct. *See Sociedad de Gananciales v. Gonzalez Padin,* 17 P.R. Offic. Trans. 111, 125 (1986). These requirements cannot be satisfied unless the plaintiff proves, inter

---

4.  The lower court perspicaciously observed that this argument was "not merely novel, but . . . perilously close to the frivolous." *Woods–Leber,* 951 F.Supp. at 1035 n. 5.

5.  In a premises case a showing of negligence under Puerto Rico law ordinarily requires a demonstration of the owner's or occupier's actual or constructive knowledge of the harm-causing condition. *See Mas v. United States,* 984 F.2d 527, 530 (1st Cir.1993).

**FIGURE 4.28**   *WOODS-LEBER v. HYATT HOTELS OF PUERTO RICO, INC.*, 124 F.3d 47 (1ST CIR. 1997) (Continued)

---

WOODS–LEBER v. HYATT HOTELS OF PUERTO RICO, INC.   **51**
Cite as 124 F.3d 47 (1st Cir. 1997)

alia, that the injury was reasonably foreseeable (and, thus, could have been avoided had the defendant acted with due care). *See Coyne*, 53 F.3d at 459–60.

[5–7] The plaintiff contends that, under Puerto Rico law, a hotel-keeper owes its guests a heightened duty of care and protection. The law so provides. *See, e.g., Mejias–Quiros v. Maxxam Property Corp.*, 108 F.3d 425, 427 (1st Cir.1997); *Coyne*, 53 F.3d at 458; *Pabon–Escabi v. Axtmayer*, 90 P.R.R. 20, 29 (1964). Nevertheless, a hotel-keeper is not an insurer of its guests' well-being. *See, e.g., Goose v. Hilton Hotels*, 79 P.R.R. 494, 499 (1956) (holding that a hotelier is liable for a guest's fall on hotel premises only if the hotelier knew or should have known of a preexisting dangerous condition). Consequently, notwithstanding the heightened duty of care and protection, the hotel-keeper is not liable for harm unless the harm is reasonably foreseeable. *See Coyne*, 53 F.3d at 460–61.

[8] In this case, the linchpin question is whether it was reasonably foreseeable at the time and place in question that a mongoose would attack a guest (for, without a foreseeable harm, Hyatt could not have breached its duty of care by failing to implement a mongoose control program before the attack). *See id.* at 460. The district court answered this question in the negative. *See Woods–Leber*, 951 F.Supp. at 1039. We think that Judge Dominguez got it right.

The evidence as to knowledge is telling. On this point, the record permits only one conclusion: that Hyatt had no knowledge, actual or constructive, either of the mongooses' existence or of the incipient danger that they presented, at any time before the attack. The hotel personnel most directly involved in the matter (such as the head grounds keeper and the chief of security) submitted affidavits which made plain that a mongoose had never before been seen on the hotel premises; that no one at the hotel

knew of the presence of mongooses in the mangrove swamp or otherwise in the vicinity; and that, prior to the assault on Woods–Leber, no wild animal of any kind had ever bitten any hotel guest. By the same token, there was no evidence from which a factfinder could conclude, without rank speculation, that the temporary food preparation and storage area presented any hazard or that Hyatt should have known the inauguration of a construction project near the mangrove swamp portended an influx of wild animals. Indeed, several previous construction projects had been undertaken near the swamp without incident. Finally, there was no evidence either that a non-rabid mongoose, unprovoked, was likely to bite a supine sunbather, or that rabies was prevalent in the area.

We do not mean to imply that, merely because a rabid mongoose had never before invaded the premises and bitten a guest, the attack could not have been foreseen. *See generally Pabon–Escabi*, 90 P.R.R. at 25 (explaining that "the requirement of foreseeability [does not require] that the precise risk or consequences have been foreseen"). If, say, an occupier of premises disregards a known general danger, or omits a precaution regularly taken by prudent persons similarly situated, a first attack might well be foreseeable (and, thus, actionable). *See Coyne*, 53 F.3d at 460; *see also State v. Francis*, 228 Conn. 118, 635 A.2d 762, 769 n. 11 (1993) (holding that liability does not require specific foreseeability); *Stevens v. Des Moines Indep. Community Sch. Dist.*, 528 N.W.2d 117, 120 (Iowa 1995) (same); *Pimentel v. Roundup Co.*, 100 Wash.2d 39, 666 P.2d 888, 891 (1983) (same). But here, the plaintiff offered no evidence to support a finding of foreseeability, electing instead to rely on the defendant's affidavits and declarations.[6] We have warned before, and today reiterate, that parties who permit the movant to configure the summary judgment record do so at their peril. *See Kelly*, 924 F.2d at 358.

---

6. This presents a marked contrast to the cases on which Woods–Leber relies. *See, e.g., Tormos–Arroyo v. Department of Ed.*, 96 J.T.S. 34, 806 n. 2 (1996) (plaintiffs submitted deposition testimony suggesting foreseeability); *J.A.D.M. v. Plaza Carolina Shopping Ctr.*, 93 J.T.S. 26, 10,435

(1993) (plaintiff submitted statistical evidence showing past incidence of crimes in the area); *Elba v. University of P.R.*, 125 P.R. Dec. 294, 306 (1990) (plaintiff submitted cartographic evidence indicating known high-risk areas).

**FIGURE 4.28**   *WOODS-LEBER v. HYATT HOTELS OF PUERTO RICO, INC.*, 124 F.3d 47 (1ST CIR. 1997) *(Continued)*

We need go no further. As the district court correctly stated, "[t]he normal rule is that a person does not have a duty to prevent an attack upon another . . . by wild animals." *Woods–Leber*, 951 F.Supp. at 1036 (citations omitted). While the rule admits of exceptions, the plaintiff in this case adduced no evidence which sufficed to bring the mongoose attack within any of those exceptions. Since a hotel-keeper, like any other owner or occupier of premises, cannot be held liable for that which it cannot reasonably foresee, the lower court did not err in granting Hyatt's motion for summary judgment.

*Affirmed.*

UNITED STATES, Appellee,

v.

Michael P. FOSHER, Defendant–
Appellant.

No. 96–1473.

United States Court of Appeals,
First Circuit.

Heard May 7, 1997.

Decided Aug. 27, 1997.

Defendant was convicted in the United States District Court for the District of Massachusetts, Nathaniel M. Gorton, J., of racketeering conspiracy, racketeering, interstate transportation of stolen property, and conspiracy, and he appealed. The Court of Appeals, Torruella, Chief Judge, held that: (1) addressing an issue of first impression, Defendant's armed bank robbery conviction under the Federal Youth Corrections Act (FYCA), that was previously set aside pursuant to the FYCA's set-aside provision, could be included in defendant's criminal history calculation; (2) remand was required to determine whether 62–year–old victim of defendant's home invasion was "unusually vul-

nerable"; and (3) individual's assistance in devising perpetrators' scheme to rob elderly victim was sufficient to find that he was participant within meaning of the Sentencing Guidelines.

Affirmed in part, reversed in part and remanded.

**1. Criminal Law ☞1181.5(8)**

Remand was required to determine whether 62–year–old victim of defendant's home invasion was "unusually vulnerable," as required to support upward adjustment at sentencing; court was required to consider victim's individual characteristics, not just her age and perpetrator's decision that use of weapons would not be necessary. U.S.S.G. § 3A1.1(b), 18 U.S.C.A.

**2. Criminal Law ☞1254**

In determining whether particularly vulnerable victim enhancement under Sentencing Guidelines applies, question is whether particular victim was less likely to thwart crime, rather than more likely to suffer harm if crime is successful. U.S.S.G. § 3A1.1(b), 18 U.S.C.A.

**3. Criminal Law ☞1158(1)**

Court of Appeals reviews district court's role in the offense determinations for clear error. U.S.S.G. § 3B1.1(a), 18 U.S.C.A.

**4. Criminal Law ☞1251**

Court making four-level role-in-the-offense adjustment under Sentencing Guidelines must first determine whether defendant acted as organizer/leader of specific criminal activity; if so, court asks separate question of whether that criminal activity involved five or more participants. U.S.S.G. § 3B1.1(a), 18 U.S.C.A.

**5. Criminal Law ☞1251**

In determining defendant's role in offense, sentencing court need not look only to elements underlying conviction, but may consider whole of defendant's relevant conduct. U.S.S.G. § 3B1.1(a), 18 U.S.C.A.

**6. Criminal Law ☞1254**

Individual's assistance in devising perpetrator's scheme to rob elderly victim

# G. CHECKLIST FOR CASE RESEARCH ∎

### 1. SELECT A PRINT DIGEST

❐ Use West's *Federal Practice Digest* to locate all federal cases.

❐ Use a state digest to locate state and federal cases from an individual state.

❐ Use a regional digest to locate state cases only within the region.

❐ Use a combined digest to locate state and federal cases from all United States jurisdictions.

### 2. LOCATE TOPICS AND KEY NUMBERS IN A PRINT DIGEST

❐ From a case on point, use the headnotes at the beginning of the decision to identify relevant topics and key numbers.

❐ From the Descriptive-Word Index, look up relevant subjects, check the pocket part for new index headings, and look up the topics and key numbers in the subject volumes.

❐ From a topic entry, review subjects included and excluded and the outline of key numbers.

### 3. READ THE CASE SUMMARIES IN THE PRINT DIGEST

❐ Use the court and date abbreviations to target appropriate cases.

### 4. UPDATE PRINT DIGEST RESEARCH

❐ Check the pocket part for the subject volume.

❐ Check any cumulative or noncumulative interim pamphlets at the end of the digest set.

❐ Check the closing table on the inside front cover of the most recent interim pamphlet (if there is no interim pamphlet, check the closing table on the inside front cover of the pocket part).

❐ If necessary, check the mini-digests in the back of each reporter volume published after the latest volume listed in the closing table.

### 5. ELECTRONIC CASE RESEARCH

❐ In Westlaw and LexisNexis, execute word searches for cases using federal, state, or combined databases.

❐ In Westlaw, use the Custom Digest function to search by digest topic and key number or the KeySearch function to search by subject.

❐ In LexisNexis, use the Search Advisor function to search by subject.

❐ Selected cases may be available on the Internet.

# RESEARCH WITH SHEPARD'S CITATIONS AND OTHER CITATORS

A. The purpose of a citator

B. Using Shepard's Citations in print for case research

C. When to use a citator in case research

D. Shepard's for additional types of authority

E. Checking citations electronically

F. Sample pages for Shepardizing a case in print

G. Checklist for case research with Shepard's Citations and other citators

## A. THE PURPOSE OF A CITATOR

Virtually all cases contain citations to legal authorities, including other cases, secondary sources, statutes, and regulations. These decisions can affect the continued validity of the authorities they cite. For example, earlier cases can be reversed or overruled, or statutes can be held unconstitutional. Even if an authority remains valid, the discussion of the authority in later cases can be helpful in your research. As a consequence, when you find an authority that helps you answer a research question, you will often want to know whether the authority has been cited elsewhere, and if so, what has been said about it.

The tool that helps you do this is called a citator. Citators catalog cases and secondary sources, analyzing what they say about the authorities they cite. Some citators also track the status of statutes and regulations, indicating, for example, whether a statute has been amended or repealed. Citators will help you determine whether an authority is still "good law," meaning it has not been changed or invalidated since it was published. They will also help you locate additional authorities that pertain to your research question. The print citator most commonly used in legal research is Shepard's Citations. Shepard's is also available electronically in LexisNexis, and Westlaw has its own citator service called KeyCite.

Using Shepard's to check legal authority is such an integral part of the research process that the term "to Shepardize" is a well-known term in the legal lexicon. At first, Shepardizing may seem like a daunting process because Shepard's uses many symbols and abbreviations that can appear undecipherable to someone unfamiliar with the service. Once you understand how the material is organized, however, you will see that Shepardizing is a fairly mechanical process that is not especially difficult.

Citators can be used in researching many types of authority, including cases, statutes, regulations, and some secondary sources. Section D outlines some of the types of authority for which Shepard's is available, and Section E discusses the scope of the citators available in LexisNexis and Westlaw. In addition, later chapters in this book discuss the use of Shepard's in researching different types of authority. The process of using a citator, however, is the same for almost any type of authority. Accordingly, for purposes of introducing you to this process, this chapter focuses on the use of citators in case research.

## B. USING SHEPARD'S CITATIONS IN PRINT FOR CASE RESEARCH

Shepardizing cases in print requires four steps:

- locating the correct set of books to Shepardize the citation
- locating the correct volumes within the set of Shepard's
- locating the entry for the case within each volume
- interpreting the entries.

This section uses the case of *Kenney v. Scientific, Inc.*, 497 A.2d 1310 (N.J. Super. L. Div. 1985), to illustrate the Shepardizing process. *Kenney* will be referred to as the original case. The later authorities that cite *Kenney* will be referred to as citing sources.

### 1. LOCATING THE CORRECT SET OF BOOKS

The first step in Shepardizing cases is locating the correct set of Shepard's books. Shepard's publishes different sets of books that correspond to various sets of reporters. Figure 5.1 identifies some of Shepard's case citators.

**FIGURE 5.1** SHEPARD'S® CITATORS FOR CASES

| IF YOUR CITATION IS FROM . . . | YOU CAN USE THIS SET OF SHEPARD'S |
|---|---|
| United States Supreme Court | *Shepard's United States Citations* |
| Any United States District Court or Court of Appeals | *Shepard's Federal Citations* |
| Any state court | Shepard's publishes a separate set for each state. An original case from a state court published in either an official reporter or a West regional reporter can be Shepardized in that state's set of Shepard's. |
| | Shepard's publishes regional sets for each of West's regional reporters. Only original cases published in West regional reporters can be Shepardized in a regional set of Shepard's. |

If you are Shepardizing a federal case, you will probably use either *Shepard's United States Citations* or *Shepard's Federal Citations*, depending on which court decided the case. Shepard's for state court decisions is a little more complex. A state set of Shepard's usually covers two sets of reporters: the state's official reporter and West's regional reporter. Thus, you can use the state books to Shepardize an original case that has been published in either type of reporter. The regional set of Shepard's, however, covers only decisions published in the regional reporter. Therefore, you will not be able to use a regional set of Shepard's unless you have a regional reporter citation for the original case. The information provided in the two sets of Shepard's also varies slightly. Although either set will give you information to determine whether the original case is still good law, you will usually find more research references in the regional set than in the state set.

In our example, *Kenney* was decided by the New Jersey Superior Court, and the case was published in the *Atlantic Reporter*, Second Series. Therefore, it can be Shepardized either in *Shepard's New Jersey Citations* or *Shepard's Atlantic Reporter Citations*.

## 2. LOCATING THE CORRECT VOLUMES

Each set of Shepard's books contains multiple volumes. Therefore, once you have located the correct set, the next step is figuring out which of the volumes you need to use to Shepardize the original case thoroughly. Unlike digests, Shepard's is not updated with pocket parts. Instead, each Shepard's volume covers a specific period of time. To update a case from the date it was decided until the present, therefore, you need to look up the citation in a series of noncumulative volumes.

In addition to publishing a series of hardbound volumes, Shepard's also publishes supplements in the form of softcover booklets and pamphlets. The most recent booklet or pamphlet on the shelf is the starting point for determining which volumes you need to check. On the front cover of the supplement, you will see a section entitled "What Your Library Should Contain." It explains which Shepard's volumes you need to use. Figure 5.2 illustrates the "What Your Library Should Contain" section. As Figure 5.2 indicates, to Shepardize *Kenney*, you would need to look in five volumes of *Shepard's Atlantic Reporter Citations*: the 1994 Bound Volumes, the 1994–1996 Bound Supplement, the 1996–1999 Bound Supplement, the April 2002 Semi–Annual Cumulative Supplement, and the August 2002 Cumulative Supplement.

### 3. LOCATING THE ENTRY FOR THE CASE WITHIN EACH VOLUME

Now that you have gathered all the books you need, you are ready to begin looking up the citation to the original case. The entries in a Shepard's volume are organized numerically, first by reporter volume number and then by the starting page number of each case, as shown in Figure 5.3.

Remember that some Shepard's sets cover more than one reporter. For example, *Shepard's New Jersey Citations* will contain references both to New Jersey's official reporter (*New Jersey Superior Court Reports*) and West's *Atlantic Reporter*. If you are using a Shepard's set covering multiple reporters, be sure to look in the section of the Shepard's volume covering the correct reporter for your citation.

Because Shepard's is not cumulative, you must repeat this process in each book you collected. Each volume covers only a specific time period, so it is important to check each one for references to the original case.

### 4. INTERPRETING THE ENTRIES

Once you have located an entry for the original case, you will need to decipher the list of numbers and letters that you find. The entry for the original case will contain a list of abbreviated citations to the citing sources (the other cases and secondary sources that have cited the original case). As shown in Figure 5.4, this information can be divided into two categories: the history of the case and the citations to the case.

The section of the entry containing the history of the original case will give you citations to decisions emanating from the same lawsuit. For example, if the original case has a parallel citation in another reporter, that citation will be listed first in parentheses.

**FIGURE 5.2**   "WHAT YOUR LIBRARY SHOULD CONTAIN"

| VOL. 87 | AUGUST 2002 | NO. 8 |

# SHEPARD'S ATLANTIC REPORTER CITATIONS

Cumulative Supplement

Check all five sources to Shepardize a case published in the *Atlantic Reporter.*

**WHAT YOUR LIBRARY SHOULD CONTAIN**

1994 Bound Volume, (Parts 1-8)
1994–1996 Bound Supplement
1996–1999 Bound Supplement*

*Supplemented with:
   –April 2002 Semi-Annual Cumulative Supplement
      Vol. 87 No. 4
   –August 2002 Cumulative Supplement Vol. 87 No. 8

**DISCARD ALL OTHER ISSUES**

LexisNexis™

Reproduced by permission of LexisNexis. Further reproduction of any kind is strictly prohibited. From *Shepard's Atlantic Reporter Citations*, Vol. 87, No. 8 (Aug. 2002), cover page.

**FIGURE 5.3** EXCERPT FROM *SHEPARD'S ATLANTIC REPORTER CITATIONS*

| Vol. 497 | | ATLANTIC REPORTER, 2d SERIES | | |
|---|---|---|---|---|
| **—1206—** | 523A2d¹24 | **—1242—** | **—1267—** | **—1291—** |
| Mayer v | d 529A2d949 | New | Robsac | New Jersey v |
| Hampton | 530A2d¹779 | Hampshire v | Industries | Sharkey |
| 1985 | 567A2d989 | Champagne | Inc. v | 1985 |
| | 571A2d1278 | 1985 | Chartpak | |
| (127NH81) | 591A2d1327 | | 1985 | (204NJS192) |
| 623A2d¹756 | 618A2d824 | (127NH266) | | 524A2d¹226 |
| **Reporter volume** | Ala | s 519A2d310 | (204NJS149) | 539A2d¹771 |
| | 529So2d1057 | 519A2d271 | f 563A2d¹41 | Iowa |
| **—1212—** | | 523A2d¹78 | Cir. 3 | 414NW94 |
| New | **—1221—** | 622A2d³1219 | 631FS⁴559 | 84A2d950n |
| Hampshire v | Dimick v Lewis | 33A21062s | | |
| Sprague | 1985 | | **—1272—** | **—1296—** |
| 1985 | | **—1249—** | In the Matter | New Jersey |
| | (127NH141) | In the Matter | of Repeal of | v Garcia |
| (127NH97) | c 532A2d⁵1389 | of Silber | N.J.A.C. 6:28 | 1985 |
| | c 532A2d⁶1389 | 1985 | 1985 | |
| **—1214—** | 547A2d¹289 | | | (204NJS202) |
| Rohde v | Ala | (100NJ517) | (204NJS158) | s 511A2d636 |
| First Deposit | 581So2d789 | 509A2d²175 | 530A2d²330 | |
| National Bank | Utah | 526A2d²665 | d 592A2d³12 | **—1298—** |
| 1985 | 765P2d868 | | 603A2d²971 | In the Matter |
| | | **—1251—** | | of D.K. |
| (127NH107) | **—1224—** | In the Matter | **—1276—** | 1985 |
| Cir. 6 | New | of Edwards | K.P. v Albanese | |
| 778FS²953 | Hampshire | 1985 | 1985 | (204NJS205) |
| Cir. 9 | v LaRose | | | 97A3780s |
| 867F2d¹525 | 1985 | (100NJ522) | (204NJS166) | |
| 867F2d²525 | | | s 508A2d225 | **—1310—** |
| c 867F2d¹526 | (127NH146) | **—1255—** | d 506A2d¹¹1294 | Kenney v |
| N J | 506A2d¹⁹348 | In the Matter | 530A2d⁴328 | Scientific Inc. |
| 521A2d³870 | 531A2d⁸331 | of Goer | 573A2d²981 | 1985 |
| R I | 552A2d592 | 1985 | 583A2d¹779 | |
| 525A2d²918 | d 581A2d73 | | 583A2d²780 | (204NJS228) |
| Ariz | 581A2d²674 | (100NJ529) | 591A2d1018 | s 512A2d1142 |
| 797P2d702 | 621A2d¹⁴443 | | j 599A2d528 | 506A2d¹⁴827 |
| Calif | 621A2d¹⁵443 | **—1258—** | 604A2d³966 | 511A2d¹³¹301 |
| 268CaR373 | | In the Matter | 604A2d¹967 | 530A2d¹⁴806 |
| Fla | **—1232—** | of Souder | | 538A2d¹455 |
| 513So2d1295 | Davis v | 1984 | **—1284—** | f 541A2d296 |
| 513So2d1297 | Barrington | | New Jersey | 546A2d575 |
| Mass | 1985 | (204NJS132) | v Davis | 558A2d482 |
| 564NE581 | | | 1985 | f 569A2d911 |
| Okla | (127NH202) | **—1265—** | | 587A2d1257 |
| 809P2d1303 | 534A2d³384 | 534 Hawthorne | (204NJS181) | 595A2d³²540 |
| | 567A2d⁵1002 | Avenue Corp. v | s 517A2d388 | 595A2d³⁴540 |
| **—1217—** | 11A2524s | Barnes | 560A2d²653 | 595A2d³⁵540 |
| New | | 1985 | 582A2d839 | e 595A2d541 |
| Hampshire v | **—1237—** | | 43A3385s | 608A2d⁴²72 |
| Whiting | Fielders v | (204NJS144) | | Cir. 3 |
| 1985 | Cunningham | 520A2d³1153 | **—1287—** | 896F2d770 |
| | 1985 | 544A2d⁶391 | Alling Street | 655FS1264 |
| (127NH110) | | 546A2d⁵588 | Urban Renewal | 711FS804 |
| | (127NH211) | d 550A2d⁴1225 | Co. v Newark | d 711FS807 |
| **—1218—** | | d 550A2d⁶1225 | 1985 | 730FS634 |
| New | **—1239—** | 559A2d³1364 | | d 811FS²⁷1053 |
| Hampshire | Corliss v Mary | 559A2d⁴1365 | (204NJS185) | Cir. 6 |
| v Westover | Hitchcock | 561A2d²694 | s 511A2d653 | 853F2d²⁵412 |
| 1985 | Memorial | 568A2d⁵543 | 543A2d13 | S C |
| | Hospital | 590A2d¹1216 | | 434SE308 |
| (127NH130) | 1985 | 628A2d⁵806 | | Wis |
| 517A2d¹1166 | | | | 476NW605 |
| | (127NH225) | | | 78A3910s |
| | 614A2d604 | | | 86A2614n |
| | | | | 86A2633n |

| **—1330—** |
|---|
| Case 1 |
| Pennsylvania |
| v Zaengle |
| 1985 |
| |
| (508Pa355) |
| s 480A2d1224 |
| s 497A2d1335 |

**Reporter name—check this when using a set of Shepard's covering multiple reporters**

| ... |
|---|
| 1985 |
| |
| (508Pa355) |
| s 491A2d237 |
| |
| **—1330—** |
| Case 3 |
| Watrel v |
| Pennsylvania |
| Department |
| of Education |
| 1985 |
| |
| (508Pa356) |
| s 488A2d378 |
| s 518A2d1158 |
| |
| **—1330—** |
| Case 4 |
| Pennsylvania |

**Starting page number of the case**

| ... |
|---|
| (508Pa356) |
| s 489A2d984 |
| |
| **—1331—** |
| Case 1 |
| Spitler v Spitler |
| 1985 |
| |
| (508Pa357) |
| s 491A2d927 |

108

Reproduced by permission of LexisNexis. Further reproduction of any kind is strictly prohibited. From *Shepard's Atlantic Reporter Citations*, 1994 Bound Volume, Part 8, p. 108.

**FIGURE 5.4** SHEPARD'S ENTRY FOR *KENNEY v. SCIENTIFIC, INC.*

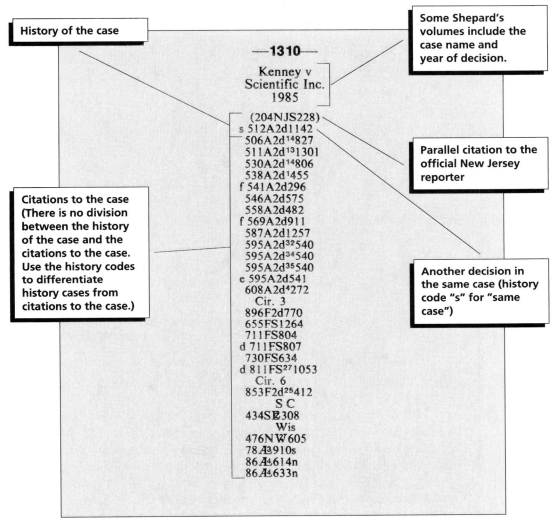

Reproduced by permission of LexisNexis. Further reproduction of any kind is strictly prohibited. From *Shepard's Atlantic Reporter Citations*, 1994 Bound Volume, Part 8, p.108.

If the original case has been reversed or affirmed, or if other decisions in the same case have been published, that information will also be listed as part of the history. These citations will be preceded by letters that form a code to help you determine what happened in the history of the case. A list of the most common history codes appears in Figure 5.5. A complete list of history codes appears in the front of each Shepard's volume.

The page numbers of the citations in the history section refer to the starting page of the citing source.

**FIGURE 5.5** SHEPARD'S® CASE HISTORY CODES

| CASE HISTORY CODES | MEANING |
| --- | --- |
| (citation in parentheses) | parallel citation to the same decision in another reporter |
| a | affirmed by a higher court |
| r | reversed by a higher court |
| m | ruling modified (usually means affirmed in part and reversed in part) |
| cc | connected case (decision either involves the same parties or arises out of the same subject matter, but is not identical to the lawsuit in the original case) |
| s | same case (decision involving the identical lawsuit as the original case, but at a different stage of the proceedings; often appears in the history of an appellate case to identify the trial court's decision) |
| v | vacated (the opinion has been rendered void and no longer has any precedential value) |
| US Cert. Den. | United States Supreme Court denied certiorari |

Following the history of the case, you will find a list of the citing sources that have cited the original case. See Figure 5.6. When you Shepardize a federal case, the citing sources will appear in this order: (1) federal cases divided according to circuit; (2) state cases listed alphabetically by state; and (3) secondary sources. When you Shepardize a state case, the list of citing sources will begin with cases from the same state as the original case. Then you will see federal cases by circuit, cases from other states, and secondary sources.

Note that the page numbers in the citations here are pinpoint citations to the specific pages on which the original case is cited, not the beginning pages of the citing sources.

Citing sources that have treated the original case in a way that may affect its validity will be marked with letters called treatment codes. A list of the more common treatment codes appears in Figure 5.7. A complete list of treatment codes appears in the front of each volume of Shepard's.

Citing sources that discuss the original case for a particular proposition of law will be identified by a superscript number appearing immediately after the reporter abbreviation, as Figure 5.8 shows. These are references to the headnotes in the original case. In the example citation,

**FIGURE 5.6**   SHEPARD'S® ENTRY FOR *KENNEY v. SCIENTIFIC, INC.*

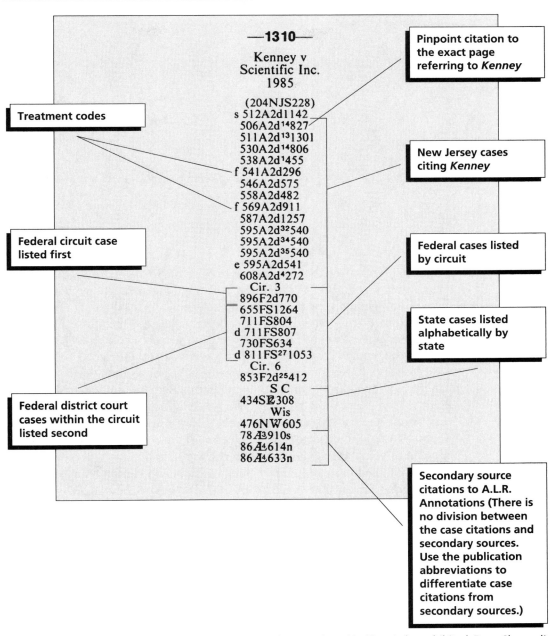

Reproduced by permission of LexisNexis. Further reproduction of any kind is strictly prohibited. From *Shepard's Atlantic Reporter Citations*, 1994 Bound Volume, Part 8, p. 108.

*Kenney* discusses a point of law that is summarized in headnote 13. A citing source, published in volume 511 of the *Atlantic Reporter*, Second Series, at page 1301, has cited *Kenney* for the same proposition of law summarized in headnote 13. Thus, the Shepard's entry includes the

**FIGURE 5.7**   SHEPARD'S® CASE TREATMENT CODES

| CASE TREATMENT CODES | MEANING |
|:---:|:---|
| c | criticized |
| d | distinguished |
| e | explained |
| f | followed |
| j | cited in a dissenting opinion |
| o | overruled |
| q | questioned |

superscript 13 after the reporter abbreviation for the citing source. The illustrations in Figures 5.9 through 5.11 trace a headnote from an original case to a Shepard's entry to a citing source.

The Shepard's entry for the original case may be quite long. The history and treatment codes and the headnote references will help you narrow down the cases you need to review to update your research. If you are only interested in determining whether your case is still good law, you should look primarily for negative history and treatment codes that might cause you to question whether the case continues to be authoritative. If you are looking for additional authority, favorable treatment codes and headnote references will help you identify the cases most likely to be relevant to your research.

If you look in a volume of Shepard's and do not find any entry for the original case, this means the original case was not cited during the time period covered by that volume. Before you conclude that the original case is still good law, however, you may want to check that you have the correct citation and that you are looking in the section of the Shepard's volume that covers the correct reporter.

## C. WHEN TO USE A CITATOR IN CASE RESEARCH

You must check every case on which you rely to answer a legal question to make sure it is still good law. In general, you will want to use Shepard's or another citator early in your research, after you have identified what appear to be a few key cases, to make sure you do not build your analysis on authority that is no longer valid. Using a citator at this stage will also help direct you to other relevant authorities. You should also check

**FIGURE 5.8**   SHEPARD'S® ENTRY FOR *KENNEY v. SCIENTIFIC, INC.*

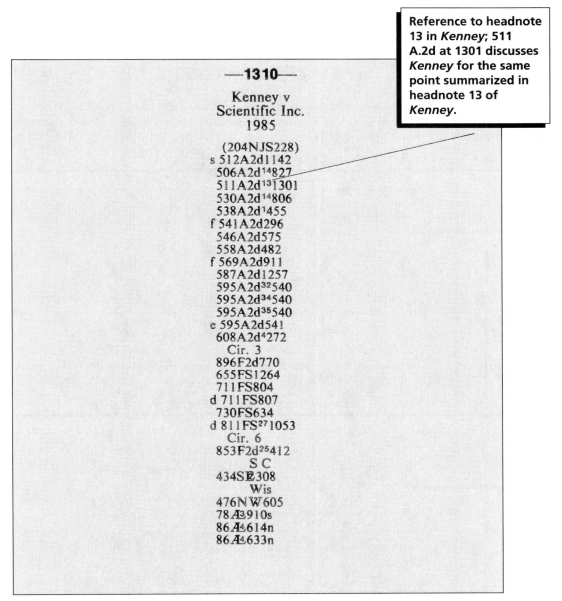

> **Reference to headnote 13 in *Kenney*; 511 A.2d at 1301 discusses *Kenney* for the same point summarized in headnote 13 of *Kenney*.**

—**1310**—

Kenney v
Scientific Inc.
1985

(204NJS228)
s 512A2d1142
506A2d¹⁴827
511A2d¹³1301
530A2d¹⁴806
538A2d¹455
f 541A2d296
546A2d575
558A2d482
f 569A2d911
587A2d1257
595A2d³²540
595A2d³⁴540
595A2d³⁵540
e 595A2d541
608A2d⁴272
Cir. 3
896F2d770
655FS1264
711FS804
d 711FS807
730FS634
d 811FS²⁷1053
Cir. 6
853F2d²⁵412
S C
434SE308
Wis
476NW605
78A3910s
86A4614n
86A4633n

Reproduced by permission of LexisNexis. Further reproduction of any kind is strictly prohibited. From *Shepard's Atlantic Reporter Citations*, 1994 Bound Volume, Part 8, p. 108.

**FIGURE 5.9**     HEADNOTE 13 FROM THE ORIGINAL CASE, *KENNEY v. SCIENTIFIC, INC.*

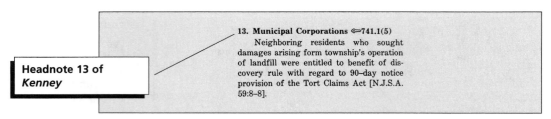

Reprinted with permission from West Group, West's *Atlantic Reporter,* 2d Ser., Vol. 497, *Kenney v. Scientific, Inc.,* 497 A.2d 1310, 1311 (N.J. Super L. Div. 1985).

**FIGURE 5.10**     SHEPARD'S® ENTRY FOR *KENNEY v. SCIENTIFIC, INC.*

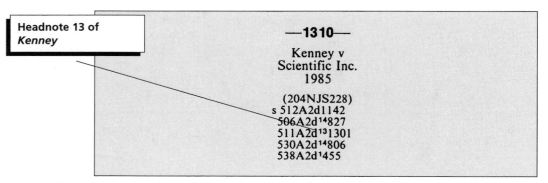

Reproduced by permission of LexisNexis. Further reproduction of any kind is strictly prohibited. From *Shepard's Atlantic Reporter Citations*, 1994 Bound Volume, Part 8, p. 108.

**FIGURE 5.11**     *SERVIS v. STATE,* CITING *KENNEY v. SCIENTIFIC, INC.*

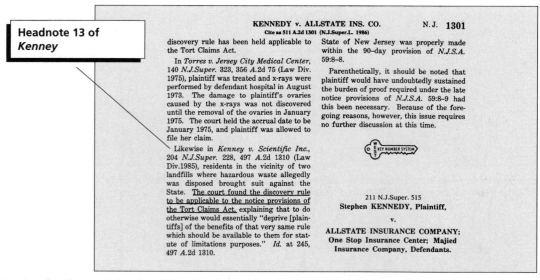

Reprinted with permission from West Group, West's *Atlantic Reporter,* 2d Ser., Vol. 511, *Servis v. State,* 511 A.2d 1299, 1301 (N.J. Super. L. Div. 1986).

every case you cite before handing in your work to make sure each one continues to be authoritative. Citing bad authority is every attorney's nightmare, and failing to check your citations can constitute professional malpractice. As a consequence, now is the time to get in the habit of updating your case research carefully.

## D. SHEPARD'S FOR ADDITIONAL TYPES OF AUTHORITY

So far, this chapter has been devoted to the process of Sheparidizing cases. Shepard's publishes a wide variety of citators, however, for almost every legal resource. Figure 5.12 lists some examples of the types of Shepard's citators available.

In general, whenever you learn to use a new research tool, you should find out whether there is a corresponding set of Shepard's. If so, Shepard's will help you locate additional authority and may help you determine the validity of the authority you have already located.

**FIGURE 5.12**  SHEPARD'S® CITATORS

| SHEPARD'S SET | ALLOWS YOU TO SHEPARDIZE . . . |
|---|---|
| Shepard's for individual states | State statutes (and sometimes administrative materials) in addition to state cases |
| Shepard's Federal Statute Citations | Federal statutes |
| Shepard's Code of Federal Regulations Citations | Federal administrative regulations |
| Shepard's Restatement of the Law Citations | Sections of the Restatement |
| Shepard's Law Review Citations | Law review and journal articles that are cited in court opinions |
| Shepard's Citations for Annotations | A.L.R. Annotations that are cited in court opinions |
| Shepard's for specific subject areas | Citations specific to the subject area. For example, in Shepard's Environmental Law Citations, you can Shepardize citations to federal decisions on environmental law, federal environmental statutes, and administrative regulations and executive orders on environmental law. |

The process of Shepardizing other forms of authority is the same as that for Shepardizing cases. The entries you find within the Shepard's volumes, however, will vary depending on the source. For example, Shepard's statutory citators do not contain a code for reversal because statutes cannot be "reversed." Instead, the codes for statutes indicate, for example, whether the statute has been repealed or held unconstitutional. You can always find a sample Shepard's entry and a list of abbreviations at the beginning of each Shepard's volume to help you interpret the entries for the set you are using.

## E. CHECKING CITATIONS ELECTRONICALLY

Shepard's is available electronically in LexisNexis, but not in Westlaw. Westlaw has its own citator service called KeyCite. Each of these services is discussed in turn.

### 1. USING SHEPARD'S IN LEXISNEXIS

A variety of authorities can be Shepardized electronically in LexisNexis, including cases, statutes, and administrative materials. Shepard's in Lexis-Nexis contains the same type of information you would find in the print version. Nevertheless, there are some differences between Shepard's in LexisNexis and Shepard's in print. Shepard's in LexisNexis is current within twenty-four hours, so it is more up to date than print versions of Shepard's. In addition, LexisNexis allows you to view the complete Shepard's entry or a restricted entry with limited information. For cases, Shepard's in LexisNexis does not automatically show headnote references, although you can find them using the Custom Restrictions function.

Shepard's is linked with other services in LexisNexis. For example, if you retrieve a case from LexisNexis, a notation at the beginning will indicate whether Shepard's contains an entry for it and, if so, what type of treatment the case has received. These notations are called Shepard's Signals. The Shepard's Signal will also appear at the beginning of the Shepard's entry for the case. LexisNexis's definitions of these signals are explained in Figure 5.13.

It is often difficult to reduce the history of a case to a single notation. Determining the continued validity of a decision often requires study of the later cases. For example, a case with a negative Shepard's Signal such as a red stop sign may no longer be good law for one of its points, but it may continue to be authoritative on other points. If you were to rely on the red stop sign without further inquiry, you might miss a case that is important for the issue you are researching. As a consequence, although Shepard's Signals can be helpful research tools, you should not rely on them in deciding whether a case is valid. Always research the

**FIGURE 5.13** SHEPARD'S® SIGNALS

| SIGNAL | MEANS |
|---|---|
| Red stop sign | The case has been reversed, overruled, or otherwise given very negative treatment. |
| Yellow triangle | The case has received some negative treatment, such as being limited or criticized, but has not been reversed or overruled. |
| Blue circle surrounding the letter A | The case has received treatment that is neither positive nor negative. |
| Blue circle surrounding the letter I | The case has been cited, but no history or treatment codes have been assigned to the citing sources. |
| Green diamond surrounding a plus sign | The case has received positive treatment, such as being affirmed or followed. |

Shepard's entry and review the citing sources carefully to satisfy yourself about the status of a case.

Figure 5.14 shows part of a Shepard's entry in LexisNexis.

## 2. USING KEYCITE IN WESTLAW

Westlaw provides its own citator service called KeyCite. KeyCite is available for cases, statutes, and administrative materials. It is similar to Shepard's in the information it provides, although it is more up to date than Shepard's in print because as soon as an authority is added to Westlaw's databases, KeyCite is updated to reflect the new information.

A KeyCite entry for a case begins with the full citation to the case and its complete direct history. After the direct history, any negative indirect history is listed. If the original case has negative indirect history, you may notice that some of the negative citations are followed by one or more stars. The star categories indicate how much discussion of the original case you will find in the citing case. There are four star categories: (a) examined (four stars); (b) discussed (three stars); (c) cited (two stars); and (d) mentioned (one star). Figure 5.15 delineates how West defines these terms.

In addition to case history, KeyCite provides a variety of research references to the original case. To locate research references, you may want to review a segment of the KeyCite entry called KC Citing Ref, which contains citations to the case. Negative cases are listed first, followed by positive cases and secondary sources. In addition, if the original case has been quoted, quotation marks will appear after the entry. You can go directly to the quoted language by clicking on the quotation marks.

KeyCite is linked with cases in Westlaw's databases with a notation

**FIGURE 5.14**   SHEPARD'S® ENTRY EXCERPT IN LEXISNEXIS FOR 552 A.2d 258

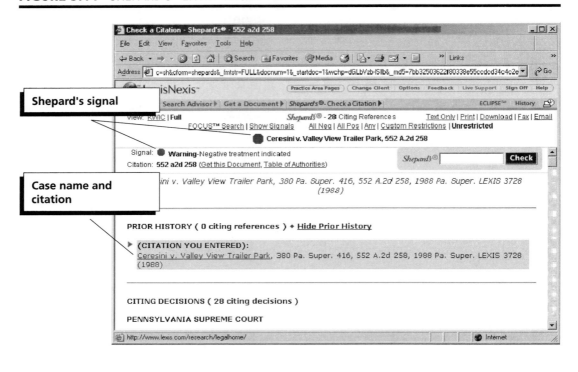

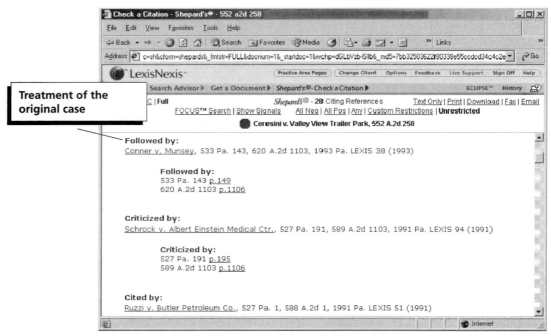

Reprinted with permission of LexisNexis. SHEPARD'S® entry for 552 A.2d 258.

**FIGURE 5.15** DEFINITIONS OF KEYCITE STAR CATEGORIES

| NUMBER OF STARS | MEANING | DEFINED |
|---|---|---|
| Four stars | Examined | Contains an extended discussion of the original case, usually more than a printed page of text |
| Three stars | Discussed | Contains a substantial discussion of the original case, usually more than one paragraph but less than a printed page |
| Two stars | Cited | Contains some discussion of the original case, usually less than a paragraph |
| One star | Mentioned | Contains a brief reference to the original case, usually in a string citation |

system similar to Shepard's Signals in LexisNexis. If a case has a KeyCite entry, a notation called a "status flag" will appear at the beginning of both the case and the KeyCite entry to give you some indication of the case's treatment in KeyCite. West's definitions of the status flags are explained in Figure 5.16.

Like Shepard's Signals, KeyCite status flags are useful research tools, but cannot substitute for your own assessment of the continued validity of a case. You should always research the KeyCite entry and review the citing sources carefully to satisfy yourself about the status of a case.

Figure 5.17 shows an excerpt from a KeyCite entry.

**FIGURE 5.16** WESTLAW STATUS FLAGS INDICATING KEYCITE HISTORY

| NOTATION | MEANS |
|---|---|
| Red flag | The case is no longer good law for at least one of the points it contains. |
| Yellow flag | The case has some negative history, but has not been reversed or overruled. |
| Blue H | The case has some history that is not known to be negative. |
| Green C | The case has citing references, but no direct or negative indirect history. |

**FIGURE 5.17**   KEYCITE ENTRY EXCERPT FOR 552 A.2d 258

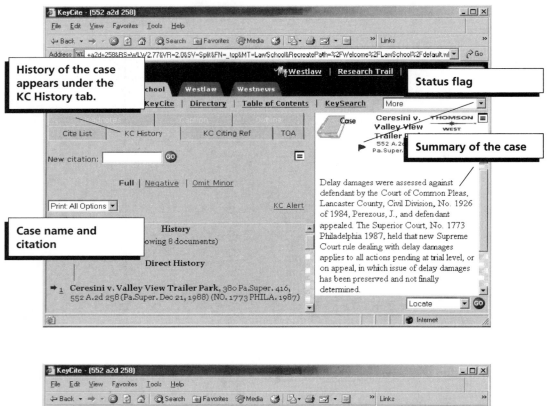

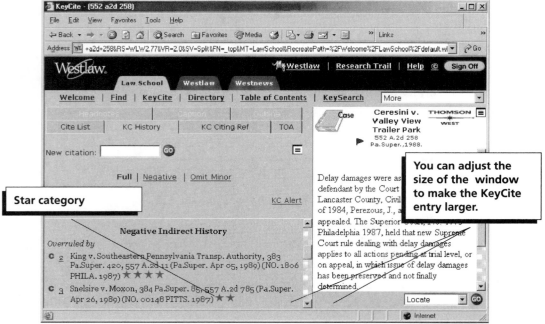

**FIGURE 5.17**   KEYCITE ENTRY EXCERPT FOR 552 A.2d 258 *(Continued)*

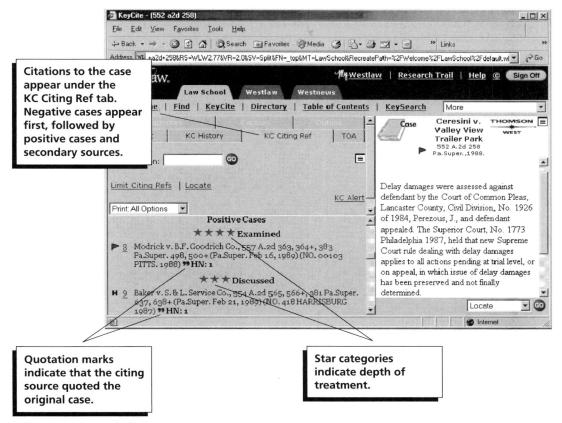

Reprinted with permission from West Group, from Westlaw, KeyCite entry for 552 A.2d 258.

## F. SAMPLE PAGES FOR SHEPARDIZING A CASE IN PRINT

Beginning on the next page, Figures 5.18 through 5.23 contain sample pages illustrating the process of Shepardizing a case in print. The case in this example is *Pennsylvania v. Smith*, 615 A.2d 321 (Pa. 1992). The first step in the process would be identifying the correct set of Shepard's for this citation. Because this case is published in the *Atlantic Reporter*, Second Series, you could use *Shepard's Atlantic Reporter Citations*. The sample pages show the entries for this case in *Shepard's Atlantic Reporter Citations*.

Once you locate Shepard's *Atlantic Reporter Citations,* you need to find the most recent supplement, which in this example is a pamphlet dated August 2002. Use the "What Your Library Should Contain" section on the front cover to identify the necessary volumes of Shepard's. This section says to use the 1994 Bound Volumes, the 1994–1996 Bound Supplement, the 1996–1999 Bound Supplement, the April 2002 Semi-Annual Cumulative Supplement, and the August 2002 Cumulative Supplement to Shepardize this citation.

**FIGURE 5.18**   "WHAT YOUR LIBRARY SHOULD CONTAIN"

**Within the August 2002 Cumulative Supplement, turn to the section with references to Volume 615 of the *Atlantic Reporter*, Second Series, and look for a reference to starting page 321. In this example, you find three references to the original case.**

**FIGURE 5.19** AUGUST 2002 CUMULATIVE SUPPLEMENT ENTRY FOR 615 A.2d 321

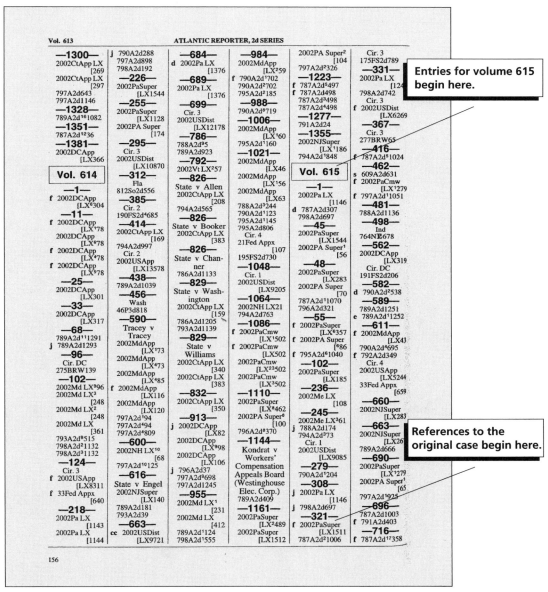

Reproduced by permission of LexisNexis. Further reproduction of any kind is strictly prohibited. From *Shepard's Atlantic Reporter Citations*, Vol. 87, No. 8 (August 2002), p. 156.

**The next step is looking up the citation in the April 2002 Semi-Annual Cumulative Supplement. In the section covering volume 615 of the *Atlantic Reporter*, Second Series, the entry under starting page 321 indicates that this case was cited a number of times during the period covered by this supplement.**

**FIGURE 5.20**   APRIL 2002 SEMI-ANNUAL CUMULATIVE SUPPLEMENT ENTRY FOR 615 A.2d 321

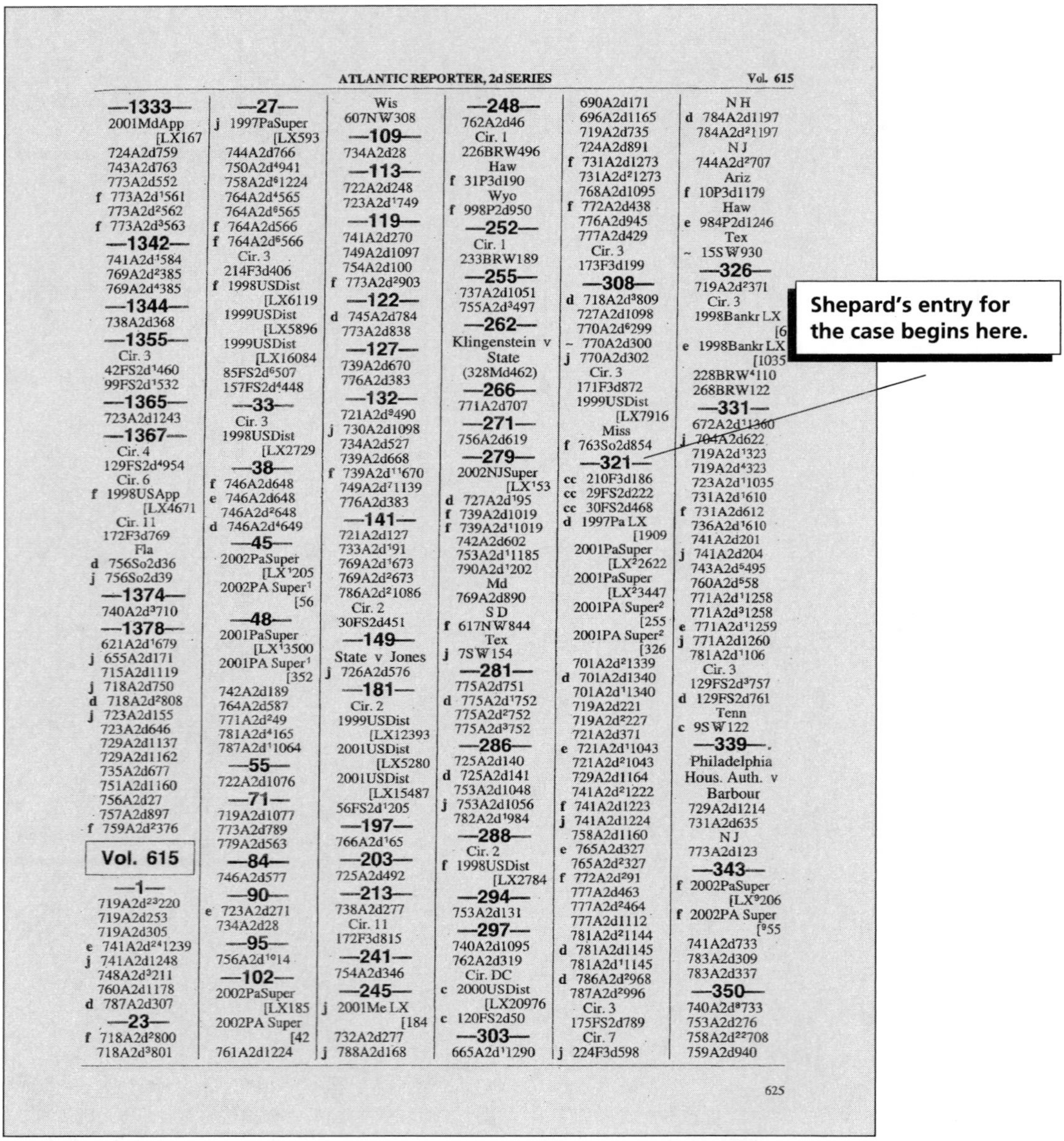

ATLANTIC REPORTER, 2d SERIES                                                      Vol. 615

Shepard's entry for the case begins here.

**The third step is looking up the citation in the 1996–1999 Bound Supplement. The entry here lists several additional citations to the case.**

**FIGURE 5.21** 1996–1999 BOUND SUPPLEMENT ENTRY FOR 615 A.2d 321

Vol. 615     ATLANTIC REPORTER, 2d SERIES

References to the original case

```
W V                 674A2d1041          —326—              Cir. 3             —505—              —611—
468SE322            690A2d171           684A2d²1053        f 105F3d148        675A2d898          693A2d826
50A2d661n           696A2d1165          Cir. 3             105F3d²148                            693A2d⁴830
                    j 697A2d585         204BRW¹888         j 105F3d151        —507—              693A2d⁸831
—248—               701A2d¹1331         216BRW¹383                            Case 1             f 702A2d439
679A2d1082          e 711A2d618         221BRW¹352         —408—              668A2d1349         ~ 707A2d820
f 715A2d937         j 711A2d624         221BRW⁴352         683A2d⁵676         710A2d814          Cir. 4
Cir. 1                                  Del                                                      202BRW³577
64F3d10             —308—               685A2d²364         —416—              —507—              D C
N J                 669A2d¹²328                            715A2d⁵461         Case 2             d 668A2d851
704A2d47            675A2d⁹1280         —331—                                 627A2d479          Tex
                    676A2d1220          672A2d¹1360        —423—              f 643A2d⁴288       936SW497
—252—               684A2d¹²645         681A2d¹788         Cir. 3             Iowa
Alk                 685A2d⁹156          686A2d³1305        970FS402           559NW9             —629—
904P2d415           690A2d⁹296          691A2d957                                                668A2d39
Fla                 690A2d¹²298         696A2d⁵1171        —432—              —530—              d 668A2d40
701So2d666          690A2d⁸1236         j 704A2d622        677A2d843          Case 11            Cir. 1
Wyo                 692A2d1035          Cir. 3             e 677A2d844        US cert den        922FS²704
920P2d660           699A2d1255          967FS²840          711A2d²1026        121LE694           922FS³704
                    701A2d⁷571          967FS³840          711A2d⁷1027        US cert den        988FS25
—253—               709A2d364           Miss               f 717A2d476        113SC823
709A2d732           711A2d475           c 692So2d100                                             —635—
S C                 714A2d⁹1037                            —438—              —533—              ~ 696A2d1123
471SE745            Cir. 3              —337—              682A2d⁵1292        672A2d²1073        697A2d936
                    903FS¹²861          Case 2             682A2d⁶1292        673A2d664
—255—               957FS⁸589           672A2d321          Cir. 3             675A2d52           —647—
698A2d³1062                                                908FS274           680A2d374          671A2d651
                    —321—               —338—              939FS⁴1194         j 694A2d446        678A2d³245
—261—               cc 87F3d108         Case 2                                Conn
Cir. 4              684A2d¹180          702A2d1082         —442—              694A2d1257         —660—
897FS236            684A2d²181                             677A2d339          Mich               f 682A2d³280
                    ~ 684A2d185         —339—              703A2d423          j 579NW131
—262—               d 685A2d101         Case 1                                                   —663—
Case 8              699A2d714           668A2d548          —452—              —555—              673A2d¹317
s 126LE259          701A2d²501         Cir. 3             715A2d446          683A2d762          685A2d⁷957
s 114SC312          701A2d²1339         221BRW351                                                694A2d247
                    d 701A2d1340                           —459—              —562—              Cir. 3
—264—               701A2d¹1340         —343—              673A2d⁹371         cc 683A2d1371      973FS470
670A2d¹590          702A2d²1032         672A2d²1334                           667A2d1348
692A2d999           712A2d²773                             —469—              691A2d65           —676—
                    f 712A2d²774        —350—              Minn               e 704A2d1201       703A2d397
—266—               Cir. 3              cc 903FS852        585NW67            704A2d¹¹1201       Cir. 3
677A2d303           f 962FS1552         682A2d⁵816         Ohio               Cir. DC            891FS¹¹1031
                    Me                  e 682A2d843        673NE1343          84F3d477           913FS³843
—279—               681A2d475           696A2d833                             j 93F3d948         913FS⁷844
l 672A2d1278        Ga                                     —476—              899FS⁷666          991FS435
672A2d1278          c 492SE920          —367—              706A2d²1316                           187BRW157
687A2d344           Iowa                Cir. 3                                 —582—
701A2d¹960          541NW539            212BRW⁷85          —481—              669A2d1294         —690—
Mass                j 541NW542                             680A2d69           f 669A2d1296       700A2d¹942
667NE267            Mass                —382—              f 695A2d1008       669A2d1297         f 700A2d943
694NE349            d 685NE1166         686A2d²831                                               712A2d¹335
Tex                 Nebr                Cir. 3             —484—              —586—              f 715A2d1138
947SW711            d 579NW549          894FS⁷190          680A2d¹102         717A2d328          j 715A2d1140
f 966SW813          N M                 S D                680A2d²⁴109
                    e 930P2d798         j 543NW794         707A2d⁶274         —589—              —696—
—286—               N D                                    707A2d⁶279         700A2d769          682A2d330
713A2d491           j 545NW159          —390—              N M                                   ~ 682A2d333
                    Tex                 693A2d⁶241         948P2d271          —600—              689A2d899
—288—               957SW12             d 699A2d727                           Cir. 1             j 700A2d1272
677A2d775           j 957SW22                              —498—              116F3d5            ~ 700A2d1281
Cir. 3              977SW581            —398—              671A2d¹1267        221BRW293          703A2d⁹1053
962FS605            j 977SW583          US cert den        692A2d395          221BRW⁸297
                    Wis                 130LE32            N Y                                   —704—
—303—               585NW180            US cert den        f 671NYS2d924      —608—              674A2d223
667A2d1190                              115SC78            44A2d218n          672A2d¹600         677A2d¹⁴325
671A2d¹762                                                                                       d 688A2d¹¹1168

600
```

**The fourth step is looking up the citation in the 1994–1996 Bound Supplement. The entry here lists further citations to the case.**

**FIGURE 5.22**   1994–1996 BOUND SUPPLEMENT ENTRY FOR 615 A.2d 321

| ATLANTIC REPORTER, 2d SERIES | | | | Vol. 615 |
|---|---|---|---|---|

—236—
658A2d235
Mont
903P2d189

—239—
635A2d961
639A2d620
642A2d855
642A2d1336
644A2d456
644A2d467
644A2d1382
649A2d1100
650A2d939
651A2d372
653A2d893
656A2d1224
663A2d1254
666A2d74

—241—
652A2d⁴651
655A2d⁴342
655A2d⁴364
657A2d⁴780

—245—
638A2d⁸720
641A2d⁸865
651A2d823
653A2d²419

—248—
661A2d²1140
Cir. 1
865FS²37
Okla
874P2d810

—252—
Alk
904P2d415

—279—
652A2d198
N M
868P2d670
884P2d517
Tex
888SW919

—281—
s 658A2d1317
666A2d1010

—286—
649A2d70

—297—
651A2d1084

—303—
f 640A2d¹890
646A2d¹691
647A2d¹977
648A2d585

656A2d¹107
f 657A2d¹1262
665A2d¹1290
j 666A2d252
667A2d1190
Cir. 3
f 4F3d234

—308—
j 637A2d272
646A2d¹588
650A2d¹²471
651A2d³139
651A2d²141
e 651A2d142
651A2d1130
658A2d⁷354
662A2d⁹1143
665A2d436
669A2d¹²328

—321—
cc 856FS229
cc 879FS436
cc 887FS752
648A2d923
f 648A2d⁵50
648A2d²52
650A2d90
652A2d322
j 662A2d1059
665A2d²1243
d 665A2d1244
Cir. 3
855FS733
Tex
j 880SW509

—326—
f 637A2d1365
655A2d127
666A2d²343

—331—
635A2d¹1050
653A2d⁵636
657A2d1315
Cir. 3
j 12F3d397
869FS1212
158FRD72

—339—
Case 1
660A2d1361
668A2d548
Cir. 2
166BRW810

—342—
cc 638A2d255
Cir. 3
859FS¹169

—343—
638A2d996
638A2d⁷997

640A2d²917
664A2d996

—350—
650A2d²⁵467
653A2d⁶709

—367—
647A2d¹578
j 648A2d579
653A2d¹642
Cir. 3
865FS⁷254

—372—
657A2d939
Ariz
d 883P2d452

—382—
636A2d⁶180
f 648A2d⁷1217
Cir. 9
878FS⁶1377
878FS²1379
878FS⁴1379

—390—
638A2d⁴967
646A2d1241
646A2d1245
j 653A2d33

—408—
639A2d⁷813
639A2d²816
639A2d³816
639A2d⁴816
639A2d⁷820
647A2d924
652A2d¹363
658A2d⁴823
Cir. 3
j 15F3d310

—416—
661A2d1393

—423—
647A2d553

—432—
665A2d476
f 666A2d659

—438—
655A2d127
Cir. 3
182BRW⁵721

—452—
648A2d²1206

—477—
f 650A2d497
651A2d1221

—484—
658A2d940
665A2d570

—498—
(159Vt31)

—505—
(224Ct1)
d 636A2d806
652A2d527

—507—
Case 1
(223Ct920)
637A2d806
668A2d1349

—507—
Case 2
s 664A2d826
f 643A2d⁴288

—512—
641A2d434
650A2d594

—533—
663A2d1221
665A2d193

—562—
cc 645A2d594
638A2d668
f 638A2d¹⁴671
667A2d1348
Wyo
881P2d287

—582—
642A2d¹123
644A2d¹448
669A2d1294
f 669A2d1296
669A2d1297

—586—
647A2d791
649A2d311

—594—
635A2d1287

—605—
637A2d²111
f 637A2d⁴112

—608—
s 649A2d20
656A2d²1216

—611—
637A2d491
644A2d514
656A2d⁸1235
Cir. DC
881FS26

Cir. 4
181BRW839
D C
d 668A2d851
Ind
633NE270

—625—
f 635A2d452

—629—
635A2d⁴1389
653A2d1121
662A2d⁵276
662A2d299
668A2d39
d 668A2d40
24A.2220n

—635—
639A2d245
652A2d679
j 652A2d1208
665A2d1075

—637—
638A2d⁴789
639A2d²244
639A2d⁴245
659A2d429

—644—
d 636A2d608
Iowa
533NW207

—647—
r 649A2d71
s 639A2d303

—654—
656A2d²1307
d 656A2d1309

—660—
638A2d891

—663—
643A2d⁷569
650A2d⁷1007
652A2d769

—676—
Cir. 3
834FS¹151
834FS¹⁰152
187BRW157

—686—
647A2d486
666A2d602

—690—
j 650A2d872

—696—
637A2d623

f 637A2d624
f 644A2d⁵752
644A2d⁶753
e 656A2d⁸1360
j 656A2d1366

—704—
f 639A2d²824
644A2d⁴1174
650A2d⁷466
j 652A2d369
662A2d¹³1075
664A2d1325
664A2d⁷1384
665A2d¹¹456

—716—
f 639A2d⁸824
639A2d³1223
640A2d⁶907
f 641A2d³327
648A2d⁶1182
f 650A2d⁶42
650A2d72
f 650A2d⁹457
j 652A2d369
654A2d³543
654A2d¹⁰1124
657A2d936
665A2d²⁶457
666A2d⁵731
668A2d⁹104

—730—
Case 1
Fla
665So2d1106

—731—
Case 2
645A2d1346

—734—
Case 3
s 666A2d319

—740—
a 648A2d1172

—743—
665A2d¹1319
c 665A2d1320

—760—
a 640A2d379
636A2d1152
656A2d163
f 656A2d²164
658A2d433

—771—
652A2d375
656A2d149
662A2d⁵18

—779—
646A2d¹1191
*Continued*

533

**More references to the original case**

**The last step is looking up the citation in the 1994 Bound Volumes. Again, in the listing for volume 615, page 321, a number of references to the case appear. At this point, you have finished Shepardizing the citation and are ready to read any cases listed in Shepard's necessary for your research. You can use the headnote references, history codes, and treatment codes to focus on the most important cases.**

**FIGURE 5.23**   1994 BOUND VOLUME ENTRY FOR 615 A.2d 321

---

ATLANTIC REPORTER, 2d SERIES                                Vol. 615

| | | | | | |
|---|---|---|---|---|---|
| —222— | 622A2d²1193 | —264— | —288— | s 591A2d730 | s 580A2d901 |
| Cafritz Co. v | 627A2d³523 | Cermele | Abella v | 617A2d1291 | |
| District of | 627A2d⁵523 | v Lawrence | Barringer | d 617A2d¹1293 | —338— |
| Columbia | | 1992 | Resources Inc. | d 617A2d²1293 | |
| Rental Housing | —248— | | 1992 | j 621A2d627 | Case 1 |
| Commission | First NH | (260NJS45) | | d 623A2d¹834 | Curran v Fiore |
| 1992 | Banks Granite | | (260NJS92) | f 625A2d642 | 1992 |
| | State v | —266— | | d 633A2d²626 | |
| —229— | Scarborough | Chrisomalis v | —294— | d 634A2d¹1071 | (532Pa210) |
| Wilson v Kelly | 1992 | Chrisomalis | Ebert v South | | s 593A2d917 |
| 1992 | Cir. 1 | 1992 | Jersey Gas Co. | —326— | |
| | e 814FS169 | | 1992 | Marra v | —338— |
| —235— | 818FS411 | (260NJS50) | | Stocker | |
| Maine v Dyer | f 818FS412 | | (260NJS104) | 1992 | Case 2 |
| 1992 | | —271— | | (532Pa187) | Herr v Booten |
| | —252— | A.C. | —297— | s 566A2d320 | 1992 |
| —236— | True v True | Construction | Knight v Ford | | (532Pa211) |
| Estate of | 1992 | Company | Motor Co. | —331— | s 580A2d1115 |
| Galluzzo | | Inc. v Kehoe | 1992 | Gouse v Cassel | |
| 1992 | —253— | 1992 | (260NJS110) | 1992 | —339— |
| | Donn-Griffin | (260NJS58) | | (532Pa197) | |
| —239— | v Donn | | —303— | s 561A2d797 | Case 1 |
| Morin Building | 1992 | —275— | Pennsylvania | 625A2d642 | Philadelphia |
| Products | 621A2d¹403 | New Jersey | State | 633A2d⁴1140 | Housing |
| Company | | v Capaci | University | | Authority v |
| Inc. v Atlantic | —255— | 1992 | v Centre | —336— | Barbour |
| Design and | Murphy v | (260NJS65) | 1992 | Case 1 | 1992 |
| Construction | Board of | | (532Pa142) | Pennsylvania | (532Pa212) |
| Company Inc. | Environmental | —277— | s 565A2d187 | v Geller | s 592A2d47 |
| 1992 | Protection | Inserra v | | 1992 | |
| 623A2d160 | 1992 | Inserra | —308— | (532Pa206) | —339— |
| 629A2d1222 | | 1992 | Pennsylvania | s 584A2d1046 | |
| 632A2d129 | —261— | (260NJS71) | v Kohl | | Case 2 |
| 634A2d963 | Montgomery | | 1992 | —336— | Gulau v Zoning |
| j 634A2d1314 | County v Jaffe | —279— | (532Pa152) | Case 2 | Hearing |
| | Raitt Heuer | New Jersey | s 576A2d1013 | Pennsylvania | Board of Allen |
| —241— | & Weiss | v Martinez | s 576A2d1049 | v Wolfe | Township |
| Security Pacific | 1992 | 1992 | 617A2d1291 | 1992 | 1992 |
| National Trust | (328Md460) | (260NJS75) | 620A2d¹¹1170 | (532Pa207) | (532Pa213) |
| Co. v Reid | | | 624A2d720 | s 570A2d592 | s 587A2d394 |
| 1992 | —263— | —281— | 624A2d725 | | |
| 626A2d935 | Case 1 | Khoudary v | 627A2d791 | —337— | —342— |
| 627A2d¹535 | In the Matter | Salem County | e 627A2d¹¹792 | Case 1 | Rivello v |
| | of Casper | Board of | d 627A2d¹¹793 | Pennsylvania | New Jersey |
| —244— | 1992 | Social Services | 629A2d³165 | v Tacey | Automobile |
| Maine v Priest | (130NJ421) | 1992 | 634A2d664 | 1992 | Full Insurance |
| 1992 | | (260NJS79) | 634A2d³665 | (532Pa208) | Underwriting |
| | —263— | f 628A2d⁴800 | 634A2d⁹665 | s 585A2d540 | Assoc. |
| —245— | Case 2 | | Ill | | 1992 |
| Mockus v | In the Matter | —286— | 607NE160 | —337— | (419PaS235) |
| Melanson | of Mulkeen | Ehrlich v | N D | Case 2 | Alloc dn |
| 1992 | 1992 | Strawbridge | 498NW152 | Pennsylvania | in 626A2d1158 |
| 617A2d³558 | (130NJ422) | & Clothier | | v Mark | —343— |
| | | 1992 | —321— | 1992 | Pennsylvania |
| | | (260NJS89) | Pennsylvania | (532Pa209) | v Munson |
| | | | v Smith | | 1992 |
| | | | 1992 | | (419PaS238) |
| | | | (532Pa177) | | |
| | | | s 568A2d600 | | |

1535

> The 1994 Bound Volume includes the case name and year of decision.

## G. CHECKLIST FOR CASE RESEARCH WITH SHEPARD'S CITATIONS AND OTHER CITATORS

### 1. LOCATE THE CORRECT SET OF SHEPARD'S IN PRINT

❒ Use a state or regional set of Shepard's to Shepardize a state case, keeping in mind that the regional set will usually contain the most complete research references.

❒ Use *Shepard's Federal Citations* or *Shepard's United States Citations* to Shepardize federal cases.

### 2. LOCATE THE CORRECT VOLUMES WITHIN THE PRINT SET

❒ Check the most recent supplement (softcover booklet or pamphlet) for the section "What Your Library Should Contain."

### 3. LOCATE THE ENTRIES FOR THE CASE WITHIN EACH VOLUME LOCATED IN STEP 2

❒ Check each noncumulative Shepard's volume for entries on the case.

❒ If the Shepard's set covers more than one reporter, check the section covering the reporter for your citation.

❒ If there is no entry for the citation within a Shepard's volume, the case was not cited during that time period.

### 4. INTERPRET THE ENTRIES

❒ Case history appears first. Parallel citations appear in parentheses. History codes signal the action taken in the history cases.

❒ Citing sources appear second. Look for authorities in this order:

  ▪ For state cases only, cases from the same state as the original case.

  ▪ Federal cases by circuit (within each circuit, appellate cases first, followed by district court cases).

  ▪ Cases from state courts listed alphabetically by state.

  ▪ Secondary sources.

❒ Treatment codes signal how the citing sources treated the original case.

❒ Headnote references signal the proposition for which a citing source refers to the original case.

### 5. CHECK CASE CITATIONS ELECTRONICALLY

❒ To Shepardize a case in LexisNexis, enter the citation in Shepard's and choose whether to view the complete or restricted entry. Interpret the entries as in Step 4.

❐ In Westlaw, use KeyCite by entering the citation.

- Review direct and negative indirect history to determine whether the case is still good law.
- Review citations to the case for both positive and negative research references.
- Use star categories and quotation marks to identify key sources.

# STATUTORY RESEARCH

## A. THE PUBLICATION OF STATUTORY LAW

Statutes enacted by a legislature are organized by subject matter into what is called a "code." Codes are published by jurisdiction; each jurisdiction that enacts statutes collects them in its own code. Thus, the federal government publishes the federal code, which contains all federal statutes. Statutes for each state are published in individual state codes. Most codes contain too many statutes to be included in a single volume. Instead, a code usually consists of a multivolume set of books containing all of the statutes passed within a jurisdiction. The federal code also includes the text of the United States Constitution. Most state codes contain the text of the state constitution, and many include the text of the United States Constitution as well.

When a federal law is enacted, it is published in three steps: (1) it is published as a separate document; (2) it is included in a chronological listing of all statutes passed within a session of Congress; and (3) it is reorganized by subject matter and placed within the code. In the first step of the process, every law passed by Congress is assigned a public law number. The public law number indicates the session of Congress in which the law was passed and the order in which it was passed. Thus, Public Law 103-416 was the 416th law passed during the 103d session of Congress. Each public law is published in a separate booklet or pamphlet containing the full text of the law as it was passed by Congress. This booklet is known as a slip law and is identified by its public law number.

In the second step of the process, slip laws for a session of Congress are compiled together in chronological order. Laws organized within this chronological compilation are called session laws because they are organized according to the session of Congress during which they were enacted. Session laws are compiled in a publication called *United States Statutes at Large*. A citation to *Statutes at Large* will tell you the volume of *Statutes at Large* containing the law and the page number on which the text of the law begins. Thus, a citation to 108 Stat. 4305 tells you that this law can be located in volume 108 of *Statutes at Large*, beginning on page 4305. Both the slip law and session law versions of a statute should be identical. The only difference is the form of publication.

The third step in the process is the codification of the law. When Congress enacts a law, it enacts a block of legislation that may cover a wide range of topics. A single bill can contain provisions applicable to many different parts of the government. For example, a drug abuse prevention law could contain provisions applicable to subject areas such as food and drugs, crimes, and public health. If federal laws remained organized chronologically by the date of passage, it would be virtually impossible to research the law by subject. Laws relating to individual subjects could have been passed at so many different times that it would be extremely difficult to find all of the relevant provisions.

In the third step of the process, therefore, the pieces of the bill are reorganized according to the different subjects they cover, and they are placed by subject, or codified, within the federal code. Once legislation is codified, it is much easier to locate because it can be indexed by subject much the way cases are indexed by subject in a digest.

Figure 6.1 illustrates the publication process.

Figure 6.2 contains an example of a statute that has been codified within the federal code.

## 1. TITLE AND SUBJECT-MATTER ORGANIZATION OF CODES

Although all codes are organized by subject, not all codes are numbered the same way. The federal code is organized into what are called "Titles." There are fifty Titles in the federal code, and each Title covers a different subject area. Title 18, for instance, contains the laws pertaining to federal crimes, and Title 35 contains the laws pertaining to patents. Each Title is subdivided into Chapters, and each Chapter is further subdivided into sections. To locate a provision of the federal code, you would need to

**FIGURE 6.1** PUBLICATION PROCESS FOR A FEDERAL STATUTE

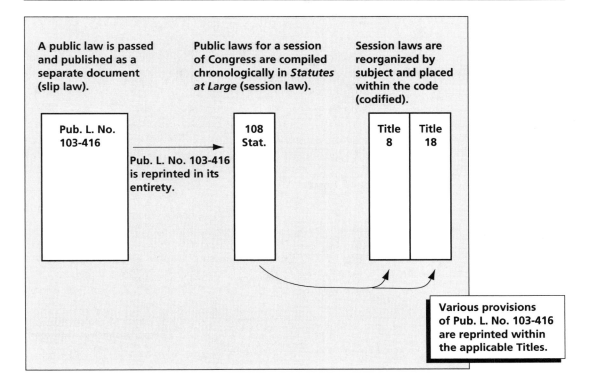

know the Title and the section number assigned to it. For example, the provision of the federal code prohibiting bank robbery is located in Title 18, section 2113.

Not all codes are organized this way. Some states organize their codes by subject name, rather than Title number. Within each subject name, the code is then usually subdivided into Chapters and sections. To find a provision of the code, you would need to know the subject area and the section number assigned to that provision. For example, the provision of New York law that prohibits issuing a bad check is located in the subject volume of the New York code containing the Penal Law, section 190.05.

## 2. OFFICIAL VS. UNOFFICIAL CODES AND ANNOTATED VS. UNANNOTATED CODES

Although there is only one "code" for each jurisdiction, in the sense that each jurisdiction has only one set of statutes in force, the text of the laws may be published in more than one set of books. Sometimes

**FIGURE 6.2**    8 U.S.C.A. § 1423

Ch. 12         NATURALIZATION        **8 § 1423**

**6. Minors**

Minority was said to be no bar to admission to citizenship. U. S. v. Stabile, C.C.A.Fla.1928, 24 F.2d 98.

Where Chinese merchants were admitted to United States prior to 1924, as permanent residents, their minor children, who were admitted after 1924, but prior to 1932, and who resided continuously in United States, were permanent residents, and could be naturalized. In re Jeu Foon, D.C.Ark.1950, 94 F.Supp. 728, affirmed 193 F.2d 117.

Where petitioner was admitted to United States in 1934 as an unmarried minor child of a resident Chinese "treaty trader", and his father resided continuously in country since their respective entries and both were merchants engaged in trade, petition's entry was for "permanent residence" within meaning of 1943 amendment to former section 703 of this title [now covered by ... is section], and he was eligible ... alization upon proof that he ... ed a United States citizen. Petition of Wong Choon Hoi, D.C.Cal.1947, 71 F.Supp. 160, appeal dismissed 164 F.2d 696.

**7. Free persons**

The word "free," originally used in recognition of the existence of slavery, no longer has any practical significance. Takao Ozawa v. U. S., 1922, 43 S.Ct. 65, 260 U.S. 178, 67 L.Ed. 199.

**8. American Indians**

The general statutes of naturalization were said not to apply to Indians, they being naturalizable by special Act of Congress or by treaty. 1856, 7 Op.Atty. Gen. 746.

An Indian born in British Columbia would not be admitted to citizenship by naturalization in the United States. In re Burton, 1900, 1 Alaska 111.

**9. Pardoned persons**

Pardons have no effect on right to naturalization. Petition for Naturalization of Quintana, D.C.Fla.1962, 203 F. Supp. 376.

Alien could not be naturaliz... he had been convicted of sec... murder, even though governor... alien full and complete pardo... restored his civil rights more than five years prior to filing of application for naturalization. Id.

**§ 1423.    Requirements as to understanding the English language, history, principles and form of government of the United States**

No person except as otherwise provided in this subchapter shall hereafter be naturalized as a citizen of the United States upon his own petition who cannot demonstrate—

(1) an understanding of the English language, including an ability to read, write, and speak words in ordinary usage in the English language: *Provided,* That this requirement shall not apply to any person physically unable to comply therewith, if otherwise qualified to be naturalized, or to any person who, on the effective date of this chapter, is over fifty years of age and has been living in the United States for periods totaling at least twenty years: *Provided further,* That the requirements of this section relating to ability to read and write shall be met if the applicant can read or write simple words and phrases to the end that a reasonable test of his literacy shall be made and that no extraordinary or unreasonable condition shall be imposed upon the applicant; and

(2) a knowledge and understanding of the fundamentals of the history, and of the principles and form of government, of the United States.

June 27, 1952, c. 477, Title III, ch. 2, § 312, 66 Stat. 239.

501

[labels: Section number | Name of the section | Text of the statute]

Reprinted with permission from West Group, *United States Code Annotated*, Title 8 (1970), p. 501.

**FIGURE 6.3** CHARACTERISTICS OF OFFICIAL AND UNOFFICIAL CODES

| OFFICIAL CODES | UNOFFICIAL CODES |
| --- | --- |
| Published under government authority (e.g., U.S.C.) | Published by a commercial publisher without government authorization (e.g., U.S.C.A. and U.S.C.S.) |
| May or may not contain research references (annotations). U.S.C. is not an annotated code. | Usually contain research references (annotations). Both U.S.C.A. and U.S.C.S. are annotated codes. |

a government arranges for the publication of its laws; this is known as an "official" code.[1] Sometimes a commercial publisher will publish the laws for a jurisdiction without government authorization; this is known as an "unofficial" code. Some jurisdictions have both official and unofficial codes, but in other jurisdictions, only one or the other type of code will be available. If both official and unofficial codes are published for a jurisdiction, they will usually be organized and numbered identically (e.g., all sets will be organized by subject or by Title). For federal laws, the government publishes an official code, *United States Code* or U.S.C. Two other sets of the federal code are also available through commercial publishers, *United States Code Annotated* (U.S.C.A.) and *United States Code Service* (U.S.C.S.).

In addition, a published code can come in one of two formats: annotated or unannotated. An annotated code contains the text of the law, as well as different types of research references. The research references may include summaries of cases or citations to secondary sources discussing a statute. An unannotated code contains only the text of the law. It may have a few references to the statutes' original public law numbers, but other than that, it will not contain research references. Most unofficial codes are annotated codes. Official codes may or may not be annotated. As you might imagine, an annotated code is much more useful as a research tool than an unannotated code.

In the federal code, U.S.C. (the official code) is an unannotated code. The two unofficial codes, U.S.C.A. and U.S.C.S., are annotated codes. See Figure 6.3 for a summary of the characteristics of official and unofficial codes.

---

[1]The government may publish the code itself, or it may arrange for a commercial publisher to publish the code. As long as the government arranges for the publication, the code is an official code, even if it is physically produced by a commercial publisher.

# B. RESEARCHING FEDERAL STATUTORY PROVISIONS IN *UNITED STATES CODE ANNOTATED*

The process of researching statutes is fairly uniform for state and federal codes. This section illustrates the research process in U.S.C.A. You should be able to adapt this process to almost any kind of statutory research.

Researching federal statutes in U.S.C.A. is a four-step process:

1. Look up the topics you want to research in the General Index.
2. Locate the relevant code section(s) in the main volumes of U.S.C.A. and evaluate the material in the accompanying annotations.
3. Update your research using the pocket part.
4. Update your research using the supplementary pamphlets at the end of the code.

Because U.S.C.A. contains the United States Constitution, you can locate federal constitutional provisions the same way you would locate any federal statute.

## 1. USING THE GENERAL INDEX

The General Index to U.S.C.A. is an ordinary subject index that consists of a series of softcover books. It is published annually, so be sure to check the most recent set of index books.

Using the General Index is just like using any other subject index. Topics are listed alphabetically. Next to each topic are references to the Title and section number(s) of the statutory provisions relevant to that topic. The abbreviation "et seq." means that the index is referring to a series of sections beginning with the section listed; often, this will be a reference to an entire Chapter within the Title. The index also contains cross-references to other subjects relevant to the topic. An example of an index page appears in Figure 6.4.

## 2. LOCATING STATUTES AND READING THE ANNOTATIONS

Once you have located relevant Title and section numbers in the General Index, the next step is finding the statute within the books. The books are organized numerically by Title, although some Titles span more than one volume. Using the Title number, you should be able to locate the correct volume. The sections within the Title will be listed in numerical

**FIGURE 6.4**   EXCERPT FROM THE U.S.C.A. GENERAL INDEX

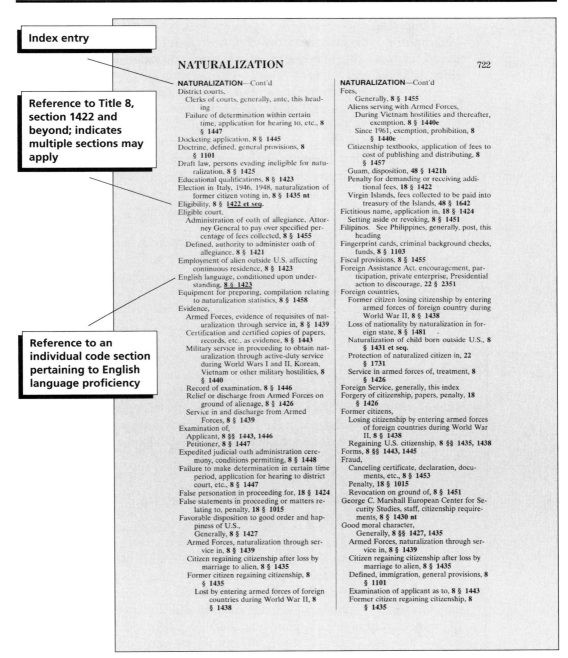

Reprinted with permission from West Group, *United States Code Annotated*, 1998 General Index, p. 722.

order within the volume.[2] At the beginning of each Chapter, you will find an outline of the code sections within the Chapter.

Following the text of the code section, you may find a series of annotations with additional information about the statute. Figure 6.5 describes some of the types of information you can find in the annotations in U.S.C.A.

Not all statutes have annotations. Those that do may not contain all of the information in Figure 6.5 or may have additional information. The information provided depends on the research references that are appropriate for that statute. If a statute has any annotations, they will always follow after the text of the code section. Figure 6.6 shows the annotations accompanying 8 U.S.C.A. § 1423.

### 3. UPDATING STATUTORY RESEARCH USING POCKET PARTS

Like other hardcover books used in legal research, U.S.C.A. volumes are updated with pocket parts. If the pocket part gets too big to fit in the back of the book, you should find a separate softcover pamphlet on the shelf next to the hardcover volume.

The pocket part is organized in the same way as the main volume. Therefore, to update your research, you need only look up the section numbers you located in the main volume. The pocket part will show any revisions to the statute, as well as additional annotations if, for example, new cases interpreting the section have been decided. If the pocket part shows new statutory language, the text in the pocket part supersedes the text in the main volume. If no reference to the section appears in the pocket part, the statute has not been amended, and no new research references are available. Figure 6.7 shows a portion of the pocket part update to 8 U.S.C.A. § 1423.

### 4. UPDATING STATUTORY RESEARCH USING SUPPLEMENTARY PAMPHLETS

The pocket part for each volume is published only once a year. Congress may change a statute after the pocket part is printed, however, and cases interpreting a statute can be published at any time. Therefore, to update your research, you need to check an additional source.

At the end of the U.S.C.A. set, you should find a series of softcover pamphlets. These are supplements that are published after the pocket part. They are noncumulative, meaning that each pamphlet covers a

---

[2]If the statute was enacted after the main volume was published, you will not find it in the hardcover book. More recent statutes will appear in the pocket part or noncumulative supplements, which are explained in the next section.

**FIGURE 6.5**   INFORMATION CONTAINED IN U.S.C.A. ANNOTATIONS

| CATEGORIES OF INFORMATION IN ANNOTATIONS | CONTENTS |
|---|---|
| Historical Note<br><br>Sometimes this section is called Historical and Statutory Notes. | Contains the history of the section, including summaries of amendments and the public law numbers and *Statutes at Large* citations for the laws containing the revisions. This section can also refer to the legislative history of the statute (for more discussion of legislative history, see Chapter 7). |
| Cross-References | Contains cross-references to related provisions of the code |
| Library References<br><br>Sometimes this section is subdivided into categories for Administrative Law, American Digest System, Encyclopedias, Law Reviews, Texts and Treatises, and Forms. | Contains references to related topics and key numbers in the West digest system, as well as references to legal encyclopedia sections with information on the subject (see Chapter 4 for more discussion of the digest system and Chapter 3 for more discussion of legal encyclopedias) |
| Code of Federal Regulations<br><br>Sometimes this appears as a separate section, and sometimes it is included with Library References, under the Administrative Law category. | Contains references to administrative agency regulations implementing the statute (for more discussion of administrative regulations, see Chapter 8) |
| Law Review Articles<br><br>Sometimes this appears as a separate section, and sometimes it is included with Library References, under the Law Reviews category. | Contains references to relevant law review articles (for more discussion of law reviews and other legal periodicals, see Chapter 3) |
| Notes of Decisions | Contains summaries of cases interpreting the statute. If the statute has been discussed in a large number of cases, the Notes of Decisions will be divided into subject categories, and each category will be assigned a number. Cases on each subject will be listed under the appropriate number. *Note that these subject and number categories do not correspond to the topics and key numbers within the West digest system.* |

**FIGURE 6.6** ANNOTATIONS ACCOMPANYING 8 U.S.C.A. § 1423

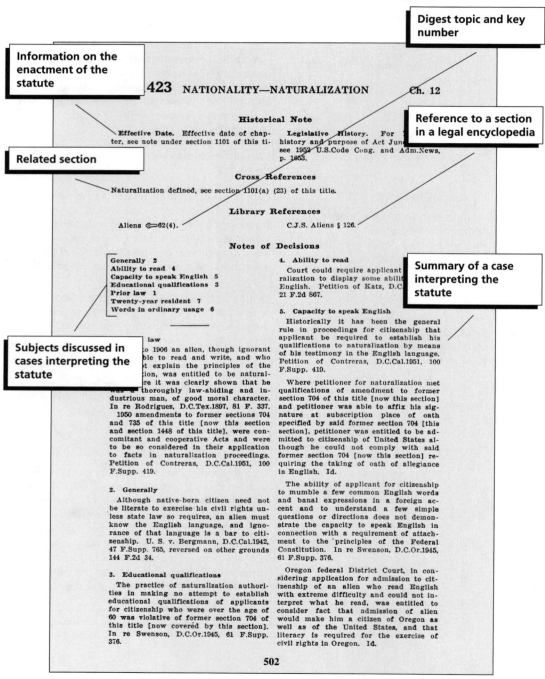

**Digest topic and key number**

**Information on the enactment of the statute**

**Reference to a section in a legal encyclopedia**

**Related section**

**Summary of a case interpreting the statute**

**Subjects discussed in cases interpreting the statute**

§ 423  NATIONALITY—NATURALIZATION  Ch. 12

**Historical Note**

**Effective Date.** Effective date of chapter, see note under section 1101 of this title.

**Legislative History.** For history and purpose of Act June see 1952 U.S.Code Cong. and Adm.News, p. 1653.

**Cross References**

Naturalization defined, see section 1101(a) (23) of this title.

**Library References**

Aliens ⊂⇒62(4).

C.J.S. Aliens § 126.

**Notes of Decisions**

Generally  2
Ability to read  4
Capacity to speak English  5
Educational qualifications  3
Prior law  1
Twenty-year resident  7
Words in ordinary usage  6

law

o 1906 an alien, though ignorant
ble to read and write, and who
t explain the principles of the
ion, was entitled to be natural-
re it was clearly shown that he
thoroughly law-abiding and industrious man, of good moral character.
In re Rodriguez, D.C.Tex.1897, 81 F. 337.

1950 amendments to former sections 704
and 735 of this title [now this section
and section 1448 of this title], were concomitant and cooperative Acts and were
to be so considered in their application
to facts in naturalization proceedings.
Petition of Contreras, D.C.Cal.1951, 100
F.Supp. 419.

**2. Generally**

Although native-born citizen need not
be literate to exercise his civil rights unless state law so requires, an alien must
know the English language, and ignorance of that language is a bar to citizenship. U. S. v. Bergmann, D.C.Cal.1942,
47 F.Supp. 765, reversed on other grounds
144 F.2d 34.

**3. Educational qualifications**

The practice of naturalization authorities in making no attempt to establish
educational qualifications of applicants
for citizenship who were over the age of
60 was violative of former section 704 of
this title [now covered by this section].
In re Swenson, D.C.Or.1945, 61 F.Supp.
376.

**4. Ability to read**

Court could require applicant
ralization to display some abili
English. Petition of Katz, D.C.
21 F.2d 867.

**5. Capacity to speak English**

Historically it has been the general
rule in proceedings for citizenship that
applicant be required to establish his
qualifications to naturalization by means
of his testimony in the English language.
Petition of Contreras, D.C.Cal.1951, 100
F.Supp. 419.

Where petitioner for naturalization met
qualifications of amendment to former
section 704 of this title [now this section]
and petitioner was able to affix his signature at subscription place of oath
specified by said former section 704 [this
section], petitioner was entitled to be admitted to citizenship of United States although he could not comply with said
former section 704 [now this section] requiring the taking of oath of allegiance
in English. Id.

The ability of applicant for citizenship
to mumble a few common English words
and banal expressions in a foreign accent and to understand a few simple
questions or directions does not demonstrate the capacity to speak English in
connection with a requirement of attachment to the principles of the Federal
Constitution. In re Swenson, D.C.Or.1945,
61 F.Supp. 376.

Oregon federal District Court, in considering application for admission to citizenship of an alien who read English
with extreme difficulty and could not interpret what he read, was entitled to
consider fact that admission of alien
would make him a citizen of Oregon as
well as of the United States, and that
literacy is required for the exercise of
civil rights in Oregon. Id.

502

Reprinted with permission from West Group, *United States Code Annotated*, Title 8 (1970), p. 502.

**FIGURE 6.7**  POCKET PART UPDATE FOR 8 U.S.C.A. § 1423

---

ALIENS AND NATIONALITY                                          8 § 1423

**32. Jurisdiction of United States courts— Generally**

Tutun v. United States, U.S.N.Y.1926, 46 S.Ct. 425, 270 U.S. 568, 70 L.Ed. 738, [main volume] conformed to 13 F.2d 541, certiorari granted 47 S.Ct. 243, 273 U.S. 685, 71 L.Ed. 839, remanded 47 S.Ct. 334, 273 U.S. 777, 71 L.Ed. 887.

**32a. —— Standing**

Child of United States citizen mother denied citizenship under statute providing citizenship only for children of citizen fathers had standing to bring constitutional challenge to statute, though courts did not have specific congressional authorization to grant citizenship, where her suit was directed at constitutional wrong. Aguayo v. Christopher, N.D.Ill.1994, 865 F.Supp. 479.

**40. —— Appellate**

In re Bogunovic, Cal.1941, 114 P.2d 581, [main volume] 18 Cal.2d 160.

**III. MANNER AND CONDITIONS OF NATURALIZATION**

Eligibility requirements  78
Waiver  79

---

**73. Naturalization as a right**

Filipino veterans, who served in the United States armed forces during World War II, were not entitled to become naturalized citizens, where statutes under which veterans applied for naturalization had expired; therefore, veterans were not entitled to mandamus relief compelling the Immigration and Naturalization Service to process their naturalization applications. Agcaoili v. Gustafson, C.A.9 (Cal.) 1989, 870 F.2d 462.

**74. Compliance with law as prerequisite to naturalization**

No alien has right to naturalization without compliance with all statutory requirements. Petition of Di Franco, S.D.N.Y.1972, 339 F.Supp. 414.

**76. Doubt, manner of resolving**

Petitioner applying for naturalization bears burden of proof; any doubts must be resolved against petitioner and in favor of government. Tan v. U.S. Dept. of Justice, I.N.S., D.Hawai'i 1996, 931 F.Supp. 725.

**78. Eligibility requirements**

This section, which provides that any naturalization petition filed after Sept. 26, 1961 would be governed by requirements of this subchapter then in effect did not bar petitioner, asserting that he had been unconstitutionally denied opportunity to apply for benefit decreed by Congress, from relying on 1940 Act's eligibility requirements of former provisions of this section. Olegario v. U. S., C.A.2 (N.Y.) 1980, 629 F.2d 204, certiorari denied 101 S.Ct. 1513, 450 U.S. 980, 67 L.Ed.2d 814.

**79. Waiver**

Alien, whose petition for naturalization had been transferred to the district court for the Eastern District of Virginia and who submitted himself to that court even though he later established residency in Washington, D.C., waived his right to assert special venue provision which states that court's jurisdiction to naturalize persons extends only to residents within court's jurisdiction. In re Duncan, C.A.9 (Cal.) 1983, 713 F.2d 538.

**§ 1422.  Eligibility for naturalization**

The right of a person to become a naturalized citizen of the United States shall not be denied or abridged because of race or sex or because such person is married.

(As amended Oct. 24, 1968, Pub.L. 100–525, § 9(t), 102 Stat. 2621.)

**HISTORICAL AND STATUTORY NOTES**

**1988 Amendment**

Pub.L. 100–525, § 9(t), struck out: "Notwithstanding section 405(b) of this Act, this section

shall apply to any person whose petition for naturalization shall hereafter be filed, or shall have been pending on the effective date of this chapter."

**LIBRARY REFERENCES**

Aliens ⊛61–66.
C.J.S. Aliens §§ 124–132.

**NOTES OF DECISIONS**

**2. Generally**

No alien has right to naturalization unless all statutory requirements have been complied

with. U. S. v. Demjanjuk, N.D.Ohio 1981, 518 F.Supp. 1362, affirmed 680 F.2d 32, certiorari denied 103 S.Ct. 447, 459 U.S. 1036, 74 L.Ed.2d 602.

**§ 1423.  Requirements as to understanding the English language, history, principles and form of government of the United States**

(a) No person except as otherwise provided in this subchapter shall hereafter be naturalized as a citizen of the United States upon his own application who cannot demonstrate—

(1) an understanding of the English language, including an ability to read, write, and speak words in ordinary usage in the English language: *Provided,* That the

391

---

> **New statutory language supersedes the language in the main volume.**

**FIGURE 6.7** POCKET PART UPDATE FOR 8 U.S.C.A. § 1423 *(Continued)*

**Annotations follow the text of the statute.**

8 § 1423               ALIENS AND NATIONALITY

requirements of this paragraph relating to ability to read and write shall be met if the applicant can read or write simple words and phrases to the end that a reasonable test of his literacy shall be made and that no extraordinary or unreasonable condition shall be imposed upon the applicant; and

(2) a knowledge and understanding of the fundamentals of the history, and of the principles and form of government, of the United States.

(b)(1) The requirements of subsection (a) of this section shall not apply to any person who is unable because of physical or developmental disability or mental impairment to comply therewith.

(2) The requirement of subsection (a)(1) of this section shall not apply to any person who, on the date of the filing of the person's application for naturalization as provided in section 1445 of this title, either—

(A) is over fifty years of age and has been living in the United States for periods totaling at least twenty years subsequent to a lawful admission for permanent residence, or

(B) is over fifty-five years of age and has been living in the United States for periods totaling at least fifteen years subsequent to a lawful admission for permanent residence.

(3) The Attorney General, pursuant to regulations, shall provide for special consideration, as determined by the Attorney General, concerning the requirement of subsection (a)(2) of this section with respect to any person who, on the date of the filing of the person's application for naturalization as provided in section 1445 of this title, is over sixty-five years of age and has been living in the United States for periods totaling at least twenty years subsequent to a lawful admission for permanent residence.

(As amended Nov. 2, 1978, Pub.L. 95–579, § 3, 92 Stat. 2474; Nov. 29, 1990, Pub.L. 101–649, Title IV, § 403, 104 Stat. 5039; Dec. 12, 1991, Pub.L. 102–232, Title III, § 305(m)(2), 105 Stat. 1750; Oct. 25, 1994, Pub.L. 103–416, Title I, § 108(a), 108 Stat. 4309.)

### HISTORICAL AND STATUTORY NOTES

**1994 Amendments**

Subsec. (a). Pub.L. 103–416, § 108(a)(1), designated existing provisions as subsec. (a).

Subsec. (a)(1). Pub.L. 103–416, § 108(a)(2), (3), struck out provisions which exempted individuals over the age of 50 and 55 years and living in the United States as permanent residents for periods totaling at least 20 and 15 years, respectively, from english language proficiency requirement, and substituted reference to this par. for reference to this section.

Subsec. (b). Pub.L. 103–416, § 108(a)(4), added subsec. (b).

**1991 Amendments**

Pub.L. 102–232 substituted reference to application for reference to petition wherever appearing.

**1990 Amendment**

Par. (1). Pub.L. 101–649 designated portion of existing text as cl. (A) and added cl. (B).

**1978 Amendment**

Par. (1). Pub.L. 95–579 substituted "person who, on the date of the filing of his petition for naturalization as provided in section 1445 of this title, is over fifty years of age and has been living in the United States for periods totaling at least twenty years subsequent to a lawful admission for permanent residence" for "person who, on the effective date of this chapter, is over fifty years of age and has been living in the United States for periods totaling at least twenty years".

**Effective Date of 1994 Amendments**

Section 108(c) of Pub.L. 103–416 provided that: "The amendments made by subsection (a) [amending this section] shall take effect on the date of the enactment of this Act [Oct. 25, 1994] and shall apply to applications for naturalization filed on or after such date and to such applications pending on such date."

**Effective Date of 1991 Amendment**

Amendments by sections 302 through 308 of Pub.L. 102–232, except as otherwise specifically provided, effective as if included in the enactment of Pub.L. 101–649, see section 310(1) of Pub.L. 102–232, set out as a note under section 1101 of this title.

Amendment by section 305(m)(2) of Pub.L. 102–232 effective as if included in section 407(d) of Pub.L. 101–649, see section 305(m) of Pub.L. 102–232, set out as a note under section 1101 of this title.

**Effective Date of 1990 Amendment; Savings Provisions**

Amendment by Title IV of Pub.L. 101–649 effective Nov. 29, 1990, with general savings provisions, see section 408(a)(3) and (d) of Pub.L. 101–649, set out as a note under section 1421 of this title.

**Promulgation of Regulations**

Section 108(d) of Pub.L. 103–416 provided that: "Not later than 120 days after the date of

392

Reprinted with permission from West Group, *United States Code Annotated*, 1997 Cumulative Pocket Part, Title 8, pp. 391–392.

**FIGURE 6.8**   NONCUMULATIVE PAMPHLET ENTRY FOR 8 U.S.C.A. § 1423

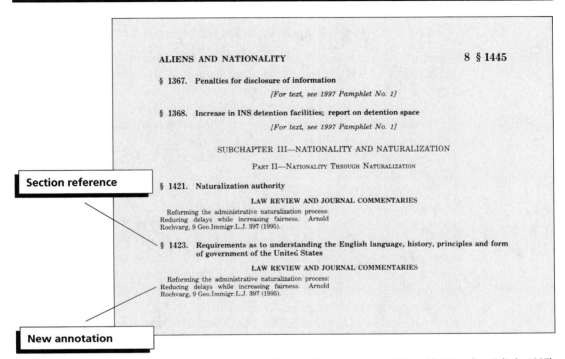

Reprinted with permission from West Group, *United States Code Annotated*, Pamphlet Number 2 (July 1997), p. 87.

specific time period. To update your research thoroughly, you must look for your code section in each pamphlet published since the pocket part.[3] The dates of coverage of each pamphlet should appear on the cover.

The noncumulative pamphlets are organized the same way as the rest of the code: by Title and section number. Therefore, you need to look up the Title and section number of the statute you are researching. The pamphlet, like the pocket part, will list any changes to the statute, as well as additional annotations. If no reference to the section appears in the noncumulative pamphlet, then there is no additional information for you to research. Figure 6.8 is an excerpt from a page in a noncumulative pamphlet updating 8 U.S.C.A. § 1423. Notice in this example that the statutory language has not changed, but there is an addition to the annotations.

---

[3] If a change to the statute appears in an earlier pamphlet, the later pamphlets will refer back to the earlier pamphlet. Later pamphlets will not, however, refer back to additional annotations. Therefore, to locate all new annotations, you must check each supplementary pamphlet.

# C. ADDITIONAL STATUTORY RESEARCH TOOLS

## 1. THE POPULAR NAME AND CONVERSION TABLES

Research using a subject-matter index is appropriate when you know the subject you want to research but do not know the exact statute you need to find. Sometimes, however, you will know which statute you need to find. In that situation, the easiest way to find the citation may be through the popular name table or the conversion tables. In U.S.C.A., the popular name table is located at the end of the last volume of the General Index. The conversion tables appear in separate softcover "Tables" volumes.

The popular name table allows you to locate statutes according to their popular names. For example, if you wanted to research the Freedom of Access to Clinic Entrances Act (FACE Act) but did not know its citation, you could look up a variety of topics in the General Index until you found it. An easier way to do this would be to look up the FACE Act according to its popular name. The popular name table lists the public law number, the *Statutes at Large* citation, and the Title and section numbers where the act is codified within U.S.C.A. Remember that when a law is first passed by a legislature, it may affect many different areas of the law and, therefore, may be codified in many different places within the code. Thus, the popular name table may refer you to a number of different Titles and sections. For many well-known statutes, however, the popular name table is an efficient way to locate the law within the code. Figure 6.9 shows the popular name table entry for the FACE Act.

Another way to locate a statute in U.S.C.A. is through the conversion tables. If you know the public law number for a statute, you can use the tables to find the *Statutes at Large* citation and the Titles and sections where the law has been codified. Figure 6.10 is an example from the conversion table showing where the FACE Act is codified.

Because the popular name and conversion tables are published annually, there is no pocket part update for the tables. At the end of each noncumulative supplement, however, you will find updates to the tables. Therefore, if you are unable to find the material you want in the General Index or Tables, check for more recent material in the noncumulative supplements.

## 2. RESEARCHING U.S.C., U.S.C.S., STATE CODES, RULES OF PROCEDURE, AND UNIFORM LAWS AND MODEL ACTS

So far, this chapter has focused on statutory research using U.S.C.A. For the most part, the same methods can also be used to research in U.S.C., U.S.C.S., and state codes. A few of the differences between U.S.C.A. and these other codes, however, are worth mentioning. In

**FIGURE 6.9** FACE ACT ENTRY, POPULAR NAME TABLE

1195                 **POPULAR NAME TABLE**

**Frank Annunzio Act**—Continued
    Pub.L. 102–390, Title II, Subtitle B, § 221(c)(2)(I), Oct. 6, 1992, 106 Stat. 1628 (31 § 5112 note)

**Fraudulent Advertising Act**
    May 29, 1916, ch. 130, 39 Stat. 165

**Frazier-Lemke Act**
    See Frazier-Lemke Farm-Mortgage Act

**Frazier-Lemke Farm-Mortgage Act (Agricultural Debt Relief Act) (Farm Bankruptcy Act) (Farm Mortgage Act) (Frazier-Lemke Act)**
    June 28, 1934, ch. 869, 48 Stat. 1289
    Aug. 28, 1935, ch. 792, 49 Stat. 942
    Mar. 4, 1940, ch. 39, §§ 1, 2, 54 Stat. 40

**Fredericksburg and Spotsylvania County Battlefields Memorial National Military Park Expansion Act of 1989**
    Pub.L. 101–214, Dec. 11, 1989, 103 Stat. 1849 (16 §§ 425k, 425k note, 425*l* to 425*o*)
    Pub.L. 102–541, § 2(a), Oct. 27, 1992, 106 Stat. 3565 (16 § 425k)

**Free Coinage of Gold Act**
    See Specie Payment Resumption Act

**Free Homestead Act**
    May 17, 1900, ch. 479, 31 Stat. 179 (43 § 179)

**Free Trade Zone Act**
    June 18, 1934, ch. 590, 48 Stat. 998 (19 §§ 81a to 81u)
    June 2, 1970, Pub.L. 91–271, Title III, § 309, 84 Stat. 292 (19 § 81c)

**Freedman's Bureau Bills**
    Mar. 3, 1865, ch. 90, 13 Stat. 507
    July 16, 1866, ch. 200, 14 Stat. 173
    July 6, 1868, ch. 135, 15 Stat. 83

**Freedman's Saving and Trust Company Acts**
    June 20, 1874, ch. 349, 18 Stat. 131
    Feb. 13, 1877, ch. 57, 19 Stat. 231
    Feb. 21, 1881, ch. 64, 21 Stat. 326
    1883, ch. 48, 22 Stat. 420
    99, ch. 440, 30 Stat. 1353

**Freedom for Russia and Emerging Eurasian Democracies and Open Markets Support Act of 1992 (FREEDOM Support Act)**
    Pub.L. 102–511, Oct. 24, 1992, 106 Stat. 3320 (7 §§ 1736*o*, 3293, 5602, 5621, 5621 note, 5622, 5622 note, 5651; 8 §§ 1157 notes, 1255 note; 18 § 955 note; 22 §§ 262d, 282m, 282n, 286e–1*l*, 286e–5b, 286e–13, 286*ll*, 286mm, 288j, 2295, 2295a, 2295b, 2295c, 2370, 2452 note, 2507, 4903a, 5402, 5801, 5811 to 5814, 5821 to 5828, 5841, 5851 to 5861, 5871 to 5874)
    Pub.L. 104–127, Title II, Subtitle C, § 276, Apr. 4, 1996, 110 Stat. 977 (7 § 5621 note)

**Freedom of Access to Clinic Entrances Act of 1994 (FACE)**
    Pub.L. 103–259, May 26, 1994, 108 Stat. 694 (18 §§ 241, 248, 248 note)

**Freedom of Information Act (FOIA)**
    Pub.L. 89–487, July 4, 1966, 80 Stat. 250 (See 5 § 552)
    Pub.L. 90–23, § 1, June 5, 1967, 81 Stat. 54 (5 § 552)
    Pub.L. 93–502, §§ 1 to 3, Nov. 21, 1974, 88 Stat. 1561 (5 § 552)

**Freedom of Information Reform Act of 1986**
    Pub.L. 99–570, Title I, Subtitle N, Oct. 27, 1986, 100 Stat. 3204–48 (5 §§ 552, 552 notes)

**FREEDOM Support Act**
    See Freedom for Russia and Emerging Eurasian Democracies and Open Markets Support Act of 1992

**French Spoliation Claims Act**
    Jan. 20, 1885, ch. 25, 23 Stat. 283

**Fresh Cut Flowers and Fresh Cut Greens Promotion and Information Act of 1993**
    Pub.L. 103–190, Dec. 14, 1993, 107 Stat. 2266 (7 §§ 6801, 6801 note, 6802 to 6814)

*Labels:* **Name** · **Public law number** · ***Statutes at Large* citation** · **Title and sections where the law is codified in U.S.C.A.**

Reprinted with permission from West Group, *United States Code Annotated*, General Index, 1998, p. 1195.

**FIGURE 6.10** CONVERSION TABLE ENTRY FOR PUB. L. NO. 103-259, THE FACE ACT

| | | | |
|---|---|---|---|
| 1994 | | | 103–260 |

| | | | |
|---|---|---|---|
| § 121(a)(1) | 108 Stat 649 | 20 § 1235c |
| § 121(a)(1) | 108 Stat 649 | 20 § 1235d |
| § 121(a)(1) | 108 Stat 649 | 20 § 1235e |
| § 121(a)(1) | 108 Stat 649 | 20 § 1235f |
| § 121(a)(1) | 108 Stat 649 | 20 § 1235g |
| § 121(a)(2)(A) | 108 Stat 649 | 20 § 1235 |
| § 121(a)(2)(B) | 108 Stat 649 | 20 § 1235c |
| § 121(a)(2)(C) | 108 Stat 649 | 20 § 1235d |
| § 121(a)(2)(D) | 108 Stat 649 | 20 § 1235e |
| § 121(b) | 108 Stat 649 | 20 § 1235a |
| § 121(c) | 108 Stat 649 | 20 § 1235e |
| § 122 | 108 Stat 650 | 42 § 9871 |
| § 123 | 108 Stat 650 | 42 § 9852a |
| § 124 | 108 Stat 650 | 42 § 10905 |
| § 125(a) | 108 Stat 650 | 42 § 9855a |
| § 125(b) | 108 Stat 650 | 42 § 1396r–5 |
| § 126 | 108 Stat 650 | 42 § 9844 nt |
| § 127 | 108 Stat 651 | 42 § 9832 nt |
| § 201(a) | 108 Stat 651 | 42 § 9901 nt. |
| § 202(a) | 108 Stat 651 | 42 § 9901 |
| § 202(b) | 108 Stat 651 | 42 § 9903 |
| § 202(c) to (g) | 108 Stat 652 | 42 § 9904 |
| § 203 | 108 Stat 654 | 42 § 9910 |
| § 204 | 108 Stat 655 | 42 § 9910a |
| § 205(1) | 108 Stat 655 | 42 § 9911 |
| § 205(1) | 108 Stat 655 | 42 § 9912 |
| § 205(2) | 108 Stat 655 | 42 § 9910c |
| § 206 | 108 Stat 656 | 42 § 11464 |
| § 207 | 108 Stat 656 | 42 § 9910b |
| § 208 | 108 Stat 657 | 42 § 9901 nt |
| § 301(a) | 108 Stat 657 | 42 § 8621 nt |
| § 302 | 108 Stat 657 | 42 § 8621 |
| § 303 | 108 Stat 658 | 42 § 8621 |
| § 304(a) | 108 Stat 658 | 42 § 8621 |
| § 304(b) | 108 Stat 658 | 42 § 8622 |
| § 304(c) | 108 Stat 659 | 42 § 8623 |
| § 305 | 108 Stat 659 | 42 § 8624 |
| § 306 to 309 | 108 Stat 659 | 42 § 8624 |
| § 310 | 108 Stat 661 | 42 § 8626 |
| § 311(a)(1) | 108 Stat 661 | 42 § 8624 |
| § 311(a)(2) | 108 Stat 661 | 42 § 8626a |
| § 311(a)(3) | 108 Stat 661 | 42 § 8628a |
| § 311(b) | 108 Stat 661 | 42 § 8624 |
| § 311(c)(1) | 108 Stat 662 | 42 § 8621 |
| § 311(c)(2) | 108 Stat 662 | 42 § 8622 |
| § 311(c)(3) | 108 Stat 662 | 42 § 8623 |
| § 311(c)(4),(5) | 108 Stat 662 | 42 § 8624 |
| § 311(c)(6) | 108 Stat 662 | 42 § 8626a |
| § 311(c)(7) | 108 Stat 662 | 42 § 8629 |
| § 312 | 108 Stat 662 | 42 § 8626b |
| § 314 | 108 Stat 666 | 42 § 8621 nt |
| § 401(a) | 108 Stat 666 | 42 § 5116 |
| § 401(a) | 108 Stat 666 | 42 § 5116a | Elim. |
| § 401(a) | 108 Stat 666 | 42 § 5116b | Elim. |
| § 401(a) | 108 Stat 666 | 42 § 5116c | Elim. |
| § 401(a) | 108 Stat 666 | 42 § 5116d | Elim. |
| § 401(a) | 108 Stat 666 | 42 § 5116e | Elim. |
| § 401(a) | 108 Stat 666 | 42 § 5116f | Elim. |
| § 401(a) | 108 Stat 666 | 42 § 5116g | Elim. |
| § 401(b)(1) | 108 Stat 672 | 42 § 12339 | Rep. |
| § 401(b)(2) | 108 Stat 672 | 42 § 5106a–1 | Rep. |
| § 402(a) | 108 Stat 672 | 42 § 12314 |
| § 402(b) | 108 Stat 673 | 42 § 12340 |
| § 403(a) | 108 Stat 673 | 42 § 12353 |
| § 403(b) | 108 Stat 673 | 42 § 12355 |
| May 19, 1994   103–254   § 1 | 108 Stat 679 | 15 § 2201 nt |
| § 2 | 108 Stat 679 | 15 § 2201 nt |
| § 3 | 108 Stat 679 | 15 § 2221 |
| § 4 | 108 Stat 682 | 15 § 2220 |
| § 5 | 108 Stat 682 | 15 § 2228 |
| § 6 | 108 Stat 682 | 15 § 2227 |
| § 7 | 108 Stat 682 | 15 § 2216 |
| § 8 | 108 Stat 683 | 15 § 2216 nt |
| 103–255   § 4 | 108 Stat 686 | 16 § 1132 nt |
| May 26, 1994   103–259   § 1, 2 | 108 Stat 694 | 18 § 248 nts |
| § 3 | 108 Stat 694 | 18 § 248 |
| § 4 | 108 Stat 697 | 18prec. 241 |
| § 5 | 108 Stat 697 | 18 § 248 nt |
| § 6 | 108 Stat 697 | 18 § 248 nt |
| 103–260   § 1 | 108 Stat 698 | 49 App. § 2201 nt |
| § 101 | 108 Stat 698 | 49 App. § 2201 | Rev.T. 49 |
| § 102 | 108 Stat 698 | 49 App. § 2206 | Rev.T. 49 |
| § 103 | 108 Stat 698 | 49 App. § 2206 | Rev.T. 49 |

**933**

**Statutes at Large citation**

**Public law number**

**Title and sections where the law is codified in U.S.C.A.**

Reprinted with permission from West Group, Tables Vol. II, *United States Code Annotated*, 1999, p. 933.

addition, brief discussions of researching rules of procedure and uniform laws and model acts are included here.

### a. U.S.C.

The index, popular name, and conversion table methods of locating statutes are all available with U.S.C. The main difference in researching U.S.C. concerns updating. The index and main volumes of the code are published every six years. In the intervening years, U.S.C. is not updated with pocket parts. Instead, it is updated with hardcover cumulative supplements. A new supplement is issued each year until the next publication of the main set.

In theory, using the supplements should be sufficient to update your research. In practice, however, the system presents some difficulties. Laws can be changed more frequently than the supplements are published, and the government is often two or three years behind in publishing the supplements. To update completely, you would need to research session and slip laws published since the latest supplement. Therefore, U.S.C. is not usually an appropriate source for locating the most current version of a statute, and because it lacks the research references contained in the annotated federal codes, it is not the most useful statutory research tool.

### b. U.S.C.S.

U.S.C.S. is organized much the same way as U.S.C.A. The index, popular name, and conversion table methods of locating statutes are all available with U.S.C.S. U.S.C.S. often has fewer references to court decisions than the Notes of Decisions in U.S.C.A., but the references to administrative materials are often more comprehensive than those in U.S.C.A.[4] The nature of your research project and the materials available in your library will determine whether it is more appropriate for you to use U.S.C.S. or U.S.C.A. for federal statutory research.

The process of updating U.S.C.S. research is basically the same as that for U.S.C.A. Hardcover main volumes are updated with pocket parts. In addition, at the end of U.S.C.S., you will find softcover supplements to the code as a whole called the Cumulative Later Case and Statutory Service. Unlike the supplements to U.S.C.A., the U.S.C.S. supplements are cumulative, so you only need to check the most recent one. The supplements are organized by Title and section number and will reflect both changes to the statutory language and additional annotations.

---

[4]Chapter 8 explains administrative materials and administrative law research.

## c. State codes

State codes have many of the same features of U.S.C.A. All have subject indices that can be used to locate statutes. Some also have popular name tables. Most do not, however, have the equivalent of the conversion tables. In addition, the updating process for state statutory research can vary. Virtually all state codes are updated with pocket parts, but some have different or additional updating tools. You may want to check with a reference librarian if you have questions about updating statutory research for a particular state. Sample pages illustrating the process of state statutory research appear in Section F of this chapter.

## d. Rules of procedure

You are probably learning about rules of procedure governing cases filed in court in your Civil Procedure class. Whenever you are preparing to file a document or take some action that a court requires or permits, the court's rules of procedure will tell you how to accomplish your task. The rules of procedure for most courts are published as part of the code for the jurisdiction where the court is located. For example, the Federal Rules of Civil Procedure appear with Title 28 in the federal code. In many states, court procedural rules are published in a separate Rules volume.

If you want to locate procedural rules, therefore, one way to find them is through the applicable code. In print, you can locate them using the subject index, or you can go directly to the rules themselves if they are published in a separate volume. Many procedural rules have been interpreted in court opinions, and you need to research those opinions to understand the rules' requirements fully. If you locate rules in an annotated code, summaries of the decisions will follow the rules, just as they do any other provision of the code. You can update your research with the pocket part and any cumulative or noncumulative supplements accompanying the code.

A couple of caveats about locating rules of procedure are in order. First, understanding the rules can be challenging. As with any other type of research, you may want to locate secondary sources for commentary on the rules and citations to cases interpreting the rules to make sure you understand them. For the Federal Rules of Civil Procedure, two helpful treatises are *Moore's Federal Practice* and Wright & Miller's *Federal Practice and Procedure*. For state procedural rules, a state "deskbook," or handbook containing practical information for lawyers practicing in the jurisdiction, may contain both the text of the rules and helpful commentary on them. If you locate the rules through a secondary source, however, be sure to update your research because the rules can be amended at any time.

Second, virtually all jurisdictions have multiple types and levels of courts, and each of these courts may have its own procedural rules. Therefore, be sure you locate the rules for the appropriate court. Determining which court is the appropriate one may require separate research into the jurisdiction of the courts.

Third, many individual districts, circuits, or divisions of courts have local rules with which you must comply. Local rules cannot conflict with the rules of procedure published with the code, but they may add requirements that do not appear in the rules of procedure. Local rules usually are not published with the code, but you can obtain them from a number of sources, including the court itself, a secondary source such as a practice "deskbook," or a web site or on-line database. To be sure that your work complies with the court's rules, do not neglect any local rules that may add to the requirements spelled out in the rules of procedure.

### e. Uniform laws and model acts

Uniform laws and model acts, as explained in Chapter 3, are proposed statutes that can be adopted by legislatures. Technically, they are secondary sources; their provisions do not take on the force of law unless they are adopted by a legislature. If your research project involves a statute based on a uniform law or model act, however, you may want to research these sources.

Many uniform laws and model acts are published in a multivolume set of books entitled *Uniform Laws Annotated, Master Edition* (ULA). The ULA set is organized like an annotated code. It contains the text of the uniform law or model act and annotations summarizing cases from jurisdictions that have adopted the statute. It also provides commentary that can help you interpret the statute. Chapter 3, on secondary sources, provides a more detailed explanation of how to use the ULA set.

### 3. SHEPARD'S FOR STATUTES

Chapter 5 discusses Shepard's Citations and how to use this service in conducting case research. Shepard's is also available as a research and updating tool for state and federal statutes. Sheardizing statutes is useful in two situations. First, if you do not have access to an annotated code, Shepard's is a useful tool for locating cases interpreting a statute. Second, Shepard's is published more frequently than pocket parts and supplementary pamphlets are, so you may find more recent research references in Shepard's. Because Shepard's for statutes uses only letter codes to provide information about the cases listed, it does not provide as much information as the case summaries in an annotated code, and many of the cases listed in Shepard's will ultimately be summarized in an annotated code. Therefore, the utility of Shepardizing a statute will depend on the type of research you are doing, the number and nature of the research references in the statutory annotations, and the research materials to which you have access.

The process of Shepardizing statutes is the same as that for Shepardizing cases: (1) locate the correct set of books; (2) locate the correct volumes within the set; (3) locate the entries for the statute within each volume; and (4) interpret the entries.

**(1) LOCATE THE CORRECT SET OF BOOKS.** *Shepard's Federal Statute Citations* contains references to federal statutes. For state statutes, the set of Shepard's for each individual state usually contains either a section or a separate volume covering state statutes.

**(2) LOCATE THE CORRECT VOLUMES WITHIN THE SET.** The section labeled "What Your Library Should Contain" will list the volumes to which you should refer to Shepardize the statute.

**(3) LOCATE ENTRIES FOR THE STATUTE WITHIN EACH VOLUME.** Shepard's for statutes will be organized the same way the code is organized. For example, *Shepard's Federal Statute Citations* is organized according to Title and section; Shepard's for state codes organized by subject matter will generally be organized alphabetically by subject and then numerically by section within each subject.

Remember that you must look up the statute in each statutory Shepard's volume listed under "What Your Library Should Contain" to Shepardize the statute thoroughly.

**(4) INTERPRET THE ENTRIES.** Shepard's entries for statutes can be divided into three components: entries reflecting action taken on the statute by the legislature, references to cases citing the statute, and references to secondary sources discussing the statute. As with Shepard's for cases, the entries may be preceded by letter codes. A complete list of letter codes can be found at the beginning of each volume of Shepard's covering statutes.

In the first category of entries, you will see references to legislation affecting the statute. Each entry in this category will be accompanied by a letter code indicating the type of action taken. For example, if a federal statute has been amended, Shepard's will list the *Statutes at Large* citation for the law effecting the change, along with the letter "A" for amended. The example in Figure 6.11 shows how the entry appears in Shepard's.

In the second category, you will see references to cases that have cited the statute. Cases that have given significant treatment to the statute

**FIGURE 6.11** SHEPARD'S® ENTRY FOR A STATUTE

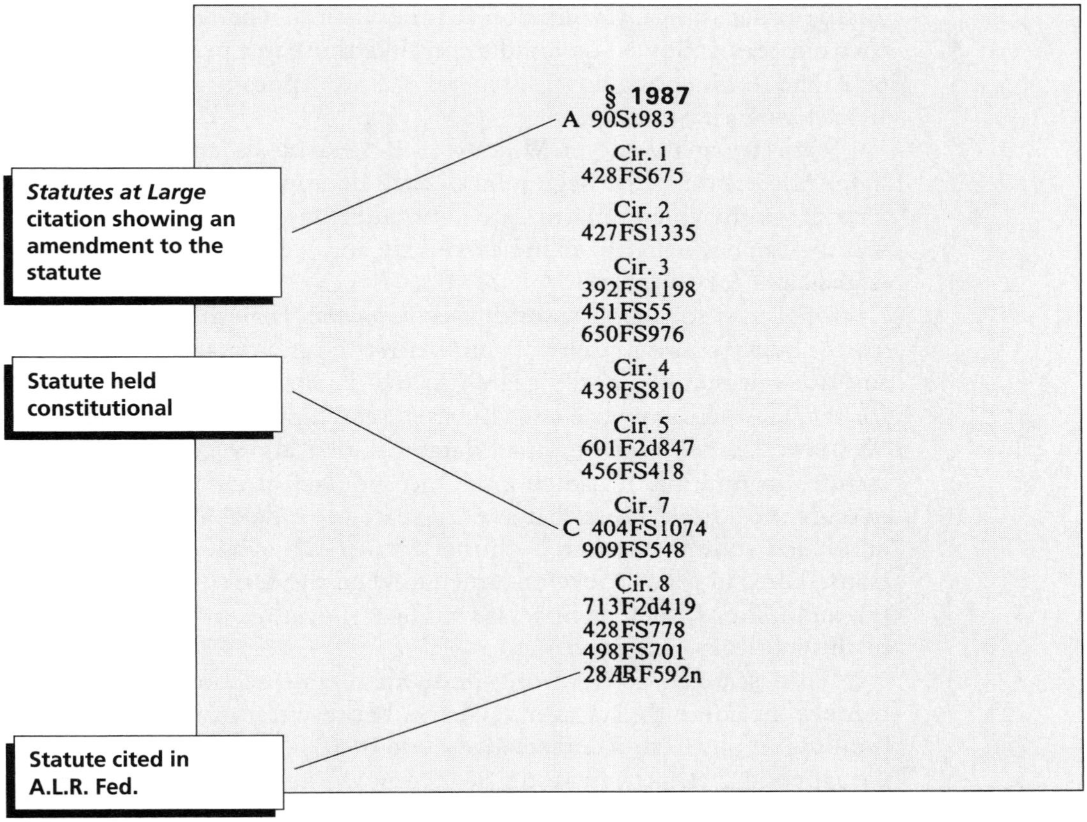

§ 1987
A 90St983

Cir. 1
428FS675

Cir. 2
427FS1335

Cir. 3
392FS1198
451FS55
650FS976

Cir. 4
438FS810

Cir. 5
601F2d847
456FS418

Cir. 7
C 404FS1074
909FS548

Cir. 8
713F2d419
428FS778
498FS701
28ARF592n

*Statutes at Large* citation showing an amendment to the statute

Statute held constitutional

Statute cited in A.L.R. Fed.

Reproduced by permission of LexisNexis. Further reproduction of any kind is strictly prohibited. From *Shepard's Federal Statute Citations*, Vol. 3, 1996, p. 240.

will be accompanied by treatment codes. In Figure 6.11, the statute was held constitutional; accordingly, the reference to that decision is accompanied by the treatment code "C" for constitutional.

The third category of information available in Shepard's for statutes is citations to secondary sources discussing the statute. An example of a reference to A.L.R. Fed. is noted in Figure 6.11.

## D. ELECTRONIC STATUTORY RESEARCH

### 1. LEXISNEXIS AND WESTLAW

LexisNexis and Westlaw contain annotated versions of many codes, including the federal code, all fifty state codes, and the District of Columbia code. In LexisNexis, the annotated version of the federal code is derived from U.S.C.S.; in Westlaw, it is derived from U.S.C.A. The display for an individual code section begins with a heading containing, among other things, the citation for the section. The text of the statute then appears, followed by annotations like those in a print code. Figures 6.12 and 6.13 show how a federal statute appears in Westlaw and LexisNexis, respectively.

Statutory materials in Westlaw and LexisNexis are usually up to date. A notation at the beginning of each document should tell you the date through which it is updated. In addition, both state and federal statutes can be Shepardized in LexisNexis, and Westlaw's KeyCite service is available for statutes.

One way to locate statutes electronically is with word searches. To conduct a word search, you must first select a database in which to search. You will ordinarily search in the database containing the code for the jurisdiction whose law you are researching. Both LexisNexis and Westlaw also contain combined databases that allow you to search for statutes in multiple jurisdictions. Once you select a database, you can execute the search. Note that a word search in a database containing an annotated code will search both the statutory language and the annotations. Thus, it will retrieve documents when the search terms appear in the annotations, such as in a case summary, even if they do not appear in the statutory language.

Word searches retrieve only individual code sections; they do not retrieve the complete statutory scheme. Because statutory analysis often requires application of interrelated code provisions, viewing only individual code sections can result in incomplete research. For example, a search might retrieve a code provision applicable to your problem but fail to retrieve a nearby section containing definitions of terms used in the applicable provision. If you relied only on the one section your initial search revealed, your research would not be accurate.

This precise difficulty causes many experienced researchers to avoid conducting statutory research solely with electronic sources. If you use the computer for statutory research, it is important to view related provisions to ensure that you consider other potentially applicable code sections.

In Westlaw, there are several ways to view a complete statutory scheme. After you retrieve a code section, you can browse preceding and subsequent code sections using the Docs in Sequence function. You can also view the code's Title (or subject) and Chapter outline along the left side of the screen by viewing the TOC tab. By clicking on the links displayed under the TOC tab, you can view the surrounding statutory material. You can also search the table of contents of a code without executing a word search by clicking on the Table of Contents link near the top of the screen. Follow the instructions on the screen to locate the table of contents for the code you want to research. Once you

**FIGURE 6.12**  TWO SCREENS SHOWING PORTIONS OF 8 U.S.C.A. § 1423 IN WESTLAW

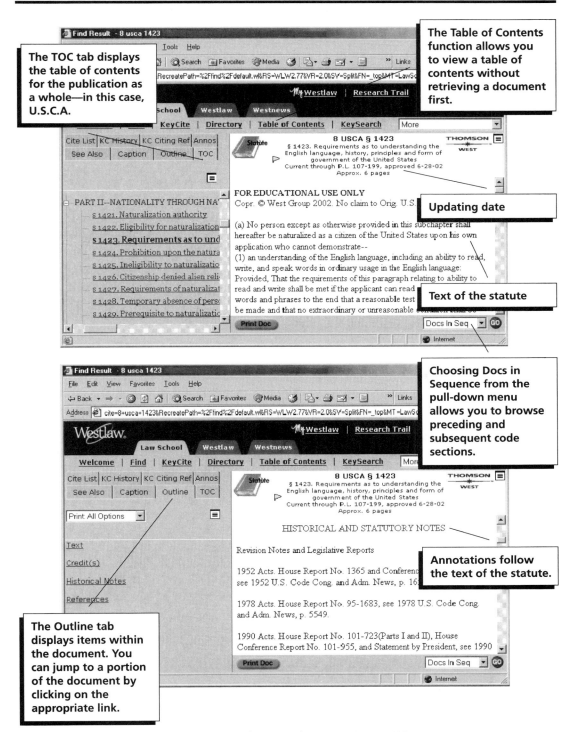

Reprinted with permission from West Group, from Westlaw, 8 U.S.C.A. § 1423.

**FIGURE 6.13**   THREE SCREENS SHOWING PORTIONS OF 8 U.S.C.S. § 1423 IN LEXISNEXIS

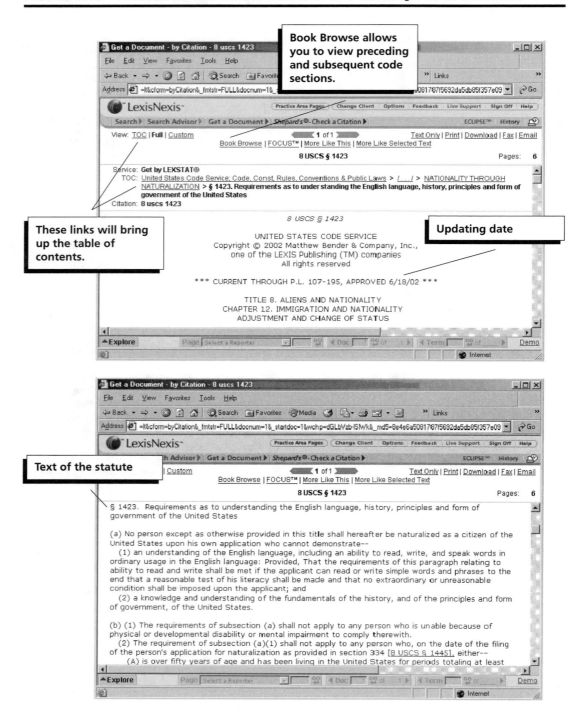

**FIGURE 6.13** THREE SCREENS SHOWING PORTIONS OF 8 U.S.C.S. § 1423 IN LEXISNEXIS
    *(Continued)*

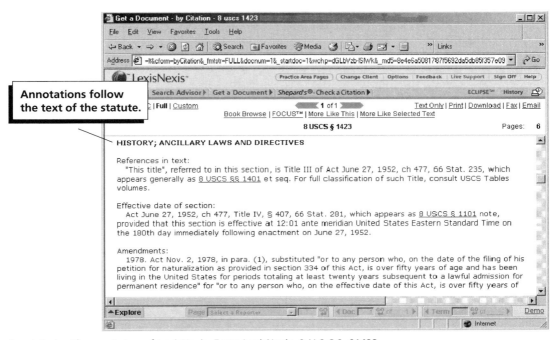

Reprinted with permission of LexisNexis. From LexisNexis, 8 U.S.C.S. §1423.

retrieve the table of contents, you can view individual code sections by clicking on the appropriate links. You can also execute a word search within selected portions of the code by checking the box next to the item(s) you want to search.

LexisNexis also has functions that allow you to view the statutory scheme. Once you retrieve a code section, you can view preceding and subsequent code sections using the Book Browse function. You can also view the code's Title (or subject) and Chapter outline by clicking on the TOC links. By clicking on the links displayed in the outline, you can view the surrounding statutory material. You can also search the table of contents of a code without executing a word search. For the federal code, the table of contents automatically appears with the search screen. For state codes, you must select the table of contents from the source directory. Once you retrieve the table of contents, you can view individual code sections by clicking on the appropriate links. You can also execute a word search within selected portions of the code by checking the box next to the item(s) you want to search.

A more thorough discussion of electronic search techniques can be found in Chapter 10.

## 2. INTERNET SOURCES

The federal code, all fifty state codes, and the District of Columbia code are available on the Internet. You can locate them through government web sites, such as the web site for the House of Representatives, or general legal research web sites. Often these sites have search functions that will allow you to retrieve statutes using word, subject, or table of contents searches. Appendix A lists the Internet addresses for web sites that may be useful for statutory research. If the code you need to research is available and up to date on the Internet, this can be an economical alternative to LexisNexis and Westlaw research.

Three caveats, however, are important to mention. First, the codes available on the Internet are usually unannotated codes, so you will only find the statutory text, not any additional research references. Second, it is important to check the date of any statutory material you use. If the material is not up to date, you will need to update your research. Third, statutory research often requires analysis of a complete statutory scheme. As with any other statutory research, you should not rely on an individual code section retrieved from a search without conducting more comprehensive research into related statutes.

## E. CITING STATUTES

The citation format for statutes is the same using either the *ALWD Manual* or the *Bluebook*. The general rules for citing statutes can be found in Rule 14 of the *ALWD Maual* and Rule 12 of the *Bluebook*.

Citations to statutes can be broken into two components: (a) information identifying the code and code section; and (b) parenthetical information containing the date of the code and any relevant supplements; this section may also include a reference to the publisher of the code. To find out the exact requirements for a citation to a particular code, you must look at Appendix 1 in the *ALWD Manual* or Table T.1 in the *Bluebook*, both of which tell you how to cite codes from every jurisdiction in the United States. Appendix 1 and Table T.1 include information on which code to cite if more than one is published, how to abbreviate the name of the code, and whether the name of the publisher must be included with the date in the parenthetical.

In a citation to a Title code, you will ordinarily give the Title number, the abbreviated name of the code, the section symbol, the section number, and a parenthetical containing the date the book was published and, if necessary, the publisher.

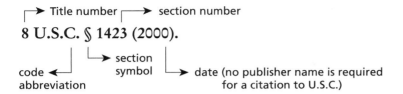

8 U.S.C. § 1423 (2000).

In a citation to a subject-matter code, you will ordinarily list the abbreviated name of the code, the section symbol, the section number, and a parenthetical containing the date the book was published and, if necessary, the publisher.

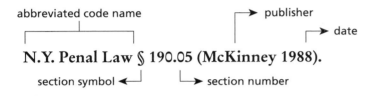

N.Y. Penal Law § 190.05 (McKinney 1988).

In this example, Appendix 1 and Table T.1 provide that citations to McKinney's *Consolidated Laws of New York Annotated* must include the name of the publisher in the parenthetical, which is why you see the reference to McKinney in this citation. In both examples, note that there is a space between the section symbol (§) and the section number.

Sometimes determining which date or dates to include in the parenthetical can be confusing. The answer is always a function of where a reader would have to look to find the full and up-to-date language of the statute. If the full statute is contained in the main volume of the code, the date in the parenthetical should refer only to the main volume. If the full statute is contained only in the pocket part, the date should refer only to the pocket part. If the reader must refer both to the main volume and to the pocket part, the parenthetical should list both dates. In making this determination, you should consider *only* the language of the statute itself, not the annotations. If the full text of the statute itself is in the main volume, you do not need to cite the pocket part even if it contains additional annotations. Once you have determined which date to place in the parenthetical, you should then refer to Appendix 1 or Table T.1 to determine whether the publisher must also be included. The following are examples of citations with different date information included in the parenthetical.

**N.Y. Penal Law § 190.05 (McKinney 1988).**

In this example, Appendix 1 and Table T.1 require the name of the publisher, and the full text of the statute can be found in the main volume.

**N.Y. Penal Law § 190.05 (McKinney Supp. 1997).**

In this example, Appendix 1 and Table T.1 require the name of the publisher, and the full text of the statute can be found in the pocket part.

**N.Y. Penal Law § 190.05 (McKinney 1988 & Supp. 1997).**

In this example, Appendix 1 and Table T.1 require the name of the publisher, and the reader must refer both to the main volume and to the pocket part to find the full text of the statute.

In citations to a code for which no publisher is required, the only difference would be the omission of the publisher's name, as in the example below.

**D.C. Code Ann. § 30-101 (1993 & Supp. 1998).**

When you look at the entries in Rule 12 and Table T.1 of the *Bluebook*, you will notice that the names of the codes are in large and small capital letters, e.g., N.Y. PENAL LAW §190.05 (McKinney 1988). Remember that this is the type style for law review footnotes, not for briefs and memoranda. Practitioners' Note P.1(h) directs that citations to statutes should be in regular type. Therefore, in briefs and memoranda, you should not use all capital letters, nor should you use large and small capital letters, even if you have the capability of printing in that font.

## F. SAMPLE PAGES FOR STATUTORY RESEARCH

Beginning on the next page, Figures 6.14 through 6.21 contain sample pages from U.S.C.A. showing the research process if you were researching federal statutes concerning the English proficiency requirements for naturalization as a United States citizen. Figures 6.22 through 6.24 contain sample pages from Vernon's *Texas Statutes and Codes Annotated* showing the research process if you were researching Texas statutes concerning assumption of the risk.

The first step in U.S.C.A. research is using the most recent General Index to locate relevant code sections. This example shows what you would find if you looked under "Naturalization."

**FIGURE 6.14** EXCERPT FROM THE U.S.C.A. GENERAL INDEX

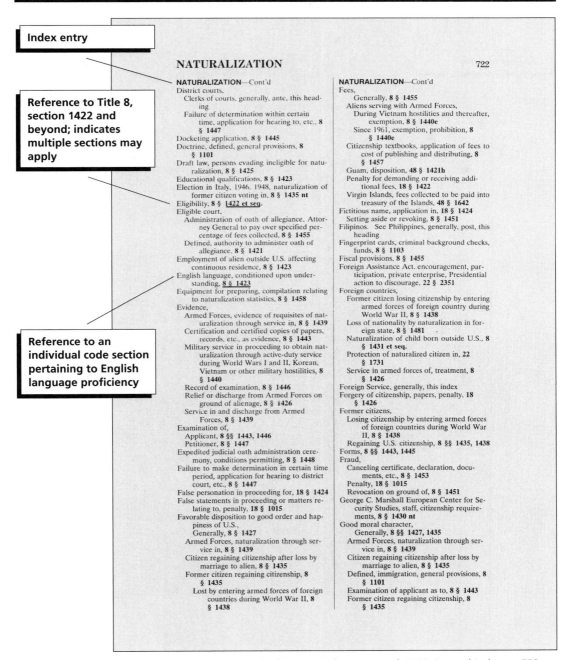

Reprinted with permission from West Group, *United States Code Annotated*, 1998 General Index, p. 722.

**The next step is looking up the statute in the main volume. Because the index indicates that several code provisions may be applicable, you might want to review the chapter outline.**

**FIGURE 6.15** EXCERPT FROM CHAPTER OUTLINE, TITLE 8, U.S.C.A.

Chapter outline

IMMIGRATION AND NATIONALITY     Ch. 12

Sec.
1406.   Persons living in and born in the Virgin Islands.
1407.   Persons living in and born in Guam.
1408.   Nationals but not citizens of the United States at birth.
1409.   Children born out of wedlock.

PART II.—NATIONALITY THROUGH NATURALIZATION

1421.   Jurisdiction to naturalize.
1422.   Eligibility for naturalization.
1423.   Requirements as to understanding the English language, history, principles and form of government of the United States.
1424.   Prohibition upon the naturalization of persons opposed to government or law, or who favor totalitarian forms of government.
1425.   Ineligibility to naturalization of deserters from the armed forces.
1426.   Citizenship denied alien relieved of service in armed forces because of alienage; conclusiveness of records.
1427.   Requirements of naturalization.
    (a) Residence.
    (b) Absences.
    (c) Physical presence.
    (d) Moral character.
    (e) Same; determination.
    (f) Restrictions.
1428.   Temporary absence of persons performing religious duties.
1429.   Prerequisite to naturalization; burden of proof.
1430.   Married persons and employees of certain non-profit organizations.
1431.   Children born outside United States of one alien and one citizen parent; conditions for automatic citizenship.
1432.   Children born outside of United States of alien parents; conditions for automatic citizenship.
1433.   Children born outside United States; naturalization on petition of citizen parent; requirements and exemptions.
1434.   Children adopted by citizens.
1435.   Former citizens regaining citizenship.
    (a) Requirements.
    (b) Additional requirements.
    (c) Oath of allegiance.
1436.   Nationals but not citizens; residence within outlying possessions.
1437.   Resident Philippine citizens excepted from certain requirements.

11

Reprinted with permission from West Group, *United States Code Annotated*, Title 8, 1970, p. 11.

**The individual code section sets out English proficiency requirements.**

**FIGURE 6.16**   8 U.S.C.A. § 1423

---

Ch. 12              NATURALIZATION              **8 § 1423**

**6. Minors**

Minority was said to be no bar to admission to citizenship. U. S. v. Stabile, C.C.A.Fla.1928, 24 F.2d 98.

Where Chinese merchants were admitted to United States prior to 1924, as permanent residents, their minor children, who were admitted after 1924, but prior to 1932, and who resided continuously in United States, were permanent residents, and could be naturalized. In re Jeu Foon, D.C.Ark.1950, 94 F.Supp. 728, affirmed 193 F.2d 117.

Where petitioner was admitted to United States in 1934 as an unmarried minor child of a resident Chinese "treaty trader", and both petitioner and his father resided continuously in country since their respective entries and both were merchants engaged in trade, petition's entry was for "permanent residence" within meaning of 1943 amendment to former section 703 of this title [now covering this section], and he was eligible for naturalization upon proof that he was a United States citizen. Petition of Wong Choon Hoi, D.C.Cal.1947, 71 F.Supp. 160, appeal dismissed 164 F.2d 696.

**7. Free persons**

The word "free," originally used in recognition of the existence of slavery, no longer has any practical significance. Takao Ozawa v. U. S., 1922, 43 S.Ct. 65, 260 U.S. 178, 67 L.Ed. 199.

**8. American Indians**

The general statutes of naturalization were said not to apply to Indians, they being naturalizable by special Act of Congress or by treaty. 1856, 7 Op.Atty. Gen. 746.

An Indian born in British Columbia would not be admitted to citizenship by naturalization in the United States. In re Burton, 1900, 1 Alaska 111.

**9. Pardoned persons**

Pardons have no effect on right to naturalization. Petition for Naturalization of Quintana, D.C.Fla.1962, 203 F. Supp. 376.

Alien could not be naturalized where he had been convicted of second degree murder, even though governor had given alien full and complete pardon and had restored his civil rights more than five years prior to filing of application for naturalization. Id.

> **Section number**

> **Name of the section**

> **Text of the statute**

**§ 1423.**   **Requirements as to understanding the English language, history, principles and form of government of the United States**

No person except as otherwise provided in this subchapter shall hereafter be naturalized as a citizen of the United States upon his own petition who cannot demonstrate—

(1) an understanding of the English language, including an ability to read, write, and speak words in ordinary usage in the English language: *Provided,* That this requirement shall not apply to any person physically unable to comply therewith, if otherwise qualified to be naturalized, or to any person who, on the effective date of this chapter, is over fifty years of age and has been living in the United States for periods totaling at least twenty years: *Provided further,* That the requirements of this section relating to ability to read and write shall be met if the applicant can read or write simple words and phrases to the end that a reasonable test of his literacy shall be made and that no extraordinary or unreasonable condition shall be imposed upon the applicant; and

(2) a knowledge and understanding of the fundamentals of the history, and of the principles and form of government, of the United States.

June 27, 1952, c. 477, Title III, ch. 2, § 312, 66 Stat. 239.

501

---

**The annotations list a variety of research references.**

**FIGURE 6.17** ANNOTATIONS ACCOMPANYING 8 U.S.C.A. § 1423

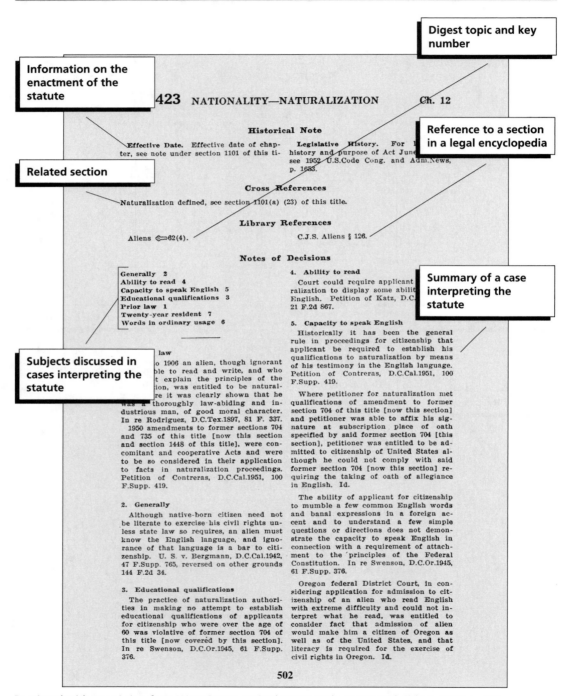

Digest topic and key number

Information on the enactment of the statute

Reference to a section in a legal encyclopedia

Related section

Summary of a case interpreting the statute

Subjects discussed in cases interpreting the statute

**423 NATIONALITY—NATURALIZATION Ch. 12**

**Historical Note**

Effective Date. Effective date of chapter, see note under section 1101 of this title.

Legislative History. For legislative history and purpose of Act June see 1952 U.S.Code Cong. and Adm.News, p. 1683.

**Cross References**

Naturalization defined, see section 1101(a) (23) of this title.

**Library References**

Aliens ⚖62(4).

C.J.S. Aliens § 126.

**Notes of Decisions**

Generally 2
Ability to read 4
Capacity to speak English 5
Educational qualifications 3
Prior law 1
Twenty-year resident 7
Words in ordinary usage 6

law

...o 1906 an alien, though ignorant ...ble to read and write, and who ...t explain the principles of the ...ion, was entitled to be natural- ...re it was clearly shown that he was a thoroughly law-abiding and industrious man, of good moral character. In re Rodriguez, D.C.Tex.1897, 81 F. 337.

1950 amendments to former sections 704 and 735 of this title [now this section and section 1448 of this title], were concomitant and cooperative Acts and were to be so considered in their application to facts in naturalization proceedings. Petition of Contreras, D.C.Cal.1951, 100 F.Supp. 419.

**2. Generally**

Although native-born citizen need not be literate to exercise his civil rights unless state law so requires, an alien must know the English language, and ignorance of that language is a bar to citizenship. U. S. v. Bergmann, D.C.Cal.1942, 47 F.Supp. 765, reversed on other grounds 144 F.2d 34.

**3. Educational qualifications**

The practice of naturalization authorities in making no attempt to establish educational qualifications of applicants for citizenship who were over the age of 60 was violative of former section 704 of this title [now covered by this section]. In re Swenson, D.C.Or.1945, 61 F.Supp. 376.

**4. Ability to read**

Court could require applicant ...ralization to display some abilit... English. Petition of Katz, D.C... 21 F.2d 867.

**5. Capacity to speak English**

Historically it has been the general rule in proceedings for citizenship that applicant be required to establish his qualifications to naturalization by means of his testimony in the English language. Petition of Contreras, D.C.Cal.1951, 100 F.Supp. 419.

Where petitioner for naturalization met qualifications of amendment to former section 704 of this title [now this section] and petitioner was able to affix his signature at subscription place of oath specified by said former section 704 [this section], petitioner was entitled to be admitted to citizenship of United States although he could not comply with said former section 704 [now this section] requiring the taking of oath of allegiance in English. Id.

The ability of applicant for citizenship to mumble a few common English words and banal expressions in a foreign accent and to understand a few simple questions or directions does not demonstrate the capacity to speak English in connection with a requirement of attachment to the principles of the Federal Constitution. In re Swenson, D.C.Or.1945, 61 F.Supp. 376.

Oregon federal District Court, in considering application for admission to citizenship of an alien who read English with extreme difficulty and could not interpret what he read, was entitled to consider fact that admission of alien would make him a citizen of Oregon as well as of the United States, and that literacy is required for the exercise of civil rights in Oregon. Id.

502

Reprinted with permission from West Group, *United States Code Annotated*, Title 8, 1970, p. 502.

**The next step is checking the pocket part. The pocket part shows new statutory language that supersedes the language in the main volume.**

**FIGURE 6.18** POCKET PART ENTRY FOR 8 U.S.C.A. § 1423

---

ALIENS AND NATIONALITY      8 § 1423

**32. Jurisdiction of United States courts— Generally**

Tutun v. United States, U.S.N.Y.1926, 46 S.Ct. 425, 270 U.S. 568, 70 L.Ed. 738, [main volume] conformed to 13 F.2d 541, certiorari granted 47 S.Ct. 243, 273 U.S. 685, 71 L.Ed. 839, remanded 47 S.Ct. 334, 273 U.S. 777, 71 L.Ed. 887.

**32a. —— Standing**

Child of United States citizen mother denied citizenship under statute providing citizenship only for children of citizen fathers had standing to bring constitutional challenge to statute, though courts did not have specific congressional authorization to grant citizenship, where her suit was directed at constitutional wrong. Aguayo v. Christopher, N.D.Ill.1994, 865 F.Supp. 479.

**40. —— Appellate**

In re Bogunovic, Cal.1941, 114 P.2d 581, [main volume] 18 Cal.2d 160.

**III. MANNER AND CONDITIONS OF NATURALIZATION**

Eligibility requirements   78
Waiver   79

**73. Naturalization as a right**

Filipino veterans, who served in the United States armed forces during World War II, were not entitled to become naturalized citizens, where statutes under which veterans applied for naturalization had expired; therefore, veterans were not entitled to mandamus relief compelling the Immigration and Naturalization Service to process their naturalization applications. Agcaoili v. Gustafson, C.A.9 (Cal.) 1989, 870 F.2d 462.

**74. Compliance with law as prerequisite to naturalization**

No alien has right to naturalization without compliance with all statutory requirements. Petition of Di Franco, S.D.N.Y.1972, 339 F.Supp. 414.

**76. Doubt, manner of resolving**

Petitioner applying for naturalization bears burden of proof; any doubts must be resolved against petitioner and in favor of government. Tan v. U.S. Dept. of Justice, I.N.S., D.Hawai'i 1996, 931 F.Supp. 725.

**78. Eligibility requirements**

This section, which provides that any naturalization petition filed after Sept. 26, 1961 would be governed by requirements of this subchapter then in effect did not bar petitioner, asserting that he had been unconstitutionally denied opportunity to apply for benefit decreed by Congress, from relying on 1940 Act's eligibility requirements of former provisions of this section. Olegario v. U. S., C.A.2 (N.Y.) 1980, 629 F.2d 204, certiorari denied 101 S.Ct. 1513, 450 U.S. 980, 67 L.Ed.2d 814.

**79. Waiver**

Alien, whose petition for naturalization had been transferred to the district court for the Eastern District of Virginia and who submitted himself to that court even though he later established residency in Washington, D.C., waived his right to assert special venue provision which states that court's jurisdiction to naturalize persons extends only to residents within court's jurisdiction. In re Duncan, C.A.9 (Cal.) 1983, 713 F.2d 538.

**§ 1422. Eligibility for naturalization**

The right of a person to become a naturalized citizen of the United States shall not be denied or abridged because of race or sex or because such person is married.

(As amended Oct. 24, 1988, Pub.L. 100–525, § 9(t), 102 Stat. 2621.)

**HISTORICAL AND STATUTORY NOTES**

**1988 Amendment**

Pub.L. 100–525, § 9(t), struck out: "Notwithstanding section 405(b) of this Act, this section shall apply to any person whose petition for naturalization shall hereafter be filed. or shall have been pending on the effective date of this chapter."

**LIBRARY REFERENCES**

Aliens ⊙61–66.
C.J.S. Aliens §§ 124–132.

**NOTES OF DECISIONS**

**2. Generally**

No alien has right to naturalization unless all statutory requirements have been complied with. U. S. v. Demjanjuk, N.D.Ohio 1981, 518 F.Supp. 1362, affirmed 680 F.2d 32, certiorari denied 103 S.Ct. 447, 459 U.S. 1036, 74 L.Ed.2d 602.

**§ 1423. Requirements as to understanding the English language, history, principles and form of government of the United States**

(a) No person except as otherwise provided in this subchapter shall hereafter be naturalized as a citizen of the United States upon his own application who cannot demonstrate—

(1) an understanding of the English language, including an ability to read, write, and speak words in ordinary usage in the English language: *Provided,* That the

391

---

**New statutory language supersedes the language in the main volume.**

**FIGURE 6.18** POCKET PART ENTRY FOR 8 U.S.C.A. § 1423 *(Continued)*

**8 § 1423** ALIENS AND NATIONALITY

requirements of this paragraph relating to ability to read and write shall be met if the applicant can read or write simple words and phrases to the end that a reasonable test of his literacy shall be made and that no extraordinary or unreasonable condition shall be imposed upon the applicant; and

(2) a knowledge and understanding of the fundamentals of the history, and of the principles and form of government, of the United States.

(b)(1) The requirements of subsection (a) of this section shall not apply to any person who is unable because of physical or developmental disability or mental impairment to comply therewith.

(2) The requirement of subsection (a)(1) of this section shall not apply to any person who, on the date of the filing of the person's application for naturalization as provided in section 1445 of this title, either—

(A) is over fifty years of age and has been living in the United States for periods totaling at least twenty years subsequent to a lawful admission for permanent residence, or

(B) is over fifty-five years of age and has been living in the United States for periods totaling at least fifteen years subsequent to a lawful admission for permanent residence.

(3) The Attorney General, pursuant to regulations, shall provide for special consideration, as determined by the Attorney General, concerning the requirement of subsection (a)(2) of this section with respect to any person who, on the date of the filing of the person's application for naturalization as provided in section 1445 of this title, is over sixty-five years of age and has been living in the United States for periods totaling at least twenty years subsequent to a lawful admission for permanent residence.

(As amended Nov. 2, 1978, Pub.L. 95–579, § 3, 92 Stat. 2474; Nov. 29, 1990, Pub.L. 101–649, Title IV, § 403, 104 Stat. 5039; Dec. 12, 1991, Pub.L. 102–232, Title III, § 305(m)(2), 105 Stat. 1750; Oct. 25, 1994, Pub.L. 103–416, Title I, § 108(a), 108 Stat. 4309.)

> **Annotations follow the text of the statute.**

### HISTORICAL AND STATUTORY NOTES

**1994 Amendments**

Subsec. (a). Pub.L. 103–416, § 108(a)(1), designated existing provisions as subsec. (a).

Subsec. (a)(1). Pub.L. 103–416, § 108(a)(2), (3), struck out provisions which exempted individuals over the age of 50 and 55 years and living in the United States as permanent residents for periods totaling at least 20 and 15 years, respectively, from english language proficiency requirement, and substituted reference to this par. for reference to this section.

Subsec. (b). Pub.L. 103–416, § 108(a)(4), added subsec. (b).

**1991 Amendments**

Pub.L. 102–232 substituted reference to application for reference to petition wherever appearing.

**1990 Amendment**

Par. (1). Pub.L. 101–649 designated portion of existing text as cl. (A) and added cl. (B).

**1978 Amendment**

Par. (1). Pub.L. 95–579 substituted "person who, on the date of the filing of his petition for naturalization as provided in section 1445 of this title, is over fifty years of age and has been living in the United States for periods totaling at least twenty years subsequent to a lawful admission for permanent residence" for "person who, on the effective date of this chapter, is over fifty years of age and has been living in the United States for periods totaling at least twenty years".

**Effective Date of 1994 Amendments**

Section 108(c) of Pub.L. 103–416 provided that: "The amendments made by subsection (a) [amending this section] shall take effect on the date of the enactment of this Act [Oct. 25, 1994] and shall apply to applications for naturalization filed on or after such date and to such applications pending on such date."

**Effective Date of 1991 Amendment**

Amendments by sections 302 through 308 of Pub.L. 102–232, except as otherwise specifically provided, effective as if included in the enactment of Pub.L. 101–649, see section 310(1) of Pub.L. 102–232, set out as a note under section 1101 of this title.

Amendment by section 305(m)(2) of Pub.L. 102–232 effective as if included in section 407(d) of Pub.L. 101–649, see section 305(m) of Pub.L. 102–232, set out as a note under section 1101 of this title.

**Effective Date of 1990 Amendment; Savings Provisions**

Amendment by Title IV of Pub.L. 101–649 effective Nov. 29, 1990, with general savings provisions, see section 408(a)(3) and (d) of Pub.L. 101–649, set out as a note under section 1421 of this title.

**Promulgation of Regulations**

Section 108(d) of Pub.L. 103–416 provided that: "Not later than 120 days after the date of

392

Reprinted with permission from West Group, *United States Code Annotated*, 1997 Cumulative Pocket Part, Title 8, pp. 391–92.

**The pocket part also shows additional research references.**

**FIGURE 6.19** POCKET PART ENTRY FOR 8 U.S.C.A. § 1423

ALIENS AND NATIONALITY                                    8 § 1424

enactment of this Act [Oct. 25, 1994], the Attorney General shall promulgate regulations to carry out section 312(b)(3) of the Immigration and Nationality Act (as amended by subsection (a)) (b)(3) of this section]."

**Legislative History**

For legislative history and purpose of Pub.L. 95–579, see 1978 U.S. Code Cong. and Adm. News, p. 5549. See also, Pub.L. 101–649, 1990 U.S. Code Cong. and Adm. News, p. 6710; Pub.L. 102–232, 1991 U.S. Code Cong. and Adm. News, p. 1362; Pub.L. 103–416, 1994 U.S. Code Cong. and Adm. News, p. 3516.

> **C.F.R. cross-references**

WEST'S FEDERAL PRACTICE MANUAL

Literacy and understanding requirements, see § 6635.

Who may be naturalized, generally, see § 6631.

CODE OF FEDERAL REGULATIONS

Educational requirements, see 8 CFR 312.1 et seq.

State impact assistance, legalization grants, see 45 CFR § 402.1 et seq.

LIBRARY REFERENCES

Aliens ⊂62(4).
C.J.S. Aliens § 126.

NOTES OF DECISIONS

Findings  9
Physical incapacity  8

> **Research references**

**5. Capacity to speak English**

Direct attack on congressional exercise of nat[uralizatio]n power, through suit challenging English language requirement of this section, was [foreclosed] as nonjusticiable in view of foreign relations powers of Congress. Trujillo-Hernandez v. Farrell, C.A.5 (Tex.) 1974, 503 F.2d 954, certiorari denied 95 S.Ct. 1976, 421 U.S. 977, 44 L.Ed.2d 468.

Even though alien could not challenge English language requirement of this section, since such direct attack on congressional exercise of naturalization power was foreclosed as nonjusticiable, alien was entitled to procedural due process in processing of his petition for naturalization, as guard against administrative arbitrariness. Trujillo-Hernandez v. Farrell, C.A.5 (Tex.) 1974, 503 F.2d 954, certiorari denied 95 S.Ct. 1976, 421 U.S. 977, 44 L.Ed.2d 468.

Naturalization petitioner who was legally blind under Connecticut law, C.G.S.A. § 10–294a, was within provision of this section barring naturalization of persons who do not have an understanding of the English language. In re Sandolo, D.C.Conn.1969, 307 F.Supp. 221.

**8. Physical incapacity**

Congress did not intend to include age within the "physically unable" exception of this section in part providing that no person shall be naturalized who cannot demonstrate an understanding of the English language, provided that "this requirement shall not apply to any per[son physi]cally unable to comply therewith, if [otherwise] qualified to be naturalized, or to a[ny person] who, on the effective date of this chap[ter, is over] fifty years of age and has been liv[ing in the] United States for periods totaling at [least twen]ty years"; rather, "physically unable" is limited to such disabilities as deafness or blindness. In re Blasko, C.A.3 (Pa.) 1972, 466 F.2d 1340.

Under this section, petitioner, who suffered from total deafness, but who was otherwise qualified, was entitled to citizenship. In re Vazquez, S.D.N.Y.1971, 327 F.Supp. 935.

**9. Findings**

District court finding, preceded by a like finding of the Immigration and Naturalization Service, that petitioner could not be naturalized for failure to comply with the writing requirement of this section providing that a person seeking naturalization must demonstrate an understanding of the English language including an ability to write words in ordinary usage in the English language, was not clearly erroneous. In re Blasko, C.A.3 (Pa.) 1972, 466 F.2d 1340.

> **Newer cases interpreting the statute**

**§ 1424.  Prohibition upon the naturalization of persons opposed to government or law, or who favor totalitarian forms of government**

(a) Notwithstanding the provisions of section 405(b) of this Act, no person shall hereafter be naturalized as a citizen of the United States—

(1) who advocated or teaches, or who is a member of or affiliated with any organization that advocates or teaches, opposition to all organized government; or

(2) who is a member of or affiliated with (A) the Communist Party of the United States; (B) any other totalitarian party of the United States; (C) the Communist Political Association; (D) the Communist or other totalitarian party of any State of the United States, of any foreign state, or of any political or geographical subdivision of any foreign state; (E) any section, subsidiary, branch, affiliate, or subdivision of any such association or party; or (F) the direct predecessors or successors of any such association or party, regardless of what name such group or organization may have used, may now bear, or may hereafter adopt, unless such alien

393

Reprinted with permission from West Group, *United States Code Annotated*, 1997 Cumulative Pocket Part, Title 8, p. 393.

**The next step is checking each of the noncumulative supplements. This page is from the May 1997 supplement. Because no reference to the statute appears, there are no changes to the statute or additional annotations.**

**FIGURE 6.20**    NONCUMULATIVE SUPPLEMENT ENTRY FOR 8 U.S.C.A. § 1423

---

8 § 1401                                                               ALIENS AND NATIONALITY

SUBCHAPTER III—NATIONALITY AND NATURALIZATION

Part I—Nationality at Birth and Collective Naturalization

§ 1401.   Nationals and citizens of United States at birth

**LAW REVIEW AND JOURNAL COMMENTARIES**

Domesticating Federal Indian Law.  Philip P. Frickey, 81 Minn.L.Rev. 31 (1996).

§ 1409.   Children born out of wedlock

**NOTES OF DECISIONS**

**½.  Constitutionality**

Additional requirements for citizenship of illegitimate child born outside United States of alien mother and American father did not represent unconstitutional denial of equal protection based on status of child or sex of parent; desire to promote early ties to United States citizen relatives and recognition that mothers and fathers of illegitimate children are not similarly situated supported additional requirements.  Miller v. Christopher, C.A.D.C.1996, 96 F.3d 1467, 321 U.S.App.D.C. 19, petition for certiorari filed.

**3.  Persons entitled to maintain action**

Nonresident alien demonstrated redressable injury for standing to challenge constitutionality of statute governing citizenship of illegitimate child born abroad of American father and alien mother; she did not request that court grant her citizenship, but instead sought declaration that statute was unconstitutional and finding by court, under general rule applicable to persons born outside United States, that she was citizen from birth.  Miller v. Christopher, C.A.D.C.1996, 96 F.3d 1467, 321 U.S.App.D.C. 19, petition for certiorari filed.

Part II—Nationality Through Naturalization

§ 1427.   Requirements of naturalization

*[See main volume and pocket part for text of (a) to (e)]*

**(f) Persons making extraordinary contributions to national security**

(1) Whenever the Director of Central Intelligence, the Attorney General and the Commissioner of Immigration determine that an applicant otherwise eligible for naturalization has made an extraordinary contribution to the national security of the United States or to the conduct of United States intelligence activities, the applicant may be naturalized without regard to the residence and physical presence requirements of this section, or to the prohibitions of section 1424 of this title, and no residence within a particular State or district of the Service in the United States shall be required: *Provided,* That the applicant has continuously resided in the United States for at least one year prior to naturalization: *Provided, further,* That the provisions of this subsection shall not apply to any alien described in clauses (i) through (iv) of section 1158(b)(2)(A) of this title.

*[See pocket part for text of (2) and (3)]*

(As amended Sept. 30, 1996, Pub.L. 104–208, Div. C, Title III, § 308(g)(7)(F), 110 Stat. 3009–624.)

**HISTORICAL AND STATUTORY NOTES**

**1996 Amendments**

Subsec. (f)(1).  Pub.L. 104–208, § 308(g)(7)(F), substituted "clauses (i) through (v) of section 1158(b)(2)(A) of this title" for "subparagraphs (A) through (D) of section 1253(h)(2) of this title".

**Effective Date of 1996 Amendments**

Amendment by section 308 of Div. C of Pub.L. 104–208 effective, with certain exceptions and subject to

certain transitional rules, on the first day of the first month beginning more than 180 days after Sept. 30, 1996, see section 309 of Div. C of Pub.L. 104–208, set out as a note under section 1101 of this title.

**NOTES OF DECISIONS**

**III.  CHARACTER, ATTACHMENT TO CONSTITUTION, ETC.**

**99.  —— Fraud**

Alien misrepresented his wartime employment, so that he was not lawfully admitted to United States and was ineligible for citizenship, where he represented to

United States Displaced Persons Commission analyst and American vice consul that he was teacher from 1940 to 1943 when he was actually serving as officer in armed Lithuanian unit assisting Germans in occupation of Lithuania and persecution of Jews there.  U.S. v. Stelmokas, C.A.3 (Pa.) 1996, 100 F.3d 302.

354

> **Any new information would have appeared here.**

---

Reprinted with permission from West Group, *United States Code Annotated,* Pamphlet Number 1 (May 1997), p. 354.

**Because the supplements are noncumulative, any supplements after May 1997 must also be checked. In this example, July 1997 is the latest supplement. The July 1997 noncumulative supplement shows a new annotation but no new statutory language.**

**FIGURE 6.21** NONCUMULATIVE SUPPLEMENT ENTRY FOR 8 U.S.C.A. § 1423

ALIENS AND NATIONALITY                                    8 § 1445

§ 1367.  Penalties for disclosure of information
*[For text, see 1997 Pamphlet No. 1]*

§ 1368.  Increase in INS detention facilities; report on detention space
*[For text, see 1997 Pamphlet No. 1]*

SUBCHAPTER III—NATIONALITY AND NATURALIZATION

PART II—NATIONALITY THROUGH NATURALIZATION

§ 1421.  Naturalization authority

LAW REVIEW AND JOURNAL COMMENTARIES

Reforming the administrative naturalization process:
Reducing delays while increasing fairness.  Arnold
Rochvarg, 9 Geo.Immigr.L.J. 397 (1995).

**Section reference**

§ 1423.  Requirements as to understanding the English language, history, principles and form
of government of the United States

LAW REVIEW AND JOURNAL COMMENTARIES

Reforming the administrative naturalization process:
Reducing delays while increasing fairness.  Arnold
Rochvarg, 9 Geo.Immigr.L.J. 397 (1995).

§ 1427.  Requirements of naturalization
*[For text, see 1997 Pamphlet No. 1]*

**New annotation**

LAW REVIEW AND JOURNAL COMMENTARIES

Reforming the administrative naturalization process:
Reducing delays while increasing fairness.  Arnold
Rochvarg, 9 Geo.Immigr.L.J. 397 (1995).

§ 1429.  Prerequisite to naturalization; burden of proof
*[For text, see 1997 Pamphlet No. 1]*

LAW REVIEW AND JOURNAL COMMENTARIES

Reforming the administrative naturalization process:
Reducing delays while increasing fairness.  Arnold
Rochvarg, 9 Geo.Immigr.L.J. 397 (1995).

§ 1430.  Married persons and employees of certain nonprofit organizations

LAW REVIEW AND JOURNAL COMMENTARIES

Reforming the administrative naturalization process:
Reducing delays while increasing fairness.  Arnold
Rochvarg, 9 Geo.Immigr.L.J. 397 (1995).

§ 1436.  Nationals but not citizens; residence within outlying possessions

LAW REVIEW AND JOURNAL COMMENTARIES

HUD shuts the door: Restrictions on housing assistance to noncitizens.  9 Geo.Immigr.L.J. 801 (1995).

§ 1445.  Application for naturalization; declaration of intention

LAW REVIEW AND JOURNAL COMMENTARIES

Reforming the administrative naturalization process:
Reducing delays while increasing fairness.  Arnold
Rochvarg, 9 Geo.Immigr.L.J. 397 (1995).

87

Reprinted with permission from West Group, *United States Code Annotated,* Pamphlet Number 2 (July 1997), p. 87.

**In state statutory research, the first step is using the subject index to locate relevant code sections. This example shows what you would find if looked under Assumption of Risk in the General Index to Vernon's *Texas Statutes and Codes Annotated.***

**FIGURE 6.22**    VERNON'S *TEXAS STATUTES AND CODES ANNOTATED* GENERAL INDEX

## ASSOCIATIONS

**ASSOCIATIONS AND SOCIETIES**—Cont'd
Prevention of cruelty to animals, tax exemption, **Tax 11.18**
Private enterprise demonstration associations, exemptions, **Tax 11.23**
Probation, **CCrP 17A.08**
Process, **CP & R 17.021**
Professional Associations and Societies, generally, this index
Property and casualty insurance guaranty association, **Ins 21.28–C**
Property Owners Associations, generally, this index
Public employees, group life insurance, **Ins 3.50**
Purporting to represent, deceptive advertising, **Bus & C 17.12**
Real estate, unknown landowner, actions, **CP & R 17.005**
Release, institutional funds, management or investment, **Prop 163.008**
Religious Organizations and Societies, generally, this index
Republic of Texas, organizations chartered by congress of, tax exemptions, **Tax 11.23**
Restraint of trade.  Monopolies and Unfair Trade, generally, this index
Risk retention groups, products liability, **Ins 21.54**
Rural Credit Unions, generally, this index
San Jacinto museum of history association, **P & W 22.016**
Savings and Loan Associations, generally, this index
School officers and employees, group insurance, **Ins 1578.001 et seq.**
Schoolteachers, this index
Sedition, **Gov 557.003**
Standards, institutional funds, management or investment, **Prop 163.007**
State officers and employees, solicitation, regulation, business entities, crimes and offenses, **Gov 572.055**
Summons, this index
Summons, **CCrP 17A.03**
Taxation,
  Gross Receipts Tax, generally, this index
  Insurance, allocation, **Ins 4.12**
  Prevention of cruelty to animals society, exemption, **Tax 11.18**
  Private enterprise demonstration associations, exemptions, **Tax 11.23**
  Youth development associations, exemptions, **Tax 11.19**
Teachers retirement system, nonprofit associations, dues, **Gov 825.516**
Title insurance guaranty association, **Ins 9.48**
Trade Associations, generally, this index
Trusts and monopolies.  Monopolies and Unfair Trade, generally, this index
Unincorporated nonprofit associations, generally.  Nonprofit Corporations, this index
Unions.  Labor Organizations, generally, this index
Venue, CCrP 13.19;  CP & R 15.001 et seq.
  Courts, CP & R 15.094

**ASSOCIATIONS AND SOCIETIES**—Cont'd
Wildlife management associations areas, **P & W 81.301 et seq.**
  Hunting lease licenses, **P & W 43.0432, 43.044**
Windstorms, insurance associations, **Ins 21.49**
Workers Compensation, this index
Youth development associations, exemptions, **Tax 11.19**

**ASSUMED BUSINESS OR PROFESSIONAL NAME ACT**
Generally, **Bus & C 36.01 et seq.**

**ASSUMED OR FICTITIOUS NAMES**
Generally, **Bus & C 36.01 et seq.**
Accountants, financial statements and reports, **Occ 901.456**
Actions and proceedings, parent child relationship, identification of parties on appeal, **Fam 109.002**
Certificates and certification, **Bus & C 36.10 et seq.**
Corporations, certificates, filing, **Corp 2.05**
Definitions, **Bus & C 36.02**
Filing, **Bus & C 36.10 et seq.**
Foreign corporations, **Corp 8.03**
Foreign insurance, **Ins 982.304**
Insurance, this index
Limited liability company, **Civ.Stat. 1528n § 2.03**
Motor vehicles, salvage vehicle dealers, licenses and permits, **Occ 2302.106**
Multiple employer welfare arrangements, **Ins 3.95–5**
Negotiable instruments, signatures, **Bus & C 3.401**
Secured transactions, filing, **Bus & C 9.402**
Signatures,
  Abandonment statement, Bus
  Certificates, **Bus & C 36.10,**
  Filing, **Bus & C 36.18**
Surveys and surveyors, license
  **Occ 1071.353**

**ASSUMED RISK ACT (RAILROAD EMPLOYEES)**
Generally, **Civ.Stat. 6437**

**ASSUMING INSURER**
Definitions,
  Fire and marine insurance, reinsurance, **Ins 6.16**
  Life, health and accident insurance, **Ins 3.10**
  Reinsurance, **Ins 5.75–1**

**ASSUMPTION OF RISK**
Affirmative defense, **CP & R 93.001**
Labor and Employment, this index
Lloyds insurance, **Ins 18.16**

**ASTHMA**
Children and minors, special health care needs, pilot programs, **H & S 35.014 et seq.**

230

*Index entry*

*Cross-reference to a related subject*

*Reference to the Civil Practice and Remedies Code, § 93.001*

Reprinted with permission from West Group, *Vernon's Texas Statutes and Codes Annotated*, 2002 General Index A-E, p. 230.

**The next step is looking up the statute in the main volume. This code section sets out the affirmative defense of assumption of the risk, and the annotations list a variety of research references.**

**FIGURE 6.23**   TEXAS CIVIL PRACTICE AND REMEDIES CODE § 93.001

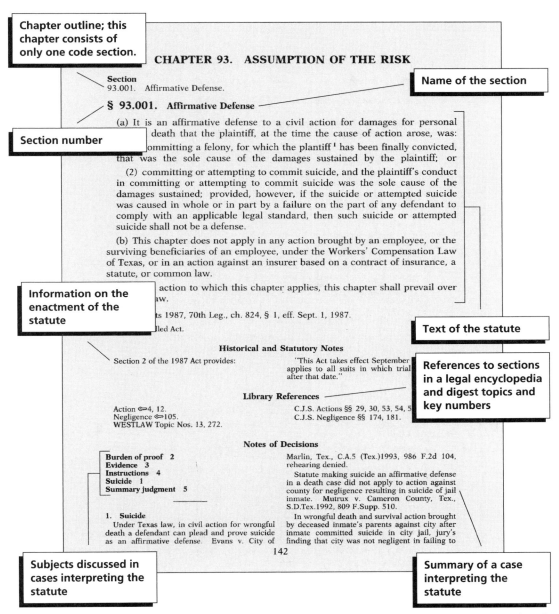

Repinted with permission from West Group, Vol. 4 *Vernon's Texas Codes Annotated* § 93.001, p. 142 (1997).

**The next step is checking the pocket part. The pocket part shows new statutory language that supersedes the language in the main volume. The state code may include cumulative or noncumulative supplements in addition to the pocket part. If so, you need to check those supplements to further update your research.**

**FIGURE 6.24**   POCKET PART ENTRY FOR TEXAS CIVIL PRACTICE AND REMEDIES CODE § 93.001

---

**§ 89.003**                                                    LIABILITY IN TORT
                                                                      Title 4

(1) knowing that use of the device would be harmful to the health or well-being of another person;

(2) with actual conscious indifference to the health or well-being of another person; or

(3) in violation of state or federal law.

(b) This chapter does not apply to a nonprofit health care organization unless the organization has liability insurance in effect that satisfies the requirements of Section 84.007(g).

Added by Acts 1997, 75th Leg., ch. 662, § 1, eff. Sept. 1, 1997.   Renumbered from § 88.003 by Acts 1999, 76th Leg., ch. 62, § 19.01(5), eff. Sept. 1, 1999.

**Notes of Decisions**

Preemption  1

---

**1. Preemption**

Provisions of the Texas Health Care Liability Act establishing an independent review process for adverse benefit determinations have a "connection with" employee benefit plans, and thus are preempted by ERISA, since the Act purports to redefine the standard for "appropriate and medically necessary" health care. Corporate Health Ins., Inc. v. Texas Dept. of Ins., S.D.Tex.1998, 12 F.Supp.2d 597, affirmed in part, reversed in part 215 F.3d 526, rehearing and rehearing en banc denied 220 F.3d 641, petition for certiorari filed.

Provisions of the Texas Health Care Liability Act establishing an independent review process for adverse benefit determinations, which are preempted by ERISA, were severable from the provisions of the Act making managed care entities liable for substandard health care treatment decisions, which are not preempted by ERISA, where the legislative history revealed that the Act had a dual purpose of addressing the distinct issues of quality of care and denial of care, though the Act lacked an express provision for severability or nonseverability. Corporate Health Ins., Inc. v. Texas Dept. of Ins., S.D.Tex.1998, 12 F.Supp.2d 597, affirmed in part, reversed in part 215 F.3d 526, rehearing and rehearing en banc denied 220 F.3d 641, petition for certiorari filed.

**CHAPTER 93.   ASSUMPTION OF THE RISK AND CERTAIN OTHER AFFIRMATIVE DEFENSES**

Section
⸺umption of the Risk: Affirmative De-          93.002.  Dry Fire Hydrants: Affirmative Defense.
⸺nse.

> **New statutory language supersedes the language in the main volume.**

**§ 93.001.   Assumption of the Risk: Affirmative Defense**

(a) It is an affirmative defense to a civil action for damages for personal injury or death that the plaintiff, at the time the cause of action arose, was:

(1) committing a felony, for which the plaintiff has been finally convicted, that was the sole cause of the damages sustained by the plaintiff; or

(2) committing or attempting to commit suicide, and the plaintiff's conduct in committing or attempting to commit suicide was the sole cause of the damages sustained; provided, however, if the suicide or attempted suicide was caused in whole or in part by a failure on the part of any defendant to comply with an applicable legal standard, then such suicide or attempted suicide shall not be a defense.

(b) This section does not apply in any action brought by an employee, or beneficiaries of an employee, under the Workers' Compensation Law of Texas, against an insurer based on a contract of insurance, a statute, or common law.

(c) In an action to which this section applies, this section shall prevail over any other law.

> **Annotations follow the text of the statute.**

Amended by Acts 1997, 75th Leg., ch. 437, § 1, eff. Sept. 1, 1997.

**Historical and Statutory Notes**

**1997 Legislation**
Acts 1997, 75th Leg., ch. 437, in the section heading, inserted "Assumption of the Risk:";

throughout the text, substituted "section" for "chapter"; and in subsec. (a)(1), corrected the spelling of "plaintiff".

54

---

# G. CHECKLIST FOR STATUTORY RESEARCH

### 1. LOCATE A STATUTE

❒ Use an index to search by subject.

❒ Use the popular name table to locate a statute from its popular name.

❒ For federal statutes, use the conversion tables to locate a statute using its *Statutes at Large* citation or public law number.

❒ In LexisNexis and Westlaw, execute word searches for statutes in the appropriate database (state, federal, or combined) or browse the table of contents for the code.

❒ On the Internet, locate statutes on government or general legal research web sites.

### 2. READ THE STATUTE AND ACCOMPANYING ANNOTATIONS

❒ Use research references to find cases, secondary sources, and other research materials interpreting the statute.

### 3. UPDATE PRINT RESEARCH

❒ Check the pocket part accompanying the main volume.

❒ Check any cumulative or noncumulative supplements accompanying the code.

### 4. SPECIAL NOTES

❒ In U.S.C.A., update entries to the popular name and conversion tables in the noncumulative supplements.

❒ In state codes, check for additional updating tools.

❒ In state or federal statutory research, update your research or find additional research references using Shepard's in print or in LexisNexis or KeyCite in Westlaw.

❒ In Internet research, check the date of the statute and update your research accordingly.

# CHAPTER 7

# FEDERAL LEGISLATIVE HISTORY RESEARCH

A. The process of enacting a law

B. Sources of federal legislative history

C. Researching federal legislative history in print

D. Researching federal legislative history electronically

E. Citing federal legislative history

F. Sample pages for federal legislative history research

G. Checklist for federal legislative history research

## A. THE PROCESS OF ENACTING A LAW

When a legislature passes a statute, it does so with a goal in mind, such as prohibiting or regulating certain types of conduct. Despite their best efforts, however, legislators do not always draft statutes that express their intentions clearly, and it is almost impossible to draft a statute that contemplates every possible situation that may arise under it. Accordingly, lawyers and judges are often called upon to determine the meaning of an ambiguous statute. Lawyers must provide guidance about what the statute permits or requires their clients to do. In deciding cases, judges must determine what the legislature intended when it passed the statute.

If you are asked to analyze an ambiguous statute, you have a number of tools available to help with the task. If the courts have already resolved the ambiguity, secondary sources, statutory annotations, Shepard's Citations, or other research resources can lead you to cases that explain the meaning of the statute.

If the ambiguity has not yet been resolved, however, you face a bigger challenge. You could research similar statutes to see if they shed light on the provision you are interpreting. You could also look to the language of the statute itself for guidance. You may have studied what are called "canons of construction" in some of your other classes. These canons are principles used to determine the meaning of a statute. For example, one canon provides that statutory terms are to be construed according to their ordinary and plain meaning. Another states that remedial statutes are to be broadly construed, while criminal statutes are to be narrowly construed.[1] Although these tools can be helpful in interpreting statutes, they rarely provide the complete answer to determining the legislature's intent.

One of the best ways to determine legislative intent is to research the paper trail of documents that legislators create during the legislative process. These documents are known as the legislative history of the statute. This chapter discusses various types of documents that make up a statute's legislative history and explains how to locate and use them. At the state level, the types of legislative history documents produced and their ease of accessibility vary widely; therefore, this chapter discusses only federal legislative history.

"Legislative history" is a generic term used to refer to a variety of documents produced during the legislative process; it does not refer to a single document or research tool. Courts consider some legislative history documents more important than others, depending on the type of information in the document and the point in the legislative process when the document was created. Understanding what legislative history consists of, as well as the value of different legislative history documents, requires an understanding of the legislative process. Figure 7.1 illustrates this process.

The legislative process begins when a bill is introduced into the House of Representatives or the Senate by a member of Congress. After the bill is introduced, it is usually referred to a committee. The committee can hold hearings on the bill to obtain the views of experts and interested parties, or it can refer the bill to a subcommittee to hold hearings. If the committee is not in favor of the bill, it usually takes no action. This ordinarily causes the bill to expire in the committee, although the sponsor is free to reintroduce the bill in a later session of Congress. If the committee is in favor of the bill, it will recommend passage to the full chamber of the House or Senate. The recommendation is presented in a committee report that contains the full text of the bill and an analysis of each provision. Because the committee presents its views in a report, this process is called "reporting out" the bill.

---

[1] *See generally* Abner J. Mikva & Eric Lane, AN INTRODUCTION TO STATUTORY INTERPRETATION AND THE LEGISLATIVE PROCESS 23–27 (Aspen Law & Business 1997).

**FIGURE 7.1**   HOW A BILL BECOMES A LAW

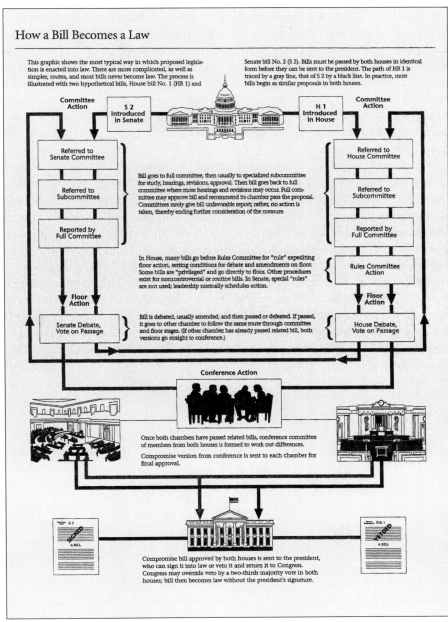

The bill then goes before the full House or Senate, where it is debated and may be amended. The members of the House or Senate vote on the bill. If it is passed, the bill goes before the other chamber of Congress, where the same process is repeated. If both chambers pass the bill, it goes to the President. The President can sign the bill into law, allow it to become law without a signature, or veto it. If the bill is vetoed, it goes back to Congress. Congress can override the President's veto if two-thirds of the House and Senate vote in favor of the bill. Once a bill is passed into law, it is assigned a public law number and proceeds through the publication process described in Chapter 6, on statutory research.

This is a simplified explanation of how legislation is enacted. A bill may make many detours along this path before becoming a law or being defeated. One situation that often occurs is that the House and Senate will pass slightly different versions of the same bill. When this happens, the bill is sent to what is called a conference committee. The conference committee consists of members of both houses of Congress, and its job is to attempt to reconcile the two versions of the bill. If the committee members are able to agree on the provisions of the bill, the compromise version is sent back to both chambers of Congress to be reapproved. If both houses approve the compromise bill, it then goes to the President.

Documents created at each stage of this process constitute the legislative history of a law. The next section describes the major sources that make up a legislative history.

## B. SOURCES OF FEDERAL LEGISLATIVE HISTORY

There are four major sources of federal legislative history:

- the bills introduced in Congress
- hearings before committees or subcommittees
- floor debates in the House and Senate
- committee reports.

These sources are listed in order from least authoritative to most authoritative. Although some of these sources are generally considered to have more weight than others, none should be viewed in isolation. Each item contributes to the documentation of the legislature's intent. In fact, you may find that the documents contain information that is either contradictory or equally as ambiguous as the underlying statute. It is rare when an inquiry into legislative history will give you a definitive answer to a question of statutory interpretation. What is more likely is that the documents will equip you with information you can use to support your arguments for the proper interpretation of the statute.

## 1. BILLS

The bill introduced into Congress, and any later versions of the bill, can be helpful in determining Congressional intent. Changes in language and addition or deletion of specific provisions may shed light on the goal the legislature was attempting to accomplish with the bill. Analysis of changes to a bill, however, requires speculation about the reasons behind the changes. Consequently, this is often considered an insufficient indication of legislative intent unless it is combined with other materials indicating intent to achieve a particular objective.

## 2. HEARINGS

Hearings before committees and subcommittees consist of the testimony of experts and interested parties called to give their views on the bill. These documents may contain transcripts of testimony, documents, reports, studies, or any other information requested by or submitted to the hearing committee. Unlike interpretation of different versions of a bill, interpretation of hearings does not require speculation. The individuals or groups providing information usually give detailed explanations and justifications for their positions.

Congress uses hearings to gather information. As a consequence, individuals or groups with opposing views are often represented, and their goal is to persuade Congress to act in a particular way. This results in the inclusion of information both for and against the legislation in the hearing documents. Sometimes it is possible to ascertain whether material from a particular source motivated Congress to act in a particular way, but this is not always the case. Therefore, hearing documents must be used carefully in determining Congressional intent.

## 3. FLOOR DEBATES

Floor debates are another source of legislative history. They are published in a daily record of Congressional proceedings called the *Congressional Record*. Unlike hearings, which include commentary that may or may not have been persuasive to the committee, floor debates consist of statements by the legislators themselves. Thus, the debates can be a good source of information about Congress's intent in passing a bill. Debates may consist of transcripts of comments or exchanges taking place on the floor of Congress. In addition, members of Congress are permitted to submit prepared statements setting forth their views. Statements by a bill's sponsors may be especially useful in determining legislative intent.

Different members of Congress may give different reasons for supporting legislation, however, and they are permitted to amend or supplement their statements after the fact. As a consequence, floor debates are not a definitive source for determining legislative intent.

## 4. COMMITTEE REPORTS

Committee reports are generally considered to be the most authoritative legislative history documents. They usually contain the committee's reasons for recommending the bill, a section-by-section analysis of the bill, and the views of any committee members who dissent from the committee's conclusions. If a bill is sent to a conference committee to work out compromise language, the conference committee usually prepares a report. This report discusses only the provisions that differed before the House and Senate. It usually contains the agreed-upon language of the bill and an explanation of the compromise.

## 5. STRATEGIES FOR APPROACHING FEDERAL LEGISLATIVE HISTORY RESEARCH

Your method of researching legislative history will depend on the type of material you need. If you are researching the history of an individual statute, your approach will be different than if you are looking for legislative activity on a particular subject, without regard for whether a statute was passed on the topic.

If you are researching the history of an individual statute, it is important to remember that not all legislation is accompanied by all of the documents described above. A committee might elect not to hold hearings. Or the bill could be amended during floor debate, in which case the amendment would not have any history to be documented elsewhere. In addition, you may not always need to look at all of these documents to resolve your research question. If you are trying to determine Congress's intent in enacting a specific provision within a statute, and a committee report sets out the goals Congress was attempting to accomplish with that provision, you might not need to go any further in your research. Often, however, the committee reports will not discuss the provision you need to interpret. In that case, you may need to delve further into the legislative history, reviewing floor debates or hearings to see if the provision was discussed in either of those sources. In other instances, you may need to compile a complete legislative history.

Your research path will depend largely on the scope of your assignment. You will almost always begin with the statute itself. From there, you should be able to use the bill number, public law number, or *Statutes at Large* citation to locate documents relating to the statute. In most cases, you will probably want to begin by reviewing committee reports. If the committee reports do not address your question, you will then need to assess which other sources of legislative history are likely to assist you and which research tools provide the most efficient means of accessing those documents. If your research takes you beyond readily accessible committee reports, you may want to consult with a reference librarian for assistance in compiling the relevant documents.

If you are trying to find out about legislative activity on a specific topic, rather than the history of an individual statute, you will need to search by subject. Because most bills are not passed into law, you may find documents relating to bills that have expired. In addition, you may locate documents unrelated to a bill. For example, committees can hold hearings on any subject within their jurisdiction, even if no legislation on the subject has been introduced.

Some research tools lend themselves more easily than others to subject searching, and some are more comprehensive in their coverage than others. Therefore, you will need to determine how much information you need, such as whether you need information on bills that have expired as well as existing legislation, and how far back in time you want to search. Again, you would be well advised to consult with a reference librarian for assistance in developing your research plan for this type of research.

The remainder of this chapter discusses methods for locating legislative history documents. The next section discusses print research tools that are accessible at many law libraries. Unlike some other sources of authority, however, legislative history is often easiest to access through electronic means. In particular, Internet research sites made available by the government and commercial providers may be the most economical and user-friendly ways to locate federal legislative history. A description of print and electronic research tools follows.

## C. RESEARCHING FEDERAL LEGISLATIVE HISTORY IN PRINT

Four print sources of legislative history are available in many law libraries:

- compiled legislative histories containing all of the legislative history documents on a statute
- *United States Code Congressional and Administrative News*, or U.S.C.C.A.N., which contains selected committee reports on bills passed into law

- Congressional Information Service (CIS) materials containing committee reports and hearings on microfiche, as well as citations to floor debates in the *Congressional Record*
- the *Congressional Record*, which contains floor debates on legislation.

You would not necessarily research each of these sources in order. Some documents may be accessible through more than one of these research tools. Therefore, you should assess the scope of your research project to determine which source is most likely to provide the information you need.

## 1. COMPILED LEGISLATIVE HISTORIES

Legislative histories for major pieces of legislation are sometimes compiled and published as separate volumes. In this situation, an author or publisher collects all of the legislative history documents on the legislation and publishes them in a single place. If a legislative history on the statute you are researching has already been compiled, your work has been done for you. Therefore, if you are researching a major piece of legislation, you should begin by looking for a compiled legislative history.

There are two ways to locate a compiled legislative history. The first is to look in the on-line catalog in your library. Compiled legislative histories can be published as individual books that are assigned call numbers and placed on the shelves. The second is to look for the statute in a reference book listing compiled legislative histories. One example of this type of reference book is *Sources of Compiled Legislative Histories: A Bibliography of Government Documents, Periodical Articles, and Books*, by Nancy P. Johnson. This book will refer you to books, government documents, and periodical articles that either reprint the legislative history for the statute or, at a minimum, contain citations to and discussion of the legislative history. This book is organized by public law number, so you would need to know the public law number of the statute to get started. You should be able to find the public law number following code sections in U.S.C. or an annotated code. Another good reference for compiled legislative histories is *Federal Legislative Histories: An Annotated Bibliography and Index to Officially Published Sources*, by Bernard D. Reams, Jr.

## 2. *UNITED STATES CODE CONGRESSIONAL AND ADMINISTRATIVE NEWS*

*United States Code Congressional and Administrative News*, or U.S.C.C.A.N., is a readily available source of committee reports on bills passed into law. For each session of Congress, U.S.C.C.A.N. publishes

**FIGURE 7.2** EXCERPT FROM ANNOTATIONS ACCOMPANYING 18 U.S.C.A. § 2441

---

### HISTORICAL AND STATUTORY NOTES

**References in Text**

Section 101 of the Immigration and Nationality Act, referred to in subsec. (b), is section 101 of Act June 27, 1952, c. 477, Title I, 66 Stat. 166, which is classified to section 1101 of Title 8, Aliens and Nationality.

**Codification**

Section 584 of Pub.L. 105–118, which directed that section 2401 of title 18 be amended, was executed to section 2441 of Title 18, despite parenthetical reference to "section 2401 of Title 18", as the probable intent of Congress.

**1997 Amendments**

Subsec. (a). Pub.L. 105–118, § 583(1), substituted "war crime" for "grave breach of the Geneva Conventions".

Subsec. (b). Pub.L. 105–118, § 583(2), substituted "war crime" for "breach" each place it appeared.

Subsec. (c). Pub.L. 105–118, § 583(3), rewrote subsec. (c). Prior to amendment, subsec. (c) read as follows: "(c) Definitions.—As used in this section, the term 'grave breach of the Geneva Conventions' means conduct defined as a grave breach in any of the international conventions relating to the laws of warfare signed at Geneva 12 August 1949 or any protocol to any such convention, to which the United States is a party."

**Short Title**

Section 1 of Pub.L. 104–192 provided [that]: "This Act [enacting this section] may be cited [as] the 'War Crimes Act of 1996'."

**Legislative History**

For legislative history and purpose of Pub.L. 104–192, see 1996 U.S. Code Cong. and Adm. News, p. 2166. See, also, Pub.L. 104–294, 1996 U.S. Code Cong. and Adm. News, p. 4021; Pub.L. 105–118, see 1997 U.S. Code Cong. and Adm. News, p. 2196.

**U.S.C.C.A.N. references**

Reprinted with permission from West Group, *United States Code Annotated*, Vol. 18, 1999 Cumulative Annual Pocket Part, p. 146.

---

a series of volumes containing, among other things, the text of laws passed by Congress (organized by *Statutes at Large* citation) and selected committee reports. References to reports in U.S.C.C.A.N. usually include the year the book was published and the starting page of the document. Thus, to find a report cited as 1996 U.S.C.C.A.N. 2166,[2] you would need to locate the 1996 edition of U.S.C.C.A.N., find the volumes labeled "Legislative History," and turn to page 2166. U.S.C.C.A.N. does not reprint all committee reports for all legislation. Nevertheless, U.S.C.C.A.N. is often a good starting place for research into committee reports because it is available at most law libraries and is fairly easy to use.

U.S.C.C.A.N. is a West publication; therefore, you can find cross-references to it in the annotations in U.S.C.A. The cross-references are usually listed in the Historical and Statutory Notes section of the annotations. If the statute has been amended, the Historical and Statutory Notes section will explain the major changes resulting from later enactments, and the legislative history section of the Historical and Statutory Notes will refer you to the year and page number of any committee reports reprinted in U.S.C.C.A.N. Figure 7.2 shows a U.S.C.C.A.N.

---

[2]This is not a complete citation. Refer to Section E below for citation rules for U.S.C.C.A.N.

reference in U.S.C.A., and Figure 7.3 shows the starting page of a committee report in U.S.C.C.A.N.

### 3. CONGRESSIONAL INFORMATION SERVICE

Congressional Information Service (CIS) is another commercial publisher of legislative history documents, but its materials are more comprehensive than those available through U.S.C.C.A.N. CIS compiles, among other documents, committee reports and hearings on microfiche.[3] In addition, CIS provides citations to floor debates published in the *Congressional Record*. CIS is a good resource for finding the complete legislative history of a statute, as well as for searching by subject.

Although CIS compiles legislative history documents on microfiche, the tools for locating these materials are published in books. The CIS finding tools consist of the Index volumes, the Abstracts volumes, and the Legislative Histories volumes. CIS publishes a new set of Index, Abstracts, and Legislative Histories[4] volumes for each calendar year. Monthly softcover booklets containing the Index and Abstracts are published for the current year. Every four years, the annual indices are combined into a Four-Year Cumulative Index, e.g., the 1991–1994 Cumulative Index.

The easiest way to locate the complete legislative history of a bill enacted into law is to use the Legislative Histories volumes. These volumes are organized by public law number. If you know the year the law was passed and the public law number, you can look it up in the appropriate volume of CIS Legislative Histories. CIS will list all of the documents in the legislative history, as well as a very brief summary of each document.

After the title of each document, a CIS citation will be listed. This citation indicates the year the document was created and the number assigned to the microfiche containing the document. Microfiche numbers will generally begin with PL for public laws, H for House documents, S for Senate documents, or J for joint documents. The microfiche should be filed in your library by year, and then by document number within each year. The only exception to this concerns references to the *Congressional Record*. CIS does not reproduce the *Congressional Record* as part of this microfiche set. Therefore, although CIS will list citations to floor

---

[3]CIS also makes this material available electronically through an Internet service called LexisNexis Congressional. Refer to Section D below for a discussion of electronic research sources.

[4]CIS began publishing a separate Legislative Histories volume in 1984. For legislation passed before 1984, the listings of legislative histories appear at the end of the Abstracts volume for each year.

**FIGURE 7.3** STARTING PAGE, HOUSE JUDICIARY COMMITTEE REPORT ON THE WAR CRIMES ACT OF 1996

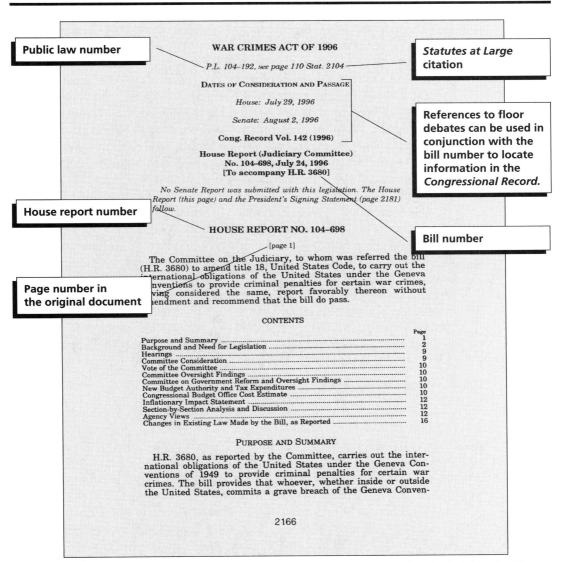

**Public law number**

**WAR CRIMES ACT OF 1996**

*P.L. 104–192, see page 110 Stat. 2104*

DATES OF CONSIDERATION AND PASSAGE

*House: July 29, 1996*

*Senate: August 2, 1996*

**Cong. Record Vol. 142 (1996)**

**House Report (Judiciary Committee)**
**No. 104–698, July 24, 1996**
**[To accompany H.R. 3680]**

*No Senate Report was submitted with this legislation. The House Report (this page) and the President's Signing Statement (page 2181) follow.*

**HOUSE REPORT NO. 104–698**

[page 1]

The Committee on the Judiciary, to whom was referred the bill (H.R. 3680) to amend title 18, United States Code, to carry out the international obligations of the United States under the Geneva Conventions to provide criminal penalties for certain war crimes, having considered the same, report favorably thereon without amendment and recommend that the bill do pass.

CONTENTS

PURPOSE AND SUMMARY

H.R. 3680, as reported by the Committee, carries out the international obligations of the United States under the Geneva Conventions of 1949 to provide criminal penalties for certain war crimes. The bill provides that whoever, whether inside or outside the United States, commits a grave breach of the Geneva Conven-

2166

**Statutes at Large citation**

**References to floor debates can be used in conjunction with the bill number to locate information in the *Congressional Record*.**

**House report number**

**Bill number**

**Page number in the original document**

Reprinted with permission from West Group, *United States Code Congressional and Administrative News*, 104th Congress-Second Session 1996, Vol. 5 (1997), p. 2166.

debates appearing in the *Congressional Record*, you will need to go to the *Congressional Record* itself to read the debates. Figure 7.4 shows a page from a CIS Legislative Histories volume.

You can also use CIS to search for legislative activity on a particular subject, rather than the history of an individual statute. To locate documents by subject, you can use the Index and Abstracts volumes. The process of locating documents using the Index and Abstracts is similar to that for researching cases with a digest. In digest research, you use the Descriptive-Word Index to find references to the subject volumes in the digest. The summaries in the subject volumes then provide you with citations to the cases themselves. Similarly, to locate documents in CIS, you use the Index to find references to document summaries in the Abstracts, which then lead to the documents themselves on CIS microfiche.

The Index is a regular alphabetical subject index that will refer you to document numbers within the Abstracts. The summaries in the Abstracts will help you assess the content of the documents and target specific pages with useful information. They are especially helpful with hearings because they allow you to determine who testified, what the witness testified about, and where to find the testimony within the document. Once you have located useful information using the Abstracts, you can read the documents in full on microfiche. Figures 7.5 and 7.6 show CIS Index and Abstracts entries, respectively.

### 4. *CONGRESSIONAL RECORD*

The *Congressional Record* is the record of all activity on the floor of the House and Senate. Therefore, it is the source you will use to find floor debates on a bill, regardless of whether the bill was passed into law. There are several ways to locate information in the *Congressional Record*, which are discussed below. First, however, it is important to understand how the *Congressional Record* is organized.

A new volume of the *Congressional Record* is published for each session of Congress. While Congress is in session, the current volume of the *Congressional Record* is published daily as a softcover pamphlet; this is called the daily edition. At the end of each session of Congress, the daily editions are compiled into a hardbound set; this is called the permanent edition.

The material in these two editions should be identical, but the pages in each are numbered differently. The daily edition is separated into different sections, including sections for House (H) and Senate (S) materials, and the pages within each section are numbered separately. In the permanent edition, all of the pages are numbered consecutively. References to the *Congressional Record* will vary, therefore, depending on whether they are to the permanent or daily edition. References to

**FIGURE 7.4** CIS LEGISLATIVE HISTORIES ENTRY FOR PUB. L. NO. 104-192

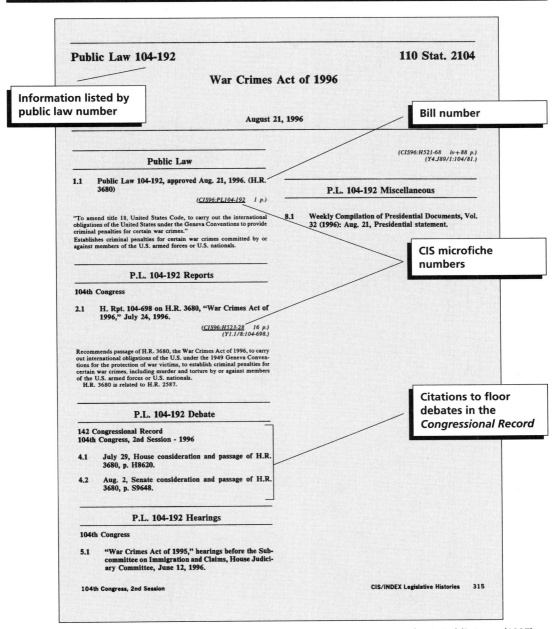

Reprinted with permission of LexisNexis, *CIS/Annual 1996*, Legislative Histories of U.S. Public Laws (1997), p. 315.

**FIGURE 7.5** CIS INDEX ENTRY

Reference to the
War Crimes Act

Abstracts entry

**Index of Subjects and Names**

**War Crimes Act**
War crimes penalties, Geneva Conventions implementation, H523–28, PL104–192
War crimes prosecution and penalties, Geneva Conventions implementation, H521–68

**War Crimes Disclosure Act**
WWII war crimes info disclosure under the Freedom of Info Act, H403–15

**War games**
China military exercises in Taiwan Strait, review and US policy issues, H461–77

**War Powers Resolution**
i restoration of democracy, US military rces assistance ops review, Pres mmunic, H460–12
peacekeeping ops in former Yugoslavia publics, US forces participation, Pres mmunic, H460–24

**War prisoners**
*see* Prisoners of war

**Ward, Benny L.**
Fed crop insurance and agric disaster assistance programs, 1994 revisions implementation issues, H161–5.3

**Ward, Mike**
hy Corps of Engrs water resources dev rograms, funding approvals and revisions, 751–26.15
T and related agencies programs, FY97 approp, H181–73.4
Energy and water resources dev programs, FY97 approp, H181–19.4
Fed bldgs and courthouses honorary designations, H751–2.3
Nomination of Jerome A Stricker to be Member, Fed Retirement Thrift Investment Bd, S401–9.2

**Ward, Peter J.**
Interior Dept and related agencies programs, FY97 approp, H181–35.1

**Ward, Sara**
Interior Dept and related agencies programs, FY97 approp, H181–34.1

**Ward, Sylvia J.**
Alaska public lands mgmt and access issues, S311–3.4

**Ward Valley, Calif.**
Land sale to Calif for use as radioactive waste repository site, S313–5

**Ward Valley Land Transfer Act**
Land sale to Calif for use as radioactive waste repository site, S313–5

**Warden, Gail L.**
Biomedical research and training programs, problems and issues, S541–22.1
Medicaid program revisions, H271–70.2

**Wardle, Lynn D.**
Marriage definition under Fed law, estab, H521–53.3, S521–33.2

**Wares Creek**
Flood control project in Fla, environmental impact assessments, H181–18.4, H181–19.7

**Warfield, William L.**
VA programs, FY97 budget proposal review, H761–11.4

**Wark, Kevin**
Bluefish fishery mgmt and conservation in Atlantic coastal areas, H651–28.2

**Warman, Timothy W.**
Agric commodity programs review, S161–19.2

Volume 27, Number 1-12

**Warner Brothers**
Trademarks intl registration system, protocol implementation; trademarks distinctive quality dilution, trademark owner standing to sue, H521–41.2

**Warner, Edward L., III**
UN intl peacekeeping ops, US involvement issues review, S201–4.1

**Warner, Isiah M.**
Natl Inst of Standards and Technology labs R&D activities review, H701–24.2

**Warner, John W.**
DC area airports operating authority restructuring, S261–19.1
DC prison facility in Lorton, Va, closure and prisoner relocation, H401–3.2
Judgeship and Justice Dept nominations, S521–21.7
Va natl parks boundary revisions; Shenandoah Valley Natl Battlefields estab, S311–46.1

**Warning systems**
*see* Emergency communication systems

**Warren, Andrew L.**
Fed hwy and surface transportation programs and policies, revision, H751–3.23
Transportation trust funds off-budget treatment estab, H751–3.20

**Warren, David R.**
DOD chemical weapons stockpile destruction programs, review, H571–6.2
DOD depot maintenance programs outsourcing issues review, H571–14.3

**Warren, Melinda**
Fed regulations impact on small business, review, H721–29.1

**Warren, William A.**
Business R&D expenditures tax credit extension and revision, H781–17.5

**Warrens, Frank R.**
Fishery conservation and mgmt programs, extension and revision, S261–1.1

**Warrick, Thomas S.**
Bosnia-Herzegovina civil conflict resolution, refugee, war crimes, and human rights issues, H461–16.1
UN mgmt and budget issues, review, H461–14.2
UN war crimes tribunal for former Yugoslavia, briefing, J892–20.1

**Warrior-Tombigbee Development Association**
Energy and water resources dev programs, FY97 approp, H181–18.1

**Warrior-Tombigbee Waterway**
Energy and water resources dev programs, FY97 approp, H181–18

**Warsaw, Poland**
Helsinki Agreement human rights commitments implementation, Warsaw meeting rpt, J892–2

**Warships**
*see* Naval vessels

**Wasem, Ruth E.**
Welfare programs reform initiatives review, H781–24.6

**Washburn, Marshall V.**
Employers classification of workers as independent contractors, tax issues, H721–24.1

**Washington**
*see* Washington State
*see* D.C. and terms beginning with D.C.

**Washington State**

**Washington Airports Task Force**
DC area airports operating authority restructuring, S261–19.3

**Washington Analysis Corp.**
Radio spectrum mgmt technical and policy issues, review, S261–15.3

**Washington Board of Rabbis**
Tax treatment of persons who relinquish US citizenship or residency, revision, H781–22.3

**Washington Cattle Feeders Association**
North Amer Free Trade Agreement implementation, Canada trade practices effects on US agric industry in Pacific Northwest, H161–8.4

**Washington County, N.Y.**
Hydroelectric projects in NY State, construction deadlines extension, PL104–242

**Washington County, Utah**
Utah land exchange with Water Conservancy Dist of Washington Cty, Utah, PL104–333

**Washington, D.C., Convention Center**
Ops and new center preconstruction activities funding authorization, S401–33

**Washington, Eric T.**
Nomination to be Assoc Judge, DC Superior Court, S401–10.1

**Washington, Frank**
Broadcast stations sale to minorities or women, spec tax rules oversight, S361–13.3

**Washington, George**
Commemorative coins minting and issuance, PL104–329

**Washington Humane Society**
Bird imports restrictions implementation, H651–2.3

**Washington Institute for Near East Policy**
Palestine Liberation Organization peace agreements with Israel, implementation issues, H461–43.3

**Washington Institute for Policy Studies**
Fed depts and agencies reorganization proposals, State, local govt, and business methods application, H401–34.8

**Washington Legal Foundation**
"Government Contracts Reform: A Critical Analysis of the Administration's Proposal", H721–18.1

**Washington Metropolitan Area Transit Authority, D.C.**
Approp, FY97, H181–45.4
Fed hwy and surface transportation programs and policies, revision, H751–3.3
Washington Metropolitan Area Transit Regulation Compact amendments, Congressional consent, PL104–322

**Washington Metropolitan Area Transit Regulation Compact**
Amendments, Congressional consent, PL104–322

**Washington Orientation and Mobility Association**
Fed hwy and surface transportation programs and policies, revision, H751–3.3

**Washington Performance Partnership**
Fed depts and agencies reorganization proposals, State, local govt, and business methods application, H401–34.8

**Washington State**
Army Corps of Engrs programs, FY97 approp, H181–13

CIS/INDEX  531

Reprinted with permission of LexisNexis, *CIS/Annual 1996*, Index to Congressional Publications and Legislative Histories (1997), p. 531.

**FIGURE 7.6** CIS ABSTRACTS ENTRY

Judiciary    H523–28

**H523–19    ANTI-CAR THEFT IMPROVEMENTS ACT OF 1995.**
June 12, 1996.  104-2.  19 p.
H Doc Rm  CIS/MF/3
•Item 1008-C; 1008-D.
H. Rpt. 104-618.
*Y1.1/8:104-618.
MC 96-16159.

Recommends passage of H.R. 2803, the Anti-Car Theft Improvements Act of 1995, to amend the Anti Car Theft Act of 1992 to revise the National Motor Vehicle Title Information System (NMVTIS), established to provide State motor vehicle departments with access to the data bases of other States in order to check whether a vehicle had been stolen before issuing the vehicle a new title.
Includes provisions to:
a.  Transfer NMVTIS operating authority from DOT to the Department of Justice.
b.  Expand NMVTIS to include title information on non-commercial light trucks and vans.
c.  Extend NMVTIS implementation deadline to Oct. 1, 1997.

**H523–20    CHURCH ARSON PREVENTION ACT OF 1996.**
June 17, 1996.  104-2.  11 p.
H Doc Rm  CIS/MF/3
•Item 1008-C; 1008-D.
H. Rpt. 104-621.
*Y1.1/8:104-621.
MC 96-16161.

Recommends passage, with an amendment in the nature of a substitute, of H.R. 3525, the Church Arson Prevention Act of 1996, to clarify and expand Federal jurisdiction over offenses relating to destruction of religious property.
Bill responds to 1996 increase in cases of arson against African-American churches.

**H523–21    ANTITRUST HEALTH CARE ADVANCEMENT ACT OF 1996.**
June 27, 1996.  104-2.  17 p.
H Doc Rm  CIS/MF/3
•Item 1008-C; 1008-D.
H. Rpt. 104-646.
*Y1.1/8:104-646.
MC 96-17606.

Recommends passage of H.R. 2925, the Antitrust Health Care Advancement Act of 1996, to modify application of antitrust laws to health care provider sponsored networks (PSNs) and require case-by-case determination on whether PSNs, which include groups of physicians, nurses, hospitals, and other health care entities, are permissible under antitrust laws.
Includes dissenting views (p. 14-17).

**H523–22    FAN FREEDOM AND COMMUNITY PROTECTION ACT OF 1996.**
June 27, 1996.  104-2.  32 p.
H Doc Rm  CIS/MF/3
•Item 1008-C; 1008-D.
H. Rpt. 104-656, pt. 1.
*Y1.1/8:104-656/PT.1.
MC 96-17614.

Recommends passage, with an amendment in the nature of a substitute, of H.R. 2740, the Fan Freedom and Community Protection Act of 1996, to revise laws relating to relocation of professional football, hockey, and basketball franchises.
Includes provisions to:
a.  Extend a limited exemption from antitrust laws to the National Football League, the National Hockey League, and the National Basketball Association to grant those leagues greater control over franchise movement by league members.
b.  Require a sports league that approves a franchise relocation to provide an expansion team to the city from which the franchise left.
c.  Require sports team owners who breach playing facility contracts with State or local governments to repay all the financial assistance received from that government.
Includes dissenting views (p. 28-32).
H.R. 2740 is similar to H.R. 2699.

**H523–23    DEFENSE OF MARRIAGE ACT.**
July 9, 1996.  104-2.
45 p. Corrected print.
H Doc Rm  CIS/MF/3
•Item 1008-C; 1008-D.
H. Rpt. 104-664.
*Y1.1/8:104-664/CORR.
MC 96-17622.

Recommends passage of H.R. 3396, the Defense of Marriage Act, to define marriage under Federal law as the legal union between one man and one woman, and to allow each State to decide individually what legal status to give to another State's same-sex marriages.
Bill responds to possible issuance by Hawaii of marriage licenses to same-sex couples.
Includes dissenting views (p. 35-44).

**H523–24    GOVERNMENT ACCOUNTABILITY ACT OF 1996.**
July 16, 1996.  104-2.  11 p.
H Doc Rm  CIS/MF/3
•Item 1008-C; 1008-D.
H. Rpt. 104-680.
*Y1.1/8:104-680.
MC 96-17634.

Recommends passage, with an amendment in the nature of a substitute, of H.R. 3166, the Government Accountability Act, to provide that individuals who make false statements to Congress or the judiciary are subject to Federal criminal prosecution.
Bill responds to May 1995 Supreme Court decision in *Hubbard v. U.S.* restricting criminal liability for false statements to statements made to the executive branch.
H.R. 3166 is similar to H.R. 1678.

**H523–25    REPEAL OF PROHIBITION ON FEDERAL EMPLOYEES CONTRACTING OR TRADING WITH INDIANS.**
July 17, 1996.  104-2.  6 p.
H Doc Rm  CIS/MF/3
•Item 1008-C; 1008-D.
H. Rpt. 104-681.
*Y1.1/8:104-681.
MC 96-19218.

Recommends passage of H.R. 3215, to repeal the prohibition barring BIA and Indian Health Service employees from contracting with Indians or purchasing or selling services or property.
H.R. 3215 is similar to S. 325.

**H523–26    PUEBLO OF ISLETA INDIAN LAND CLAIMS.**
July 22, 1996.  104-2.  6 p.
H Doc Rm  CIS/MF/3
•Item 1008-C; 1008-D.
H. Rpt. 104-694.
*Y1.1/8:104-694.
MC 96-19223.

Recommends passage of H.R. 740, to confer jurisdiction on the U.S. Court of Federal Claims to hear and render judgment on claims by the Pueblo of Isleta Indian Tribe of New Mexico against the U.S. for lands taken without adequate compensation to the tribe.

**H523–27    CONTINUED PARTICIPATION OF SENIOR JUDGES IN AN IN BANC PROCEEDINGS.**
July 23, 1996.  104-2.
H Doc Rm  CIS/MF/3
•Item 1008-C; 1008-D.
H. Rpt. 104-697.
*Y1.1/8:104-697.
MC 96-19226.

Recommends passage of S. 531, to authorize active circuit judges who take senior status while an in banc case is pending to continue to participate in the pending in banc case.

> Description of the Committee's report

**H523–28    WAR CRIMES ACT OF 1996.**
July 24, 1996.  104-2.  16 p.
H Doc Rm  CIS/MF/3
•Item 1008-C; 1008-D.
H. Rpt. 104-698.
*Y1.1/8:104-698.
MC 96-19227.

Recommends passage of H.R. 3680, the War Crimes Act of 1996, to implement U.S. obligations under the 1949 Geneva Conventions and the laws of warfare by establishing criminal penalties for war crimes, including murder and torture by or against members of the U.S. armed forces or U.S. citizens.
H.R. 3680 is related to H.R. 2587.

Volume 27, Number 1-12

CIS/INDEX    207

Reprinted with permission of LexisNexis, *CIS/Annual 1996*, Abstracts from Congressional Publications (1997), p. 207.

both editions will give the volume and page number, but the page numbering will differ for each edition. Thus, 142 Cong. Rec. H8620[5] refers to volume 142 of the *Congressional Record*, page 8,620 of the House section of the daily edition. The "H" before the page number alerts you that the reference is to the daily edition. By contrast, a citation to 142 Cong. Rec. 11,352 refers to volume 142 of the *Congressional Record*, page 11,352 of the permanent edition. Because the page number contains no letter designation, the reference is to the permanent edition. Figure 7.7 is an excerpt from the daily edition.

There are several ways to find citations to material in the *Congressional Record*. If you are looking for debates on a specific statute, you will find *Congressional Record* citations in the CIS Legislative Histories volumes. In the listing summarizing the statute's legislative history documents, CIS provides the dates and page numbers of references to the legislation in the *Congressional Record*.

You can also use U.S.C.C.A.N. to find *Congressional Record* references. At the beginning of each report published in U.S.C.C.A.N., you will find a list of the dates when the House and Senate considered the bill, which you can use in conjunction with the bill number to locate material in the daily edition of the *Congressional Record*. At the end of each issue of the daily edition of the *Congressional Record*, you will find a Daily Digest of Congressional activity for that day. If you know the date on which the bill was considered, you can look up the bill number in the Daily Digest to find references to the legislation within that issue of the *Congressional Record*.

The index to the *Congressional Record* will allow you to find information on a piece of legislation or to search by subject. If you are researching the permanent edition of the *Congressional Record*, the index will be published in a separate volume. During the current session of Congress, softcover interim indices for the daily edition are published roughly every two weeks. The interim indices are not cumulative; thus, you would need to check each one to find out if activity on the bill or subject you are researching has taken place.

The index is divided into two sections, one with a subject index, and the other containing the history of bills and resolutions. Either section will refer you to pages with relevant material. In using the section with the history of bills and resolutions, a couple of caveats are in order. First, you will need to know the House and Senate bill numbers of the legislation, not the public law number. A bill cannot be assigned a public law number until it is passed into law, and floor debates, by definition, take place before the passage of a bill. The CIS Legislative Histories

---

[5]The citations here are not complete. Refer to Section E below for citation rules for the *Congressional Record*.

**FIGURE 7.7** *CONGRESSIONAL RECORD*, DAILY EDITION

**Comments on the War Crimes Act in the House of Representatives**

H8620        CONGRESSIONAL RECORD — HOUSE        *July 29, 1996*

Mr. Speaker, H.R. 740, introduced by the gentleman from New Mexico [Mr. Richardson] and the gentleman from New Mexico [Mr. Skeen] would permit the Pueblo of Isleta Indian Tribe to file a claim in the U.S. Court of Federal Claims for certain aboriginal lands accrued from the tribe by the United States. The tribe was erroneously advised by the Bureau of Indian Affairs in regard to this claim, and as a result never filed a claim for aboriginal lands before the expiration of the statute of limitations.

The court's jurisdiction would apply only to claims accruing on or before August 13, 1946, as provided in the Indian Claims Commission Act.

The Pueblo of Isleta Tribe seeks the opportunity to present the merits of its aboriginal land claims, which otherwise would be barred as untimely. The tribe cites numerous precedents for conferring jurisdiction under similar circumstances, such as the case of the Zuni Indian Tribe in 1978.

An identical bill passed the Senate in the 103d Congress, but was not considered by the House. In the 102d Congress, H.R. 1206, amended to the current language, passed the House, but was not considered by the Senate before adjournment. On June 11, 1996, the Judiciary Committee favorably reported this bill by unanimous voice vote.

Mr. Speaker, I reserve the balance of my time.

Mr. SCOTT. Mr. Speaker, I yield myself such time as I may consume.

Mr. Speaker, I think the bill has been explained that was introduced by the gentleman from New Mexico [Mr. Skeen] and the gentleman from New Mexico [Mr. Schiff]. It is a fair bill, and I would just urge colleagues to support it at this time.

Mr. Speaker, I yield back the balance of my time.

Mr. RICHARDSON. Mr. Speaker, I wish to extend my strong support for H.R. 740 which deals with the Pueblo of Isleta Indian land claims. H.R. 740 comes before Congress for a vote which will correct a 45-year-old injustice. In 1951, the Pueblo of Isleta was given erroneous advice by employees of the Bureau of Indian Affairs regarding the nature of the claim the Pueblo could mount under the Indian Claims Commission Act of 1946. This is documented and supported by testimony. The Pueblo was not made aware of the fact that a land claim could be made based upon aboriginal use and occupancy. As a result, it lost the opportunity to make such a claim.

The Pueblo of Isleta was a victim of circumstances beyond its control, and this bill is an opportunity for us to correct this wrong. No expenditure or appropriations of funds are provided for in this bill; only the opportunity for the Pueblo to make a claim for aboriginal lands which the Isletas believe to be rightfully theirs. This bill may be the last chance for the United States to correct an injustice which occurred many years ago because of misinformation from the BIA.

Therefore, I urge my colleagues to support H.R. 740.

Mr. SMITH of Texas. Mr. Speaker, I have no further requests for time, and I yield back the balance of my time.

The SPEAKER pro tempore. The question is on the motion offered by the gentleman from Texas [Mr. Smith] that the House suspend the rules and pass the bill, H.R. 740.

The question was taken; and (two-thirds having voted in favor thereof) the rules were suspended and the bill was passed.

A motion to reconsider was laid on the table.

## WAR CRIMES ACT OF 1996

Mr. SMITH of Texas. Mr. Speaker, I move to suspend the rules and pass the bill (H.R. 3680) to amend title 18, United States Code, to carry out the international obligations of the United States under the Geneva Conventions to provide criminal penalties for certain war crimes.

The Clerk read as follows:

H.R. 3680

*Be it enacted by the Senate and House of Representatives of the United States of America in Congress assembled,*

**SECTION 1. SHORT TITLE.**

This Act may be cited as the "War Crimes Act of 1996".

**SEC. 2. CRIMINAL PENALTIES FOR CERTAIN WAR CRIMES.**

(a) IN GENERAL.—Title 18, United States Code, is amended by inserting after chapter 117 the following:

"**CHAPTER 118—WAR CRIMES**

"Sec.

"2401. War crimes.

"**§ 2401. War crimes**

"(a) OFFENSE.—Whoever, whether inside or outside the United States, commits a grave breach of the Geneva Conventions, in any of the circumstances described in subsection (b), shall be fined under this title or imprisoned for life or any term of years, or both, and if death results to the victim, shall also be subject to the penalty of death.

"(b) CIRCUMSTANCES.—The circumstances referred to in subsection (a) are that the person committing such breach or the victim of such breach is a member of the armed forces of the United States or a national of the United States (as defined in section 101 of the Immigration and Nationality Act).

"(c) DEFINITIONS.—As used in this section, the term 'grave breach of the Geneva Conventions' means conduct defined as a grave breach in any of the international conventions relating to the laws of warfare signed at Geneva 12 August 1949 or any protocol to any such convention, to which the United States is a party."

(b) CLERICAL AMENDMENT.—The table of chapters for part I of title 18, United States Code, is amended by inserting after the item relating to chapter 117 the following new item:

"118. War crimes .................... 2401."

The SPEAKER pro tempore. Pursuant to the rule, the gentleman from Texas [Mr. Smith] and the gentleman from Virginia [Mr. Scott] each will control 20 minutes.

The Chair recognizes the gentleman from Texas [Mr. Smith].

GENERAL LEAVE

Mr. SMITH of Texas. Mr. Speaker, I ask unanimous consent that all Members may have 5 legislative days to revise and extend their remarks on the bill under consideration.

The SPEAKER pro tempore. Is there objection to the request of the gentleman from Texas?

There was no objection.

Mr. SMITH of Texas. Mr. Speaker, I yield myself such time as I may consume.

Mr. Speaker, H.R. 3680 is designed to implement the Geneva conventions for the protection of victims of war. Our colleague, the gentleman from North Carolina, WALTER JONES, should be commended for introducing this bill and for his dedication to such a worthy goal.

□ 1445

Mr. Speaker, the Geneva Conventions of 1949 codified rules of conduct for military forces to which we have long adhered. In 1955 Deputy Under Secretary of State Robert Murphy testified to the Senate that—

The Geneva Conventions are another long step forward towards mitigating the severity of war on its helpless victims. They reflect enlightened practices as carried out by the United States and other civilized countries, and they represent largely what the United States would do, whether or not a party to the Conventions. Our own conduct has served to establish higher standards and we can only benefit by having them incorporated in a stronger body of wartime law.

Mr. Speaker, the United States ratified the Conventions in 1955. However, Congress has never passed implementing legislation.

The Conventions state that signatory countries are to enact penal legislation punishing what are called grave breaches, actions such as the deliberate killing of prisoners of war, the subjecting of prisoners to biological experiments, the willful infliction of great suffering or serious injury on civilians in occupied territory.

While offenses covering grave breaches can in certain instances be prosecutable under present Federal law, even if they occur overseas, there are a great number of instances in which no prosecution is possible. Such nonprosecutable crimes might include situations where American prisoners of war are killed, or forced to serve in the Army of their captors, or American doctors on missions of mercy in foreign war zones are kidnapped or murdered. War crimes are not a thing of the past, and Americans can all too easily fall victim to them.

H.R. 3680 was introduced in order to implement the Geneva Conventions. It prescribes severe criminal penalties for anyone convicted of committing, whether inside or outside the United States, a grave breach of the Geneva Conventions, where the victim or the perpetrator is a member of our Armed Forces. In future conflicts H.R. 3680 may very well deter acts against Americans that violate the laws of war.

Mr. Speaker, I urge my colleagues to support this legislation, and I reserve the balance of my time.

Mr. SCOTT. Mr. Speaker, I yield myself such time as I may consume.

Mr. Speaker, as the gentleman from Texas has fully explained, H.R. 3680 implements this country's international

Reprinted from U.S. Government Printing Office, *Congressional Record*, Vol. 142, No. 113, Monday, July 29, 1996, H8620.

volumes and the committee reports in U.S.C.C.A.N. will provide the bill numbers. Second, be sure to check both the House and Senate listings for activity on the bill; either chamber of Congress could act at any time on a piece of pending legislation.

## D. RESEARCHING FEDERAL LEGISLATIVE HISTORY ELECTRONICALLY

As noted earlier in this chapter, electronic sources are often easier to use in locating legislative history than print sources. In particular, Internet sources can be extremely useful in legislative history research. No matter which electronic tool you use, your research strategy will still largely be governed by whether you are looking for information on an individual statute or searching by subject.

As with print research, electronic research into the legislative history of an individual statute is easiest if you have a citation identifying the legislation. Most electronic tools will allow you to search using a public law number, bill number, or *Statutes at Large* citation. Conducting a word search using the popular name of the act is also an effective strategy. Searching simply by topic or with general keywords is the least efficient means of researching for material on an individual statute. It is possible that you could miss important documents if you do not have the correct terms in the search; in addition, you are likely to retrieve material on other pieces of legislation unrelated to your research. By contrast, topic or keyword searching is most effective when you want to find out about legislative activity on a particular subject.

One exception to these general approaches concerns electronic research in the *Congressional Record*. Conducting *Congressional Record* research on-line is easiest if you have the House and Senate bill numbers or the dates and page numbers of *Congressional Record* references to the bill. You can locate this information using the print sources described above or some of the electronic tools described below. You can also conduct a word search using the popular name of the act or general keywords.

More information on electronic searching generally is available in Chapter 10.

### 1. LEXISNEXIS AND WESTLAW

Both LexisNexis and Westlaw provide access to many legislative history documents. Both services have databases that allow you to search the full text of bills introduced in Congress, selected committee reports and hearings, and floor debates in the *Congressional Record*. Both also have databases containing compiled legislative histories for certain major pieces of legislation.

## 2. INTERNET SOURCES

Both government and commercial Internet web sites now contain a significant amount of legislative history. Government-operated sites can be used free of charge. One commercial source, LexisNexis Congressional (formerly known as Congressional Universe), is an excellent Internet resource available by subscription. This service provides electronic access to CIS legislative histories. If you are conducting research at a library that maintains a subscription to this service, you can access it through the library's computer network.

Two sources of legislative history provided by the federal government are Thomas, a site maintained by the Library of Congress, and GPO Access, a site maintained by the Government Printing Office (GPO). The Internet addresses for both of these sites are listed in Appendix A. One potential drawback to using either of these sites is that some of their databases do not yet go back very far. As of this writing, some information on these sites dates back only to the early 1990s. For each category of information available, you should be able to determine the period of time covered, and you will want to check this carefully before you begin your research. If you are researching the legislative history of a fairly recent statute, however, these are excellent tools to use. In addition, these sites will become more comprehensive over time as new material is added to them.

Thomas will provide you with the text of bills introduced, House and Senate roll call votes, public laws, the text of the *Congressional Record*, committee reports, and other information on the legislative process. Thomas will also allow you to search in several ways. You can search by public law number, report number, or committee name, or you can conduct word searches. The introductory screens for the Thomas site appear in Figure 7.8.

GPO Access also makes some legislative history documents available. Here, you will find the text of bills introduced into Congress, selected reports and hearings, and the *Congressional Record*. You can conduct word searches in any of these databases, and many of them allow you to include a date restriction if you know the session of Congress you want to research. If you know the bill number, you can enter it as your word search to locate documents related to a specific piece of legislation. In addition, if you know the committee that issued the report you want, you can select the name of the committee to retrieve a list of its documents available on-line. Figure 7.9 shows the introductory screens for the legislative information section of GPO Access.

LexisNexis Congressional, a commercial research service, is both more comprehensive than the government sites and in some ways more user-friendly. LexisNexis Congressional is an electronic version of the CIS microfiche set. Its database includes committee reports, hearings,

**FIGURE 7.8**   INTRODUCTORY SCREENS FOR THOMAS

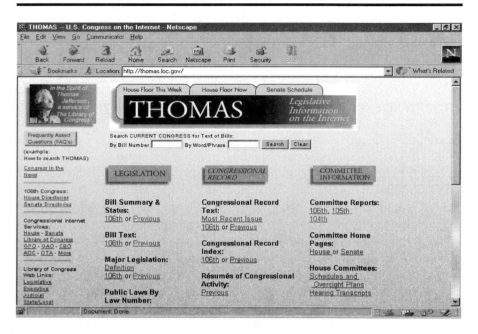

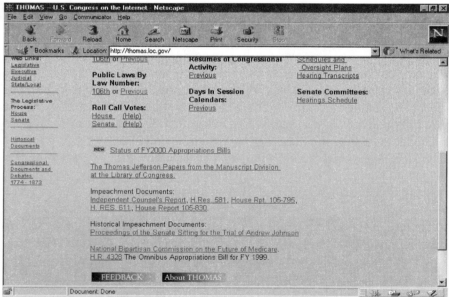

Reprinted from <http://thomas.loc.gov>.

**FIGURE 7.9**   INTRODUCTORY SCREENS FOR GPO ACCESS, LEGISLATIVE
INFORMATION

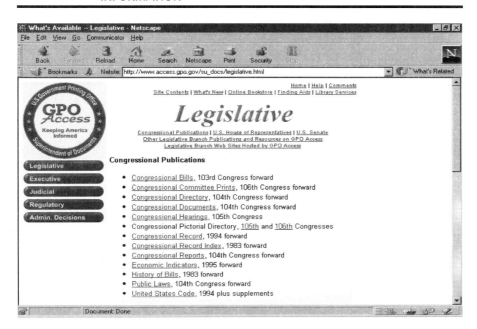

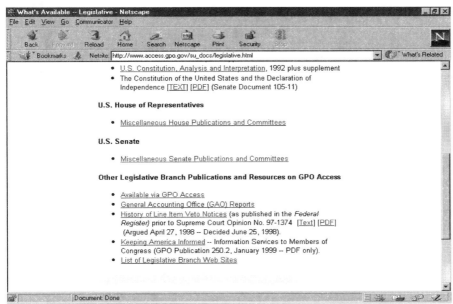

Reprinted from <http://www.gpo.gov/su_docs/legislative.html>.

bills, and the *Congressional Record*. The introductory screen in Figure 7.10 shows some of the types of information available through this service.

There are two important differences between the CIS legislative history microfiche set and LexisNexis Congressional. First, LexisNexis Congressional does not contain complete information on Congressional hearings. Unlike the CIS microfiche, LexisNexis Congressional includes only the text of prepared statements and transcripts of testimony, but not any attachments or documents submitted to the committee. The second difference concerns access to the *Congressional Record*. Although CIS provides citations to the *Congressional Record* in its Legislative Histories volumes, it does not reproduce the *Congressional Record* as part of the legislative history microfiche set. LexisNexis Congressional, by contrast, does provide electronic access to the *Congressional Record* from 1985 forward.

Within LexisNexis Congressional, you can search the full text of the documents available on-line, or you can search through the CIS Index. The easiest way to locate all of the available documents on a piece of legislation is to search within the Index. Searching this way retrieves the same information you would find in the print Index and Abstracts. Your search will first retrieve index entries. You can click on these to retrieve abstracts (summaries) of the documents available, and

**FIGURE 7.10**   INTRODUCTORY SCREEN FOR LEXISNEXIS CONGRESSIONAL

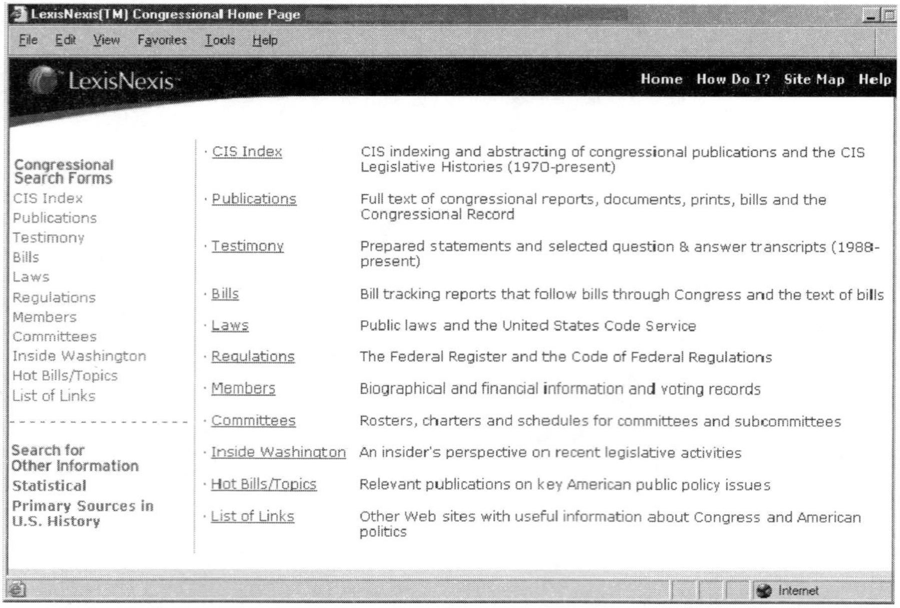

Reprinted with permission of LexisNexis, LexisNexis Congressional Introductory screen.

you can retrieve the full text of a document by clicking on the appropriate link.[6] You can search in the CIS Index by number using the public law number, *Statutes at Large* citation, or bill number. As you can see from Figure 7.11, however, other searching options are also available.

Full-text searching, by contrast, requires you to search separate databases for each type of legislative history document (reports, hearings, etc.) that you want to retrieve. If you are compiling the legislative history for one piece of legislation, searching in the CIS Index database is usually preferable to this piecemeal approach. If you are researching legislative activity by subject, however, you may want to conduct full-text searches for each type of document.

LexisNexis Congressional contains a wealth of legislative material beyond what is described here and can be searched using a variety of techniques. If you have any questions about how to find information in this service, the How Do I? option in the top right corner of the screen should lead you in the right direction. In addition, the Help function, which also appears in the top right corner, provides a link to the coverage and update schedule for all of the LexisNexis Congressional databases.

## E. CITING FEDERAL LEGISLATIVE HISTORY

Citations to legislative history documents are covered in *ALWD Manual* Rule 15 and *Bluebook* Rule 13. This chapter discusses citations to committee reports and floor debates because those are the sources you are most likely to cite in a brief or memorandum.

In the *Bluebook,* the examples contained in Rule 13 show some of the Congressional document abbreviations in large and small capital letters. Practitioners' Note P.1(b), however, provides that legislative documents in briefs and memoranda should appear in ordinary type.

### 1. COMMITTEE REPORTS

Using either the *ALWD Manual* or the *Bluebook,* a citation to a committee report consists of four elements: (1) the abbreviation for the type of document; (2) the report number; (3) the pinpoint reference to the cited material; and (4) a parenthetical containing the date of the report.

Although citations to reports in both formats contain the same elements, the document abbreviations, report number, and date differ in

---

[6]Sometimes LexisNexis Congressional will provide a reference to a document that is not contained within its database. If that happens, you can use the citation provided by LexisNexis Congressional to locate the document in the CIS microfiche set.

**FIGURE 7.11**   SEARCH OPTIONS FOR CONGRESSIONAL PUBLICATIONS IN LEXISNEXIS CONGRESSIONAL

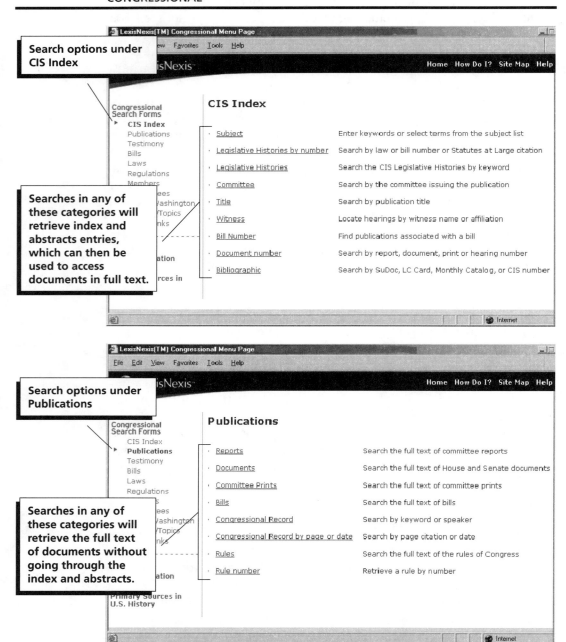

Reprinted with permission of LexisNexis, LexisNexis Congressional search options.

their presentation, as illustrated in the following examples. Here is an example of a citation to a report issued by the House of Representatives in *ALWD Manual* format:

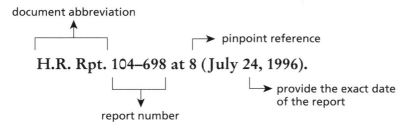

Here is an example in *Bluebook* format:

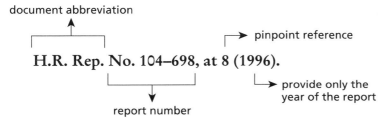

Both the *ALWD Manual* and the *Bluebook* require a parallel citation to U.S.C.C.A.N. if the report is reprinted there. A citation to a report reprinted in U.S.C.C.A.N. consists of six elements: (1) the report citation, as discussed above; (2) the notation "reprinted in;" (3) the year of the U.S.C.C.A.N. volume; (4) the publication name (U.S.C.C.A.N.); (5) the starting page of the report in U.S.C.C.A.N.; and (6) the pinpoint reference to the page in U.S.C.C.A.N. containing the cited material.

Although the elements of a U.S.C.C.A.N. citation in either *ALWD Manual* or *Bluebook* format are the same, the presentation of the citation varies slightly depending on which format you use. Here is an example in *ALWD Manual* format:

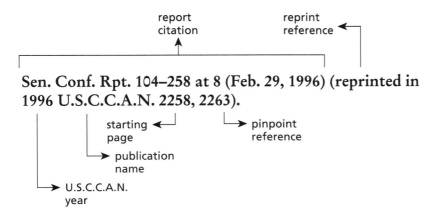

Here is an example in *Bluebook* format:

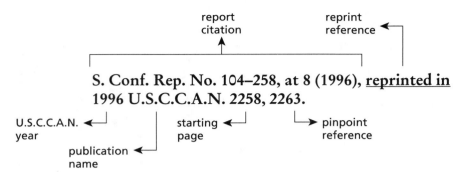

If you locate a report in U.S.C.C.A.N., you can still find the page numbers for the original document. Throughout the report, U.S.C.-C.A.N. provides the page numbers of the original document in brackets.

## 2. FLOOR DEBATES

Floor debates are published in the *Congressional Record*. As explained earlier in this chapter, two versions of the *Congressional Record* are published. The daily edition is published during the current session of Congress, and the permanent edition is published at the close of the session. Both the *ALWD Manual* and the *Bluebook* require citation to the permanent edition if possible. A citation to the permanent edition using either the *ALWD Manual* or the *Bluebook* consists of four elements: (1) the volume number of the *Congressional Record*; (2) the abbreviation Cong. Rec.; (3) the page number with the information cited; and (4) a parenthetical containing the year.

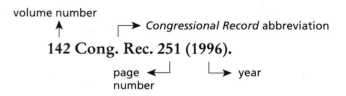

A citation to the daily edition contains the same elements, except that the parenthetical must indicate that the citation is to the daily edition and provide the exact date of the daily edition.

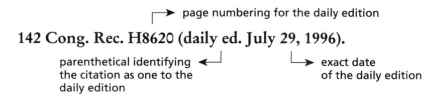

## F. SAMPLE PAGES FOR FEDERAL LEGISLATIVE HISTORY RESEARCH

Beginning on the next page, Figures 7.12 through 7.22 contain sample pages illustrating what you would find if you researched committee reports on the War Crimes Act of 1996 in print using U.S.C.C.A.N. and electronically using Thomas and LexisNexis Congressional.

**The first step is locating the statute to find the public law number. U.S.C. or any annotated code will provide the public law number. If you locate the statute in U.S.C.A., the annotations will also provide citations to U.S.C.C.A.N.**

**FIGURE 7.12**    18 U.S.C.A. § 2441 AND ACCOMPANYING ANNOTATIONS

CRIMES AND CRIMINAL PROCEDURE                    18 § 2441

LAW REVIEW AND JOURNAL COMMENTARIES

Use of Title III electronic surveillance to in-    gambling casinos. Emil A. Tonkovich, 16 Rut-
vestigate organized crime's hidden interest in    gers L.J. 811 (1985).

LIBRARY REFERENCES

1 Am Jur 2d, Abduction and Kidnapping § 5.      3A Am Jur 2d, Aliens and Citizens
31A Am Jur 2d, Extortion, Blackmail, and        §§ 1855-1860.
Threats § 141.                                   63A Am Jur 2d, Prostitution § 31.

**§ 2425.  Use of interstate facilities to transmit information about a minor**

Whoever, using the mail or any facility or means of interstate or foreign commerce, or within the special maritime and territorial jurisdiction of the United States, knowingly initiates the transmission of the name, address, telephone number, social security number, or electronic mail address of another individual, knowing that such other individual has not attained the age of 16 years, with the intent to entice, encourage, offer, or solicit any person to engage in any sexual activity for which any person can be charged with a criminal offense, or attempts to do so, shall be fined under this title, imprisoned not more than 5 years, or both.

(Added Pub.L. 105–314, Title I, § 101(a), Oct. 30, 1998., 112 Stat. 2975.)

**§ 2426.  Repeat offenders**

(a) **Maximum term of imprisonment.**—The maximum term of imprisonment for a violation of this chapter [18 U.S.C.A. § 2421 et seq.] after a prior sex offense conviction shall be twice the term of imprisonment otherwise provided by this chapter.

(b) **Definitions.**—In this section—

(1) the term "prior sex offense conviction" means a conviction for an offense—

(A) under this chapter [18 U.S.C.A. § 2421 et seq.], chapter 109A [18 U.S.C.A. § 2251 et seq.], or chapter 110 [18 U.S.C.A. § 2241 et seq.]; or

(B) under State law for an offense consisting of conduct that would have been an offense under a chapter referred to in paragraph (1) if the conduct had occurred within the special maritime and territorial jurisdiction of the United States; and

(2) the term "State" means a State of the United States, the District of Columbia, and any commonwealth, territory, or possession of the United States.

(Added Pub.L. 105–314, Title I, § 104(a), Oct. 30, 1998., 112 Stat. 2976.)

**§ 2427.  Inclusion of offenses relating to child pornography in definition of sexual activity for which any person can be charged with a criminal offense**

In this chapter [18 U.S.C.A. § 2421 et seq.], the term "sexual activity for which any person can be charged with a criminal offense" includes the production of child pornography, as defined in section 2256(8).

(Added Pub.L. 105–314, Title I, § 105(a), Oct. 30, 1998., 112 Stat. 2977.)

**CHAPTER 118—WAR CRIMES**

Sec.
2441.  War crimes.

HISTORICAL AND STATUTORY NOTES

**1996 Amendments**
Pub.L. 104–294, Title VI, § 605(p)(2), Oct. 11, 1996, 110 Stat. 3510, redesignated former item 2401 as 2441.

**§ 2441.  War crimes**

(a) **Offense.**—Whoever, whether inside or outside the United States, commits a war crime, in any of the circumstances described in subsection (b), shall be fined under this title or imprisoned for life or any term of years, or both, and if death results to the victim, shall also be subject to the penalty of death.

145

Section 2441 is so recent that it does not appear in the main volume of U.S.C.A. It appears only in the pocket part.

**FIGURE 7.12** 18 U.S.C.A. § 2441 AND ACCOMPANYING ANNOTATIONS *(Continued)*

18 § 2441        CRIMES AND CRIMINAL PROCEDURE

**(b) Circumstances.**—The circumstances referred to in subsection (a) are that the person committing such breach or the victim of such war crime is a member of the Armed Forces of the United States or a national of the United States (as defined in section 101 of the Immigration and Nationality Act).

**(c) Definition.**—As used in this section the term 'war crime' means any conduct—

(1) defined as a grave breach in any of the international conventions signed at Geneva 12 August 1949, or any protocol to such convention to which the United States is a party;

(2) prohibited by Article 23, 25, 27, or 28 of the Annex to the Hague Convention IV, Respecting the Laws and Customs of War on Land, signed 18 October 1[...]

(3) which constitutes a violation of common Article 3 of the international conventions signed at Geneva, 12 August 1949, or any protocol to such convention to w[...] the United States is a party and which deals with non-international armed-conf[...] or

(4) of a person who, in relation to an armed conflict and contrary to the provisions of the Protocol on Prohibitions or Restrictions on the Use of Mines, Booby-Traps and Other Devices as amended at Geneva on 3 May 1996 (Protocol II as amended on 3 May 1996), when the United States is a party to such Protocol, willfully kills or causes serious injury to civilians.

(Added Pub.L. 104–192, § 2(a), Aug. 21, 1996, 110 Stat. 2104, § 2401; renumbered § 2441, Pub.L. 104–294, § 605(p)(1), Oct. 11, 1996, 110 Stat. 3510, and amended Pub.L. 105–118, Title V, § 583, Nov. 26, 1997, 111 Stat. 2436.)

> **Public law number of an amendment**

> **Public law number of statute as originally passed**

HISTORICAL AND STATUTORY NOTES

**References in Text**

Section 101 of the Immigration and Nationali[...] [...]t, referred to in subsec. (b), is section 101 [...]t June 27, 1952, c. 477, Title I, 66 Stat. 166, [...] is classified to section 1101 of Title 8, [...]s and Nationality.

**[...]fication**

[...]ction 584 of Pub.L. 105–118, which directed [...] section 2401 of title 18 be amended, was executed to section 2441 of Title 18, despite parenthetical reference to "section 2401 of Title 18", as the probable intent of Congress.

**1997 Amendments**

Subsec. (a). Pub.L. 105–118, § 583(1), substituted "war crime" for "grave breach of the Geneva Conventions".

Subsec. (b). Pub.L. 105–118, § 583(2), substituted "war crime" for "breach" each place it appeared.

Subsec. (c). Pub.L. 105–118, § 583(3), rewrote subsec. (c). Prior to amendment, subsec. (c) read as follows: "(c) Definitions.—As used in this section, the term 'grave breach of the Geneva Conventions' means conduct defined as a grave breach in any of the international conventions relating to the laws of warfare signed [...] Geneva 12 August 1949 or any protocol to such convention, to which the United States [...] party."

**Short Title**

Section 1 of Pub.L. 104–192 provided "This Act [enacting this section] may be cited as the 'War Crimes Act of 1996'."

**Legislative History**

For legislative history and purpose of Pub.L. 104–192, see 1996 U.S. Code Cong. and Adm. News, p. 2166. See, also, Pub.L. 104–294, 1996 U.S. Code Cong. and Adm. News, p. 4021; Pub.L. 105–118, see 1997 U.S. Code Cong. and Adm. News, p. 2196.

> **Annotations provide references to U.S.C.C.A.N.**

CHAPTER 119—WIRE AND ELECTRONIC COMMUNICATIONS INTERCEPTION AND INTERCEPTION OF ORAL COMMUNICATIONS

| Sec. | | Sec. | |
|---|---|---|---|
| 2510. | Definitions. | 2516. | Authorization for interception of wire, oral, or electronic communications. |
| 2511. | Interception and disclosure of wire, oral, or electronic communications prohibited. | 2517. | Authorization for disclosure and use of intercepted wire, oral, or electronic communications. |
| 2512. | Manufacture, distribution, possession, and advertising of wire, oral, or electronic communication intercepting devices prohibited. | 2518. | Procedure for interception of wire, oral, or electronic communications. |
| | | 2519. | Reports concerning intercepted wire, oral, or electronic communications. |
| 2513. | Confiscation of wire, oral, or electronic communication intercepting devices. | 2520. | Recovery of civil damages authorized. |
| [2514. | Repealed.] | 2521. | Injunction against illegal interception. |
| 2515. | Prohibition of use as evidence of intercepted wire or oral communications. | 2522. | Enforcement of the Communications Assistance for Law Enforcement Act. |

146

**To locate a report in U.S.C.C.A.N., locate the edition of U.S.C.C.A.N. for the appropriate year, locate the volumes labeled "Legislative History," and turn to the page number provided in the annotations. In this case, the committee report is in 1996 U.S.C.C.A.N. beginning on page 2166.**

**FIGURE 7.13**   HOUSE JUDICIARY COMMITTEE REPORT REPRINTED IN U.S.C.C.A.N.

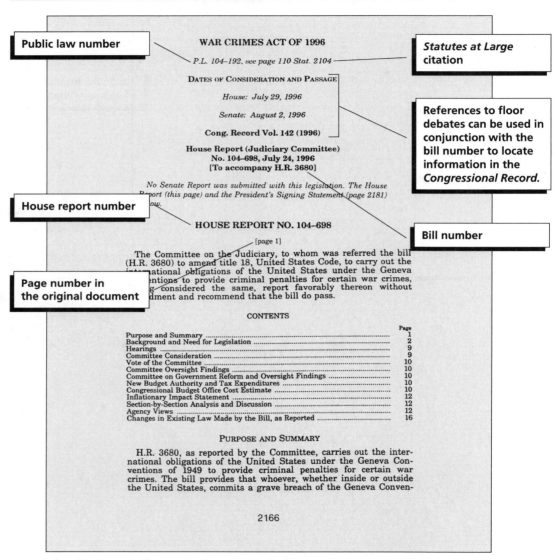

Reprinted with permission from West Group, *United States Code Congressional and Administrative News*, 104th Congress-Second Session 1996, Vol. 5 (1997), p. 2166.

**Reports on this Act are also available through Thomas. Selecting the option to search for committee reports for the 104th Congress brings up a search screen.**

**FIGURE 7.14** SEARCH SCREEN IN THOMAS

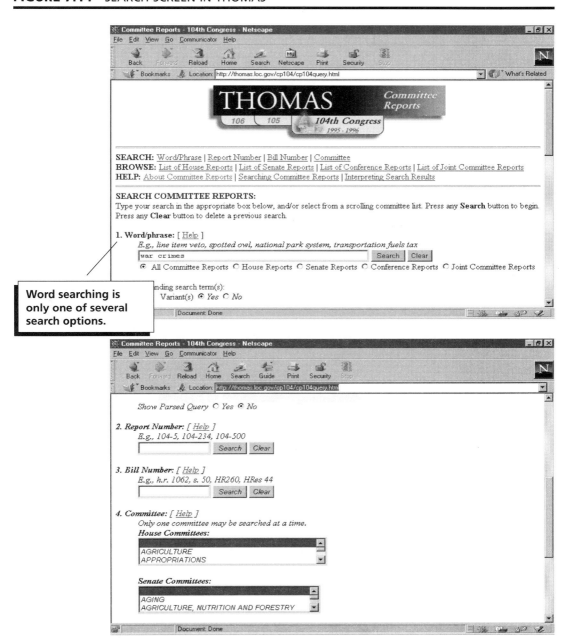

Reprinted from <http://thomas.loc.gov>.

**Searching for the terms "war crimes" retrieves the following results. To access the report for the War Crimes Act of 1996, click on the link for that document.**

**FIGURE 7.15** SEARCH RESULTS IN THOMAS

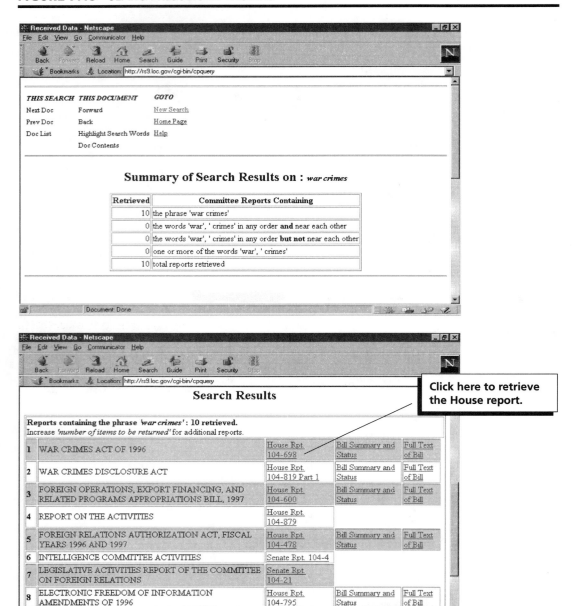

Reprinted from <http://thomas.loc.gov>.

**The report begins with a table of contents.**

**FIGURE 7.16**   HOUSE JUDICIARY COMMITTEE REPORT RETRIEVED THROUGH THOMAS

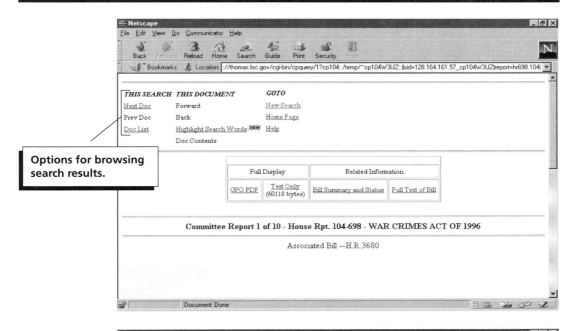

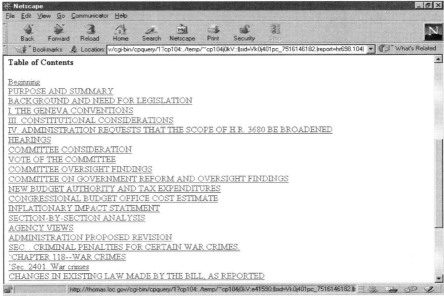

Reprinted from <http://thomas.loc.gov>.

**To locate legislative history in LexisNexis Congressional, access the LexisNexis Congressional web site from your library's computer network. Select the option to search in the "CIS Index."**

**FIGURE 7.17**    SEARCH OPTIONS, LEXISNEXIS CONGRESSIONAL

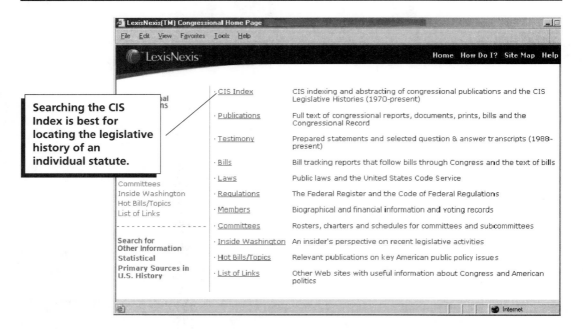

**Select the option for "Legislative Histories by number."**

**FIGURE 7.18**    SEARCH OPTIONS, LEXISNEXIS CONGRESSIONAL

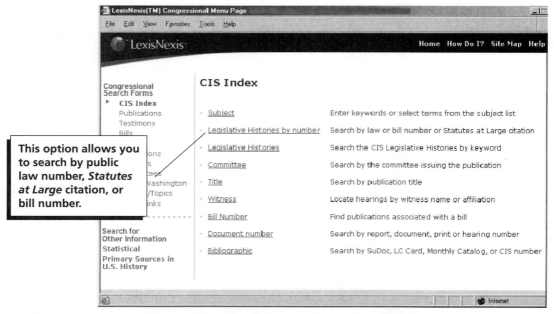

Both figures are reprinted with permission of LexisNexis, LexisNexis Congressional search options.

**Enter the public law number, *Statutes at Large* citation, or bill number.**

**FIGURE 7.19**   SEARCH SCREEN, LEXISNEXIS CONGRESSIONAL

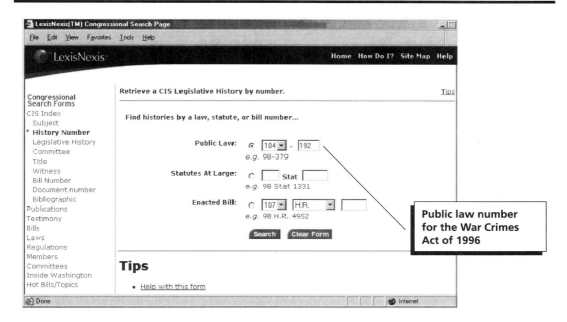

**This search produced one document, an entry for the legislative history of the War Crimes Act of 1996. Click on the link to view a list of documents**

**FIGURE 7.20**   SEARCH RESULTS, LEXISNEXIS CONGRESSIONAL

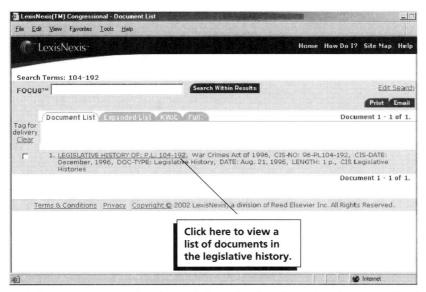

Both figures are reprinted with permission of LexisNexis, LexisNexis Congressional search screen and results.

**Clicking on the index entry or Full tab takes you to an abstract containing a summary of the bill and a list of documents that make up its legislative history. You can access the full text of a document by clicking on the appropriate link.**

**FIGURE 7.21** ABSTRACTS ENTRIES FROM LEXISNEXIS CONGRESSIONAL

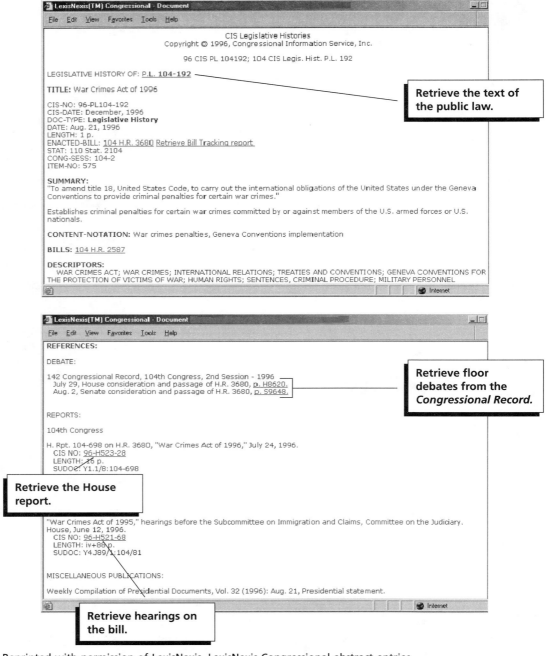

Reprinted with permission of LexisNexis, LexisNexis Congressional abstract entries.

**By following the links, you can retrieve the full text of the House report.**

**FIGURE 7.22** HOUSE JUDICIARY COMMITTEE REPORT RETRIEVED FROM LEXISNEXIS CONGRESSIONAL

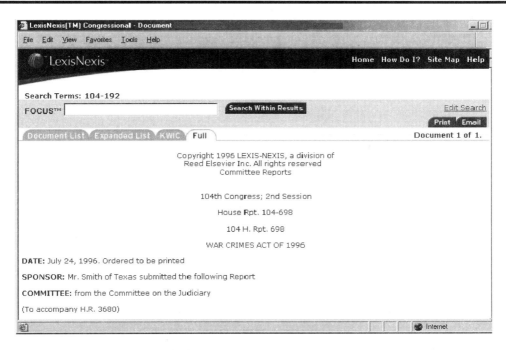

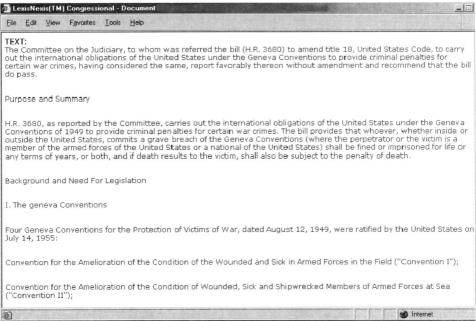

Reprinted with permission of LexisNexis, LexisNexis Congressional house report.

## G. CHECKLIST FOR FEDERAL LEGISLATIVE HISTORY RESEARCH

Because the same legislative documents can be accessed through a variety of print and electronic resources, this section provides both a research checklist and a summary chart in Figure 7.23 setting out where you can locate legislative history documents.

### 1. IDENTIFY THE SCOPE OF YOUR RESEARCH

❐ Determine whether you need the history of an individual statute or material on a general subject.

❐ To research the history of an individual statute, begin by locating the statute.

  ▪ The public law number should follow the statute in U.S.C. or an annotated code.

  ▪ To determine Congressional intent, start with committee reports; use U.S.C.C.A.N., a compiled legislative history, the CIS microfiche set, or an electronic source to locate committee reports.

  ▪ For more comprehensive legislative history research, locate hearings, floor debates, and prior versions of the bill in addition to committee reports; use a compiled legislative history, the CIS microfiche set (in conjunction with the *Congressional Record*), or an electronic source to locate a statute's complete legislative history.

❐ To research material on a general subject, use the CIS microfiche set or an electronic source.

❐ If necessary, consult a reference librarian for assistance in determining the appropriate scope of your research and locating necessary documents.

### 2. LOCATE A COMPILED LEGISLATIVE HISTORY

❐ Search the library's on-line catalog for separately published legislative histories.

❐ Use Johnson, *Sources of Compiled Legislative Histories*, or Reams, *Federal Legislative Histories*.

### 3. LOCATE COMMITTEE REPORTS IN U.S.C.C.A.N.

❐ Use annotations in U.S.C.A. to locate cross-references to committee reports reprinted in U.S.C.C.A.N.

### 4. LOCATE COMPLETE LEGISLATIVE HISTORIES IN THE CIS MICROFICHE SET

❐ Look up the public law number in the Legislative Histories volumes (after 1984) to locate listings of all legislative history documents for an individual statute.

❐ Before 1984, locate the same information in the legislative histories section in the annual Abstracts volumes.

❐ Use the Index and Abstracts volumes if you do not have the public law number or need to locate information by subject.

### 5. LOCATE FLOOR DEBATES IN THE *CONGRESSIONAL RECORD* USING PRINT RESOURCES

❐ Locate references to floor debates using the CIS Legislative Histories volumes or reports reprinted in U.S.C.C.A.N.

❐ Use the *Congressional Record* index to locate information by subject or bill number.

### 6. SEARCH FOR LEGISLATIVE HISTORY ELECTRONICALLY

❐ Search by public law number, *Statutes at Large* citation, or bill number to locate the legislative history of an individual piece of legislation.

❐ Use subject or word searches to locate information by subject.

❐ Use Westlaw and LexisNexis to locate legislative documents.

❐ Use Thomas or GPO Access for free Internet access to legislative documents.

❐ Use LexisNexis Congressional if your library subscribes to this service for electronic access to the CIS microfiche set.

**FIGURE 7.23** RESEARCH SUMMARY FOR FEDERAL LEGISLATIVE HISTORY

| TO LOCATE THIS TYPE OF DOCUMENT | USE THIS PRINT RESOURCE | OR THIS ELECTRONIC RESOURCE |
|---|---|---|
| Bills | Compiled legislative histories, CIS microfiche | LexisNexis, Westlaw, LexisNexis Congressional, Thomas, GPO Access |
| Hearings | Compiled legislative histories, CIS microfiche | LexisNexis, Westlaw, LexisNexis Congressional, Thomas, GPO Access |
| Floor debates | Compiled legislative histories, *Congressional Record* | *Congressional Record* accessed through LexisNexis, Westlaw, LexisNexis Congressional, Thomas, GPO Access |
| Committee reports | Compiled legislative histories, U.S.C.C.A.N., CIS microfiche | LexisNexis, Westlaw, LexisNexis Congressional, Thomas, GPO Access |

# FEDERAL ADMINISTRATIVE LAW RESEARCH

A. Administrative agencies and regulations

B. Researching federal regulations in print

C. Shepard's for the *Code of Federal Regulations*

D. Electronic research of federal regulations

E. Citing federal regulations

F. Sample pages for federal administrative law research

G. Checklist for federal administrative law research

## A. ADMINISTRATIVE AGENCIES AND REGULATIONS

Administrative agencies exist at all levels of government. Examples of federal administrative agencies include the Food and Drug Administration (FDA), the Environmental Protection Agency (EPA), and the Federal Communications Commission (FCC). Agencies are created by statute, but they are part of the executive branch because they "enforce" or implement a legislatively created scheme. In creating an agency, a legislature will pass what is known as "enabling" legislation. Enabling legislation defines the scope of the agency's mission and "enables" it to perform its functions, which may include promulgating regulations and adjudicating controversies, among other functions. If an agency is empowered to create regulations, those regulations cannot exceed the authority granted by the legislature. Thus, for example, while the FCC may be able to establish regulations concerning television licenses, it would not be able to promulgate regulations concerning the labeling of drugs because that would exceed the authority granted to it by Congress in its enabling legislation.

Federal agencies often create regulations to implement statutes passed by Congress. Sometimes Congress cannot legislate with the level of detail necessary to implement a complex legislative scheme. In those circumstances, Congress charges an agency with enforcing the statute, and the agency will develop procedures for implementing more general legislative mandates. In the Family and Medical Leave Act, for instance, Congress mandated that an employer allow an employee with a "serious health condition" to take unpaid medical leave. Pursuant to the statute, the Department of Labor has promulgated more specific regulations defining what "serious health condition" means.

In format, a regulation looks like a statute. It is, in essence, a rule created by a government entity, and many times administrative regulations are called "rules." In operation, they are indistinguishable from statutes, although the methods used to create, modify, and repeal them are different from those applicable to statutes. Federal administrative agencies are required to conform to the procedures set out in the Administrative Procedure Act (APA) in promulgating regulations. State agencies may be required to comply with similar statutes at the state level. Without going into too much detail, the APA frequently requires agencies to undertake the following steps: (1) notify the public when they plan to promulgate new regulations or change existing ones; (2) publish proposed regulations and solicit comments on them before the regulations become final; and (3) publish final regulations before they go into effect to notify the public of the new requirements.

Regulations and proposed regulations, along with other information on the executive branch of government, are published daily in the *Federal Register*. After final regulations are published in the *Federal Register*, they are codified in the *Code of Federal Regulations* (C.F.R.). Like U.S.C., the C.F.R. is divided into fifty "Titles." The C.F.R. Titles are subdivided into Chapters, which are usually named for the agencies issuing the regulations. Chapters are subdivided into Parts covering specific regulatory areas, and Parts are further subdivided into sections. To find a regulation, you would need to know its Title, Part, and section number. Thus, a citation to 16 C.F.R. §1700.1 tells you that the regulation is published in Title 16 of the C.F.R. in Part 1700, section number 1700.1. Figure 8.1 illustrates what a federal regulation looks like.

## B. RESEARCHING FEDERAL REGULATIONS IN PRINT

Researching federal regulations entails two steps:

1. locating regulations
2. updating your research.

This section describes how to complete these steps using print research resources.

**FIGURE 8.1** 16 C.F.R., BEGINNING OF PART 1700

---

**Consumer Product Safety Commission** §1700.1

## SUBCHAPTER E—POISON PREVENTION PACKAGING ACT OF 1970 REGULATIONS

*Outline of the Part*

### PART 1700—POISON PREVENTION PACKAGING

Sec.
1700.1  Definitions.
1700.2  Authority.
1700.3  Establishment of standards for special packaging.
1700.4  Effective date of standards.
1700.5  Noncomplying package requirements.
1700.14  Substances requiring special packaging.
1700.15  Poison prevention packaging standards.
1700.20  Testing procedure for special packaging.

AUTHORITY: Pub. L. 91–601, secs. 1–9, 84 Stat. 1670–74, 15 U.S.C. 1471–76. Secs. 1700.1 and 1700.14 also issued under Pub. L. 92–573, sec. 30(a), 88 Stat. 1231, 15 U.S.C. 2079(a).

SOURCE: 38 FR 21247, Aug. 7, 1973, unless otherwise noted.

### §1700.1  Definitions.

(a) As used in this part:

(1) *Act* means the Poison Prevention Packaging Act of 1970 (Pub. L. 91–601, 84 Stat. 1670–74; 15 U.S.C. 1471–75), enacted December 30, 1970.

(2) *Commission* means the Consumer Product Safety Commission established by section 4 of the Consumer Product Safety Act (86 Stat. 1210; 15 U.S.C. 2053).

(3) *Dietary supplement* means any vitamin and/or mineral preparation offered in tablet, capsule, wafer, or other similar uniform unit form; in powder, granule, flake, or liquid form; or in the physical form of a conventional food but which is not a conventional food; and which purports or is represented to be for special dietary use by humans to supplement their diets by increasing the total dietary intake of one or more of the essential vitamins and/or minerals.

(b) Except for the definition of "Secretary," which is obsolete, the definitions given in section 2 of the act are applicable to this part and are repeated herein for convenience as follows:

(1) [Reserved]

(2) *Household substance* means any substance which is customarily produced or distributed for sale for con-

sumption or use, or customarily stored, by individuals in or about the household and which is:

(i) A hazardous substance as that term is defined in section 2(f) of the Federal Hazardous Substances Act (15 U.S.C. 1261(f));

(ii) A food, drug, or cosmetic as those terms are defined in section 201 of the Federal Food, Drug, and Cosmetic Act (21 U.S.C. 321); or

(iii) A substance intended for use as fuel when stored in a portable container and used in the heating, cooking, or refrigeration system of a house.

*Statutory authority for promulgating the regulations*

(3) *Package* means the immediate container or wrapping in which any household substance is contained for consumption, use, or storage by individuals in or about the household and, for purposes of section 4(a)(2) of the act, also means any outer container or wrapping used in the retail display of any such substance to consumers. "Package" does not include:

*Citation to the Federal Register where the regulations were originally published*

(i) Any shipping container or wrapping used solely for the transportation of any household substance in bulk or in quantity to manufacturers, packers, or processors, or to wholesale or distributors thereof; or

(ii) Any shipping container or wrapping used by retailers to ship or deliver any household substance to consumers unless it is the only such container or wrapping.

*An individual regulation*

(4) *Special packaging* means packaging that is designed or constructed to be significantly difficult for children under 5 years of age to open or obtain a toxic or harmful amount of the substance contained therein within a reasonable time and not difficult for normal adults to use properly, but does not mean packaging which all such children cannot open or obtain a toxic or harmful amount within a reasonable time.

(5) *Labeling* means all labels and other written, printed, or graphic matter upon any household substance or

669

## 1. LOCATING REGULATIONS

The C.F.R. is published as a set of softcover books. Once you locate the C.F.R. set, the next question is how to find regulations relevant to your research issue. There are two ways to accomplish this. One way is to use the cross-references to the C.F.R. in U.S.C.S. or U.S.C.A. The other is to go directly to the C.F.R. itself, using a subject index to refer you to relevant C.F.R. provisions.[1]

### a. Using an Annotated Code

Because regulations are often used to implement statutory schemes, U.S.C.S. and U.S.C.A. frequently contain cross-references to applicable regulations. Thus, if your research leads you to statutes, the annotations are a useful tool to guide you toward regulations that bear on the area of law you are researching. You may recall from Chapter 6 that U.S.C.S. contains more extensive regulatory annotations than U.S.C.A. does. Figure 8.2 shows C.F.R. cross-references in U.S.C.S. annotations.

### b. Using an Index

Another way to locate regulations is to use a subject index. There are at least two indices you can use to locate federal regulations:

1. CFR Index and Finding Aids. This is a volume within the C.F.R. set itself. Like all other C.F.R. volumes, it is a softcover book, and it is published annually.
2. CIS Index to the *Code of Federal Regulations*. This is a separate subject index to the C.F.R. published by Congressional Information Service (CIS). It is a hardcover book and is also published annually.

Figure 8.3 shows a page from the CFR Index and Finding Aids.

## 2. UPDATING REGULATIONS

The C.F.R. is updated once a year in four separate installments. Titles 1 through 16 are updated on January 1 of each year, Titles 17 through 27 on April 1, Titles 28 through 41 on July 1, and Titles 42 through 50 on October 1. Because a new set of C.F.R. volumes is published annually, the C.F.R. is not updated with pocket parts. Instead, new or amended regulations are published in the *Federal Register*. They are not codified

---

[1] Subject-matter services used for researching specific subject areas of the law may also contain the text of regulations. Researching with subject-matter services is covered in Chapter 9.

**FIGURE 8.2** ANNOTATIONS TO 15 U.S.C.S. § 1476

> **PACKAGING FOR CHILD PROTECTION** **15 USCS § 1476**
>
> [Cross-references to applicable regulations in U.S.C.S. statutory annotations]
>
> he Poison Prevention Packaging Act of 1970 [enacting 15 USCS §§ 1471 et seq. and amending 7 USCS § 135; 15 USCS § 1261; 21 USCS §§ 343, 52, 353, 362] were transferred to the Consumer Product Safety Commission by 15 USCS § 2079(a).
>
> **Other provisions:**
> **Effective date of regulations promulgated under Act.** For effective date of regulations promulgated under 15 USCS §§ 1471 et seq., see other provisions note to 15 USCS § 1471.
>
> **CODE OF FEDERAL REGULATIONS**
>
> Consumer Product Safety Commission–General–Notice of Agency activities, 16 CFR Part 1011.
>
> Consumer Product Safety Commission–General–Meetings policy–Meetings between Agency personnel and outside parties, 16 CFR Part 1012.
>
> Consumer Product Safety Commission–General–Policies and procedures for information disclosure and Commission employee testimony in private litigation, 16 CFR Part 1016.
>
> Consumer Product Safety Commission–General–Applications for exemption from preemption, 16 CFR Part 1061.
>
> Consumer Product Safety Commission–Poison Prevention Packaging Act Regulations–Poison prevention packaging, 16 CFR Part 1700.
>
> Consumer Product Safety Commission–Poison Prevention Packaging Act Regulations–Statements of policy and interpretation, 16 CFR Part 1701.
>
> **RESEARCH GUIDE**
> **American Law of Products Liability 3d:**
> 4 Am Law Prod Liab 3d, Consumer Product Safety Laws §§ 62:11; 64:50.

Reprinted with permission from LexisNexis, *United States Code Service*, Title 15 Commerce and Trade §§ 1151–1600 (1993), p. 391.

within the C.F.R. until a new set is published. Because agencies can act at any time during the year, updating C.F.R. research is essential. Updating is a two-step process:

- Use the List of CFR Sections Affected to find any *Federal Register* notices indicating that the regulation has been affected by agency action.
- Update from the date of the List of CFR Sections Affected until the present.

### a. Using the List of CFR Sections Affected

The List of CFR Sections Affected (LSA) is a monthly publication listing each C.F.R. section affected by agency action. The LSA is a cumulative

**FIGURE 8.3**    INDEX ENTRY, CFR INDEX AND FINDING AIDS

---

**Plutonium**                                                              **CFR Index**

Pears, plums, and peaches grown in
California, 7 CFR 917
Prunes grown in designated counties in
Washington and in Umatilla County,
Oregon, 7 CFR 924

**Plutonium**
Air transportation of plutonium, 10 CFR 871

**Pneumoconiosis**
*See* Black lung benefits

**Poison prevention**
*See also* Lead poisoning
Federal Caustic Poison Act, 21 CFR 1230
Formal evidentiary public hearing
procedures, 16 CFR 1502
Poison prevention packaging, 16 CFR 1700
Applications for exemption from
preemption of State and local
requirements, 16 CFR 1061
Exemption petitions procedures and
requirements, 16 CFR 1702
Policy and interpretation statements, 16
CFR 1701
Public Health Service, requests for health
hazard evaluations, 42 CFR 85
substances control, administrative
assessment of civil penalties and
revocation or suspension of permits,
consolidated practice rules, 40 CFR 22

**Police**
*See* Law enforcement officers

**Political activities (Government
employees)**
ACTION, prohibitions on electoral and
lobbying activities, 45 CFR 1226
Civil service
Political activity of Federal employees, 5
CFR 734
Residing in designated localities, 5 CFR
733
Prohibited practices, 5 CFR 4
Community Services Office, grantee
personnel management, 45 CFR 1069
General Accounting Office, 4 CFR 7
Legal Services Corporation, 45 CFR 1608
State or local officers or employees, 5 CFR
151

**Political affiliation discrimination**
ACTION, 45 CFR 1225

Job Training Partnership Act,
nondiscrimination and equal opportunity
requirements, 29 CFR 34
Prisons Bureau, 28 CFR 551

**Political candidates**
*See also* Campaign funds
Air carriers, credit extension to political
candidates, 14 CFR 374a
Aircraft operators, carriage of candidates in
Federal elections, 14 CFR 91
Cable television service, 47 CFR 76
Candidate status and designations for Federal
office, 11 CFR 101
Communications common carriers,
miscellaneous rules, 47 CFR 64
Debts owed by candidates and political
committees, 11 CFR 116
Election campaign documents, filing, 11
CFR 105
Federal office candidates or their
representatives, credit extension for
transportation, 49 CFR 1325
Radio broadcast services, 47 CFR 73

**Political committees and parties**
Campaign fund allocations of candidate and
committee activities, 11 CFR 106
Campaign fund reports by political
committees, 11 CFR 104
Debts owed by candidates and political
committees, 11 CFR 116
Depositaries for campaign funds, 11 CFR
103
Election campaign documents, filing, 11
CFR 105
Income taxes, exempt organizations, political
organizations, 26 CFR 1 (1.527-1—
1.527-9)
Political committees registration,
organization, and recordkeeping, 11
CFR 102
Presidential election campaign financing,
contribution and expenditure limitations
and prohibitions, 11 CFR 110
Presidential nominating conventions
Federal financing, 11 CFR 9008
Registration, and reports, 11 CFR 107

Reference to C.F.R.
Title and Part with
regulations on poison
prevention packaging

552

publication; thus, you only need to check the most recent issue to determine whether any changes to a regulation have taken place since the date the relevant Title of the C.F.R. was last published.

Once you have located the most recent LSA, the first step in using it is checking the time period it covers. This information is on the inside front cover. In the illustration in Figure 8.4, the LSA for September 1995 contains changes to Titles 1 through 16 of the C.F.R. from January 3 through September 29, 1995.

The next step is looking up the regulation in the LSA. The LSA is organized numerically by Title number, and within each Title, numerically by Part and section number. If you do not find the section listed in the LSA, there have been no changes to the regulation. If you do find the section listed, the LSA will refer you to the page or pages of the *Federal Register* containing information on the agency's action. Figure 8.5 is an example of a page from the September 1995 LSA.

The *Federal Register* is a daily publication. It begins on the first business day of the new year with page one and is consecutively paginated from that point on until the last business day of the year. Because the *Federal Register* is consecutively paginated throughout the year, locating an individual page number can be difficult. The LSA has a table in the back listing the range of page numbers contained in each daily issue. You can use this table to identify the precise day on which the change was reported in the *Federal Register*. An example of the table appears in Figure 8.6.

Once you know the date of the *Federal Register* issue containing the page with changes to the regulation, you can go directly to that issue and read about the change. Figure 8.7 shows the page from the *Federal Register* with the revised language of 16 C.F.R. § 1700.15.

### b. Updating Beyond the List of CFR Sections Affected

Although the LSA is published monthly, agency action can affect federal regulations after the latest LSA was published. Therefore, the next step in updating is using the *Federal Register* to update your research from the last day covered by the LSA through the most current issue of the *Federal Register*.

For purposes of illustrating this process, assume that the most current issue of the *Federal Register* is dated October 20, 1995. In the earlier example, the September 1995 LSA provided updates through September 29, 1995, according to the information on the inside front cover. Therefore, you would still need to update your research for the period from September 29 through October 20. To update for this period, you would need to use a table on the inside back cover of the October 20 *Federal Register* called CFR Parts Affected During October. The table of CFR Parts Affected appears in the back of each issue of the *Federal Register*

**FIGURE 8.4**   INSIDE FRONT COVER, SEPTEMBER 1995 LIST OF CFR SECTIONS AFFECTED

# LSA

List of CFR Sections Affected

## September 1995

**Dates of coverage**

**Title 1–16**
Changes January 3, 1995
through September 29, 1995

**Title 17–27**
Changes April 3, 1995
through September 29, 1995

**Title 28–41**
Changes July 3, 1995
through September 29, 1995

**Title 42–50**
Changes October 3, 1994
through September 29, 1995

**FIGURE 8.5**   SEPTEMBER 1995 LIST OF CFR SECTIONS AFFECTED

---

**SEPTEMBER 1995**                                        **63**

**CHANGES JANUARY 3, 1995 THROUGH SEPTEMBER 29, 1995**

4.11  Heading,  (e)  heading,  (1)
    through (5) revised; (b) and
    (c) amended ..............................37750
4.12 (a) and (c) revised ...................37751
14.2 Removed .................................42033
14.4 Removed .................................42033
14.7 Removed .................................42033
14.11 Removed................................42033
14.16 Revised.................................42033
14.17 Removed................................42033
24 Removed....................................48027
231 Removed...................................48027
234 Removed ..................................40262
236 Guide rescission.....................37334
237 Removed ..................................40265
242 Removed ..................................40267
247 Removed ..................................48027
248 Removed ..................................40270
252 Removed ..................................40453
305 Energy efficiency ranges ..........15198
305.8 (a)(4)(v) revised ......................14210
305.9 (a) revised ..............................9296
305.11 (f)(1) amended .....................14210
    (e)(1)(iii), (iv) and (vi) revised
    .................................................. 31081
305.13 (a)(4) revised .........................14211
305.14 (d) revised ............................14211
305 Appendix F revised..........19845, 27691
    Appendixes C and D4 revised
    .................................................. 43368
    ~~..~~ )5, D6, E and J1
    ..................................................43369
    ~~..~~ revised....................43370
    ..................................................26955
    ..................................................43864
600 Appendix amended....................45660
800 Removed ..................................40706
803 Appendix amended....................40706

**Chapter   II—Consumer   Product
Safety   Commission   (Parts
1000—1799)**

1000.7 (b) amended ..........................26825
1000.12 Revised................................26825
1000.19 Amended ............................26825
1000.24 Amended; heading revised
    ..................................................26825
1000.26 Revised................................26825
1000.32 Revised................................26825
1117 Added ......................................10493
1117.2 (a) revised; (h) added.............41801
1203 Added; interim .........................15232

1500 Authority citation revised
    .................................................. 10752
1500.14 (b)(8)(iv) added ....................8193
1500.18   (a)   introductory   text;
    (a)(17) added ............................10752
1500.19 Added .................................10752
    (b)(1) introductory text revised
    .................................................. 41802
1700 Authority citation revised

1700.14 (a)(22) added.......
    (a)(23) and (24) added ..
    (a) introductory text
    ..................................................
    (a)(25) added; eff. 2–6–9(
    Regulation at 60 FR 37739 eff.
    date corrected to 7–22–96 ..........48890
1700.15 (b)(2) revised; eff. 7–22–96
    .................................................. 37734
1700.20 (a) revised; eff. in part 1–
    24–96 and in part 7–22–96..........37734
    (d) added...................................37738

*Proposed Rules:*

0—999 (Ch. I)...................................6463
3..........................................................42481
24.........................................15724, 48056
231......................................................15724
247......................................................15724
248......................................................17032
260......................................................38978
305......................................................15200
307........................................................8312
310..............................................8312, 30406
311......................................................44712
400......................................27240, 48063
402......................................27241, 48065
404......................................27242, 48067
405......................................15725, 48070
409......................................17491, 28554
413......................................27243, 48071
417......................................27244, 48073
418......................................27245, 48075
419......................................................38474
436......................................17656, 34485
444......................................................24805
460......................................................17492
801......................................................38930
802......................................................38930
1307....................................................29518
1500....................................34922, 40785
1507....................................................34922
1700....................2716, 9654, 12165, 17660

> *Federal Register* page
> number showing a
> change to
> § 1700.15(b)(2)

> Changes to Part 1700
> are included in this
> section.

**FIGURE 8.6**   SEPTEMBER 1995 LIST OF CFR SECTIONS AFFECTED, TABLE OF *FEDERAL REGISTER* ISSUE PAGES AND DATES

## TABLE OF FEDERAL REGISTER ISSUE PAGES AND DATES     249

| Pages | Date | Pages | Date |
|---|---|---|---|
| 14891–15026 | 21 | 31227–31369 | 14 |
| 15027–15227 | 22 | 31371–31622 | 15 |
| 15229–15455 | 23 | 31623–31905 | 16 |
| 15457–15648 | 24 | 31907–32097 | 19 |
| 15649–15853 | 27 | 32099–32255 | 20 |
| 15855–16034 | 28 | 32557–32420 | 21 |
| 16035–16361 | 29 | 32421–32575 | 22 |
| 16363–16564 | 30 | 32577–32898 | 23 |
| 16565–16764 | 31 | 32899–33096 | 26 |
| 16765–16977 | Apr. 3 | 33097–33321 | 27 |
| 16979–17190 | 4 | 33323–33676 | 28 |
| 17191–17432 | 5 | 33677–34086 | 29 |
| 17433–17624 | 6 | 34087–34452 | 30 |
| 17625–17890 | 7 | 34453–34842 | July 3 |
| 17891–18342 | 10 | 34843–35111 | 5 |
| 18343–18538 | 11 | 35113–35320 | |
| 18539–18725 | 12 | 35321–35460 | |
| 18727–18948 | 13 | 35461–35690 | 1 |
| 18949–19152 | 14 | 35691–35827 | 1 |
| 19158–19342 | 17 | 35829–36026 | 1 |
| 19343–19483 | 18 | 36027–36202 | 13 |
| 19485–19664 | 19 | 36203–36338 | 14 |
| 19665–19843 | 20 | 36339–36634 | 17 |
| 19845–19997 | 21 | 36635–36949 | 18 |
| 19999–20169 | 24 | 36951–37321 | 19 |
| 20171–20389 | 25 | 37323–37553 | 20 |
| 20391–20622 | 26 | 37555–37801 | 21 |
| 20623–20878 | 27 | 37803–37932 | 24 |
| 20879–21032 | 28 | 37933–38226 | 25 |
| 21033–21424 | May 1 | 38227–38474 | 26 |
| 21425–21697 | 2 | 38475–38663 | 27 |
| 21699–21971 | 3 | 38665–38945 | 28 |
| 21973–22245 | 4 | 38947–39099 | 31 |
| 22247–22453 | 5 | 39101–39239 | Aug. 1 |
| 22455–24534 | 8 | 39241–39624 | 2 |
| 24535–24759 | 9 | 39625–39834 | 3 |
| 24761–25117 | 10 | 39835–40051 | 4 |
| 25119–25600 | 11 | 40053–40257 | 7 |
| 25601–25837 | 12 | 40259–40452 | 8 |
| 25839–25976 | 15 | 40453–40735 | 9 |
| 25983–26338 | 16 | 40737–40992 | 10 |
| 26339–26666 | 17 | 40993–41792 | 11 |
| 26667–26821 | 18 | 41793–42024 | 14 |
| 26823–26975 | 19 | 42025–42423 | 15 |
| 26977–27220 | 22 | 42425–42766 | 16 |
| 27221–27400 | 23 | 42767–42999 | 17 |
| 27401–27655 | 24 | 43001–43346 | 18 |
| 27657–27866 | 25 | 43347–43512 | 21 |
| 27867–28026 | 26 | 43513–43703 | 22 |
| 28027–28316 | 30 | 43705–43952 | 23 |
| 28317–28508 | 31 | 43953–44252 | 24 |
| 28509–28699 | June 1 | 44253–44413 | 25 |
| 28701–29461 | 2 | 44415–44725 | 28 |
| 29463–29745 | 5 | 44727–45309 | 29 |
| 29749–29957 | 6 | 45041–45323 | 30 |
| 29959–30181 | 7 | 45325–45646 | 31 |
| 30183–30456 | 8 | 45647–46016 | Sept. 1 |
| 30457–30771 | 9 | 46017–46212 | 5 |
| 30773–31045 | 12 | 46213–46495 | 6 |
| 31047–31226 | 13 | 46497–46748 | 7 |

Page 37,734 was published on July 21.

**FIGURE 8.7**  *FEDERAL REGISTER*, JULY 21, 1995

37734     Federal Register / Vol. 60, No. 140 / Friday, July 21, 1995 / Rules and Regulations

protocol), to use standard (supplier stocked, on-the-shelf) SAUE packaging, or to reformulate or withdraw a product. Some SAUE packaging is available now; other SAUE package types, including those for products having formulations that impose unusual requirements on packaging, are expected to become available. Changes in packaging may require associated equipment purchases or modifications. Costs of testing some products to meet the requirements of government agencies other than CPSC may be required if packaging is changed. Incremental costs associated with new SAUE packaging should not add materially to the costs of a product and are expected to be passed on to the consumer.

CPSC does not anticipate that any substantial number of small businesses will be significantly affected, however, because of the current and expected future availability of SAUE packaging for all types of product formulations. If necessary, companies can apply for a temporary stay of enforcement to comply with the rule.

*D. Pharmaceutical Packagers*

There are an estimated 1,200 pharmaceutical packagers, according to an FDA spokesperson, an unknown number of which are small. [236] Also unknown is the number of small firms that provide consumer-ready pharmaceuticals; some firms provide products only in bulk packages. The Commission expects that many of the small firms can use standard SAUE packaging. However, firms that use reclosable packaging may have to find new suppliers, and may also have to pay more for SAUE packaging. Films, foils, and other materials used for SAUE non-reclosable packaging also may cost more than the materials used for existing CRP. No comments were received from any small company regarding the possible need for stability testing to meet FDA requirements. Incremental costs for new packaging are expected to be modest and most likely will be passed on to users. CPSC does not anticipate that a significant number of packagers will be severely or permanently affected.

*E. Pharmacies*

There are over 40,000 independent pharmacies, according to a representative of the National Association of Retail Druggists, most of which are small businesses. [236] (There are an additional 25,000 chain pharmacies, including those associated with drug and food stores and mass merchandisers. *Id.*) Retail establishments may have to find new suppliers if old suppliers abandon the

market or do not offer acceptable sizes of containers. Pharmacies may also have to pay more for SAUE packaging than for existing CRP. Pharmacy staff probably will spend additional time instructing customers in the use of new packaging. Modest incremental costs for SAUE packaging and for staff time are likely to be passed on to the consumer, and there should not be a big impact on most pharmacies.

*F. Conclusion*

The Commission concludes that the action to revise the testing protocol for special packaging under the PPPA will not have a significant adverse impact on a substantial number of small businesses.

**IX. Environmental Considerations**

Pursuant to the National Environmental Policy Act, and in accordance with the Council on Environmental Quality regulations and CPSC procedures for environmental review, the Commission has assessed the possible environmental effects associated with the revisions to the PPPA protocols.

The Commission assessed the possible environmental effects of rulemaking associated with the revisions to the protocol for testing CRP under the PPPA and presented its findings in a paper dated April 2, 1990. [123, Tab D] Reassessment of the possible environmental effects confirms the original determination that the rule will have no significant effects on the environment. [236] The revisions to the rule involve a test method and establish new test standards. They will not change the number of CRP in use. Since the rule will not become effective until 1 year after its publication and there will be a subsequent 18-month blanket exemption from compliance, there is time to use up existing inventories of unfilled non-SAUE packaging. Additionally, SAUE packaging is made of basically the same materials and in basically the same way as older styles of CRP. Much of the existing equipment involved in the production and filling of non-SAUE packaging can be modified to produce SAUE packaging, rather than replaced.

**EFFECTIVE DATES:** Revised §§ 1700.15(b)(2), 1700.20(a)(3), and 1700.20(a)(4) are effective July 22, 1996. Until then, current §§ 1700.15(b)(2), 1700.20(a)(4), and 1700.20(a)(5) remain in effect.

Revised §§ 1700.20(a) (1) and (2) are effective January 24, 1996. Until then, current §§ 1700.20(a)(1)–(3) remain in effect.

New § 1700.20(d) is effective August 21, 1995.

For mandatory provisions, the effective dates specified above apply to all products subject to the respective sections that are packaged on or after the effective date.

**List of Subjects in 16 CFR Part**

Consumer protection, Drugs, and children, Packaging and co Poison prevention, Toxic subst

**V. Conclusion**

For the reasons given above, the Commission amends 16 CFR 1700.20 as follows:

**PART 1700—[AMENDED]**

1. The authority citation for Part 1700 is revised to read as follows:

**Authority:** 15 U.S.C. 1471–76. Secs. 1700.1 and 1700.14 also issued under 15 U.S.C. 2079(a).

2. Section 1700.15(b)(2) is revised to read as follows:

**§ 1700.15   Poison prevention packaging standards.**

\* \* \* \* \*

(b) \* \* \*

(2) Ease of adult opening. (i) Senior-adult test. Except for products specified in paragraph (b)(2)(ii) of this section, special packaging shall have a senior adult use effectiveness (SAUE) of not less than 90% for the senior-adult panel test of § 1700.20(a)(3).

(ii) *Younger-adult test.* (A) When applicable. Products that must be in aerosol form and products that require metal containers, under the criteria specified below, shall have an effectiveness of not less than 90% for the younger-adult test of § 1700.20(a)(4). The senior-adult panel test of § 1700.20(a)(3) does not apply to these products. For the purposes of this paragraph, metal containers are those that have both a metal package and a reclosable metal closure, and aerosol products are self-contained pressurized products.

(B) Determination of need for metal or aerosol container.

(*1*) *Criteria.* A product will be deemed to require metal containers or aerosol form only if:

(*i*) No other packaging type would comply with other state or Federal regulations,

(*ii*) No other packaging can reasonably be used for the product's intended application,

(*iii*) No other packaging or closure material would be compatible with the substance,

> **New regulatory language**

and is cumulative for the current month. Thus, the table in the back of the October 20 issue covers the period from October 2 through October 20.

Remember that the C.F.R. is divided into Titles, Parts, and sections. The cumulative table in the back of the *Federal Register* will not tell you which sections have been affected, only which Parts. Therefore, you must know the Part of the C.F.R. containing the section you are updating. If you do not see this Part referenced in the table, no action has been taken during the month to date. If you do see a reference to the Part, however, you have some additional work to do. The table will refer you to page numbers within that month's *Federal Register* with information affecting the C.F.R. Part. You cannot tell from this table which sections within the Part have been affected. Therefore, you must look up each page number reference to see which sections have been affected. When you look up each reference, if you do not find any mention of the section you are researching, your research is complete. If you do find a reference to the section, read about the change to see how it affects your research. Figure 8.8 shows an excerpt from the table of CFR Parts Affected from the October 20, 1995, *Federal Register*.

Although the *Federal Register* is a daily publication, today's edition is not immediately available in print like a newspaper. It takes time for the daily issues to be printed and distributed. Accordingly, if you want to update your research through the current date without using electronic resources, the final step is contacting the agency directly to find out whether any action has been taken recently or is contemplated in the near future. At the beginning of any *Federal Register* notice regarding rule making, you will find the name and telephone number of a contact person at the agency. In administrative law research, agency staff can be one of your best resources, and you should not hesitate to use the telephone as one of your research tools.

**FIGURE 8.8** *FEDERAL REGISTER*, OCTOBER 20, 1995, TABLE OF CFR PARTS AFFECTED DURING OCTOBER

i

## Reader Aids

Federal Register
Vol. 60, No. 203
Friday, October 20, 1995

**Cumulative table**

### CUSTOMER SERVICE AND INFORMATION

**Federal Register/Code of Federal Regulations**
General information, indexes and other finding aids    202–523–5227
Public inspection announcement line    523–5215

**Laws**
Public Laws Update Services (numbers, dates, etc.)    523–6641
For additional information    523–5227

**Presidential Documents**
Executive orders and proclamations    523–5227
The United States Government Manual    523–5227

**Other Services**
Electronic and on-line services (voice)    523–4534
Privacy Act Compilation    523–3187
TDD for the hearing impaired    523–5229

### ELECTRONIC BULLETIN BOARD

Free **Electronic Bulletin Board** service for Public Law numbers, Federal Register finding aids, and list of documents on public inspection.    202–275–0920

### FAX-ON-DEMAND

You may access our Fax-On-Demand service. You only need a fax machine and there is no charge for the service except for long distance telephone charges the user may incur. The list of documents on public inspection and the daily Federal Register's table of contents are available using this service. The document numbers are 7050-Public Inspection list and 7051-Table of Contents list. The public inspection list will be updated immediately for documents filed on an emergency basis.

NOTE: YOU WILL ONLY GET A LISTING OF DOCUMENTS ON FILE AND NOT THE ACTUAL DOCUMENT. Documents on public inspection may be viewed and copied in our office located at 800 North Capitol Street, N.W., Suite 700. The Fax-On-Demand telephone number is:    301–713–6905

### FEDERAL REGISTER PAGES AND DATES, OCTOBER

| | |
|---|---|
| 51321–51666 | 2 |
| 51667–51876 | 3 |
| 51877–52062 | 4 |
| 52063–52290 | 5 |
| 52291–52608 | 6 |
| 52609–52830 | 10 |
| 52831–53100 | 11 |
| 53101–53246 | 12 |
| 53247–53502 | 13 |
| 53503–53690 | 16 |
| 53691–53846 | 17 |
| 53847–54026 | 18 |
| 54027–54150 | 19 |
| 54151–54290 | 20 |

### CFR PARTS AFFECTED DURING OCTOBER

At the end of each month, the Office of the Federal Register publishes separately a List of CFR Sections Affected (LSA), which lists parts and sections affected by documents published since the revision date of each title.

**3 CFR**

**Proclamations:**
| | |
|---|---|
| 6828 | 51877 |
| 6829 | 51879 |
| 6830 | 52291 |
| 6831 | 52827 |
| 6832 | 53097 |
| 6833 | 53099 |
| 6834 | 53101 |
| 6835 | 53103 |
| 6836 | 53105 |
| 6837 | 53107 |
| 6838 | 53247 |
| 6839 | 53249 |
| 6840 | 53843 |
| 6841 | 54023 |
| 6842 | 54025 |

**Executive Orders:**
| | |
|---|---|
| 4410 (Revoked in part by PLO 7165) | 52846 |
| 11145 (Continued by EO 12974) | 51875 |
| 11183 (Continued by EO 12974) | 51875 |
| 11287 (Continued by EO 12974) | 51875 |
| 11776 (Continued by EO 12974) | 51875 |
| 12131 (Continued by EO 12974) | 51875 |
| 12196 (Continued by EO 12974) | 51875 |
| 12216 (Continued by EO 12974) | 51875 |
| 12345 (Continued by EO 12974) | 51875 |
| 12367 (Continued by EO 12974) | 51875 |
| 12382 (Continued by EO 12974) | 51875 |
| 12844 (Revoked in part by EO 12974) | 51876 |
| 12869 (Superseded by EO 12974) | 51876 |
| 11871 (Continued by EO 12974) | 51875 |
| 11876 (Continued by EO 12974) | 51875 |
| 12878 (Revoked by EO 12974) | 51876 |
| 12882 (Continued by EO 12974) | 51875 |
| 12887 (See EO 12974) | 51876 |
| 12900 (Continued by EO 12974) | 51875 |
| 12901 (Amended by EO 12973) | 51665 |
| 12905 (Continued by EO 12974) | 51875 |
| 12912 (See EO 12974) | 51876 |

| | |
|---|---|
| 12958 (See Order of October 13, 1995) | 53845 |
| 12973 | 51665 |
| 12974 | 51875 |
| 12975 | 52063 |
| 12976 | 52829 |

**Administrative Orders:**
Memorandums:
| | |
|---|---|
| September 29, 1995 | 52061 |
| October 2, 1995 | 52821 |
| October 3, 1995 | 52289 |
| October 10, 1995 | 53251 |
| October 13, 1995 | 53845 |

Presidential Determinations:
| | |
|---|---|
| No. 95–45 of September 29, 1995 | 52823 |
| No. 95–46 of September 29, 1995 | 53089 |
| No. 95–47 of September 29, 1995 | 53091 |
| No. 95–48 of September 29, 1995 | 53677 |
| No. 95–49 of September 28, 1995 | 53093 |
| No. 95–50 of September 30, 1995 | |

**C.F.R. Title**

**5 CFR**
| | |
|---|---|
| 315 | 53503 |
| 532 | 51881 |
| 870 | 51881 |
| 871 | 51881 |
| 872 | 51881 |
| 874 | 51881 |
| 2608 | |
| 2612 | |
| 2635 | |

**C.F.R. Part affected**

**Proposed Rules:**
| | |
|---|---|
| 251 | 51371 |
| 531 | 53545 |
| 591 | 53716 |

**7 CFR**
| | |
|---|---|
| 8 | 52293 |
| 301 | 52831, 52833 |
| 400 | 51321 |
| 810 | 51667 |
| 916 | 52067 |
| 917 | 52067 |
| 920 | 52834 |
| 982 | 51668 |
| 1150 | 53253 |
| 1212 | 52835 |
| 1443 | 51885 |
| 1477 | 52609 |
| 1478 | 52609 |

**FIGURE 8.9**    UPDATING C.F.R. RESEARCH IN PRINT

| DATE | JANUARY 3, 1995 | JANUARY 3, 1995–SEPTEMBER 29, 1995 | OCTOBER 2, 1995–OCTOBER 20, 1995 | OCTOBER 20, 1995–PRESENT |
|------|-----------------|-----------------------------------|----------------------------------|--------------------------|
| **Source** | Title 16, C.F.R. | September 1995 List of CFR Sections Affected (LSA) | October 20, 1995, *Federal Register* | Agency personnel |
| **Use** | Locate regulations in the C.F.R. using an annotated code or a C.F.R. index. The date of the C.F.R. is listed on the front cover. | Use the latest monthly issue. Dates of coverage are on the inside front cover. Look up the Title and section number of the regulation. If it is listed, use the table in the back to find the date of the *Federal Register* containing the change. Look up the page in the *Federal Register* to locate the change. | Use the latest daily issue. The monthly cumulative table of CFR Parts Affected is in the back of the issue. If the C.F.R. Part is not listed, no changes have taken place during the month to date. If the C.F.R. Part is listed, each page reference must be checked to see which individual sections have been affected. | Call the agency to find more recent information. |

The chart in Figure 8.9 summarizes the process of updating, using the example of a regulation within Title 16 of the C.F.R. published on January 3, 1995, an LSA dated September 29, 1995, and the most current *Federal Register* dated October 20, 1995.

## C. SHEPARD'S FOR THE *CODE OF FEDERAL REGULATIONS*

Shepard's is available for the C.F.R., as it is for many other publications. Because the C.F.R. is not annotated,[2] Shepard's can be an invaluable research tool. Shepard's will provide references to cases that have cited the regulation, which can help you determine whether the regulation remains valid and how it has been interpreted. The process of Shepardizing should be familiar to you by now: locate the correct set of Shepard's,

---

[2]Some administrative regulations are reproduced as part of the U.S.C.S. and U.S.C.A. sets and may have limited annotations; however, U.S.C.S. and U.S.C.A. do not contain all Titles of the C.F.R.

**FIGURE 8.10** SHEPARD'S® ENTRY FOR 16 C.F.R. § 1700.15

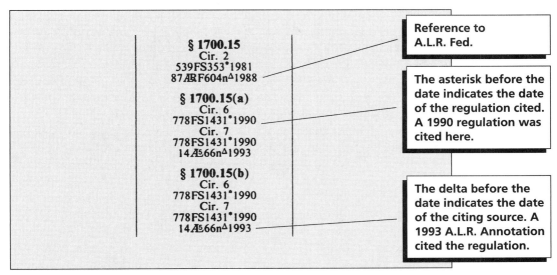

Reference to A.L.R. Fed.

The asterisk before the date indicates the date of the regulation cited. A 1990 regulation was cited here.

The delta before the date indicates the date of the citing source. A 1993 A.L.R. Annotation cited the regulation.

Reproduced by permission of LexisNexis. Further reproduction of any kind is strictly prohibited. From *Shepard's Code of Federal Regulations Citations*, Titles 1–27; 1994, Part 1, p. 397.

in this case, *Shepard's Code of Federal Regulations Citations*; locate the correct volumes by checking the "What Your Library Should Contain" section on the front of the most recent softcover supplement; and check each noncumulative volume for references to the regulation. Shepard's will refer you to cases and secondary sources that cite the regulation. A list of the treatment codes applicable to Shepard's entries for C.F.R. provisions can be found in the front of each volume of *Shepard's Code of Federal Regulation Citations*. A sample entry appears in Figure 8.10.

## D. ELECTRONIC RESEARCH OF FEDERAL REGULATIONS

LexisNexis, Westlaw, and the Internet are all excellent sources for regulatory research. The C.F.R. is available in LexisNexis and Westlaw, and it is usually up to date. You can check the date through which the regulation is updated by looking at the heading on the first screen displaying the regulation. The *Federal Register* is also available in both services. Administrative regulations in LexisNexis and Westlaw can be located either in the general administrative materials databases or in the databases for specific subject areas, if regulations have been promulgated in those subject areas. Once you select a database, you can find regulations by executing a word search using the techniques described in Chapter 10. You can also browse the table of contents of the C.F.R. In Westlaw, you can access the table of contents by clicking on the Table of Contents link near the top of the screen. In LexisNexis, selecting the

C.F.R. from the source directory brings up a search screen that also displays the table of contents. In addition, both Shepard's in LexisNexis and KeyCite in Westlaw are available for federal regulations.

Because the C.F.R. and *Federal Register* are government publications, they are widely available on the Internet free of charge. The Government Printing Office's GPO Access service is one of the best places to research federal regulations. Sites for individual agencies can also be good sources for federal regulations. Internet addresses for several useful sites for federal regulatory research are listed in Appendix A.

If you use the Internet to locate C.F.R. provisions, you should pay careful attention to the date of the material you are using. Unlike LexisNexis and Westlaw, Internet sources of regulations often are no more up to date than the print version of the C.F.R. In GPO Access, for example, the C.F.R. databases are only updated four times per year as the new print editions of the C.F.R. become available, although the *Federal Register* database is updated daily. To update C.F.R. research in GPO Access, you would need to follow the same steps electronically that you would use to update print research. You would begin by searching for the regulation in the database containing the most recent LSA to find *Federal Register* references affecting the regulation. To update from the last day of the LSA to the present, you would need to search the *Federal Register* database for additional changes, using a date restriction to limit your search to the appropriate time period. If these searches revealed any changes to the regulation, you could then access the relevant pages from the *Federal Register* through GPO Access. Figure 8.11 shows some of the C.F.R. research options in GPO Access.

## E. CITING FEDERAL REGULATIONS

Citations to administrative materials are governed by Rule 19 of the *ALWD Manual* and Rule 14 of the *Bluebook*, and the citation is the same using either format. A citation to the C.F.R. is very similar to a citation to a statute. It consists of the Title number, the abbreviation C.F.R., the pinpoint reference to the Part or section number, and a parenthetical containing the year.

Title ◄──┐     ┌──► abbreviated name  ┌──► year of the C.F.R. volume

**16 C.F.R. pt. 1700 (1995).**

abbreviation for Part ◄──┘     └──► Part number

Title ◄──┐     ┌──► abbreviated name  ┌──► year of the C.F.R. volume

**16 C.F.R. § 1700.15 (1995).**

└──► section number

**FIGURE 8.11** INTRODUCTORY SCREENS FOR C.F.R. RESEARCH IN GPO ACCESS

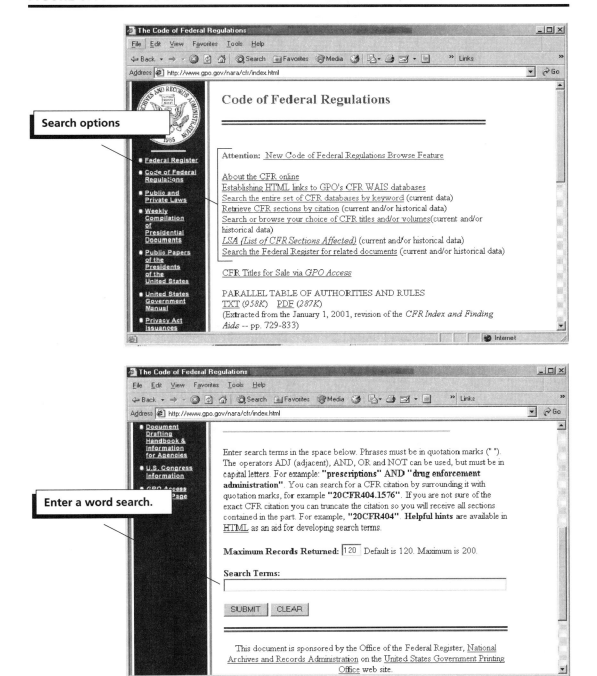

The preceding examples did not involve a regulation commonly known by name. If they had, the citation would have begun with the name of the regulation, pursuant to *ALWD Manual* Rule 19.1 and *Bluebook* Rule 14.2.

Citations to the *Federal Register* are also fairly simple and are the same using either the *ALWD Maual* or the *Bluebook*. They require the volume number, the abbreviation Fed. Reg., the page number, and a parenthetical containing the exact date.

volume    ←⌐     ⌐→ abbreviated name     ⌐→ exact date

### 60 Fed. Reg. 7734 (Feb. 28, 1995).

               └→ page number

If appropriate, you should also provide a pinpoint reference to the specific page or pages containing the cited material.

## F. SAMPLE PAGES FOR FEDERAL ADMINISTRATIVE LAW RESEARCH

Beginning on the next page, Figures 8.12 through 8.25 contain sample pages from the C.F.R. showing the process of print research into regulations pertaining to the packaging of poisonous materials, as well as several samples from GPO Access.

**The first step is locating relevant regulations. You could use a subject index such as the CFR Index and Finding Aids, as illustrated in this example. You could also use statutory annotations to locate relevant regulations.**

**FIGURE 8.12** INDEX ENTRY, CFR INDEX AND FINDING AIDS

---

### Plutonium | CFR Index

Pears, plums, and peaches grown in California, 7 CFR 917
Prunes grown in designated counties in Washington and in Umatilla County, Oregon, 7 CFR 924

**Plutonium**
Air transportation of plutonium, 10 CFR 871

**[oconiosis]**
[ck] lung benefits

**prevention**
*[ ]* Lead poisoning
[Federal] Caustic Poison Act, 21 CFR 1230
Formal evidentiary public hearing procedures, 16 CFR 1502
Poison prevention packaging, 16 CFR 1700
  Applications for exemption from preemption of State and local requirements, 16 CFR 1061
  Exemption petitions procedures and requirements, 16 CFR 1702
  Policy and interpretation statements, 16 CFR 1701
Public Health Service, requests for health hazard evaluations, 42 CFR 85
Toxic substances control, administrative assessment of civil penalties and revocation or suspension of permits, consolidated practice rules, 40 CFR 22

**Police**
*See* Law enforcement officers

**Political activities (Government employees)**
ACTION, prohibitions on electoral and lobbying activities, 45 CFR 1226
Civil service
  Political activity of Federal employees, 5 CFR 734
  Residing in designated localities, 5 CFR 733
  Prohibited practices, 5 CFR 4
Community Services Office, grantee personnel management, 45 CFR 1069
General Accounting Office, 4 CFR 7
Legal Services Corporation, 45 CFR 1608
State or local officers or employees, 5 CFR 151

**Political affiliation discrimination**
ACTION, 45 CFR 1225

Job Training Partnership Act, nondiscrimination and equal opportunity requirements, 29 CFR 34
Prisons Bureau, 28 CFR 551

**Political candidates**
*See also* Campaign funds
Air carriers, credit extension to political candidates, 14 CFR 374a
Aircraft operators, carriage of candidates in Federal elections, 14 CFR 91
Cable television service, 47 CFR 76
Candidate status and designations for Federal office, 11 CFR 101
Communications common carriers, miscellaneous rules, 47 CFR 64
Debts owed by candidates and political committees, 11 CFR 116
Election campaign documents, filing, 11 CFR 105
Federal office candidates or their representatives, credit extension for transportation, 49 CFR 1325
Radio broadcast services, 47 CFR 73

**Political committees and parties**
Campaign fund allocations of candidate and committee activities, 11 CFR 106
Campaign fund reports by political committees, 11 CFR 104
Debts owed by candidates and political committees, 11 CFR 116
Depositaries for campaign funds, 11 CFR 103
Election campaign documents, filing, 11 CFR 105
Income taxes, exempt organizations, political organizations, 26 CFR 1 (1.527-1—1.527-9)
Political committees registration, organization, and recordkeeping, 11 CFR 102
Presidential election campaign financing, contribution and expenditure limitations and prohibitions, 11 CFR 110
Presidential nominating conventions
  Federal financing, 11 CFR 9008
  Registration, and reports, 11 CFR 107

---

Reference to C.F.R. Title and Part with regulations on poison prevention packaging

552

**The next step is locating C.F.R. sections. In this example, you can find applicable sections within the C.F.R. by looking in the volume with Title 16 and locating Part 1700.**

**FIGURE 8.13**    16 C.F.R., BEGINNING OF PART 1700

---

**Consumer Product Safety Commission**                                        **§ 1700.1**

Outline of the Part

## SUBCHAPTER E—POISON PREVENTION PACKAGING ACT OF 1970 REGULATIONS

**PART 1700—POISON PREVENTION PACKAGING**

Sec.
1700.1  Definitions.
1700.2  Authority.
1700.3  Establishment of standards for special packaging.
1700.4  Effective date of standards.
1700.5  Noncomplying package requirements.
1700.14  Substances requiring special packaging.
1700.15  Poison prevention packaging standards.
1700.20  Testing procedure for special packaging.

AUTHORITY: Pub. L. 91–601, secs. 1–9, 84 Stat. 1670–74, 15 U.S.C. 1471–76. Secs. 1700.1 and 1700.14 also issued under Pub. L. 92–573, sec. 30(a), 88 Stat. 1231, 15 U.S.C. 2079(a).

SOURCE: 38 FR 21247, Aug. 7, 1973, unless otherwise noted.

**§ 1700.1  Definitions.**

(a) As used in this part:
(1) *Act* means the Poison Prevention Packaging Act of 1970 (Pub. L. 91–601, 84 Stat. 1670–74; 15 U.S.C. 1471–75), enacted December 30, 1970.
(2) *Commission* means the Consumer Product Safety Commission established by section 4 of the Consumer Product Safety Act (86 Stat. 1210; 15 U.S.C. 2053).
(3) *Dietary supplement* means any vitamin and/or mineral preparation offered in tablet, capsule, wafer, or other similar uniform unit form; in powder, granule, flake, or liquid form; or in the physical form of a conventional food but which is not a conventional food; and which purports or is represented to be for special dietary use by humans to supplement their diets by increasing the total dietary intake of one or more of the essential vitamins and/or minerals.
(b) Except for the definition of "Secretary," which is obsolete, the definitions given in section 2 of the act are applicable to this part and are repeated herein for convenience as follows:
(1) [Reserved]
(2) *Household substance* means any substance which is customarily produced or distributed for sale for con-

sumption or use, or customarily stored, by individuals in or about the household and which is:
(i) A hazardous substance as that term is defined in section 2(f) of the Federal Hazardous Substances Act (15 U.S.C. 1261(f));
(ii) A food, drug, or cosmetic as those terms are defined in section 201 of the Federal Food, Drug, and Cosmetic Act (21 U.S.C. 321); or
(iii) A substance intended for use as fuel when stored in a portable container and used in the heating, cooking, or refrigeration system of a house.
(3) *Package* means the immediate container or wrapping in which any household substance is contained for consumption, use, or storage by individuals in or about the household and, for purposes of section 4(a)(2) of the act, also means any outer container or wrapping used in the retail display of any such substance to consumers. "Package" does not include:
(i) Any shipping container or wrapping used solely for the transportation of any household substance in bulk or in quantity to manufacturers, packers, or processors, or to wholesale or retail distributors thereof; or
(ii) Any shipping container or wrapping used by retailers to ship or deliver any household substance to consumers unless it is the only such container or wrapping.
(4) *Special packaging* means packaging that is designed or constructed to be significantly difficult for children under 5 years of age to open or obtain a toxic or harmful amount of the substance contained therein within a reasonable time and not difficult for normal adults to use properly, but does not mean packaging which all such children cannot open or obtain a toxic or harmful amount within a reasonable time.
(5) *Labeling* means all labels and other written, printed, or graphic matter upon any household substance or

Statutory authority for promulgating the regulations

Citation to the *Federal Register* where the regulations were originally published

An individual regulation

**If you were interested in researching packaging standards, you might want to read 16 C.F.R. § 1700.15.**

**FIGURE 8.14** 16 C.F.R. § 1700.15

---

**Consumer Product Safety Commission** §1700.20

retail or user level, drugs listed under paragraph (a) of this section as requiring special packaging.

(c) *Applicability.* Special packaging standards for drugs listed under paragraph (a) of this section shall be in addition to any packaging requirements of the Federal Food, Drug, and Cosmetic Act or regulations promulgated thereunder or of any official compendia recognized by that act.

**Regulation on poison prevention packaging standards**

ecs. 2(4), 3, 5, 85 Stat. 1670–
), 1472, 1474; Pub. L. 92–573,
S.C. 2079(a))

7, 1973]

E: For FEDERAL REGISTER citations affecting §1700.14, see the List of CFR Sections Affected in the Finding Aids section of this volume.

**§1700.15  Poison prevention packaging standards.**

To protect children from serious personal injury or serious illness resulting from handling, using, or ingesting household substances, the Commission has determined that packaging designed and constructed to meet the following standards shall be regarded as "special packaging" within the meaning of section 2(4) of the act. Specific application of these standards to substances requiring special packaging is in accordance with §1700.14.

(a) *General requirements.* The special packaging must continue to function with the effectiveness specifications set forth in paragraph (b) of this section when in actual contact with the substance contained therein. This requirement may be satisfied by appropriate scientific evaluation of the compatibility of the substance with the special packaging to determine that the chemical and physical characteristics of the substance will not compromise or interfere with the proper functioning of the special packaging. The special packaging must also continue to function with the effectiveness specifications set forth in paragraph (b) of this section for the number of openings and closings customary for its size and contents. This requirement may be satisfied by appropriate technical evaluation based on physical wear and stress factors, force required for activation, and other such relevant factors which establish that, for the duration

of normal use, the effectiveness specifications of the packaging would not be expected to lessen.

(b) *Effectiveness specifications.* Special packaging, tested by the method described in §1700.20, shall meet the following specifications:

(1) Child-resistant effectiveness of not less than 85 percent without a demonstration and not less than 80 percent after a demonstration of the proper means of opening such special packaging. In the case of unit packaging, child-resistant effectiveness of not less than 80 percent.

(2) Adult-use effectiveness of not less than 90 percent.

(c) *Reuse of special packaging.* Special packaging for substances subject to the provisions of this paragraph shall not be reused.

(d) *Restricted flow.* Special packaging subject to the provisions of this paragraph shall be special packaging from which the flow of liquid is so restricted that not more than 2 milliliters of the contents can be obtained when the inverted, opened container is taken or squeezed once or when the container is otherwise activated once.

(Secs. 2(4), 3, 5, 84 Stat. 1670–72; 15 U.S.C. 1471(4), 1472, 1474)

**§1700.20  Testing procedure for special packaging.**

(a) The protocol for testing "special packaging" as defined in section 2(4) of the act shall be as follows:

(1) Use 200 children between the ages of 42 and 51 months inclusive, evenly distributed by age and

**Statutory authority for this individual regulation**

ability of the special p
sist opening by childre
distribution shall be
having 20 children (pl
percent) whose nearest age is 42 months, 20 whose nearest age is 43 months, 20 at 44 months, etc., up to and including 20 at 51 months of age. There should be no more than a 10 percent preponderance of either sex in each age group. The children selected should be healthy and normal and should have no obvious or overt physical or mental handicap.

(2) The children shall be divided into groups of two each. The testing shall be done in a location that is familiar to the children; for example, their cus-

675

To begin updating § 1700.15, locate the most recent List of CFR Sections Affected (LSA), which in this example is the LSA for September 1995. Look on the inside front cover to see the dates covered.

**FIGURE 8.15**    INSIDE FRONT COVER, SEPTEMBER 1995 LIST OF CFR SECTIONS AFFECTED

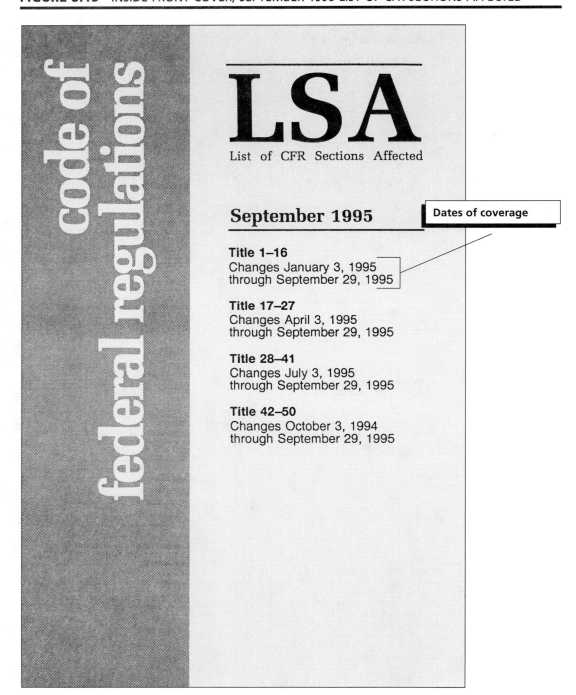

**Look up the regulation within the LSA. If the regulation is not listed, the agency has not taken action affecting the regulation. If the regulation is listed, the page of the *Federal Register* containing the change will be listed.**

**FIGURE 8.16**   SEPTEMBER 1995 LIST OF CFR SECTIONS AFFECTED

---

### SEPTEMBER 1995                                                    63

### CHANGES JANUARY 3, 1995 THROUGH SEPTEMBER 29, 1995

4.11 Heading, (e) heading, (1)
  through (5) revised; (b) and
  (c) amended ...............................37750
4.12 (a) and (c) revised ...................37751
14.2 Removed .................................42033
14.4 Removed .................................42033
14.7 Removed .................................42033
14.11 Removed.................................42033
14.16 Revised.................................42033
14.17 Removed.................................42033
24 Removed ....................................48027
231 Removed ...................................48027
234 Removed ...................................40262
236 Guide rescission.......................37334
237 Removed ...................................40265
242 Removed ...................................40267
247 Removed ...................................48027
248 Removed ...................................40270
252 Removed ...................................40453
305 Energy efficiency ranges ..........15198
305.8 (a)(4)(v) revised ......................14210
305.9 (a) revised .............................9296
305.11 (f)(1) amended ......................14210
  (e)(1)(iii), (iv) and (vi) revised
  ....................................................31081
305.13 (a)(4) revised ......................14211
305.14 (d) revised ..........................14211
305 Appendix F revised...........19845, 27691
  Appendixes C and D4 revised
  ....................................................43368

> **Changes to Part 1700 are included in this section.**

  ]05, D6, E and J1
  ....................................................43369
  evised....................43370
  ....................................................26955
  ....................................................43864
600 Appendix amended.....................45660
800 Removed .................................40706
803 Appendix amended...................40706

### Chapter II—Consumer Product Safety Commission (Parts 1000—1799)

1000.7 (b) amended .........................26825
1000.12 Revised...............................26825
1000.19 Amended ............................26825
1000.24 Amended; heading revised
  ....................................................26825
1000.26 Revised...............................26825
1000.32 Revised...............................26825
1117 Added .....................................10493
1117.2 (a) revised; (h) added.............41801
1203 Added; interim ........................15232

1500 Authority citation revised
  ....................................................10752
1500.14 (b)(8)(iv) added.......................8193
1500.18 (a) introductory text;
  (a)(17) added .............................10752
1500.19 Added .................................10752
  (b)(1) introductory text revised
  ....................................................41802
1700 Authority citation revised

1700.14 (a)(22) added.......
  (a)(23) and (24) added ..
  (a) introductory text
  (a)(25) added; eff. 2-6-96
  Regulation at 60 FR 3739 eff.
  date corrected to 7-22-96 ..........48890
1700.15 (b)(2) revised; eff. 7-22-96
  ....................................................37734
1700.20 (a) revised; eff. in part 1-
  24-96 and in part 7-22-96............37734
  (d) added....................................37738

> ***Federal Register* page number showing a change to § 1700.15(b)(2)**

### *Proposed Rules:*

0—999 (Ch. I).....................................6463
3.....................................................42481
24..........................................15724, 48056
231.................................................15724
247.................................................15724
248.................................................17032
260.................................................38978
305.................................................15200
307...................................................8312
310..........................................8312, 30406
311.................................................44712
400..........................................27240, 48063
402..........................................27241, 48065
404..........................................27242, 48067
405..........................................15725, 48070
409..........................................17491, 28554
413..........................................27243, 48071
417..........................................27244, 48073
418..........................................27245, 48075
419.................................................38474
436..........................................17656, 34485
444.................................................24805
460.................................................17492
801.................................................38930
802.................................................38930
1307...............................................29518
1500........................................34922, 40785
1507...............................................34922
1700...................2716, 9654, 12165, 17660

**A table in the back of the LSA indicates the date on which the relevant *Federal Register* page was published.**

**FIGURE 8.17**   SEPTEMBER 1995 LIST OF CFR SECTIONS AFFECTED, TABLE OF *FEDERAL REGISTER* ISSUE PAGES AND DATES

### TABLE OF FEDERAL REGISTER ISSUE PAGES AND DATES    249

| Pages | Date | Pages | Date |
|---|---|---|---|
| 14891–15026 | 21 | 31227–31369 | 14 |
| 15027–15227 | 22 | 31371–31622 | 15 |
| 15229–15455 | 23 | 31623–31905 | 16 |
| 15457–15648 | 24 | 31907–32097 | 19 |
| 15649–15853 | 27 | 32099–32255 | 20 |
| 15855–16034 | 28 | 32557–32420 | 21 |
| 16035–16361 | 29 | 32421–32575 | 22 |
| 16363–16564 | 30 | 32577–32898 | 23 |
| 16565–16764 | 31 | 32899–33096 | 26 |
| 16765–16977 | Apr. 3 | 33097–33321 | 27 |
| 16979–17190 | 4 | 33323–33676 | 28 |
| 17191–17432 | 5 | 33677–34086 | 29 |
| 17433–17624 | 6 | 34087–34452 | 30 |
| 17625–17890 | 7 | 34453–34842 | July 3 |
| 17891–18342 | 10 | 34843–35111 | 5 |
| 18343–18538 | 11 | 35113–35320 | |
| 18539–18725 | 12 | 35321–35460 | |
| 18727–18948 | 13 | 35461–35690 | 1 |
| 18949–19152 | 14 | 35691–35827 | 1 |
| 19158–19342 | 17 | 35829–36026 | 1 |
| 19343–19483 | 18 | 36027–36202 | 13 |
| 19485–19664 | 19 | 36203–36338 | 14 |
| 19665–19843 | 20 | 36339–36634 | 17 |
| 19845–19997 | 21 | 36635–36949 | 18 |
| 19999–20169 | 24 | 36951–37321 | 19 |
| 20171–20389 | 25 | 37323–37553 | 20 |
| 20391–20622 | 26 | 37555–37801 | 21 |
| 20623–20878 | 27 | 37803–37932 | 24 |
| 20879–21032 | 28 | 37933–38226 | 25 |
| 21033–21424 | May 1 | 38227–38474 | 26 |
| 21425–21697 | 2 | 38475–38663 | 27 |
| 21699–21971 | 3 | 38665–38945 | 28 |
| 21973–22245 | 4 | 38947–39099 | 31 |
| 22247–22453 | 5 | 39101–39239 | Aug. 1 |
| 22455–24534 | 8 | 39241–39624 | 2 |
| 24535–24759 | 9 | 39625–39834 | 3 |
| 24761–25117 | 10 | 39835–40051 | 4 |
| 25119–25600 | 11 | 40053–40257 | 7 |
| 25601–25837 | 12 | 40259–40452 | 8 |
| 25839–25976 | 15 | 40453–40735 | 9 |
| 25983–26338 | 16 | 40737–40992 | 10 |
| 26339–26666 | 17 | 40993–41792 | 11 |
| 26667–26821 | 18 | 41793–42024 | 14 |
| 26823–26975 | 19 | 42025–42423 | 15 |
| 26977–27220 | 22 | 42425–42766 | 16 |
| 27221–27400 | 23 | 42767–42999 | 17 |
| 27401–27655 | 24 | 43001–43346 | 18 |
| 27657–27866 | 25 | 43347–43512 | 21 |
| 27867–28026 | 26 | 43513–43703 | 22 |
| 28027–28316 | 30 | 43705–43952 | 23 |
| 28317–28508 | 31 | 43953–44252 | 24 |
| 28509–28699 | June 1 | 44253–44413 | 25 |
| 28701–29461 | 2 | 44415–44725 | 28 |
| 29463–29745 | 5 | 44727–45309 | 29 |
| 29749–29957 | 6 | 45041–45323 | 30 |
| 29959–30181 | 7 | 45325–45646 | 31 |
| 30183–30456 | 8 | 45647–46016 | Sept. 1 |
| 30457–30771 | 9 | 46017–46212 | 5 |
| 30773–31045 | 12 | 46213–46495 | 6 |
| 31047–31226 | 13 | 46497–46748 | 7 |

Page 37,734 was published on July 21.

**Look up the page number within the *Federal Register* to determine how the regulation was changed.**

**FIGURE 8.18**   *FEDERAL REGISTER,* JULY 21, 1995

---

**37734**     Federal Register / Vol. 60, No. 140 / Friday, July 21, 1995 / Rules and Regulations

protocol), to use standard (supplier stocked, on-the-shelf) SAUE packaging, or to reformulate or withdraw a product. Some SAUE packaging is available now; other SAUE package types, including those for products having formulations that impose unusual requirements on packaging, are expected to become available. Changes in packaging may require associated equipment purchases or modifications. Costs of testing some products to meet the requirements of government agencies other than CPSC may be required if packaging is changed. Incremental costs associated with new SAUE packaging should not add materially to the costs of a product and are expected to be passed on to the consumer.

CPSC does not anticipate that any substantial number of small businesses will be significantly affected, however, because of the current and expected future availability of SAUE packaging for all types of product formulations. If necessary, companies can apply for a temporary stay of enforcement to comply with the rule.

*D. Pharmaceutical Packagers*

There are an estimated 1,200 pharmaceutical packagers, according to an FDA spokesperson, an unknown number of which are small. [236] Also unknown is the number of small firms that provide consumer-ready pharmaceuticals; some firms provide products only in bulk packages. The Commission expects that many of the small firms can use standard SAUE packaging. However, firms that use reclosable packaging may have to find new suppliers, and may also have to pay more for SAUE packaging. Films, foils, and other materials used for SAUE non-reclosable packaging also may cost more than the materials used for existing CRP. No comments were received from any small company regarding the possible need for stability testing to meet FDA requirements. Incremental costs for new packaging are expected to be modest and most likely will be passed on to users. CPSC does not anticipate that a significant number of packagers will be severely or permanently affected.

*E. Pharmacies*

There are over 40,000 independent pharmacies, according to a representative of the National Association of Retail Druggists, most of which are small businesses. [236] (There are an additional 25,000 chain pharmacies, including those associated with drug and food stores and mass merchandisers. *Id.*) Retail establishments may have to find new suppliers if old suppliers abandon the

market or do not offer acceptable sizes of containers. Pharmacies may also have to pay more for SAUE packaging than for existing CRP. Pharmacy staff probably will spend additional time instructing customers in the use of new packaging. Modest incremental costs for SAUE packaging and for staff time are likely to be passed on to the consumer, and there should not be a big impact on most pharmacies.

*F. Conclusion*

The Commission concludes that the action to revise the testing protocol for special packaging under the PPPA will not have a significant adverse impact on a substantial number of small businesses.

**IX. Environmental Considerations**

Pursuant to the National Environmental Policy Act, and in accordance with the Council on Environmental Quality regulations and CPSC procedures for environmental review, the Commission has assessed the possible environmental effects associated with the revisions to the PPPA protocols.

The Commission assessed the possible environmental effects of rulemaking associated with the revisions to the protocol for testing CRP under the PPPA and presented its findings in a paper dated April 2, 1990. [123, Tab D] Reassessment of the possible environmental effects confirms the original determination that the rule will have no significant effects on the environment. [236] The revisions to the rule involve a test method and establish new test standards. They will not change the number of CRP in use. Since the rule will not become effective until 1 year after its publication and there will be a subsequent 18-month blanket exemption from compliance, there is time to use up existing inventories of unfilled non-SAUE packaging. Additionally, SAUE packaging is made of basically the same materials and in basically the same way as older styles of CRP. Much of the existing equipment involved in the production and filling of non-SAUE packaging can be modified to produce SAUE packaging, rather than replaced.

**EFFECTIVE DATES:** Revised §§ 1700.15(b)(2), 1700.20(a)(3), and 1700.20(a)(4) are effective July 22, 1996. Until then, current §§ 1700.15(b)(2), 1700.20(a)(4), and 1700.20(a)(5) remain in effect.

Revised §§ 1700.20(a) (1) and (2) are effective January 24, 1996. Until then, current §§ 1700.20(a)(1)–(3) remain in effect.

New § 1700.20(d) is effective August 21, 1995.

For mandatory provisions, the effective dates specified above apply to all products subject to the respective sections that are packaged on or after the effective date.

**List of Subjects in 16 CFR Part ‖**

Consumer protection, Drugs, ‖ and children, Packaging and c‖ Poison prevention, Toxic subst‖

**V. Conclusion**

For the reasons given above, the Commission amends 16 CFR 1700.20 as follows:

**PART 1700—[AMENDED]**

1. The authority citation for Part 1700 is revised to read as follows:

**Authority:** 15 U.S.C. 1471–76. Secs. 1700.1 and 1700.14 also issued under 15 U.S.C. 2079(a).

2. Section 1700.15(b)(2) is revised to read as follows:

**§ 1700.15   Poison prevention packaging standards.**

\*    \*    \*    \*    \*

(b) \*    \*    \*

(2) Ease of adult opening. (i) Senior-adult test. Except for products specified in paragraph (b)(2)(ii) of this section, special packaging shall have a senior adult use effectiveness (SAUE) of not less than 90% for the senior-adult panel test of § 1700.20(a)(3).

(ii) *Younger-adult test.* (A) When applicable. Products that must be in aerosol form and products that require metal containers, under the criteria specified below, shall have an effectiveness of not less than 90% for the younger-adult test of § 1700.20(a)(4). The senior-adult panel test of § 1700.20(a)(3) does not apply to these products. For the purposes of this paragraph, metal containers are those that have both a metal package and a recloseable metal closure, and aerosol products are self-contained pressurized products.

(B) Determination of need for metal or aerosol container.

(*1*) *Criteria.* A product will be deemed to require metal containers or aerosol form only if:

(*i*) No other packaging type would comply with other state or Federal regulations,

(*ii*) No other packaging can reasonably be used for the product's intended application,

(*iii*) No other packaging or closure material would be compatible with the substance,

> New regulatory language

**Update beyond the LSA with the *Federal Register*. In this example, the most recent *Federal Register* is dated October 20, 1995. The table of CFR Parts Affected During October appears in the back of the *Federal Register* and is cumulative for the month to date.**

**FIGURE 8.19** *FEDERAL REGISTER*, OCTOBER 20, 1995, TABLE OF CFR PARTS AFFECTED DURING OCTOBER

---

i

# Reader Aids

Federal Register

Vol. 60, No. 203

Friday, October 20, 1995

**Cumulative table**

## CUSTOMER SERVICE AND INFORMATION

**Federal Register/Code of Federal Regulations**

| | |
|---|---|
| General Information, indexes and other finding aids | 202–523–5227 |
| Public inspection announcement line | 523–5215 |

**Laws**

| | |
|---|---|
| Public Laws Update Services (numbers, dates, etc.) | 523–6641 |
| For additional information | 523–5227 |

**Presidential Documents**

| | |
|---|---|
| Executive orders and proclamations | 523–5227 |
| The United States Government Manual | 523–5227 |

**Other Services**

| | |
|---|---|
| Electronic and on-line services (voice) | 523–4534 |
| Privacy Act Compilation | 523–3187 |
| TDD for the hearing impaired | 523–5229 |

## ELECTRONIC BULLETIN BOARD

Free **Electronic Bulletin Board** service for Public Law numbers, Federal Register finding aids, and list of documents on public inspection. **202–275–0920**

## FAX-ON-DEMAND

You may access our Fax-On-Demand service. You only need a fax machine and there is no charge for the service except for long distance telephone charges the user may incur. The list of documents on public inspection and the daily Federal Register's table of contents are available using this service. The document numbers are 7050-Public Inspection list and 7051-Table of Contents list. The public inspection list will be updated immediately for documents filed on an emergency basis.

**NOTE:** YOU WILL ONLY GET A LISTING OF DOCUMENTS ON FILE AND NOT THE ACTUAL DOCUMENT. Documents on public inspection may be viewed and copied in our office located at 800 North Capitol Street, N.W., Suite 700. The Fax-On-Demand telephone number is: **301–713–6905**

## FEDERAL REGISTER PAGES AND DATES, OCTOBER

| | |
|---|---|
| 51321–51666 | 2 |
| 51667–51876 | 3 |
| 51877–52062 | 4 |
| 52063–52290 | 5 |
| 52291–52608 | 6 |
| 52609–52830 | 10 |
| 52831–53100 | 11 |
| 53101–53246 | 12 |
| 53247–53502 | 13 |
| 53503–53690 | 16 |
| 53691–53846 | 17 |
| 53847–54026 | 18 |
| 54027–54150 | 19 |
| 54151–54290 | 20 |

## CFR PARTS AFFECTED DURING OCTOBER

At the end of each month, the Office of the Federal Register publishes separately a List of CFR Sections Affected (LSA), which lists parts and sections affected by documents published since the revision date of each title.

**3 CFR**

**Proclamations:**

| | |
|---|---|
| 6828 | 51877 |
| 6829 | 51879 |
| 6830 | 52291 |
| 6831 | 52827 |
| 6832 | 53097 |
| 6833 | 53099 |
| 6834 | 53101 |
| 6835 | 53103 |
| 6836 | 53105 |
| 6837 | 53107 |
| 6838 | 53247 |
| 6839 | 53249 |
| 6840 | 53843 |
| 6841 | 54023 |
| 6842 | 54025 |

**Executive Orders:**

| | |
|---|---|
| 4410 (Revoked in part by PLO 7165) | 52846 |
| 11145 (Continued by EO 12974) | 51875 |
| 11183 (Continued by EO 12974) | 51875 |
| 11287 (Continued by EO 12974) | 51875 |
| 11776 (Continued by EO 12974) | 51875 |
| 12131 (Continued by EO 12974) | 51875 |
| 12196 (Continued by EO 12974) | 51875 |
| 12216 (Continued by EO 12974) | 51875 |
| 12345 (Continued by EO 12974) | 51875 |
| 12367 (Continued by EO 12974) | 51875 |
| 12382 (Continued by EO 12974) | 51875 |
| 12844 (Revoked in part by EO 12974) | 51876 |
| 12869 (Superseded by EO 12974) | 51876 |
| 11871 (Continued by EO 12974) | 51875 |
| 11876 (Continued by EO 12974) | 51875 |
| 12878 (Revoked by EO 12974) | 51876 |
| 12882 (Continued by EO 12974) | 51875 |
| 12887 (See EO 12974) | 51876 |
| 12900 (Continued by EO 12974) | 51875 |
| 12901 (Amended by EO 12973) | 51665 |
| 12905 (Continued by EO 12974) | 51875 |
| 12912 (See EO | |

| | |
|---|---|
| 12974) | 51876 |
| 12958 (See Order of October 13, 1995) | 53845 |
| 12973 | 51665 |
| 12974 | 51875 |
| 12975 | 52063 |
| 12976 | 52829 |

**Administrative Orders:**

**Memorandums:**

| | |
|---|---|
| September 29, 1995 | 52061 |
| October 2, 1995 | 52821 |
| October 3, 1995 | 52289 |
| October 10, 1995 | 53251 |
| October 13, 1995 | 53845 |

**Presidential Determinations:**

| | |
|---|---|
| No. 95–45 of September 29, 1995 | 52823 |
| No. 95–46 of September 29, 1995 | |
| No. 95–47 of September 29, 1995 | 53089 |
| No. 95–48 of September 29, 1995 | 53091 |
| No. 95–49 of September 28, 1995 | 53677 |
| No. 95–50 of September 30, 1995 | 53093 |

**C.F.R. Title**

**5 CFR**

| | |
|---|---|
| 315 | 53503 |
| 532 | 51881 |
| 870 | 51881 |
| 871 | 51881 |
| 872 | 51881 |
| 874 | 51881 |
| 2608 | |
| 2612 | |
| 2635 | |

**C.F.R. Part affected**

**Proposed Rules:**

| | |
|---|---|
| 251 | 51371 |
| 531 | 53545 |
| 591 | 53716 |

**7 CFR**

| | |
|---|---|
| 8 | 52293 |
| 301 | 52831, 52833 |
| 400 | 51321 |
| 810 | 51667 |
| 916 | 52067 |
| 917 | 52067 |
| 920 | 52834 |
| 982 | 51668 |
| 1150 | 53253 |
| 1212 | 52835 |
| 1443 | 51885 |
| 1477 | 52609 |
| 1478 | 52609 |

**The table shows a reference to 16 C.F.R. Part 1700 on page 53,699. The table does not indicate which section was affected, so the reference must be checked to see if § 1700.15 was changed.**

**FIGURE 8.20**  *FEDERAL REGISTER*, OCTOBER 20, 1995, CFR PARTS AFFECTED DURING OCTOBER

> 16 C.F.R. Part 1700 was affected by action reported on page 53,699.

ii    **Federal Register** / Vol. 60, No. 203 / Friday, October 20, 1995 / Reader Aids

1942....52838
1980....52838, 53254
2610....52840
2620....52842
**Proposed Rules:**
54....53283
300....51373
318....51373
985....52869
1280....51737
1413....52634
3015....53717
3016....53717
3017....54103
3050....53717

**8 CFR**
204....54027
208....52068
212....52068, 52248
214....52068, 52248
236....52068
242....52068
245....52068, 52248
248....52068
274a....52068
299....52068

**9 CFR**
[Proposed R]ules:
....52635
....53505
....53505
....53505
....53507
....54151
**Proposed Rules:**
50....51936
52....51936, 53883
100....51936

**11 CFR**
100....52069
106....52069
109....52069
110....52069
114....52069

**12 CFR**
229....51669
701....51886
722....51889
Ch. XVIII....54110
1805....54110
1806....54110
1815....54110
**Proposed Rules:**
Ch. II....53546
22....53962
208....53692
339....53692
563....53692
572....53692
614....53692
701....51936
760....53692

**14 CFR**
25....53691
39....51321, 51703, 51705, 51707, 51709, 51713, 52073, 52618, 52620, 52622, 52843, 52844, 53109, 53110, 53112,

53265, 53507, 53847, 54849,
53851, 53853, 53855, 53857,
53859, 53860, 53862, 53864,
53866, 53868, 53869
61....51850
63....51850
65....51850
71....52293, 52624, 52846, 53870, 53871, 53872
97....51715, 51717
107....51854, 53830
108....51850, 51854, 53830
121....51850, 52625
125....52625
135....51850, 52625
**Proposed Rules:**
39....51375, 51376, 51942, 51944, 52130, 52131, 52636, 52870, 52872, 53148, 53150, 53307, 53309, 53310, 53312, 53314, 53548, 53550, 53552, 53554, 53556, 53558, 53883, 53888, 54202, 54203
71....51747, 52133, 52134, 52637, 52638, 52639, 53724, 54205, 54206
77....53680

**15 CFR**
773....54030
778....54030
799....53698, 54030
**Proposed Rules:**
929....53890
937....53890

**16 CFR**
429....54185
436....51895
1500....53266
1700....53699

**17 CFR**
36....51323
200....52626
231....53458
241....53458
271....53458
**Proposed Rules:**
230....53468
232....53468
239....53468
240....52792, 53468, 53832
270....53152, 53468

**18 CFR**
2....53019
154....52960
157....53019
158....53019
201....53019
250....53019
260....53019
284....53019
357....53114
381....53019
382....53114
385....53019
**Proposed Rules:**
35....52874

**19 CFR**
10....52294
19....52294
54....52294

101....52627
123....54187
125....52294
141....52294
144....52294
148....54187
210....53117
**Proposed Rules:**
101....52347
201....51748
207....51748

**20 CFR**
404....53267
702....51346
703....51346

**21 CFR**
73....52628
100....53480
101....53480
103....53480
104....53480
105....53480
109....53480
137....53480
161....53480
163....53480
173....54035
177....54188
182....53480
184....54190
186....53480
197....53480
200....53480
250....53480
310....52474, 53480
355....52474
369....52474
500....53480
505....53480
507....53480
508....53480
510....53480, 54193
522....51718, 53509
558....53509, 53701, 54193
570....53480
573....53702
601....53480
620....53480
630....53480
640....53480
650....53480
660....53480
680....53480
700....53480
801....53480
1310....53121
**Proposed Rules:**
2....53725
330....52058
801....53560
803....53560
804....53560
888....51946
897....53560

**22 CFR**
92....51719
514....53122
**Proposed Rules:**
51....51760, 54103

**24 CFR**
291....52296
**Proposed Rules:**
882....51658

**25 CFR**
163....52250
164....51723
165....51723

**26 CFR**
1....52077, 53126
31....53509
52....52848
301....51724
602....52848, 53126, 53509
**Proposed Rules:**
31....53561

**27 CFR**
9....51896

**28 CFR**
0....53267
2....51348, 51349, 51350
501....53490
549....52278
**Proposed Rules:**
16....51962
549....54288
551....54289

**29 CFR**
4....51725
1602....51350
1910....52856
2610....53268
2619....53269
2622....53268
2644....53272
2676....53269
**Proposed Rules:**
Ch. XIV....54207
1625....51762
1910....54047
2615....52135

**30 CFR**
914....53511
948....51900
**Proposed Rules:**
6....52640
18....52640, 53891
19....52640
20....52640
21....52640
22....52640
23....52640
26....52640
27....52640
29....52640
33....52640
35....52640
75....53891
206....51963
906....53562
934....53564
938....53565
943....53567, 53569

**31 CFR**
515....54194
**Proposed Rules:**
103....53316

**32 CFR**
199....52078
311....54197
505....51918
706....52860, 53272, 54198

**Page 53,699 discusses an exemption to the packaging regulations.**

**FIGURE 8.21**   *FEDERAL REGISTER*, OCTOBER 17, 1995

---

Federal Register / Vol. 60, No. 200 / Tuesday, October 17, 1995 / Rules and Regulations   **53699**

---

2. *General Software Note*. General License GTDR, without written assurance, is available to all destinations, except Country Groups S and Z, Iran, and Syria, for release of software that is generally available to the public by being:

\*   \*   \*   \*   \*

*Supplement No. 1 to § 799.2 [Amended]*

3. In Supplement No. 1 to § 799.2 (Interpretations), interpretations Nos. 24, 25, and 26 are removed.

Dated: October 12, 1995.

**Sue E. Eckert,**

*Assistant Secretary for Export Administration.*

[FR Doc. 95–25742 Filed 10–16–95; 8:45 am]

**BILLING CODE 3510–DT–P**

---

**CONSUMER PRODUCT SAFETY COMMISSION**

**16 CFR Part 1700**

**Poison Prevention Packaging Requirements; Exemption of Certain Iron Containing Dietary Supplement Powders**

**AGENCY:** Consumer Product Safety Commission.

**ACTION:** Final rule.

**SUMMARY:** The Commission is amending its regulations to exempt from child-resistant packaging requirements those dietary supplement powders that have no more than the equivalent of 0.12 percent weight-to-weight elemental iron. The Commission issues this exemption because there are no known poisoning incidents with these products, and the dry powdered form deters children from ingesting them in harmful amounts.

**DATES:** The exemption is effective on October 17, 1995.

**FOR FURTHER INFORMATION CONTACT:** Michael Bogumill, Division of Regulatory Management, Consumer Product Safety Commission, Washington, DC 20207; telephone (301) 504–0400 ext. 1368.

**SUPPLEMENTARY INFORMATION:**

**A. Background**

In 1978, the Consumer Product Safety Commission ("the Commission") required child-resistant packaging ("CRP") for drugs and dietary supplements that contain iron. 16 CFR 1700.14(a) (12) and (13). The Commission issued these rules under the Poison Prevention Packaging Act ("PPPA"), 15 U.S.C. 1471–1476, which authorizes the Commission to require CRP to protect children under 5 years of age from poisoning hazards posed by harmful household substances.

Specifically, CRP is required for dietary supplements "that contain an equivalent of 250 milligrams or more of elemental iron, from any source, in a single package in concentrations of 0.025 percent or more on a weight-to-volume basis for liquids and 0.05 percent or more on a weight-to-weight basis for nonliquids." 16 CFR 1700.14(a)(13). This requirement does not apply if iron is present only as a colorant. *Id.*

On May 11, 1994, Nutritech, Inc. ("Nutritech"), petitioned the Commission to exempt unflavored, unsweetened iron powders from CRP requirements for dietary supplements containing iron. Nutritech manufactures an unsweetened, unflavored vitamin, mineral, and amino acid powder intended to be mixed with fruit juice. The petitioner stated several reasons why CRP is unnecessary for this dietary supplement. (1) [1] The Commission published a notice in the **Federal Register** on August 4, 1994, soliciting comments on the petition, 59 FR 39747, and received no responses.

**B. Proposed Rule and Comment**

On April 7, 1995, the Commission published a notice granting Nutritech's petition to initiate rulemaking and proposing to exempt certain powdered iron-containing dietary supplements from CRP requirements. 60 FR 17660. The Commission proposed that the exemption would apply to dietary supplement powders, both flavored and unflavored, with no more than the equivalent of 0.12 percent w/w elemental iron.

In response to the proposed rule, the Commission received one comment. The comment, submitted on behalf of an organization called SI Metric, objected that the proposed regulation did not use proper SI metric terminology. The Commission has considered the comment and has made some changes in the preamble to ensure that measurements are presented in metric terminology. However, the Commission declines to make some changes suggested by the commenter—for example, using the term mass rather than weight. The Commission also believes that its expression of the percentage of concentration of iron for liquids and non-liquids as weight-to-volume ("w/v") or weight-to-weight ("w/w") measurements is appropriate. Based on the United States Pharmacopeia guidelines, the percent

[1] Numbers in parentheses identify documents listed at the end of this notice.

w/v refers to the number of grams of a constituent in 100 milliliters of solution, and the percent w/w is the number of grams of a constituent in 100 grams of solution or mixture. The Commission believes that its use of terminology is consistent with use throughout the Federal government. Moreover, the terminology is consistent with other regulations under the PPPA.

**C. Toxicity Data**

The minimum ██████ of iron are not we██████ doses of elementa██████ milligrams per ki██████ ("mg/kg") may produce mild symptoms of poisoning, 60 mg/kg is the minimal dose for serious toxicity, and approximately 180 to 250 mg/kg is considered a lethal dose. However, fatalities of young children have been reported at lower doses. (2)(3)

According to the relevant scientific and medical literature, where information on the formulation was available, the majority of pediatric poisoning incidents involved solid iron—in the form of tablets or capsules—with the remaining cases involving liquid preparations. Among the reported ingestion incidents, fatalities and serious cases of toxicity usually involve ingestion of adult preparations (such as prenatal vitamins) that contain 60 mg or more of elemental iron per tablet. The literature search did not identify a single case of pediatric poisoning involving powdered iron formulations. (2)(3)(5)

When the Food and Drug Administration ("FDA") ██████ proposed labeli██████ requirements fo██████ supplements an██████ (October 6, 1994), it decided to limit the proposed rules to products in solid oral dosage forms (capsules and tablets) and not include liquid or powder products. (2)

The Commission's own 1994 study of pediatric iron poisonings and fatalities found that the majority of serious outcomes involved products in solid or capsule forms. T██████ all 36 of the in-d██████ iron ingestion de██████ 5 years old occurring between 1986 and 1993 involved solid capsule or tablet formulations. In 1993, 57 hospital emergency room ██████ through NEISS i██████ iron capsules or██████ under 5 years ol██████ liquid iron. As noted, there were no known pediatric poisonings that involved powde██████ study was based██████ Commission's N██████

Reading through the *Federal Register*, page 53,701 indicates that the change is to 16 C.F.R. § 1700.14, not § 1700.15. Therefore, the updating process is now complete. A telephone call to the agency would confirm that no further action on § 1700.15 has taken place.

**FIGURE 8.22**  *FEDERAL REGISTER*, OCTOBER 17, 1995

---

*Federal Register* / Vol. 60, No. 200 / Tuesday, October 17, 1995 / Rules and Regulations    **53701**

availability of dietary supplement powders with no more than the equivalent of 0.12 percent weight-to-weight elemental iron are such that special packaging is not required to protect children from serious personal injury or serious illness resulting from handling, or ingesting such substance. Accordingly, the Commission voted to grant the petition and proposed to amend 16 CFR 1700.14(a)(13) to exempt from requirements for child resistant packaging those dietary supplement powders with no more than the equivalent of 0.12 percent weight-to-weight elemental iron. 60 FR 17660 (April 7, 1995).

After considering all available and relevant information, the Commission determines to issue the proposed exemption on a final basis.

**G. Regulatory Flexibility Certification**

Under the Regulatory Flexibility Act (Pub. L. 96–354, 5 U.S.C. 601 *et seq.*), when an agency issues proposed and final rules, it must examine the rules' potential impact on small businesses.

**After the explanation, the revised regulation is set forth.**

requires agencies to prepare available for public comment regulatory flexibility analysis sed rule would have a t impact on a substantial f small businesses, small ions, and small governmental jurisdictions.

When the Commission proposed to exempt powdered iron-containing dietary supplements from CRP requirements, it found that the exemption would not have any significant economic impact on a substantial number of small entities. The exemption will give manufacturers of these products the option of packaging products using any packaging they choose. As far as CPSC is aware, powdered iron-containing dietary supplements are not currently packaged in CRP. The Commission's Compliance staff is exercising its enforcement discretion regarding these products pending completion of this rulemaking. Thus, the exemption will bring no change in the current packaging of products subject to the exemption. The Commission is not aware of any information that would alter its conclusion that this exemption will not have any significant economic effect on a substantial number of small entities.

**H. Environmental Considerations**

The Commission's regulations at 16 CFR 1021.5(c)(3) state that rules exempting products from child-resistant packaging requirements under the PPPA normally have little or no potential for affecting the human environment. The

Commission did not foresee any special or unusual circumstances surrounding the proposed rule and found that exempting these products from the PPPA requirements would have little or no effect on the human environment. For this reason, when the Commission issued the proposed exemption, it concluded that no environmental assessment or impact statement is required in this proceeding. That conclusion remains unchanged.

**I. Effective Date**

Because this rule provides for an exemption, no delay in the effective date is required. 5 U.S.C. 553(d)(1). Accordingly, the rule shall become effective upon publication of the final rule in the **Federal Register**.

**List of Subjects in 16 CFR Part 1700**

Consumer protection, Infants and children, Packaging and containers, Poison prevention, Toxic substances.

**Conclusion**

For the reasons given above, the Commission amends Title 16 of the Code of Federal Regulations to read as follows:

**PART 1700—[AMENDED]**

1. The authority citation for part 1700 continues to read as follows:

**Authority:** 15 U.S.C. 1471–1476. Secs. 1700.1 and 1700.14 also issued under 15 U.S.C. 2079(a).

2. Section 1700.14(a)(13) is revised to read as follows:

**§ 1700.14  Substances requiring special packaging.**

(a) * * *

(13) *Dietary supplements containing iron.* Dietary supplements, as defined in § 1700.1(a)(3), that contain an equivalent of 250 mg or more of elemental iron, from any source, in a single package in concentrations of 0.025 percent or more on a weight-to-volume basis for liquids and 0.05 percent or more on a weight-to-weight basis for nonliquids (e.g., powders, granules, tablets, capsules, wafers, gels, viscous products, such as pastes and ointments, etc.) shall be packaged in accordance with the provisions of § 1700.15 (a), (b), and (c), except for the following:

(i) Preparations in which iron is present solely as a colorant; and

(ii) Powdered preparations with no more than the equivalent of 0.12 percent weight-to-weight elemental iron.

* * * * *

Dated: October 6, 1995.
**Sadye E. Dunn,**
*Secretary, Consumer Product Safety Commission.*

**Reference Documents**

The following documents contain information relevant to this rulemaking proceeding and are available for inspection at the Office of the Secretary, Consumer Product Safety Commission, Washington, Room 502, 4330 East-West Highway, Bethesda, Maryland 20814.

1. Briefing Memorandum with attached briefing package, March 14, 1995.

2. Memorandum from Sandra E. Inkster, Ph.D., HSPS, to Jacqueline N. Ferrante, Ph.D., HSPS, "Review of Iron Toxicity: Relevance to a Petition Requesting Exemption for Powdered, Iron-Containing Dietary Supplements," February 15, 1995.

3. Memorandum from Catherine A. Sedney, EPHF, to Jacqueline N. Ferrante, Ph.D., HSPS, "Petition to Exempt Iron-Containing Supplement Powders from PPPA Requirements," February 16, 1995.

4. Memorandum from Marcia P. Robins, EPSS, to Jacqueline N. Ferrante, Ph.D., HSPS, "Preliminary Market Information: Petition for Exemption from Child-Resistant Packaging Requirements for Powdered Iron-Containing Dietary Supplements," March 10, 1995.

5. Briefing Memorandum with attached briefing package, September 19, 1995.

6. Memorandum from Marcia P. Robins, EPSS, to Jacqueline N. Ferrante, Ph.D., HSPS, Final Regulatory Flexibility Act Issues: Petition for Exemption from Child-Resistant Packaging Requirements for Powdered Iron-Containing Dietary Supplements," July 5, 1995.

[FR Doc. 95–25322 Filed 10–16–95; 8:45 am]
**BILLING CODE 6355–01–P**

---

**DEPARTMENT OF HEALTH AND HUMAN SERVICES**

**Food and Drug Administration**

**21 CFR Part 558**

**New Animal Drugs For Use In Animal Feeds; Decoquinate**

**AGENCY:** Food and Drug Administration, HHS.

**ACTION:** Final rule.

**SUMMARY:** The Food and Drug Administration (FDA) is amending the animal drug regulations to reflect approval of a supplemental new animal drug application (NADA) filed by Rhone-Poulenc, Inc. The supplemental NADA provides for use of decoquinate Type A medicated articles to make Type C medicated feeds for young sheep for the prevention of certain forms of coccidiosis.

**EFFECTIVE DATE:** October 17, 1995.

**FOR FURTHER INFORMATION CONTACT:** Melanie R. Berson, Center for Veterinary

**If you had retrieved 16 C.F.R. § 1700.15 from GPO Access, it would appear in this format.**

**FIGURE 8.23**   EXCERPT FROM 16 C.F.R. § 1700.15 RETRIEVED FROM GPO ACCESS

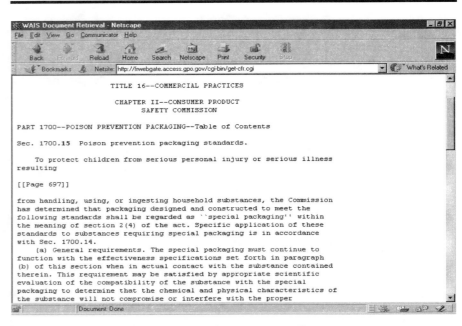

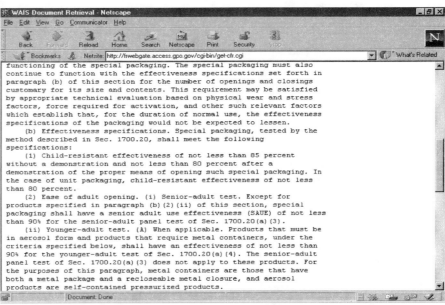

**To update this regulation through GPO Access, you would need to search for it in the database for the most recent LSA.**

**FIGURE 8.24**    EXCERPT FROM THE LSA SEARCH SCREEN IN GPO ACCESS

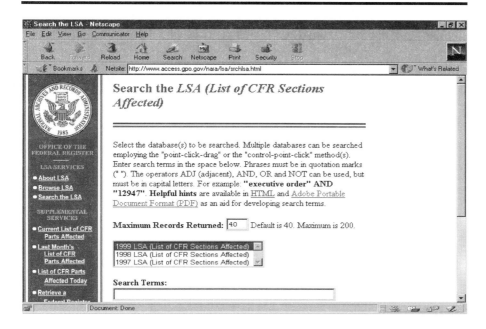

**To update beyond the LSA with the *Federal Register,* you would need to search for the regulation in the *Federal Register* database. You could use a date restriction to limit the search to the appropriate period of time.**

**FIGURE 8.25**    EXCERPT FROM THE *FEDERAL REGISTER* SEARCH SCREEN IN GPO ACCESS

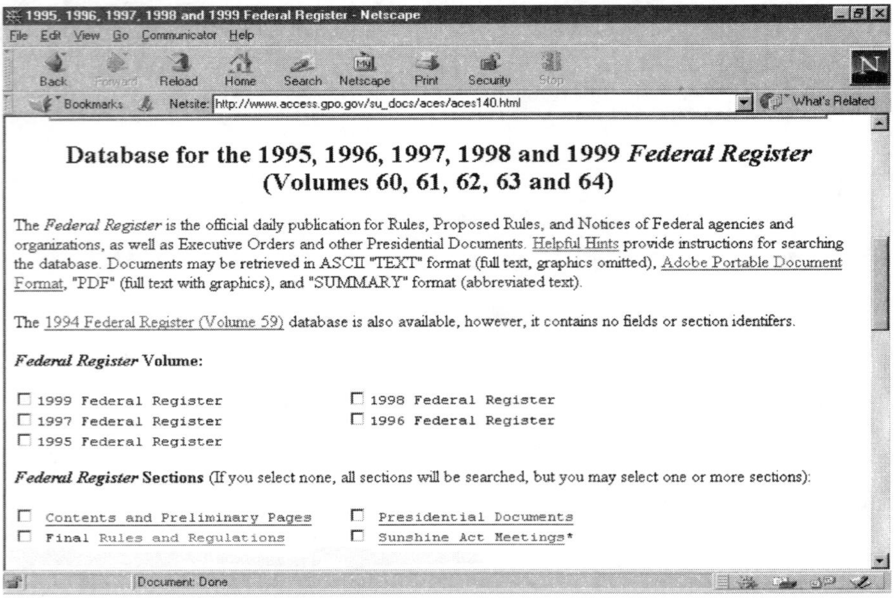

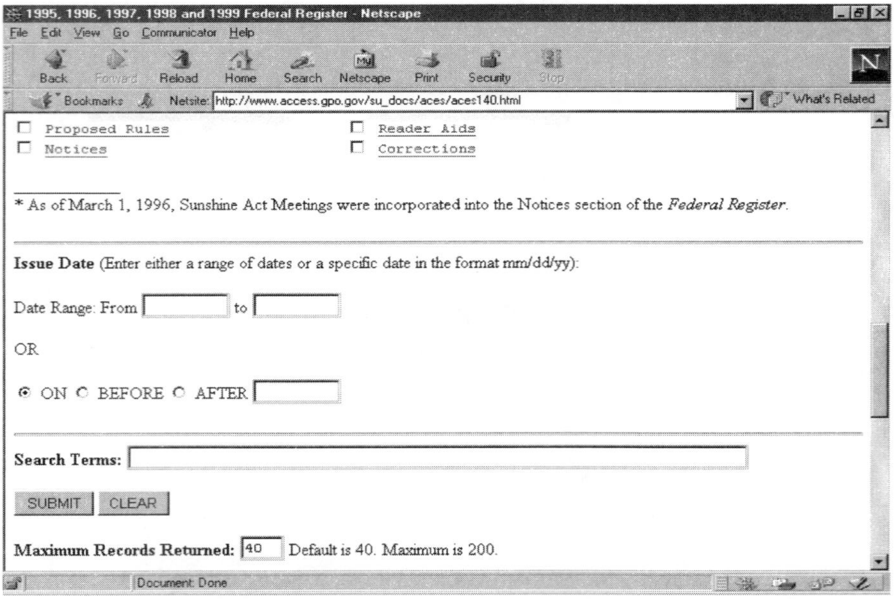

# G. CHECKLIST FOR FEDERAL ADMINISTRATIVE LAW RESEARCH

### 1. LOCATE PERTINENT REGULATIONS

❏ Use the cross-references to the C.F.R. in the annotations in U.S.C.S. and U.S.C.A.

❏ Use a subject index, such as the CFR Index and Finding Aids or CIS Index to the *Code of Federal Regulations.*

❏ Use LexisNexis and Westlaw by executing word searches in the databases for the C.F.R. or specific subject areas or by browsing the table of contents.

❏ Use GPO Access or other Internet web sites to locate regulations.

### 2. UPDATE PRINT OR INTERNET MATERIALS WITH THE LSA AND *FEDERAL REGISTER*

❏ To update in print:

■ Look up the regulation in the most recent LSA to locate page numbers in the *Federal Register* reflecting changes to the regulation.

■ Use the table in the back of the LSA to find the date of the *Federal Register* issue containing the change.

■ Read the material in the *Federal Register* to see how it affects the regulation.

❏ To update in GPO Access, use the electronic versions of the LSA and *Federal Register.*

### 3. UPDATE BEYOND THE LSA

❏ Use the *Federal Register* to update beyond the LSA.

❏ In print:

■ Use the cumulative table of CFR Parts Affected on the inside back cover of the latest issue of the *Federal Register.*

■ If the Part in which the section appears is listed, look up each page number referenced in the table to see if the section has been affected.

❏ In GPO Access, search the *Federal Register* electronically to update beyond the LSA.

❏ Contact the agency for additional information on recent or proposed regulatory changes.

### 4. USE SHEPARD'S IN PRINT OR IN LEXISNEXIS, OR KEYCITE IN WESTLAW, TO UPDATE YOUR RESEARCH OR LOCATE RESEARCH REFERENCES

# CHAPTER 9

# Subject-Matter Service Research

A. Overview of subject-matter services

B. Locating subject-matter services

C. Conducting subject-matter research using print, CD-ROM, and Internet resources

D. Subject-matter research in LexisNexis and Westlaw

E. Citing subject-matter services

F. Sample pages for subject-matter service research

G. Checklist for subject-matter service research

Many research tools are organized by type of authority and jurisdiction. Some, however, are organized by subject. They may contain only one type of authority, such as cases, but include authority from many jurisdictions. Alternatively, they may collect multiple types of authority from multiple jurisdictions in a defined subject area. These services may also compile information not available in other sources, including cases not reported in general case reporters or news and analysis in the field not available elsewhere. As a consequence, if you are researching an area of law for which subject-matter services are available, complete research requires that you consult them.

Unlike the other chapters in this book, this chapter will not take you step-by-step through the process of using different types of subject-matter services. Subject-matter services are published by many different commercial publishers. As a consequence, no uniform method of organization or research process applies to all of them. Instead, each one contains its own explanation of how to use the service. This chapter, therefore, focuses on more general information about these resources, rather than on step-by-step instructions. The sample pages in Section

F show the process for researching materials relating to the Americans with Disabilities Act so you can see how some of these services are organized.

## A. OVERVIEW OF SUBJECT-MATTER SERVICES

Subject-matter research services are often called "looseleaf" services. This is because many of them are actually published in looseleaf binders. By putting the information in a binder, the publisher is able to update individual pages or sections as necessary. Not all services are published in binders, however. They are available in many formats, including bound print volumes, CD-ROMs, and Internet databases. Thus, this chapter refers to them as subject-matter services, rather than looseleaf services.

A subject-matter service may contain some or all of the following types of information:

- news or analysis of current events in the field
- statutory material, including
    federal statutes
    state statutes
    legislative history of pertinent statutes
- administrative materials, including
    federal regulations and agency decisions
    state regulations and agency decisions
- cases, including
    federal cases
    state cases

A few subject-matter services contain all of this information, but most contain some combination of these items. Some, but by no means all, of the areas for which subject-matter services are available include environmental law, tax, bankruptcy, government contracts, intellectual property, employment and labor law, and securities law. Some of the best known publishers of subject-matter services are the Bureau of National Affairs (BNA), CCH, Inc. (CCH), Clark Boardman Callaghan (CBC), Matthew Bender (MB), Pike & Fischer (P & F), and Research Institute of America (RIA).

The statutes, regulations, and legislative history documents contained in a subject-matter service could be located through other resources, such as an annotated code or LexisNexis Congressional. The advantage of the subject-matter service, however, is that it compiles all of this information in one place, which is easier and more efficient than re-searching each item individually. This is especially true because many subject-matter services focus on complex, highly regulated areas of the law for which it might be difficult to compile all of the relevant information.

Many of the cases in a subject-matter service could also be located through digests or other general legal research resources, but again, the compilation of material from many different jurisdictions makes the subject-matter service easier to use. In addition, some of the opinions reported in the service may not be reported elsewhere, so the service may give you access to cases you would not have been able to locate in other sources.

In short, "one-stop shopping" and access to authority not published elsewhere make subject-matter services an invaluable research tool.

## B. LOCATING SUBJECT-MATTER SERVICES

Locating a subject-matter service is not unlike locating a treatise—it is much easier to find if you already know what you are looking for. The difficult part is figuring out whether a subject-matter service exists for your research issue when you have not previously conducted research in that area of law.

One quick place to check for subject-matter services is the *Bluebook*. Table T.16 contains an alphabetical list of some of the more commonly used services.

Another place to look is in a directory of subject-matter services. Two that are especially helpful are *Legal Looseleafs in Print* and *Directory of Law-Related CD-ROMs*, both of which are compiled and edited by Arlene L. Eis. These reference books list subject-matter services by publisher, title, and subject.[1] Sample entries from these publications appear in Figures 9.1 and 9.2. Once you know the name of a pertinent subject-matter service, you can locate it using your library's on-line catalog or computer network.

## C. CONDUCTING SUBJECT-MATTER RESEARCH USING PRINT, CD-ROM, AND INTERNET RESOURCES

Although no uniform process applies to using subject-matter services, this section provides some general information that may help you get started with your research. It also discusses ways you can use publicly available information on the Internet for researching in specific subject areas of the law.

---

[1] Both of these publications, plus Legal Newsletters in Print, are indexed electronically in a subscription service called LawTRIO. If your library subscribes to this service, you should be able to access it from the library's computer network.

**FIGURE 9.1**  SAMPLE ENTRY FROM *LEGAL LOOSELEAFS IN PRINT*

Title List

**Blue Sky Guide**
2. Investment Company Institute, ed.
3. Investment Company Institute
4. 1981
5. 1 vol.
6. $175/yr.-members, $775/yr.-nonmembers
7. annual
8. renewal - $125/yr.-members, $525/yr.-nonmembers
9. OCLC 10204625;  LC call # KF1435.B58
● www
*On Internet:* www.ici.org

**Blue Sky Law Desk Reference**
2. -
3. CCH INCORPORATED
4. 1999
5. 1 vol.
6. $372/yr.
7. monthly supp.
● CD-ROM; www
*On Internet:* business.cch.com

**Blue Sky Law Reports**
2. -
3. CCH INCORPORATED
4. 1928
5. 6 vols.
6. $1,214/yr.
7. semimonthly supp.
9. LC # 47-2581;  OCLC 1564311
● CD-ROM; www
*On Internet:* business.cch.com

**Blue Sky Law (Securities Law Series, Vol. 12 & 12A)**
2. Long, Joseph C.
3. West Group
4. 1996
5. 3 vols.
6. $477 incl. 3 mos. supp.
7. semiannual supp.
8. 1997 - $351; 1999 - $372
9. LC # 85-11377;  OCLC 37766086;  LC call # KF1070.Z95L66
● CD-ROM

**Blue Sky Regulation**
2. Sommer, A. A., Jr.
3. Matthew Bender & Co., Inc.
4. 1977
5. 4 vols.
6. $1,017 incl. 1 yr. supp.
7. supp. as needed
8. renewal - $827/yr.
9. LC # 77-365432;  OCLC 3273572;  LC call # KF1440.Z95S69
● CD-ROM; www
*On Internet:* www.bender.com

**BNA/ACCA Compliance Manual: Prevention of Corporate Liability**
2. Moore, Mike, ed.
3. Bureau of National Affairs, Inc.
4. 1993
5. 2 vols.
6. $893/yr.
7. monthly supp.

**BNA Criminal Practice Manual**
2. Mroczka, Judith, ed.
3. Pike & Fischer, Inc.
4. 1987
5. 2 vols.
6. $570/yr.
7. quarterly supp.
9. OCLC 36281089;  LC call # KF9655.B88

● CD-ROM

**BNA Policy and Practice Series**
2. Day, Jeff
3. Bureau of National Affairs, Inc.
4. 1945
5. 19 vols.
6. $1,965/yr.
7. weekly supp. and newsletters
8. renewal - $1,898/yr.
9. LC # sf79-10252;  OCLC 3463998;  LC call # HD4802.B952
● CD-ROM; www
*On Internet:* hrlaw.bna.com

**BNA's Americans with Disabilities Act Manual**
2. Goldman, Leslie
3. Bureau of National Affairs, Inc.
4. 1992
5. 3 vols.
6. $997/yr.
7. bimonthly supp.
9. OCLC 25146276;  LC call # KF480.A95
● Online - WESTLAW; CD-ROM

**BNA's Environmental Due Diligence Guide**
2. Fetherston, Kevin
3. Bureau of National Affairs, Inc.
4. 1992
5. 2 vols.
6. $865/yr.
7. monthly supp.
8. renewal - $742/yr.
9. OCLC 25724616;  LC call # KF1298.A6B63

**BNA's Health Law & Business Series**
2. Herman, Robin, ed.
3. Bureau of National Affairs, Inc.
4. 1996
5. 1 vol. & current portfolios
6. $1,636/yr.
7. monthly supp.
9. LC # 97-660778;  OCLC 34381941;  LC call # KF3821.A73B58

**\*Board Service for the Community Association**
2. Clark, William D.
3. Revere Legal Publishers
4. 1996
5. 1 vol.
6. $60
7. annual supp.
8. 2000 - $40; 2001 - $40
9. LC # 96-113851;  OCLC 34546093;  LC call # KFF114.C6C547

**\*The Book on D.U.I.**
2. Fowlkes, C. Edward
3. M. Lee Smith Publishers LLC
4. 1999
5. 1 vol.
6. $137
7. periodic supp.
8. no supp. yet
9. OCLC 42057745;  LC call # KFT297.8.F64B66
● Diskette of forms incl.

**Boston Stock Exchange Guide**
2. -
3. CCH INCORPORATED
4. 1970
5. 1 vol.
6. $440/yr.
7. bimonthly supp.
9. LC # 75-26412;  OCLC 151746;  LC call # HG5131.B7A5

**Brady on Bank Checks**
2. Bailey, Henry J. and Richard B. Hagedorn

Reprinted with permission from Arlene L. Eis, *Legal Looseleafs in Print 2002*, Title List (Infosources Publ'g 2002), p. 37.

**FIGURE 9.2**   SAMPLE ENTRY FROM *DIRECTORY OF LAW-RELATED CD-ROMS*

---

**CD-ROM Product List**

AMC's patented headnote system, table of cases and cross reference tables.
*Toll-free support*

### American Stock Exchange Guide

*Publisher:* CCH INCORPORATED
*Search Software:* Proprietary
*Compatible Drives:* All supporting Microsoft Extensions
*Min. Equip. Specs:* Windows - IBM-compatible 386 or higher, 4MB RAM (8MB recommended), Windows 3.1, Windows for Workgroups 3.11, Windows 95, Windows NT 3.51 or Windows NT 4.0. DOS 5.0 (or higher) is required for Windows 3.x, VGA or better video, 12 MB hard disk space
*Networks:* Yes
*Site License:* Inquire
*Language:* English
*Print Equiv.:* Available in print
*On Internet:* business.cch.com
*Coverage Dates:* Current
*Updated:* Monthly
*Price:* $524/yr.
*No. of Discs:* 1
*Description:* Includes membership list, listing of securities on the ASE, ASE constitution and rules, and rules of procedure in disciplinary matters. Available on web.
*Toll-free support*

### Americans With Disabilities LawDesk

*Publisher:* West Group
*Search Software:* LawDesk
*Compatible Drives:* Double-speed CD-ROM drive
*Min. Equip. Specs:* Windows - 95, 98, or NT, 486 or higher processor, 24MB RAM, 32MB free hard disk space.
*Networks:* Contact Customer Service 1-800-888-9907
*Site License:* Inquire
*Language:* English
*Print Equiv.:* Available in print
*Coverage Dates:* Current
*Updated:* Quarterly
*Price:* Inquire
*No. of Discs:* 1
*Description:* Contains all the statutes, regulations, and requirements for complying with the ADA, the Rehabilitation Act, Individuals with Disabilities Education Act and more. Also includes all relevant federal disability law cases and decisions, and hundreds of forms.
*Toll-free support*

### AmJur Legal Forms 2d on LawDesk

*Publisher:* West Group
*Search Software:* PREMISE (West); LawDesk
*Compatible Drives:* Double-speed CD-ROM drive
*Min. Equip. Specs:* Windows - 3.1 or higher, DOS 3.3, 486 processor, 4MB RAM (8MB recommended), 15MB free hard disk space. Macintosh - System 7.1 or higher (7.6 recommended), 68020 or higher processor, 4MB RAM (8MB recommended), 11.4MB free hard disk space. For LawDesk 5.1 - Windows 95, 98, or NT, 486 or higher processor, 24MB RAM, 32MB free hard disk space.
*Networks:* Contact Customer Service 1-800-888-9907
*Site License:* Inquire
*Language:* English
*Print Equiv.:* See description
*Coverage Dates:* Current
*Updated:* Quarterly
*Price:* Inquire
*No. of Discs:* 1
*Description:* Contains forms from American Jurisprudence Legal Forms 2d and the Federal Tax Guide to Legal Forms. Includes checklists, research references, and other drafting tools to help fill out the form. Hypertext-linked to AmJur.

*Reviews: Legal Times*, Sept. 26, 1994, p.63; *Legal Times*, June 17, 1996, p. 24
*Toll-free support*

### AmJur Pleading and Practice Forms on LawDesk

*Publisher:* West Group
*Search Software:* PREMISE (West); LawDesk
*Compatible Drives:* Double-speed CD-ROM drive
*Min. Equip. Specs:* Windows - 3.1 or higher, DOS 3.3, 486 processor, 4MB RAM (8MB recommended), 15MB free hard disk space. Macintosh - System 7.1 or higher (7.6 recommended), 68020 or higher processor, 4MB RAM (8MB recommended), 11.4MB free hard disk space. For LawDesk 5.1 - Windows 95, 98, or NT, 486 or higher processor, 24MB RAM, 32MB free hard disk space.
*Networks:* Contact Customer Service 1-800-888-9907
*Site License:* Inquire
*Language:* English
*Print Equiv.:* Available in print
*Coverage Dates:* Current
*Updated:* Quarterly
*Price:* Inquire
*No. of Discs:* 1
*Description:* More than 30,000 forms for every stage of litigation, from pre-trial motions to appeals. Covers 360 topics. Includes checklists, timetables, and practice tips.
*Reviews: Legal Times*, June 19, 1995, p.36; *Legal Times*, June 17, 1996, p.24
*Toll-free support*

### AmJur Proof of Facts on LawDesk

*Publisher:* West Group
*Search Software:* PREMISE (West); LawDesk
*Compatible Drives:* Double-speed CD-ROM drive
*Min. Equip. Specs:* Windows - 3.1 or higher, DOS 3.3, 486 processor, 4MB RAM (8MB recommended), 15MB free hard disk space. Macintosh - System 7.1 or higher (7.6 recommended), 68020 or higher processor, 4MB RAM (8MB recommended), 11.4MB free hard disk space. For LawDesk 5.1 - Windows 95, 98, or NT, 486 or higher processor, 24MB RAM, 32MB free hard disk space.
*Networks:* Contact Customer Service 1-800-888-9907
*Site License:* Inquire
*Language:* English
*Print Equiv.:* Available in print
*Coverage Dates:* Current
*Updated:* Quarterly
*Price:* Inquire
*No. of Discs:* 1
*Description:* More than 1,000 expert authored articles that cover case preparation procedure and technique for all major areas of civil litigation and selected criminal defense topics. Links to other LawDesk products.
*Toll-free support*

### AmJur 2d on LawDesk

*Publisher:* West Group
*Search Software:* PREMISE (West); LawDesk
*Compatible Drives:* Double-speed CD-ROM drive
*Min. Equip. Specs:* Windows - 3.1 or higher, DOS 3.3, 486 processor, 4MB RAM (8MB recommended), 15MB free hard disk space. Macintosh - System 7.1 or higher (7.6 recommended), 68020 or higher processor, 4MB RAM (8MB recommended), 11.4MB free hard disk space. For LawDesk 5.1 - Windows 95, 98, or NT, 486 or higher processor, 24MB RAM, 32MB free hard disk space.
*Networks:* Contact Customer Service 1-800-888-9907
*Site License:* Inquire
*Language:* English
*Print Equiv.:* See description
*Coverage Dates:* Current
*Updated:* Quarterly

---

DIRECTORY OF LAW-RELATED CD-ROMS 2002                                    9

Reprinted with permission from Arlene L. Eis, *Directory of Law-Related CD-ROMs 2002*, CD-ROM Product List (Infosources Publ'g 2002), p. 9.

## 1. PRINT RESOURCES

In print form, most subject-matter services have a section at the beginning of the binder or in the front of a bound volume entitled "Overview" or "How to use this service." This section should first explain the scope of the service. Does it contain statutes, cases, news bulletins, or some combination of materials? Knowing the scope will help you determine how the service fits with your overall research strategy. This section should also explain how to find and update material within the service, and some contain sample research problems illustrating the research process. Subject-matter services that contain cases are often organized in a digest format similar to the format of West digests, although they do not use the West topic and key number system. Regardless of how they are organized, however, all subject-matter services have some type of indexing method that you can use to locate information.

## 2. CD-ROM RESOURCES

Some subject-matter services are available in CD-ROM format. Your library may have special terminals for using CD-ROM resources, or these services may be accessible through the library's computer network. As with the print versions of these services, the CD-ROM versions vary in their scope, organization, and searching options. CD-ROM services, like other electronic research tools, require you to execute searches to retrieve information contained within the database. Chapter 10 explains general techniques that you can use to create effective word searches in CD-ROM services. Accordingly, you may want to review Chapter 10 in conjunction with this chapter.

Although each service is somewhat different, a number of them operate on one of two types of search platforms: Premise and Folio. Premise is similar to Westlaw. In a Premise-based product, you can select a database and execute a word search. The search screen should be similar to the Westlaw search screen, and you should be able to use a number of Westlaw search options, including terms and connectors, natural language, and field searching. An example of a Premise search screen appears in Figure 9.3.

Folio is slightly different. Folio organizes the information within a subject-matter service into databases called "infobases," and infobases are subdivided into individual items of information called "records." The amount and type of information contained in a "record" is not standardized; it could consist of a statutory code section, a case, or some other subdivision of the total information in the infobase.

When you are using a Folio-based service, you must select the infobase you want to search. Once you have selected an infobase, you will have several searching options for retrieving individual records. You can

**FIGURE 9.3** PREMISE SEARCH SCREEN

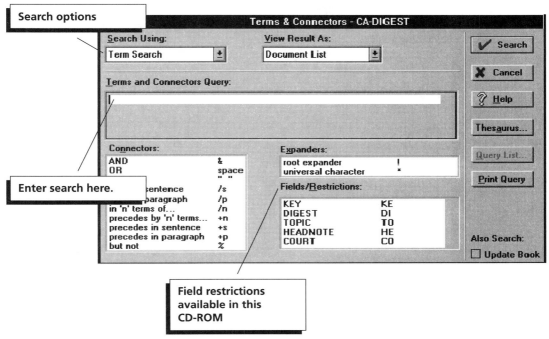

Reprinted with permission from West Group, from Westlaw, Premise-based product—California Digest, 2002.

browse the full text of the infobase, view the table of contents for the infobase, or execute a query, which is the term Folio uses to describe word searches. Depending on the type of information contained within the infobase, other searching options may be available.

Of the three basic searching options, browsing the full text of the infobase is least likely to be a useful technique. If you want to review the contents of the infobase, viewing the table of contents is more likely to lead you to useful information.

The query option allows you to execute a word search. The appearance of the search screen for querying differs depending on the service you are using and the infobase you have selected. Generally, however, you will find these common features on the screen:

- A box for you to enter your search information.
- A "Word Wheel," which is a box that lists every term that appears in the infobase. You can enter a search in the search box by typing in terms or selecting terms from the list.
- A "results map," which tells you how many records contain the information in your search.

**FIGURE 9.4**   FOLIO SEARCH COMMANDS

| TO RETRIEVE . . . | USE SEARCH TECHNIQUE |
|---|---|
| Two words that appear in the same record | Type the word AND between the words (movie and theater).<br><br>Leave a space between the words (movie theater). |
| Two words in the alternative | Type the word OR between the words (movie or theater).<br><br>Insert a vertical slash between the words (movie\|theater). |
| A phrase | Place the words in quotation marks ("movie theater"). |
| Alternative forms of base words | Use "wildcard" characters.<br><br>An asterisk (*) at the end of a word retrieves multiple suffixes (theat* will retrieve theater, theaters, theatre, theatres, theatrical, etc.).<br><br>A question mark (?) takes the place of each unknown letter (theat?? will retrieve theater and theatre). |

Word searching in Folio is similar to word searching in other types of computer databases. The rules for constructing searches are similar to those in LexisNexis and Westlaw. Figure 9.4 illustrates some of the more common search commands; you should refer to the "Help" or "How to use" functions in the CD-ROM or the printed manual for more detailed searching instructions for a specific service. Once you have created your search, the results map will tell you the number of records with "hits" containing your search terms. When you execute the search, the computer will display the search results.

Figure 9.5 shows a sample search screen from a Folio-based CD-ROM. Although this screen shows features common to many Folio-based products, it has been customized in some respects. Therefore, search screens for other Folio-based products may look different.

This is only a brief introduction to searching in Folio and Premise. Both platforms have additional techniques for searching and navigating through the information in the CD-ROM, and as noted earlier, the features in any given service will vary even if it is a Premise- or Folio-based product. Whenever you use a CD-ROM subject-matter service for the first time, you should plan to spend a few minutes reviewing the printed manual or reading through the help function to use the features of the service effectively.

**FIGURE 9.5** FOLIO SEARCH SCREEN

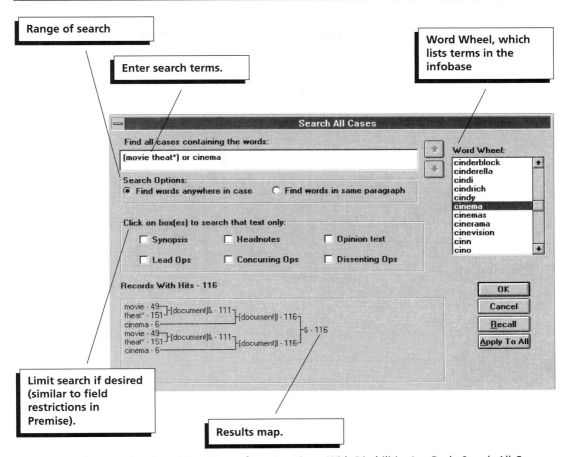

Reprinted with permission from West Group, from Americans With Disabilities LawDesk, Search All Cases screen, 1998.

## 3. INTERNET RESOURCES

The Internet may be useful in two ways for searching in defined subject areas of the law. First, many publishers of subject-matter services are converting their print and CD-ROM products into Internet format. In some cases, the web-based versions are in addition to the print or CD-ROM products, but increasingly, they are replacing the print and CD-ROM versions. Although these services are available on the Internet, access to them is limited to subscribers. They should be accessible through a subscriber's computer network, although you may need a password to retrieve information. A reference librarian will be able to give you instructions for accessing the Internet version of any subject-matter service available at your library. As with the print versions of these services, the Internet versions are all organized differently. You

will need to refer to the instructions provided with the service to understand the search options available.

The second way the Internet may prove useful is through publicly
available information. Although the Internet, by itself, is not yet a useful
tool for completing a research project from start to finish, it can be an
excellent starting point for research into defined subject areas of the law.
This is because many government, educational, nonprofit, trade, and
civic organizations that are engaged in public education efforts make
useful information on many areas of law available for free on the Internet.
You may find background information on the area of law, references to
significant legal authorities, legislative initiatives pending at the local,
state, or federal level, and links to other sites with useful information
on the subject. Although you would certainly have to supplement your
Internet research with more traditional legal research to make sure your
information is complete, accurate, and up to date, Internet searching
may be a good starting point for your project.

For example, if you were asked to research a problem in bankruptcy,
you might want to spend a few minutes looking over the web site for
the American Bankruptcy Institute. The screen reproduced in Figure
9.6 shows the kinds of information you would find there. Obviously,

**FIGURE 9.6**   INTRODUCTORY SCREEN, AMERICAN BANKRUPTCY INSTITUTE
WEB SITE

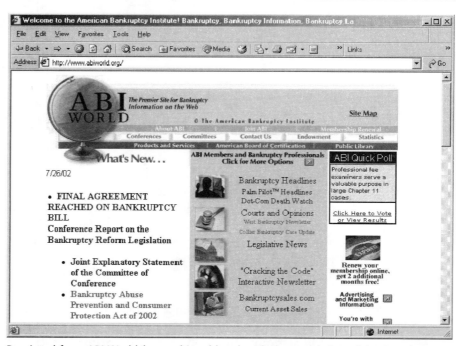

Reprinted from ABI World (www.abiworld.org) with the permission of the American
Bankruptcy Institute, 2002.

you would not want to rely solely on the information provided here for your research project, but you might be able to find useful information for getting started.

If you use the Internet in this way, you should plan to undertake three steps: (1) locate web sites with useful information; (2) verify the source of the information; and (3) verify and update any legal authorities identified on the web site.

You can locate information on the Internet in a variety of ways. Print or other resources may refer you to web sites maintained by organizations with useful information on your topic. You can also use a general or law-related search engine to search for web sites on a particular issue. Appendix A lists Internet sites that may be helpful in this regard.

Once you have located one or more useful web sites, you may want to verify that the source of this information is reputable. Because of the way Internet addresses, or "domain names," are assigned,[2] only United States government sites will end in .gov, and only United States military sites will end in .mil. Beyond that, however, addresses are not so certain. Domain names for educational institutions will usually end in .edu and those for nonprofit organizations in .org. Other entities have domain names ending in .com, .net, and .info, among others. These categories, however, are not absolute, and even when they do apply, you may want to verify independently who is maintaining the web site.

A domain name registration service can help you verify who maintains a web site by allowing you to conduct a domain name search. By entering the site address, you can find out to whom the domain name is registered, as well as limited contact information. This will allow you to verify that a site claiming to be the product of a particular organization is in fact maintained by that group. Conducting a domain name (WHOIS) search for <abiworld.org> shows that that domain name is, in fact, registered to the American Bankruptcy Institute. The result of the domain name search appears in Figure 9.7.

Of course, just because a site is maintained by the person or entity purporting to maintain it does not mean that the information there is reliable or accurate. Many groups post information on the Internet to advance their social or policy agendas. Therefore, you need to make a separate assessment of how much weight to give to information posted on an individual's or organization's web site.

If you find references to legal authorities on the Internet, the next step is updating your research. You should not assume that the authorities

---

[2]A complete explanation of how domain names are assigned is beyond the scope of this chapter. For more information on how addresses are assigned, see InterNIC, *InterNIC Frequently Asked Questions (FAQs)* <http://www.internic.org/faqs/index.html> (last updated Mar. 19, 2002).

**FIGURE 9.7** SEARCH RESULTS FOR ABIWORLD.ORG SHOWING THE DOMAIN NAME REGISTRANT

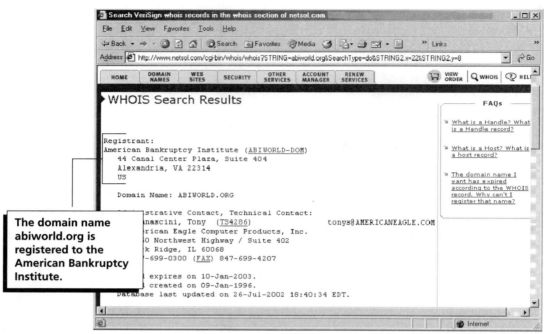

© 2002 VeriSign, Inc. Reprinted with permission from VeriSign, Inc.

you have located are correct, complete, or up to date. Use the information you have found as a springboard into more traditional avenues of legal research to make sure you have located all pertinent information and updated it completely.

## D. SUBJECT-MATTER RESEARCH IN LEXISNEXIS AND WESTLAW

Both LexisNexis and Westlaw have databases devoted to subject areas of the law. You will find them in the Westlaw directory under "Topical Materials by Area of Practice" and in the LexisNexis source directory under "Area of Law—By Topic." These databases allow you to search cases, statutes, regulations, secondary sources, and other materials in a subject area, instead of by jurisdiction. Once within the database for a subject area, you can limit your search to a particular jurisdiction. Thus, for example, if you were to select the database for insurance, you could search all jurisdictions in that subject area, or you could choose to search only materials for an individual state. In addition, some of the subject-matter services published by BNA, CCH, and other publishers are available in the LexisNexis and Westlaw subject-area databases.

## E. CITING SUBJECT-MATTER SERVICES

Citations to subject-matter services contain the same elements using either the *ALWD Manual* or the *Bluebook*, although as noted below, abbreviations for some items within the citation will vary depending on which format you use. In the *ALWD Manual*, subject-matter service citations are governed by Rule 28, and in the *Bluebook*, they are governed by Rule 19.

A citation to a subject-matter service consists of six components: (1) the title of the item; (2) the volume of the service; (3) the abbreviated title of the service; (4) the abbreviated name of the publisher of the service in parentheses; (5) the pinpoint reference to the subdivision in the service where the cited item begins; and (6) a parenthetical containing the exact date and, for case citations, the jurisdiction and level of court deciding the case. When citing cases, be sure to refer to the rules for case citations. The following example shows how to cite a case reported in a subject-matter service.

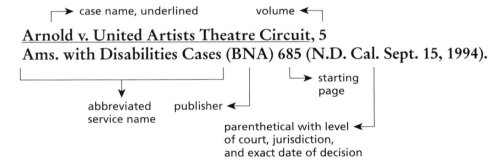

Determining the abbreviated name of the service requires you to use Appendix 3 in the *ALWD Manual* and several Tables in the *Bluebook*. For the example above, Appendix 3 in the *ALWD Manual* abbreviates "American" (singular) as "Am." but directs you to add an "s" to form an abbreviation of the plural form of the word. Appendix 3 does not abbreviate any other words in the title of the service. Thus, the service is cited as Ams. with Disabilities Cases.

Using the *Bluebook*, determining the proper abbreviation is more challenging. Rule 19 refers you to Table T.16, which contains abbreviations for commonly used services. Americans with Disabilities Cases is not listed in Table T.16. If a publication does not appear in Table T.16, Rule 19.1 directs you to use the periodical abbreviations in Table T.14 to determine the abbreviation for the service. Although Table T.14 does not list a specific abbreviation for "Americans" (plural), the abbreviation for "American" (singular) appears in the titles of several publications as "Am." According to Table T.6, containing case name abbreviations, you can form a plural abbreviation by adding an "s" unless the *Bluebook* specifically indicates that an abbreviation refers to both the singular and the plural forms of the word. Accordingly, although the *Bluebook* is not entirely clear, it appears that the word "Americans" in the title of the service should be abbreviated as "Ams." Table T.14 does not abbreviate any other words in the title of the service. Thus, the service can be abbreviated as Ams. with Disabilities Cases.

## F. SAMPLE PAGES FOR SUBJECT-MATTER SERVICE RESEARCH

Figures 9.8 through 9.15 illustrate some of the features of two different subject-matter services, the *Americans with Disabilities Act Manual* (hereinafter ADA Manual) and *Americans with Disabilities Cases* (hereinafter A.D. Cases[3]), both published by BNA. The ADA Manual is a three-binder set containing, among other items, news, the full text of the federal Americans with Disabilities Act (ADA), federal regulations, summaries of state disability laws, technical assistance and resources for employers and businesses, and summaries of disability cases from federal and state courts.

BNA's A.D. Cases is a reporter service that publishes the full text of disability decisions. The A.D. Cases service also has its own digesting system. The finding tool for locating cases in the reporter is the Cumulative Digest and Index. Each Cumulative Digest and Index volume covers a specific period of time, so you would need to use several volumes to research cases over a period of years.

Like many other BNA reporter services, the A.D. Cases service divides material into different topics called "classifications," and each classification is assigned a number. You can find a classification number applicable to your research issue in two ways. In the front of each volume of the Cumulative Digest and Index, you will find an "Outline of Classifications," which is similar to the key number outline at the beginning of a West digest topic. You can review this outline to locate classification numbers. Each volume of the Cumulative Digest and Index also contains an alphabetical subject index called the "Topic Finder," which will refer you to classification numbers.

Once you have identified classification numbers relevant to your research, you can look them up within the Cumulative Digest and Index to locate case summaries, just as you would find case summaries under key numbers in a West digest. The Cumulative Digest and Index will give you the full citations to the cases, which you can find in the A.D. Cases reporter volumes. The cases in the A.D. Cases reporter volumes also contain "headnotes" listing the applicable classification numbers.

---

[3]This is not the correct abbreviation for a citation to this service. See Section E above for a discussion of citation rules for subject-matter services.

In BNA's *Americans with Disabilities Act Manual*, you would begin by reviewing the information in the "Overview" section to see what is included in the service and how it is organized.

**FIGURE 9.8** EXCERPT FROM THE OVERVIEW, *BNA'S AMERICANS WITH DISABILITIES ACT MANUAL*

---

No. 116
10:0003

# How to Use ADAM

## Overview

The Americans with Disabilities Act of 1990 prohibits the exclusion of people from jobs, services, activities, or benefits based on disability. To that end, the ADA's five sections, or titles, cover employment, state and local governments and transportation, public accommodations, telecommunications, and miscellaneous provisions. The ADA is modeled in large part on the Rehabilitation Act of 1973, which prohibits discrimination on the basis of disability by federal contractors and subcontractors and employers that receive federal funds.

BNA's *American's with Disabilities Act Manual* provides detailed information and practical guidance on all aspects of the ADA, allowing subscribers to:

- keep up-to-date on federal and state laws and regulations,
- monitor emerging trends in disability law, and
- simplify and speed research.

## How ADAM Is Organized

**[Identifies finding tools for this service]**

### One

*Newsletter*

The newsletter contains news on the ADA and its implementation, regulatory and legal developments, case summaries, and articles relevant to disabilities issues.

*Index and Table of Cases*

The index, which is updated every four months, organizes the manual's contents by subject and cross-references subject areas to other relevant sections. A table of cases allows rapid location of pertinent federal and state court decisions.

*Tab 20–Employment (Title I)*

This section addresses issues covered under Title I, the employment section of the ADA, such as coverage, definition of disability, prohibited actions, reasonable accommodation, exceptions and defenses, and interaction of the ADA with other laws and programs.

**[Describes an individual section]** *State and Local Governments and rtation (Title II)*

ection covers prohibitions against discrimina-tate and local governments and explains accessibility standards for public transportation services. The section addresses issues such as coverage, program accessibility, communications with people with disabilities, administrative requirements, accessibility requirements for vehicles, and paratransit services.

*Tab 30–Public Accommodations (Title III)*

This section covers prohibitions against discrimination by private entities in places of public accommodation, such as hotels, restaurants, stores, theaters, and other service establishments. Issues such as accessibil-ity standards for buildings and facilities, barrier removal, examinations and courses, auxiliary aids and services, service animals, and direct threat exceptions are addressed.

*Tab 35–Telecommunications (Title IV)*

This section covers Title IV, which requires that people with speech and/or hearing disabilities have equal access to telecommunication systems. The section includes information on telecommunications relay services, hearing-aid-compatible telephones, and TRS telephone numbers.

*Tab 40–Definitions and Terms*

This section includes definitions of key terms in the ADA and its implementing regulations.

*Tab 50–Policy and Practice*

This section describes policies and practices that employers use to comply with reasonable accommodation requirements.

### Binder Two

*Tab 70–Statutes and Regulations*

This section includes the full text of the ADA and other federal laws, agency regulations implementing the ADA, and policy guidance documents issued by the Equal Employment Opportunity Commission and other agencies.

### Binder Three

*Tab 80–State Disability Laws*

This section includes summaries of state laws that prohibit discrimination on the basis of disability.

9–13–01                Copyright © 2001 by The Bureau of National Affairs, Inc.

**FIGURE 9.8** EXCERPT FROM THE OVERVIEW, *BNA'S AMERICANS WITH DISABILITIES ACT MANUAL* (Continued)

---

10:0004 OVERVIEW

*Tab 90–Technical Assistance and Resources*

This section includes Technical Assistance Manuals for Titles I, II, and III of the ADA issued by EEOC and the Justice Department; directories of ADA-related federal offices and information sources; sample forms, policies, and job descriptions; and information on disability-related tax incentives.

*Tab 100–Legal Developments*

This section contains summaries of federal and state court decisions.

9–13–01       BNA's Americans with Disabilities Act Manual

---

Reproduced with permission from *BNA's Americans with Disabilities Act Manual*, pp. 10:0003–0004. Copyright 2001 by The Bureau of National Affairs, Inc. (800-372-1033) <http://www.bna.com>.

**Once you know the scope of the service, you could use the Master Index to find sections and pages with information on various topics.**

**FIGURE 9.9**   EXCERPT FROM THE MASTER INDEX, *BNA'S AMERICANS WITH DISABILITIES ACT MANUAL*

---

INDEX - 1

Explains index entries

## MASTER INDEX
## BNA'S AMERICANS WITH DISABILITIES ACT MANUAL

*(Covers through Supplement No. 122)*

### How to Use This Index

This topical index provides references to the material in **BNA's AMERICANS WITH DISABILITIES ACT MANUAL.** The number preceding the colon in each citation indicates the tabbed divider, and the number following the colon gives the page number in that tabbed divider on which the information may be found, e.g., 70:0101.

Editor's Notes [*Ed. Note:*] clarify the scope of a particular heading and, where appropriate, refer the researcher to related headings. The phrase "et seq." after a page citation indicates a series of three or more pages relating to the subject entry.

Federal act and law references include in parentheses detailed section numbers (e.g., §12102(2)) to facilitate research. Federal regulation references include in parentheses the Code of Federal Regulations title and regulation number (e.g., 29 CFR 1630.2(k)). Architectural Guidelines under Title III (Appendix to Justice Department's Final Rules Implementing Title III) are cited in index references to specific sections of Appendix A (e.g., ADAAG 4.2).

This index is arranged alphabetically word-by-word. For example, the heading DRUG TESTING precedes the heading DRUGSTORES. Moreover, hyphenated words are treated as two separate words, not as single words. For example, CHECK-OUT AISLES precedes the heading CHECKLISTS. Also, it is important to note that most headings appear in plural form.

To help researchers locate quickly the text of federal acts and laws, the phrase "Full text" with its tab and page citation is printed first under certain subject headings. See example below:

**REHABILITATION ACT**
Full text, 70:0301 et seq.

Cross-references assist users by linking related information within the index. They refer researchers from one topic heading to another topic heading or to a subheading under another topic heading where relevant information is found. They also suggest related topic headings.

Types of cross-references are:

* *See* .................................................................. all information at other location
* *See also* ........................................................... more information at other location
* *See generally* .................................................. all related information at other location
* *See now* ........................................................... change of terminology or agency name

Cross-references to another main topic heading are indicated by the use of CAPITAL LETTERS. The word *"subheading"* may be included in the cross-reference to pinpoint the exact subentry language used for particular information. Internal cross-references are also used to link one subheading to another under the same topic heading. The phrase *"this heading"* appears at the end of these cross-references.

This index, which is updated every four months, provides in-depth analysis of disability law topics. The *NEWSLETTER* is indexed separately, and that index is filed with the newsletters.

See also the Table of Cases for a listing of court decisions.

---

**A**

**ABSENCES**
*See* LEAVES OF ABSENCE

**ACCESS BOARD**
*See* ARCHITECTURAL AND TRANSPOR-TATION BARRIERS COMPLIANCE BOARD (ACCESS BOARD)

**ACCESS ROUTES**
*See* ACCESSIBILITY GUIDELINES (ADAAG), *subheading:* Routes

**ACCESS TO INFORMATION**
*See also* CONFIDENTIALITY
Federal contractor records, OFCCP regulation (41 CFR 60-741.81), 70:0331

**ACCESSIBILITY GUIDELINES (ADAAG)**
*See also* ACCESSIBILITY REQUIRE-MENTS; *specific facilities*
*Ed. Note: Numbers prefixed by ADAAG refer to sections of Appendix A to 28 CFR Part 36.*
Full text, Appx. A to 28 CFR Part 36, 70:0201 et seq.
—Proposed amendments, interim final guidelines, 70:2041 et seq.
—Advisory committee recommendations, Spl Supp (11/14/96)
Additions
—Definition (ADAAG 3.5), 70:0204 et seq.
—DOJ technical assistance manual, 90:0951
—Generally (ADAAG 4.1.5), 70:0212
—State and local government facilities (ADAAG 4.1.5), 70:2229
Adults, provisions based on (ADAAG 2.1), 70:0203
Airports (ADAAG 10.4), 70:0274
Alarms. *See* ALARMS

Alterations
—Bus stops (ADAAG 10.2.2), 70:0271
—Curb ramps (ADAAG 4.1.6(3)(a)), 70:0214
—Definition (ADAAG 3.5), 70:0204 et seq.
—DOJ regulation (28 CFR 36.406), 70:0194
—DOJ technical assistance manual, 90:0951
—Doors (ADAAG 4.1.6(3)(d)), 70:0214
—Dressing rooms (ADAAG 4.1.6(3)(h)), 70:0215
—Entrances (ADAAG 4.1.6(1)(h), A4.1.6(1)(h)), 70:0213, 0284
—Escalators (ADAAG 4.1.6(1)(f)), 70:0213
—Exceptions (ADAAG 4.1.6(1)(i-k)), 70:0213-14
—Generally (ADAAG 4.1.6), 70:0213 et seq.
—Primary function areas (ADAAG 4.1.6(2)), 70:0214
—Ramps (ADAAG 4.1.6(3)(a)), 70:0214
—Social service establishments, transient lodging (ADAAG 9.5.2), 70:0269-70
—Stairways (ADAAG 4.1.6(1)(d),(3)(b)), 70:0213-14

---

**If you were interested in researching "Public Accommodations," you might review the section that describes the ADA's public accommodation requirements.**

**FIGURE 9.10**   EXCERPT FROM PUBLIC ACCOMMODATIONS, *BNA'S AMERICANS WITH DISABILITIES ACT MANUAL*

No. 117
30:0001

## Introduction to Title III

Textual description of ADA statutory and regulatory provisions on public accommodations

### Overview

III of the ADA prohibits discrimination on the basis of disability by private entities in places of public odation—facilities open to the public, including certain mixed-use and commercial facilities. According III, places of public accommodation must remove barriers to access and must provide appropriate ive services when physical barriers cannot be removed.

chapter explains what types of public accommodations are covered, compliance requirements, and what Title III requires for new construction and alterations.

### Title III Basics

#### Who Is Covered?

Title III prohibits disability-based discrimination in the "full and equal enjoyment" of goods, services, privileges, advantages, or accommodations of any place of public accommodation by anyone who owns, leases, leases to, or operates a place of public accommodation (42 U.S.C. § 12182(a); see Tab 70). Private entities are considered public accommodations if their operations "affect commerce" among states, between a state and a foreign country, or between points in the same state but through another state or foreign country (42 U.S.C. § 12181(1); see Tab 70).

Title III is enforced by the Justice Department, which issued implementing regulations (28 C.F.R. Part 36; see Tab 70). DOJ also issued a Technical Assistance Manual to help employers and businesses comply with the law (see Tab 90).

Federal government facilities are not covered by the ADA, but are covered by the 1973 Rehabilitation Act.

Cross-reference to a C.F.R. Part. It can be located in the C.F.R. or within this service under Tab 70.

#### What Is a Public Accommodation?

gh the terminology can sometimes be confus-
e III covers public accommodations—that is,
that are open to the public—but are owned or
by private entities—meaning nongovernmen-
s. Public facilities and services of state and
ernmental bodies are covered by Title II. (See
or information on Title II.)

rm "public accommodations" encompasses a
wide range of facilities, including:

- hotels, motels, and other places of lodging, unless they contain five rooms or less for rental and are occupied by the proprietor as a residence;
- restaurants, bars, and other establishments serving food or drink;
- theaters, concert halls, stadiums, and other places of entertainment;
- stores and shopping centers;
- service establishments such as laundromats, drycleaners, banks, travel services, funeral parlors, and

professional offices of lawyers and health care providers;

- terminals and stations used for public transportation;
- parks, zoos, and other places of recreation;
- daycare centers, senior citizen centers, homeless shelters, and social service establishments; and
- health spas, bowling alleys, and other places of exercise.

Title III also applies to courses and examinations related to licensing and certification for professional or trade purposes.

Both the landlord who owns a public accommodation and the tenant who operates a public accommodation are subject to the ADA's requirements. A lease or contract may be used to determine the extent of each party's responsibility. However, allocations made in a lease or other contract are effective only between the parties; both landlord and tenant remain fully liable for ADA compliance (28 C.F.R. § 36.201(b); see Tab 70).

*Mixed-Use Facilities*

Mixed-use facilities are those that include facilities and services that are open to the public. The public portions are covered by Title III, while the other portions are exempt.

For example, a private childcare center operating in space leased from a church is covered by Title III, while the church itself is exempt from ADA coverage as a "religious entity" (28 C.F.R. § 36.102(e), see Tab 70; TAM § III-1.5000, see Tab 90).

Similarly, a private club is not covered by Title III. However, private club facilities lose their exemption to the extent that they are made available to nonmembers as places of public accommodation. For example, a meeting room rented to an outside organization must comply with the act.

A mixed-use hotel with residential and lodging wings is covered by Title III requirements as to the short-term lodging portion of the establishment, while the residential portion is covered by the Fair Housing Act (42 U.S.C. §§ 3601-3631). If "separate and discrete

10–11–01          Copyright © 2001 by The Bureau of National Affairs, Inc.

Reproduced with permission from *BNA's Americans with Disabilities Act Manual*, p. 30:0001. Copyright 2001 by The Bureau of National Affairs, Inc. (800-372-1033) <http://www.bna.com>.

**Working either from the Master Index or the cross-references in the discussion of public accommodations, you could find regulations defining public accommodation.**

**FIGURE 9.11**   28 C.F.R. Pt. 36, *REPRINTED IN BNA'S AMERICANS WITH DISABILITIES ACT MANUAL*

---

No. 93
70:0185

### Justice Department: Americans with Disabilities Act Public Accommodations Regulations

*Following is the text of rules issued by the Justice Department to implement Title III, the public accommodations portion, of the Americans with Disabilities Act. Codified as 28 CFR Part 36, the rules were issued July 26, 1991, at 56 FR 35592, and became effective January 26, 1992. The rules read as last amended Aug. 30, 1999 (64 FR 47099), effective Sept. 29, 1999. The preamble to the rules starts on p. 70:0131.*

Regulations

**PART 36 — NONDISCRIMINATION ON THE BASIS OF DISABILITY BY PUBLIC ACCOMMODATIONS AND IN COMMERCIAL FACILITIES**

**Table of Contents**

**Subpart A—General**

Section
36.101   Purpose.
36.102   Application.
36.103   Relationship to Other Laws.
36.104   Definitions.
36.105-36.200 [Reserved]

**Subpart B—General Requirements**
36.201   General.
36.202   Activities.
36.203   Integrated Settings.
36.204   Administrative Methods.
36.205   Association.
36.206   Retaliation or Coercion.
36.207   Places of Public Accommodations Located in Private Residences.
36.208   Direct Threat.
36.209   Illegal Use of Drugs.
36.210   Smoking.
36.211   Maintenance of Accessible Features.
36.212   Insurance.
36.213   Relationship of subpart B to subparts C and D of This Part.
36.214-36.300 [Reserved]

**Subpart C—Specific Requirements**
36.301   Eligibility Criteria.
36.302   Modifications in Policies, Practices, or Procedures.
36.303   Auxiliary Aids and Services.
36.304   Removal of Barriers.
36.305   Alternatives to Barrier Removal.
36.306   Personal Devices and Services.
36.307   Accessible or Special Goods.
36.308   Seating in Assembly Areas.
36.309   Examinations and Courses.
36.310   Transportation Provided by Public Accommodations.
36.311-36.400 [Reserved]

**Subpart D—New Construction and Alterations**

36.401   New Construction.
36.402   Alterations.
36.403   Alterations: Path of Travel.
36.404   Alterations: Elevator Exemption.
36.405   Alterations: Historic Preservation.
36.406   Standards for New Construction and Alterations.
36.407   Temporary Suspension of Certain Detectable Warning Requirements.
36.408-36.500 [Reserved]

**Subpart E—Enforcement**
36.501   Private Suits.
36.502   Investigations and Compliance Reviews.
36.503   Suit by the Attorney General.
36.504   Relief.
36.505   Attorney's Fees.
36.506   Alternative Means of Dispute Resolution.
36.507   Effect of Unavailability of Technical Assistance.
36.508   Effective Date.
36.509-36.600 [Reserved]

**Subpart F—Certification of State Laws or Local Building Codes**
36.601   Definitions.
36.602   General rule.
36.603   Filing a Request for Certification.
36.604   Preliminary Determination.
36.605   Procedure Following Preliminary Determination of Equivalency.
36.606   Procedure following Preliminary Denial of Certification.
36.607   Effect of Certification.
36.608   Guidance Concerning Model Codes.
36.609-36.999 [Reserved]
Appendix A to Part 36—Standards for Accessible Design
Appendix B to Part 36—Preamble to Regulation on Nondiscrimination on the Basis of Disability by Public Accommodations and in Commercial Facilities (Published July 26, 1991)

**Authority:** 5 U.S.C. 301; 28 U.S.C. 509, 510; sec. 306(b), Pub. L. 101-336, 104 Stat. 361, 362 (42 U.S.C. 12186).

**Subpart A—General**

**Sec. 36.101. Purpose**

The purpose of this part is to implement title III of the Americans with Disabilities Act of 1990 (42 U.S.C. 12181), which prohibits discrimination on the basis of disability by public accommodations and requires places of public accommodation and commercial facilities to be designed, constructed, and altered in compliance with the accessibility standards established by this part.

**Sec. 36.102. Application**

(a) *General.* This part applies to any —
(1) Public accommodation;
(2) Commercial facility; or
(3) Private entity that offers examinations or courses related to applications, licensing, certification, or credentialing for secondary or postsecondary education, professional, or trade purposes.

(b) *Public accommodations.*
(1) The requirements of this part applicable to public accommodations are set forth in subparts B, C, and D of this part.
(2) The requirements of subparts B and C of this part obligate a public accommodation only with respect to the operations of a place of public accommodation.
(3) The requirements of subpart D of this part obligate a public accommodation only with respect to —
(i) A facility used as, or designed or constructed for use as, a place of public accommodation; or
(ii) A facility used as, or designed and constructed for use as, a commercial facility.

(c) *Commercial facilities.* The requirements of this part applicable to commercial facilities are set forth in subpart D of this part.

(d) *Examinations and courses.* The requirements of this part applicable to private entities that offer examinations or courses as specified in paragraph (a) of this section are set forth in Sec. 36.309.

10–14–99

Copyright © 1999 by The Bureau of National Affairs, Inc.

BNA's *Americans with Disabilities Cases* (A.D. Cases) is a reporter service. You can locate cases in A.D. Cases using the Cumulative Digest and Index accompanying that service. The "Introduction" in the front of each volume of the Cumulative Digest and Index explains how to locate cases.

**FIGURE 9.12**   CUMULATIVE DIGEST AND INDEX, BNA'S A.D. CASES

---

Description of the organization of A.D. Cases

## INTRODUCTION

This Americans with Disabilities Cases Cumulative Digest and Index (CDI) volume organizes, under AD Cases classification numbers (e.g., ▸333.29), concise descriptions of case holdings on points of disability law.

Case references (e.g., 6 AD Cases 1865) are to volumes and page numbers of cases reported in Americans with Disabilities Cases volumes 1-6, covering the period 1974 - August 18, 1997.

The Outline of Classifications (page 1) provides descriptions of the classification numbers. Scope notes under the descriptions of the classification number indicate other classification numbers where related cases may be found. Additionally, an Outline in Brief is provided at the beginning of each section. A Star (⋆) appearing after a classification number in the Outline in Brief indicates that there are no reported cases for the period covered.

The Topic Finder (page 51) is an alphabetical arrangement by descriptive words and phrases of all material covered in the classification scheme. References in the Topic Finder are to classification numbers.

The Table of Cases (page 1869) lists court decisions by both forward and reverse titles, and indicates the court or agency that handed down the opinion, the history of the case, official parallel citations, and the volume and page number where the case appears in AD Cases volumes.

Instructions for researching begin here.

## RESEARCHING BY SUBJECT

1. Turn first to the Topic Finder to locate your subject. Note the classification number and turn to it in the Cumulative Digest and Index (CDI) to find concise descriptions of all decisions on point.

2. Alternatively, turn to the Outline of Classifications. A quick survey of the main sections will lead you to the general subject in which you are interested. Note the applicable classification number(s), turn to the CDI, and proceed to the description of the decisions.

## RESEARCHING BY CASE NAME

Turn to the Table of Cases to get the page citation in AD Cases volumes, and proceed to the volume and page indicated. Related decisions may be obtained by using the classification numbers assigned to the headnotes appearing at the start of every decision. Proceed to the CDI using these classification numbers.

v

**FIGURE 9.12** CUMULATIVE DIGEST AND INDEX, BNA'S A.D. CASES *(Continued)*

## ORDER OF DIGESTS

Rulings of law in the Cumulative Digest and Index volumes are grouped under the various classification numbers by tribunal in the following order:

1. Supreme Court of the United States.

2. United States Court of Appeals, in order of circuit number (including Court of Appeals for the District of Columbia and Court of Appeals for the Federal Circuit).

3. Federal District Courts, in alphabetical order of states in which courts are sitting, U.S. Court of Federal Claims, U.S. Bankruptcy Courts, and Judicial Panel on Multi-district Litigation (JPML).

4. State, county, and city courts, in alphabetical order of states.

5. EEOC decisions.

Under each tribunal, rulings appear in the order of the volume and page where the case was reported in AD Cases.

## CITATIONS

Each entry in the CDI is followed by the name of the case, the tribunal that made the ruling, the date of the decision, and the volume and page number where the case can be found in AD Cases.

vi

**A.D. Cases organizes cases according to "classification numbers." One way to locate classification numbers is through the "Topic Finder," an alphabetical subject index near the beginning of each volume of the Cumulative Digest and Index.**

**FIGURE 9.13**   A.D. CASES TOPIC FINDER

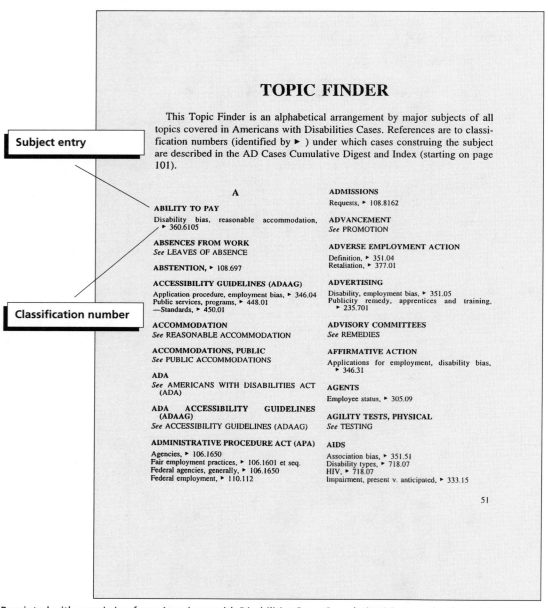

Reprinted with permission from *Americans with Disabilities Cases Cumulative Digest and Index*, Table of Cases, Vol. 1–6 (1974–1997), p. 51. Copyright 2002 by The Bureau of National Affairs, Inc. (800-372-1033) <http://www.bna.com>.

**Once you have identified useful classification numbers, you can find case summaries by looking up the classification numbers in the digest section of the Cumulative Digest and Index. Because each volume of the Cumulative Digest and Index covers only a certain period of time, you may need to look through several volumes to complete your research.**

**FIGURE 9.14** CASE SUMMARIES, A.D. CASES CUMULATIVE DIGEST AND INDEX

---

AD CDI        ENFORCEMENT        ▶575.01

▶ **567.01 In general**

**U.S. Courts of Appeals**

NLRB's decision that employer, which provides transportation services to elderly and disabled clients, violated §8(2)(1) of LMRA by its work rule providing for immediate dismissal of employees who discuss problems and complaints about employer with passengers does not violate ADA or Minn. Vulnerable Adults Act, since decision does not prevent employer from taking steps to protect passengers with disabilities. —*Handicabs Inc. v. National Labor Relations Bd.* (CA 8, 9/11/96) 5 AD Cases 1484

**U.S. District Courts**

Blind couple who were refused boarding by tour bus driver because of their guide dog lack standing to seek injunctive relief against tour bus company, there being no real and immediate threat that they will be subject to repeated injury by tour bus company, as they have not shown that they are likely to use same buses in near future or that, if they do use them, company is likely to violate their rights under ADA again. —*O'Brien v. Werner Bus Lines Inc.* (DC EPa, 2/26/96) 5 AD Cases 444

Blind couple who seek injunction against tour bus company whose driver refused to let them board with their guide dog have not shown likelihood that they are going to use company's buses in near future, where record does not show that couple used its buses regularly or even on occasion before incident.—*Id.*

Blind couple who seek injunctive relief against tour bus company whose driver refused to let them board with their guide dog have not shown that company is likely to violate their rights under ADA again, where company president immediately recognized error, apologized to couple, and took corrective measures by addressing issue with his drivers through memorandum, individual communication, discussion at drivers' meetings, and drivers' handbook.—*Id.*

Tour bus company's evidence of its efforts to instruct its drivers on its non-biased policy regarding disabled passengers shifts burden in summary judgment proceeding to blind couple, who had not been allowed to board tour bus because of their guide dog, to provide evidence that those efforts are inadequate, such as by showing that incidents of bias have occurred following its efforts, by introducing expert testimony of inadequacy of those efforts, or by showing pattern of past conduct so permeated with bias that inadequacy of simple corrective procedures is obvious.—*Id.*

▶ **575. Enforcement**

▶ **575.01 In general**

**U.S. Courts of Appeals**

Lower court was warranted in concluding that DOJ regulation concerning duty of newly constructed public facility to provide wheelchair seats with lines of sight over standing spectators required only substantial compliance rather than 100% compliance, where DOJ never indicated in technical assistance manual whether every wheelchair location must be afforded view over standing spectators. —*Paralyzed Veterans of America v. D.C. Arena L.P.* (CA DC, 7/1/97) 6 AD Cases 1614

Doubts about scope of injunction that disabled individuals who seek total ban on smoking at all of two companies' fast-food restaurants could be entitled to do not justify dismissal of ADA action in view of fact that they have alleged cognizable claims, at least with respect to restaurants that they expect to visit.

—*Staron v. McDonald's Corp.* (CA 2, 4/4/95) 4 AD Cases 353

Beer brewery did not establish that proposed modification of its blanket "no animals" policy to permit guide dogs to accompany blind visitors on its public brewery tour would either fundamentally alter its nature or would jeopardize safety, and it was thus required to make modification under ADA. —*Johnson v. Gambrinus Co./Spoetzl Brewery* (CA 5, 3/27/97) 6 AD Cases 1115

Lower court had no duty to delineate exact nature of changes that beer brewery must make before concluding that it violated ADA in not modifying its blanket "no animals" policy to allow guide dog to accompany blind visitor on its public brewery tour, where visitor met his burden of showing that modification of policy is reasonable in run of cases, and it therefore must make modification unless it can establish affirmative defense.—*Id.*

*For Guidance see Introduction*        1527

**Classification numbers**

**Case summary**

---

**The full text of cases summarized in the Cumulative Digest and Index appear in the A.D. Cases reporter volumes.**

**FIGURE 9.15**   *ARNOLD v. UNITED ARTISTS THEATRE CIRCUIT*

---

ARNOLD v. UNITED ARTISTS THEATRE CIRCUIT     5 AD Cases 685

**YOUNG v. ST. LUKE'S-ROOSEVELT HOSPITAL CTR.**

**U.S. District Court, Southern District of New York**

SONJA YOUNG, Plaintiff v. ST. LUKE'S-ROOSEVELT HOSPITAL CENTER, Defendant, No. 95 CIV 6077(HB), March 25, 1996

**AMERICANS WITH DISABILITIES ACT**

**Amendment of complaint** ▶108.7221 ▶708.01

Former employee, to avoid dismissal of her ADA action, must amend complaint by providing statements or other documentation from former supervisor and from emergency room doctor who treated her for epiglottal attack that focuses on nature and severity of her bronchitis and upper respiratory impairment, duration or expected duration of bronchitis, and its permanent or long-term impact on her health; among matters that would be relevant would be number of absences that she took in five-year period before her last absence, length of those absences, and type of treatment that she received.

---

Sonja Young, New York, N.Y., plaintiff pro se.
Michael L. Stevens and Jennifer Pitarresi (Arent, Fox, Kintner, Plotkin & Kahn), Washington, D.C., for defendant.

*Full Text of Opinion*

HAROLD BAER, Jr., District Judge: — Plaintiff Sonja Young filed this employment discrimination claim pursuant to the Americans with Disabilities Act ("ADA") of 1990. Defendants St. Luke's-Roosevelt Hospital Center moves this Court pursuant to Fed. R. Civ. Pro. 12(b)(6) to dismiss plaintiff's complaint.

Papers having been filed and oral argument having been heard on these motions on March 21, 1996 and due deliberation having been had, defendant St. Luke's motion to dismiss plaintiff's complaint is held in abeyance. Plaintiff has thirty days from the date hereof to amend her complaint and submit additional information in support of her claim. Should the plaintiff fail to do so within this thirty day period the motion will be granted.

During this thirty day period, plaintiff will obtain statements or other

documentation from her former supervisor during her employment at St. Luke's from the 1988 to 1993 and from a doctor who treated her in the emergency room for an epiglottal attack. Defendant is to provide plaintiff with the addresses of these former St. Luke's employees as soon as conveniently possible. Plaintiff should focus her inquiry on three areas. First, the nature and severity of her bronchitis and upper respiratory impairment. Instances regarding how many absences due to bronchitis plaintiff took from 1988 to 1993 prior to her twelve day absence in 1993, this to evidence how debilitating the attacks were. Second, the duration or expected duration of plaintiff's bronchitis. The length of plaintiff's prior absences in the 1988 to 1993 period and what type of treatment plaintiff received would be relevant. Third, the permanent or long term impact, or the projected permanent or long term impact of or resulting from the bronchitis and upper respiratory infections to plaintiff's health.

Unless plaintiff provides the Court with additional information obtained from these or other prospective witnesses within the thirty day period, defendant's motion to dismiss plaintiff's claim will be granted.

SO ORDERED.

---

**ARNOLD v. UNITED ARTISTS THEATRE CIRCUIT**

**U.S. District Court, Northern District of California**

CONNIE ARNOLD, et al., Plaintiffs v. UNITED ARTISTS THEATRE CIRCUIT, INC., Defendant, No. C 93-0079 TEH, April 26, 1994; Memorandum Opinion and Order September 15, 1994

**AMERICANS WITH DISABILITIES ACT**

1. **Title III — Class action** ▶519.01 ▶575.01 ▶700.38

Action under Title III of ADA challenging movie theater company's alleged failure to comply, in both existing and new theaters, with regulations concerning seating for wheelchair users and other mobility-impaired persons satisfies requirements for certification of class, where number of persons af-

> The case begins here.

**FIGURE 9.15** *ARNOLD v. UNITED ARTISTS THEATRE CIRCUIT (Continued)*

---

5 AD Cases 686       ARNOLD v. UNITED ARTISTS THEATRE CIRCUIT

fected by alleged access violations at more than 70 theaters numbers in thousands, company's accommodations at particular theaters are very likely to affect all wheelchair users or semi-ambulatory persons in same way, class representatives possess same interests and rely on same legal theories as other members of proposed class, and they have no individual claims different from those of other class members.

**2. Title III — Class action ▸575.01 ▸700.38**

Class action under Title III of ADA challenging movie theater company's alleged failure to comply, in both existing and new theaters, with regulations concerning seating for wheelchair users and other mobility-impaired persons will be certified under Rule 23(b)(2) of Federal Rules of Civil Procedure, even though damages are sought ... te law, since class is remark-... ogeneous in that all members ... enging company's refusal to ... ertain architectural features ... its various theaters that af-... of them in almost precisely ...

... **action ▸575.01 ▸700.38**

... mbulatory persons cannot be included within class of persons who can challenge movie theater company's alleged failure to comply, in both existing and new theaters, with regulations concerning seating for wheelchair users and other mobility-impaired persons, since Title III of ADA does not impose any specific requirements regarding semi-ambulatory seating.

**4. Bifurcation ▸575.01**

Class action under Title III and state law against movie theater company for allegedly failing to comply with regulations concerning seating for wheelchair users and other mobility-impaired persons will be bifurcated, with issues of liability, injunctive and declaratory relief, and damages for named class representatives being tried in first phase and damages for other class members being tried in second phase.

**5. Title III ▸503.01**

Showing of intent to discriminate is not element of cause of action under Title III of ADA.

**6. Enforcement ▸575.01**

Use of separate juries to hear liability and classwide damages phases of class action under Title III of ADA is constitutionally permissible.

Lawrence W. Paradis (Miller Starr & Regalia), Oakland, Calif., and Elaine Feingold, Berkeley, Calif., for plaintiffs Connie Arnold and Ann Cupulo.

Lawrence W. Paradis (Miller Starr & Regalia), Oakland, Calif., and Brad Seligman, Berkeley, Calif., for plaintiffs Howard Ripley, Julianna Cyril, Cynde Soto, and Cyrus Berlowitz.

Peter I. Ostroff (Sidley & Austin), Los Angeles, Calif., Michael W. O'Neil, Orinda, Calif., for defendant United Artists Theatre Circuit, Inc.

David H. Raizman, Los Angeles, Calif., for California Assn. of Persons with Handicaps and California Foundation of Independent Living Centers, amici curiae.

Jane C. Pandell and Randy Wright (Pandell Norvich & Borsuk), Walnut Creek, Calif., for Raad/Uesugi & Associates, Stan Stanovich, and Heidenfrost/Harowits & Associates.

Patrick M. Glenn (Hanson Bridgett Marcus Vlahos & Rudy), San Francisco, Calif., for Irwin Seating Co.

Stephen Goldberg (Spierer Woodward Denis & Furstman), Redondo Beach, Calif., and Thomas L. Wolf (Myer Swanson & Adams), ... Colo., for Proctor Co.

Timothy L. McInerney (... & Dillon, P.C.), Oakland, ... Tolladay Construction Co., ...

*Full Text of Opinion*

THELTON E. HENDERSON, Chief Judge: — This case is a suit by disabled persons who use wheelchairs or who walk using aids such as crutches, brought against United Artists Theatre Circuit, Inc. ("United Artists" or "UA"). Plaintiffs charge that defendant's movie theaters do not afford disabled persons full and equal access to their accommodations, in violation of California and federal law.

Plaintiffs have filed motions seeking certification of the suit as a class action under Rule 23(b)(2) of the Federal Rules of Civil Procedure ("Rules") and bifurcation of the trial. The Court heard oral argument on this matter on March 7, 1994. After consideration of the parties' written and oral arguments, the Court, for the reasons set forth below, GRANTS plaintiffs' motion for certification of this suit as a Rule 23(b)(2) class action, and GRANTS plaintiffs' motion for bifurcation of the trial.

**I. PLAINTIFFS' MOTION
FOR CLASS CERTIFICATION**

**A. NATURE OF THE MOTION**

Plaintiffs seek certification of this lawsuit as a class action under subpart

---

> **AD Cases headnote with a classification number. This does not correspond to a West topic or key number.**

> **The opinion begins here.**

## G. CHECKLIST FOR SUBJECT-MATTER SERVICE RESEARCH

### 1. LOCATE A SUBJECT-MATTER SERVICE FOR YOUR RESEARCH ISSUE

❐ Look in Table T.16 in the back of the *Bluebook*.

❐ Check a reference source such as *Legal Looseleafs in Print* or *Directory of Law-Related CD-ROMs*.

❐ Locate subject area databases in LexisNexis and Westlaw.

### 2. DETERMINE HOW TO USE THE SERVICE

❐ In print services, look for the "Overview" or "How to use this service" section.

❐ In CD-ROM services, follow the service's instructions for locating information.

- In Premise-based services, search as you would in Westlaw.
- In Folio-based services, choose an infobase and locate information by browsing the full text, reviewing the table of contents, or executing a query.

❐ In LexisNexis and Westlaw, execute word searches.

### 3. USE THE INTERNET TO LOCATE INFORMATION ON THE SUBJECT

❐ Search subscription subject-matter services available on your library's computer network.

❐ Use publicly available information in your research.

- Locate helpful web sites.
- Verify who maintains the site.
- Update authorities located on the Internet and continue researching in traditional legal research tools.

# CHAPTER 10

# Electronic Legal Research

A. Introduction to electronic legal research

B. Selecting an electronic legal research service

C. Constructing, executing, and reviewing an electronic word search

D. Researching effectively in Westlaw and LexisNexis

E. Citing electronic legal research services

F. Sample pages for electronic legal research

G. Checklist for electronic legal research

As Chapter 1 explains, legal research can be accomplished using both print and electronic research tools. Frequently, you will use some combination of these tools in completing a research project. Although print and electronic resources are often used together, this chapter introduces you to some search techniques unique to electronic research. Earlier chapters discussed both print and electronic research in the context of individual types of authority, such as cases or statutes. This chapter explains some of the basics of electronic searching that can be used effectively in a number of services, regardless of the type of authority you need to locate. In doing so, it focuses on research in Westlaw and LexisNexis, two of the most commonly available commercial services containing a wide variety of legal authority. Although Westlaw and LexisNexis are featured in this chapter, they are only two of many electronic research services available, and you should be able to adapt the techniques described here to other electronic research services.

This chapter describes electronic search techniques in general terms and provides few specific commands for executing them. Electronic research providers update their services regularly, thus making it impossible to describe commands with any accuracy. In fact, you will likely receive training through your law school on the use of at least Westlaw and LexisNexis, if not other electronic services, and those training sessions will cover the commands necessary to execute the functions in those services. In addition, print or on-line instructions should be available for any electronic service you use, and these instructions should contain up-to-date information for executing search commands. A single instruction session on any electronic service cannot convey all of the nuances involved in researching with it, so you should plan to review additional instructional material for any electronic service you learn to use.

## A. INTRODUCTION TO ELECTRONIC LEGAL RESEARCH

### 1. OVERVIEW OF ELECTRONIC LEGAL RESEARCH SERVICES

Electronic legal research services can be divided into three categories. Fee-based services charge individual users a fee every time the service is used. Subscription services charge the subscriber for access, but individual users ordinarily are not charged for researching in the service. Publicly available services are those available for free on the Internet to anyone with a modem and a web browser. Appendix A contains the Internet addresses for a number of publicly available research sites, including those discussed in this chapter and elsewhere in this text. A brief overview of some popular electronic legal research services follows.

#### a. Fee-Based Services

**WESTLAW AND LEXISNEXIS.** As noted earlier, Westlaw and LexisNexis are two of the most commonly available electronic services for conducting legal research. Both of these services contain the full text of a broad range of primary and secondary authorities.

**LOISLAW.** Loislaw is similar to Westlaw and LexisNexis, in that it contains the full text of many legal authorities. It also contains treatises on a number of subjects and has its own citator service, GlobalCite. Although Loislaw has less comprehensive coverage than either Westlaw or LexisNexis, it can be a cost-effective alternative to those services if it contains the information you need. Loislaw is available on the Internet.

**VERSUSLAW.** VersusLaw is similar to Loislaw. It also offers access to the full text of a range of legal authorities, and like Loislaw, it can be a cost-effective alternative to Westlaw and LexisNexis. As of this writing, however, its coverage is also less comprehensive than that of Westlaw and LexisNexis. VersusLaw is available on the Internet.

#### b. Subscription Services

**LEXISNEXIS CONGRESSIONAL.** This service is described in more detail in Chapter 7, on federal legislative history research. It is a subscription service available at many law libraries. LexisNexis Congressional contains a wealth of legislative information, including federal statutes, Congressional documents generated during the legislative process, administrative regulations, and news about activities taking place on Capitol Hill.

**INDEX TO LEGAL PERIODICALS AND LEGALTRAC.** These are index services, meaning that they will generate lists of citations to authority but will not retrieve the full text of the documents. They provide citations to secondary sources and are described in more detail in Chapter 3.

**SUBJECT-MATTER SERVICES.** Chapter 9 discusses research in defined subject areas of the law using specialized subject-matter services. A number of subject-matter services are available electronically, either on the Internet or in CD-ROM format. Many CD-ROM services use research platforms called Premise or Folio, both of which are explained in more detail in Chapter 9. The techniques for drafting searches described in this chapter can be used effectively in many electronic subject-matter services.

## c. Publicly Available Services

**WEB SITES OPERATED BY GOVERNMENT OR PRIVATE ENTITIES.** Government web sites can provide access to local, state, and federal legal information. Some examples of useful sites for federal law include Thomas, which is maintained by the Library of Congress, and GPO Access, a site operated by the Government Printing Office. These services are described in Chapters 7 and 8. Many courts also maintain web sites where they publish the full text of opinions, local court rules, and other useful information. In addition, as noted in Chapter 9, web sites operated by trade, civic, educational, or other groups may provide useful information in their specialized fields.

**LEGAL RESEARCH WEB SITES.** A number of Internet sites collect legal information, and these can be useful research sources. Examples of legal research web sites include FindLaw and American Law Sources Online. In addition, several law schools have developed "virtual law library" sites, such as Cornell Law School's Legal Information Institute.

**INTERNET SEARCH ENGINES.** A search engine is a point of entry into the Internet. It is a service that allows you to execute a search or query to locate publicly available Internet sites, much as you would search for individual documents in Westlaw or LexisNexis. Services such as Google, AltaVista, and Yahoo process queries by searching throughout the Internet for web sites that contain some or all of the terms specified. Another service, LawCrawler, limits its searches to law-related web sites, and a service known as MetaCrawler has a function that links several search engines together. This allows you to run your search through several search engines simultaneously.

An Internet search engine is not likely to be an effective tool for locating individual legal authorities. It may, however, help you locate government, educational, legal research, or other web sites with useful information.

## 2. OVERVIEW OF ELECTRONIC SEARCH TECHNIQUES

Before you undertake the process of electronic research, you need to assess the search options available to you. This will help you decide whether electronic research is your best option or whether print resources are a better choice. Chapter 11, on creating a research plan, touches on this issue. This section explains four techniques for searching electronically and compares them with techniques for print research.

The four primary methods of locating information in an electronic research service are: (1) retrieving a document when you know its citation; (2) browsing a publication's table of contents; (3) searching by subject; and (4) searching for documents that contain words relevant to your research issue, otherwise known as "word searching." These are not the only ways of researching electronically, but they are the most common.

If you have a citation to a document contained in an electronic service's database, you can retrieve it using its citation. There is not much difference from a process perspective between retrieving a document in print or electronically using its citation. Your decision about how to obtain the document will probably turn on other considerations. Print resources are often more economical to use and easier to read than computer resources. In addition, many secondary sources are only available in print. By contrast, electronic resources can be more up to date than print materials and can give you access to documents unavailable in your library's print collection.

Browsing a publication's table of contents is another way to search. Often you can follow links, or drill down, through a publication's table of contents to view the text of individual sections of the document. Table of contents searching usually is not available for every publication in a service's database, but statutory codes and selected secondary sources can often be searched this way. From a process perspective, there is not much difference between browsing a table of contents in print and browsing it electronically. The same considerations that affect whether to use a print or an electronic source for citation searching will also influence your decision about which type of source to use for table of contents searching.

Another option is searching by subject. With this technique, you ordinarily select a subject from an alphabetical menu of topics and then select the source or type of authority that you want to search for information on the subject. To select a subject, you can drill down through menu options for general subjects to more specific subtopics. If you do not know which subject is most relevant to your research, many services will allow you to execute a search within the menu options to identify relevant subjects or subtopics. After you drill down through the menu options, you will often also have the choice of adding a word search to further refine the search.

Searching electronically by subject combines aspects of searching a print table of contents and a print index. The menu options you can select will usually be broad subjects like those in a table of contents, but you will usually be able to drill down through the menu options to specific subtopics like entries in a print index. Electronic subject searching can be an effective search technique when you know the general subject area you want to search. In addition, you can often use electronic subject searches to search several publications simultaneously, whereas with print research you must search one publication at a time.

There are, however, limitations on electronic subject searching. The content and organization of subject categories vary by service, as do the precision and accuracy with which authorities are assigned to the categories. You should also be aware that many services will not allow you to search for all types of authority by subject. Subject searching may be limited to cases and selected secondary sources. Therefore, if you need to search for a type of authority that is not searchable by subject, or if you need to tailor your search more specifically, using a print index or electronic word search may be more effective.

Electronic word searching is available for virtually any source contained in an electronic service's database. It is most like searching in a print index, although there are significant differences between word searches and print indices. Most print indices are organized around subjects or concepts, rather than individual words in a document. This distinguishes them from electronic word searches, which locate documents based on individual terms, rather than by subject. Obviously, there is a fair amount of overlap between subjects or concepts and the words used to express them, and some entries in a print index are generated from specific terms or key words within the document. Nevertheless, electronic word searching and print index searching are not identical.

For example, if you were trying to find information on cars in a book that uses the term "automobile" instead of "car," you still might find the word "car" in the index, perhaps with a cross-reference to an entry for "automobile." If you researched the same publication in electronic form, a word search for the term "car" would not retrieve any information because the word search is limited to the exact terms you specify. This difference is one of the main factors that will determine whether you should use a word search. Word searches can be very effective for locating unique terms, but electronic subject searching (if it is available for the authority you need to locate) and print index searching can be better choices for searching by topic.

Experienced researchers rarely rely exclusively on either print or electronic research to complete a research project. Electronic research can be especially useful for locating one or two good "hits," or relevant documents, which you can then use as a springboard into other avenues of research. Understanding electronic search techniques will help you determine the mix of print and electronic research appropriate for your research project.

## 3. OVERVIEW OF THE ELECTRONIC RESEARCH PROCESS

Electronic research, like print research, is a process. You need to follow an organized plan to research effectively using electronic research tools. Effective electronic searching usually involves the following four steps.

### a. Selecting a Service

You want to choose the service or services most likely to contain the information you need. In addition, although you may not be concerned with the cost of research while you are in law school, in practice, selecting a cost-effective service is also an important consideration.

### b. Selecting a Search Technique

Once you have selected a service, you will probably have several options for searching for authority, including citation, table of contents, subject, and word searching. To search effectively, you must decide which method is most likely to retrieve the information you need. If you decide to use a word search, you will also need to construct a query that will retrieve the information you need.

### c. Selecting a Category of Information in Which to Execute a Search

After you select a search technique (and construct a word search if necessary), you are ready to sign on to a service and execute a search. Most of the time, you will not search through the entire contents of the service. The majority of services divide their contents into categories based on subjects, such as torts or criminal law, or on the sources of information they contain, such as federal cases or cases from an individual state. These categories of information may be called databases, libraries, files, infobases, or something similar. To retrieve information, you will need to select a category of information in which to execute the search.

### d. Reviewing the Search Results

Once you have executed a search, you will need to manipulate the results in a way that allows you to determine whether the search has been successful. You may need to view a list of documents retrieved, read the text of individual documents, find specific terms within a document, or use links to other documents. You may also need to refine the search to improve the search results.

Following these steps is not always a linear process. You might decide first on your search technique, which could influence the service you select. Even if you follow the steps in order initially, you may repeat some of them based on the search results. For example, after reviewing your search results, you might go back to the second step and select a different search technique. A single search is unlikely to retrieve exactly the desired information, except when you are retrieving a document you need from its citation. One provider offers the following explanation of the search process in the context of word searching:

> Searching is a process, not an event. This should be your mantra when using [electronic research services]. Searching . . . is not about spending time and mental energy formulating the "golden query" that retrieves your desired information in a single stroke. In practice, good online searching involves formulating a succession of queries until you are satisfied with the results. As you view results from one search, you will come across additional leads that you did not identify in your original search. You can incorporate these new terms into your existing query or create a new one. After each query, evaluate its success by asking:
> - Did I find what I was looking for?
> - What better information could still be out there?
> - How can I refine my query to find better information?
>
> Issuing multiple queries can be frustrating or rewarding, depending on how long it takes you to identify the key material you need to answer your research problem.[1]

Sections B, C, and D below discuss the electronic research process in greater detail. Section B discusses how to select an electronic research service. Section C discusses the remaining steps of the electronic research process in the context of word searching. Section D discusses techniques available in Westlaw and LexisNexis for reviewing and refining your search results.

---

[1]VersusLaw, Inc. Research Manual, Part 1, *Electronic Searching Strategy*, http://www.versuslaw.com/V/part1.asp (visited Dec. 28, 1998).

## B. SELECTING AN ELECTRONIC LEGAL RESEARCH SERVICE

Because many electronic legal research services exist, you must determine which service or services you should consult for your research project. Two important considerations are scope and cost.

The scope of the service is clearly a paramount consideration. You want to be sure to choose a service that contains the type of material you need. The more you know about your research issue, the easier this will be. For example, if you know you need to retrieve a United States Supreme Court case from the last term, you could research in Westlaw, LexisNexis, Loislaw, VersusLaw, or a publicly available legal research site containing Supreme Court decisions. If you know you need to research federal administrative regulations, you could research in Westlaw, LexisNexis, Loislaw, VersusLaw, LexisNexis Congressional, or GPO Access. Conversely, if you do not know the precise jurisdiction or type of authority you need, you might limit yourself to Westlaw or LexisNexis because those services contain a broad range of authorities.

After you have identified services with the proper scope of information, you should consider the cost of use. The cost of electronic research is something you might not notice as a law student because most, if not all, of the cost is subsidized. In practice, however, cost is an important consideration. You cannot use research services for which your client cannot or will not pay. Even if your client is willing and able to pay for some electronic research, you may not have unlimited ability to use fee-based services.

Of course, just because a service is fee-based does not mean it is a bad research option. It can be less expensive to locate authority through a fee-based service than it is to purchase books that would rarely be used, and some tasks can be accomplished more quickly through electronic research. In those situations, increased efficiency can justify the cost of using a fee-based service. You should not shy away from fee-based services simply because using them costs money. You should, however, be aware of cost issues and select the most cost-effective research options for your client, whether they are print or electronic, fee-based or free of charge.

It is difficult to generalize about the cost of fee-based services because many pricing options exist. Generally speaking, use of Westlaw and LexisNexis will result in the most direct expense to your client. Although some large organizations negotiate flat rates for use of these services, more frequently, charges will be based on the amount of time spent on-line, the number of searches executed, or both. Premiums may be charged for accessing certain sources, especially those containing multiple types of authority, and separate charges for printing or downloading information also may apply. Loislaw and VersusLaw charge for use of their services as well, but their rates are generally lower than those for Westlaw and LexisNexis. Therefore, if the scope of information available in one of those services is sufficient to meet your research needs, you might choose one of them over Westlaw or LexisNexis.

Because pricing varies widely among fee-based services, it is important to investigate cost issues before you get on-line. Regardless of the method of billing, efficient searching can reduce the cost associated with the use of fee-based services. Cost-cutting strategies for searching efficiently in Westlaw and LexisNexis are discussed in Section D below. These strategies can be used when searching in other fee-based services as well.

Subscription and publicly available services are economical choices for your client if they will give you the information you need. Although charges for access to subscription services are usually paid by the subscriber, rather than the user, users can be charged for printing or downloading information. Publicly available services on the Internet are the least expensive option because they involve only the cost of access to the Internet.

If scope and cost do not dictate which service you should use, use the service with which you are most familiar. The more familiar you become with a service, the more comfortable you will feel using it and the more efficient you will be. Although you should try to gain experience using as many services as possible while you are in law school, you may find in practice that you gravitate toward certain services that meet your research needs on a regular basis.

## C. CONSTRUCTING, EXECUTING, AND REVIEWING AN ELECTRONIC WORD SEARCH

Once you have selected a service, you are ready to begin searching for information. As noted earlier, one electronic search technique is word searching. To locate information using a word search, you will need to construct a search, select a category of information in which to execute the search, and review the results. This section discusses each of these topics.

### 1. CONSTRUCTING A WORD SEARCH

In word searching, the computer will search for the words in your query and retrieve documents containing the requested information. Most electronic services recognize two types of word searches: Boolean searches (sometimes called terms and connectors searches) and natural language searches. Figures 10.1 and 10.2 show the search screens from Westlaw and LexisNexis, respectively. The search features identified in these figures are explained in this section.

**FIGURE 10.1** WESTLAW SEARCH SCREEN

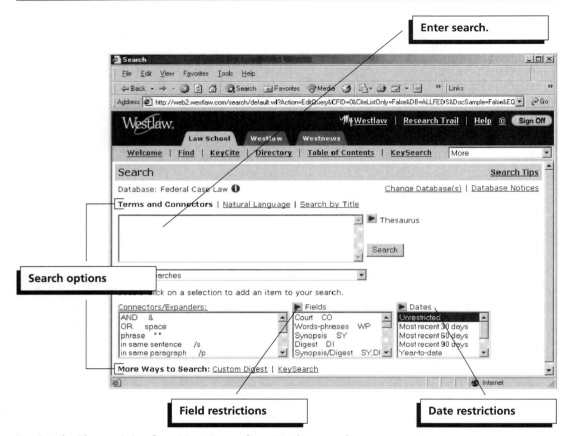

Reprinted with permission from West Group, from Westlaw, search screen.

## a. Boolean Searching

Boolean searching retrieves information based on the relationships among words in a document. Using specific commands, you can ask the computer to locate documents that contain certain words in defined relationships to other words. For example, you could search for documents that contain both the term "ice cream" and the term "sundae." Alternatively, you could search for documents that contain either the term "ice cream" or the term "sundae," but not necessarily both. In a Boolean search, the computer looks for documents containing the precise terms you identify, in the precise relationships you request.

### (1) Boolean search commands

In Boolean searching, you define the relationships among the terms in the search using "connectors." The most common connectors are AND and OR. AND retrieves documents containing all of the specified terms.

**FIGURE 10.2** LexisNexis SEARCH SCREEN

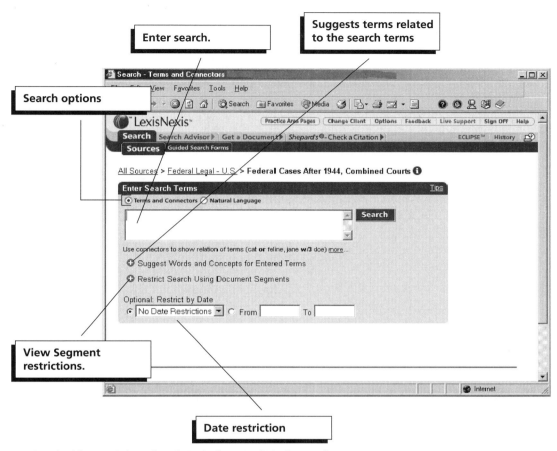

Reprinted with permission of LexisNexis, from LexisNexis, search screen.

OR retrieves documents containing any one of the specified terms. In addition to indicating relationships among words within the document as a whole, connectors can also indicate more specific relationships, such as terms appearing within a certain number of words of each other (/N), or within the same paragraph (/P) or sentence (/S). Some services use the connector ADJ (for adjacent) or NEAR to indicate words in proximity to each other, instead of allowing you to specify the proximity. The help function or search tips section of the service should indicate how close adjacent or near terms have to be to be captured by the search. Connectors can also be used to exclude terms. For example, the AND NOT connector allows you to search for documents that include one term and exclude another. The chart in Figure 10.3 shows some of the more common connectors.

You can search for individual terms within a Boolean search, or you

**FIGURE 10.3**   BOOLEAN SEARCH CONNECTORS

| CONNECTOR OR COMMAND | WESTLAW | LEXISNEXIS | OTHER SERVICES OR SEARCH ENGINES |
|---|---|---|---|
| Search for terms as a phrase. | "Place phrase in quotation marks." | Create a phrase by joining words in sequence without a connector. | Options vary by service; single or double quotation marks are common ways to denote a phrase. |
| Segregate terms and connectors within a search. | (Place in parentheses.) | (Place in parentheses.) | Options vary by service; parentheses are often used to segregate parts of a search. |
| Search for terms in the alternative. | Connect terms with **or**; leave a space between terms. | Connect terms with **or**. | Connect terms with **or**; other options vary by service. |
| Search for, or exclude, terms in proximity to each other.<br><br>(**n** = a specific number) | Term1 **+n** Term2 (Term1 appears a certain number of words before Term2.)<br><br>Term1 **/n** Term2 (Term1 appears within a certain number of words of Term2; Term1 can occur before or after Term2.)<br><br>Term1 **/s** Term2 (Term1 appears within the same sentence as Term2.)<br><br>Term1 **/p** Term2 (Term1 appears within the same paragraph as Term2.) | Term1 **/n** Term2 (Term1 appears within a certain number of words of Term2; Term1 can occur before or after Term2.)<br><br>Term1 **pre/n** Term2 (Term1 appears a certain number of words before Term2.)<br><br>Term1 **not /n** Term2 (Term1 does not appear within a certain number of words of Term2.)<br><br>Term1 **/s** Term2 (Term1 appears within the same sentence as Term2; can also be used to exclude terms, using **not /s**.)<br><br>Term1 **/p** Term2 (Term1 appears within the same paragraph as Term2; can also be used to exclude terms, using **not /p**.) | Often, proximity is indicated with **/n**, **/s**, or **/p**, depending on the service.<br><br>Some services use **adj** (for adjacent) or **near** (for nearby terms). |
| Search for all terms. | Connect terms with **and** or **&**. | Connect terms with **and** or **&**. | Connect terms with **and**; other options vary by service. |
| Exclude terms. | Connect terms with **but not** or **%**. | Connect terms with **and not**. | Options vary by service. |

can search for phrases. The way you indicate that terms should be searched together as a phrase will depend on the service you are using. In some services, such as LexisNexis, words in a sequence are automatically treated as a phrase unless separated by a connector. In a search for ICE CREAM, therefore, LexisNexis would search for the phrase ICE CREAM as a single unit. Other services automatically treat words in a sequence as though they have a particular connector between them. Westlaw, for example, automatically applies the OR connector between words in a sequence. A Westlaw search for ICE CREAM operates as a search for ICE OR CREAM. Other services may automatically apply the AND, ADJ, or NEAR connectors between words in a sequence. In services that automatically apply a particular connector, you can usually create a phrase using quotation marks or some other type of punctuation. You can search for a phrase in Westlaw by placing the words in quotation marks: "ICE CREAM".

Most searches contain several terms and several connectors. When the search is executed, Boolean logic will process the connectors in a specific sequence. In Westlaw and LexisNexis, the OR connector is processed first, followed by the proximity connectors (/N, /P, /S), the AND connector, and finally, the exclusion connectors (AND NOT, BUT NOT). It is important to understand this hierarchy of connectors to create an effective search.

If you executed a search for ICE AND CREAM OR SUNDAE, the search for the terms CREAM OR SUNDAE would be processed first. After documents with one or the other of those terms were identified, the search for the term ICE would begin. In effect, the query would be processed as a search for ICE AND CREAM OR ICE AND SUNDAE. This is probably not the intended search, and it could miss documents containing the terms you want or retrieve irrelevant documents.

Here, you probably intended to search for the phrase "ice cream" or the term "sundae." There are two ways you could have modified this search to achieve that result. One is by searching for "ICE CREAM" as a phrase, instead of connecting the words with AND. That would result in a search for the phrase "ICE CREAM" or the term "SUNDAE," which was the intended search.

Another way to vary the search would have been to segregate the ICE AND CREAM portion of the search. In Westlaw or LexisNexis, you can accomplish this by placing a portion of the search in parentheses: (ICE AND CREAM) OR SUNDAE. The terms within parentheses would be treated as a separate unit. Thus, the AND connector would apply only to the terms within the parentheses. In this example, adding parentheses would result in a search for the terms ICE AND CREAM as a unit, and then in the alternative, for the individual term SUNDAE. This again would achieve the intended search result. The chart in Figure

10.3, containing common connectors, lists them in the order in which they are processed in Boolean searches in Westlaw and LexisNexis.

The hierarchy of connectors, as well as the precise connectors and punctuation used to create a search, can vary in any given service. You should consult the help or search tips function when you are using a service for the first time to make sure you use the appropriate search commands.

### (2) Constructing a basic Boolean search

Once you understand the concept of Boolean searching, your next task is creating an effective search that is tailored to find the information you need. Constructing a basic search involves three steps:

- developing the initial search terms
- expanding the breadth and depth of the search and adding wildcard characters
- adding connectors and parentheses to clarify the relationships among the search terms.

In developing the initial search terms, you should use the process described in Chapter 2. Think about the problem in terms of the parties, any places or things, potential claims and defenses, and the relief sought. You may recall the example factual scenario in Chapter 2, which involved the issue of whether a hotel operator is liable in negligence to a guest who was bitten by a parrot living on the hotel premises. To develop a Boolean search on this issue, you might begin with the following words:

hotel negligence guest bite parrot

Having identified the relevant terms, your next step would be expanding the search. This can be done in two ways. First, unless you are searching for terms of art that need to appear precisely as written to be useful, you need to expand the breadth and depth of the search, as explained in Chapter 2. Expanding the breadth of the search involves generating synonyms and terms related to the initial search terms. Expanding the depth involves expressing the terms with varying degrees of abstraction. Recall that a Boolean search is limited to the exact terms you identify. If an object, idea, concept, or action is expressed in a document using different terminology, a Boolean search will not locate it. Therefore, it is especially important to expand your search terms with this type of searching.

The second way to expand your search is to use wildcard characters. Wildcard characters substitute for variable letters within a word. Westlaw and LexisNexis use two wildcard characters: the asterisk (*) to substitute for individual letters, and the exclamation point (!) to substitute for variable word endings. Thus, in the example above, you might change NEGLIGENCE to NEGLIGEN! to expand the search to include negligence, negligent, negligently, and any other variation on the word.

Although many services use wildcard characters, the functions of the characters are not standard. For example, the asterisk (*) in some services is used for variable word endings, not the exclamation point (!). You should review the search commands in any service with which you are unfamiliar. In addition, some services will not search for plurals, which means you need to use wildcard characters to capture them, e.g., hotel! for hotel or hotels, wom*n for woman or women. Both Westlaw and LexisNexis will search for plural forms of words automatically if they end in "s" or "es." Westlaw will also automatically search for irregular plurals, such as "mice" or "children," but LexisNexis will not.

The example search might be expanded in the following ways:

hotel motel inn! lodg! negligen!
guest visitor tourist bit! peck! parrot bird animal

Now that a series of terms has been developed and expanded, the next step is identifying the appropriate relationships among the terms using connectors and, if appropriate, parentheses. The closer the connections you require among the terms, the more restrictive the search will be, and the broader the connections, the more open the search will be. For example, the AND connector, which requires only that both words appear somewhere within the same document, will retrieve more documents than a proximity connector such as /P, which requires the words to appear within the same paragraph. Parentheses should be used to group categories of terms that you want to search together.

In the example search, the terms might be connected as follows:

(hotel or motel or inn! or lodg!) /p
negligen! /p (guest or visitor or tourist) and
(bit! or peck! /s parrot or bird or animal)

The parentheses group related terms together within the search. Thus, the terms relating to the premises (hotel, motel, inn, etc.) will be searched together, as will the terms relating to the injured party and the nature of the injury. The query will then proceed to the relationships among the groups of terms (within the same paragraph, sentence, or document).

The /P proximity connector is used in the example search to connect the terms relating to the premises, the legal theory, and the injured party. Hotels can be involved in many types of claims, so requiring the premises terms to appear within the same paragraph as the legal theory (NEGLIGEN!) helps target cases involving hotel negligence. Because hotels can be subject to liability in negligence to many parties, requiring terms relating to the injured party to occur within the same paragraph also helps focus the search. By contrast, the terms relating to the parrot that bit the guest could occur anywhere within the document and still be relevant to the search. Therefore, the AND connector is used for that part of the search.

### (3) Constructing a more sophisticated search

In addition to allowing you to search for terms within the body of a document, some services will allow you to limit your search to individual components of the document, such as words in the title, the name of the author, or the date of the document. Although you will not always use this search option, it is an important feature to understand.

In Westlaw, the document components are called "fields"; in Lexis-Nexis, they are called "segments." Both services will allow you to add field or segment restrictions using menu options or by typing commands into the search. The chart in Figure 10.4 sets out some of the more common fields and segments recognized in Westlaw and LexisNexis.

In the example search, the search results could be limited to cases from a particular jurisdiction or time period. In the hypothetical set out in Chapter 2, the hotel was located in Puerto Rico. Therefore, you might want to limit your search to cases from courts in Puerto Rico. You could do that in Westlaw by choosing the option for "Court" under the "Fields" section on the search screen or typing the field command CO for court, and then typing the search terms in parentheses:

> (hotel or motel or inn! or lodg!) /p
> negligen! /p (guest or visitor or tourist) and
> (bit! or peck! /s parrot or bird or animal)
> and co("puerto rico")

The same connectors and commands that apply to other Boolean searches also apply to field and segment searches. Therefore, in the Westlaw search above, "Puerto Rico" is placed in quotation marks so that Westlaw will treat it as a phrase. Without quotation marks, Westlaw would search for PUERTO OR RICO.

As another example, you can search for a document by name or title by limiting the search to terms within the name or title. If you wanted to search for the United States Supreme Court case of *Roe v. Wade*, you could search in LexisNexis using the query ROE AND WADE. This search, however, would retrieve every case within the database that ever mentioned *Roe v. Wade*, which could be hundreds of cases. The search would be more successful with a segment restriction. A search for NAME(ROE AND WADE) would limit the search to

**FIGURE 10.4**   FIELD AND SEGMENT COMMANDS IN WESTLAW AND LEXISNEXIS

| DOCUMENT COMPONENT | WESTLAW FIELD COMMAND | LEXISNEXIS SEGMENT COMMAND |
| --- | --- | --- |
| title | TI | NAME |
| author | AU | AUTHOR |
| date | The Westlaw search screen contains a separate section for date restrictions. | The LexisNexis search screen contains a separate section for date restrictions. |
| attorney | AT | COUNSEL |
| court | CO | COURT |
| opinions written by a particular judge | JU (retrieves any opinion written by that judge) | WRITTENBY (retrieves any opinion written by that judge)<br><br>OPINIONBY (retrieves majority or plurality opinions)<br><br>CONCURBY (retrieves concurring opinions)<br><br>DISSENTBY (retrieves dissenting opinions) |
| terms occurring within a concurring opinion | CON | CONCUR |
| terms occurring within a dissenting opinion | DIS | DISSENT |

cases in which the terms ROE and WADE both appear only in the name of the document.

### b. Natural Language Searching

Boolean searching requires you to understand various commands and connectors, and as a consequence, can be challenging to master. Another way to execute a word search is to use what is called "natural language" searching. This is what many Internet search engines use as their default search option. It is also available in Westlaw, LexisNexis, and other electronic research services.

With natural language searching, you simply enter your search as a question, without concern for connectors, parentheses, or wildcard characters. The computer converts the terms in the question into a search format to retrieve documents. In Westlaw and LexisNexis, natural language searching retrieves a fixed number of documents. In LexisNexis, you can manually increase or decrease that number by clicking on "Options" along the top of the screen.

To construct a natural language search, you begin by developing the initial query. The example search might look like this:

> Is a hotel liable in negligence if a guest is bitten
> by a parrot living on the premises?

Like a Boolean search, a natural language search will be limited to the terms you specify. Therefore, the initial search must be expanded:

> Is a hotel, motel, inn, innkeeper, or lodging liable
> in negligence if a guest, visitor, or tourist suffers a bite or peck
> from a parrot, bird, or animal living on the premises?

Both Westlaw and LexisNexis have additional options for refining a natural language search. Natural language searching can be helpful if you are researching an area of law with which you are unfamiliar. If you know some relevant terms, but are uncertain about how to construct an effective Boolean query, you can use a natural language search as a starting point. If the search retrieves relevant authorities, you can use them as an access point into other electronic search functions, such as the table of contents for a code or the Custom Digest or Core Concepts functions for case research. In addition, reading the authorities that the search retrieves can give you enough knowledge about the subject to construct an effective Boolean search.

Although natural language searching can be a useful way to get started with some research projects, it is not likely to be effective as your sole electronic searching technique. The program that converts the question into a search is not perfect. The results can be inconsistent, especially because you do not specify the connectors used to define the relationships among the search terms or add parentheses to group terms together. Boolean searching offers more flexibility in tailoring the search to your needs. You will generally get better search results if you work on becoming proficient in Boolean search techniques.

## 2. SELECTING A CATEGORY OF INFORMATION IN WHICH TO EXECUTE THE SEARCH

Once you have constructed a word search, you are ready to execute it in the electronic service you have chosen to use. As noted earlier, most services divide their contents into categories based on subjects or on the sources of information they contain. Therefore, you will need to select the category of information in which to execute your search. Selecting *a* category is not difficult. What is more challenging is selecting *the best* category to obtain the information you need.

Generally speaking, you should select the narrowest category that contains all of the information you need. For example, if you were researching Maryland statutes on-line, you should not choose a category that contains statutes from all fifty states. Instead, if possible, search a category that contains only Maryland statutes. Searching in an overly broad category requires you to sort through information that is not relevant to your search, making it difficult to determine whether your search was successful. Choosing a category tailored to your research needs will improve the efficiency of your electronic searching.

## 3. REVIEWING THE SEARCH RESULTS

Sometimes when you execute a word search, the results may not be quite what you expected. Specifically, you may retrieve too many documents, not enough documents, or documents that simply are not useful in resolving your research issue.

If your word search does not retrieve useful information, consider the following options:

- searching in a narrower or broader category of information
- subtracting less essential terms or expanding the breadth and depth of the search
- excluding terms from the search (AND NOT or BUT NOT can be used as connectors in a Boolean search or as part of a textual query with natural language searching).

In a Boolean search, you have additional options for revising your search:

- making the proximity connectors more restrictive or less restrictive
- subtracting or adding wildcard characters
- subtracting or adding field or segment restrictions.

You may need to browse some of the documents you have retrieved to see why the search was not successful. For example, if you conducted a Boolean search for cases involving diving accidents and included the term DIV! in your search, you could be retrieving cases concerning divestiture of assets or diversity jurisdiction in addition to cases about diving and divers. Browsing can also help you identify additional terms that should be added to your search.

If the search seems completely off the mark, you might not be searching in an appropriate category of information or for the correct terms. In that case, you may need to consult secondary sources to obtain background information on your research issue, and print resources organized by subject may prove easier to use at this stage of your research. Chapter 3 discusses the use of secondary sources. In addition, Chapter 11, on creating a research plan, discusses ways to improve your research results if your initial efforts prove fruitless.

## D. RESEARCHING EFFECTIVELY IN WESTLAW AND LEXISNEXIS

This section provides some information on how to retrieve and refine the results of a word search in Westlaw and LexisNexis. It also provides some techniques for cost-effective Westlaw and LexisNexis searching.

### 1. SEARCH RESULTS IN WESTLAW

To retrieve information using a word search in Westlaw, you must select a database and execute your search. Westlaw will automatically display the first page of the first document retrieved and will highlight the search terms within the document. It will also display a list of citations along the left side of the screen. You can view the text of a document by selecting it from the citation list. You can also adjust the display to increase the size of the document you are viewing.

The Term function provides another way to browse your search results. Term will move the cursor forward or backward to each occurrence of one of your search terms. Instead of browsing the full text of a document, you can use Term to jump to passages that are likely to have relevant information.

After you have browsed your search results, you may want to refine your query, which you can do in a couple of ways. The first is to edit your query, which allows you to change or add terms or field restrictions to the search. If you edit the query, Westlaw will execute the edited search within the original database you selected. You can also choose to run the search in a different database. If the search has retrieved too many documents, another alternative is to use the Locate command. Locate allows you to search for terms within the documents retrieved in the initial query. In effect, it operates as a search within a search. A Locate request can be submitted using Boolean or natural language searching. Once you have executed a Locate request, the citation list will show only the documents containing the Locate term(s), and the Term function will move the cursor to the Locate term(s). An example of a Westlaw search result screen appears in Figure 10.5.

**FIGURE 10.5** WESTLAW SEARCH RESULTS SCREEN

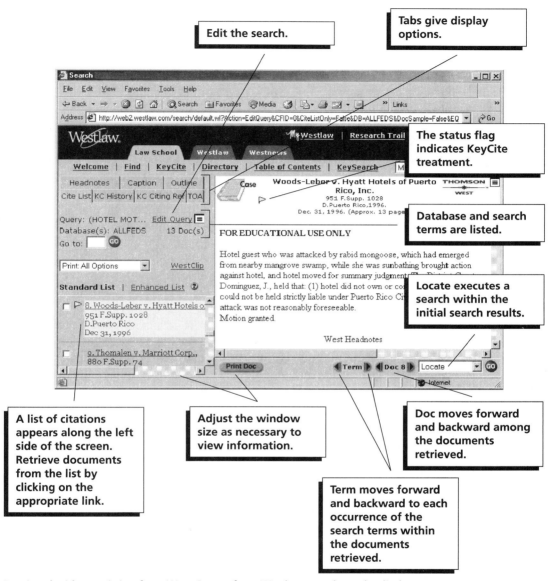

Reprinted with permission from West Group, from Westlaw, search results display.

### 2. SEARCH RESULTS IN LEXISNEXIS

Word searching in LexisNexis requires you to select a source in which to search. After you select a source, you can execute a Boolean or natural language search.

Once you have executed your search, LexisNexis offers three options for viewing the results: Full, KWIC, and Cite. Full retrieves the full text of each document. KWIC displays portions of the document containing your search terms, along with the immediately surrounding text. In both Full and KWIC formats, your search terms will be highlighted. When you are viewing a document in Full or KWIC, you can move to the previous or next document using the arrows above the title of the document, and you can use Term to move to each occurrence of one of your search terms. Cite displays a list of citations to the documents retrieved by the search. From the citation list, you can view individual documents in Full or KWIC format by clicking on the citation.

LexisNexis offers several ways to refine your search results if necessary. One way is by editing the initial search. Another option is the FOCUS function, which is similar to Locate in Westlaw. By selecting FOCUS, you can search for new terms within the documents retrieved by the initial search.

LexisNexis also has a search function called More Like This. You may be familiar with this function if you have used other Internet search engines. This function creates a new search using terms within a document you have retrieved. Thus, if you found a document that was especially helpful, the More Like This function would allow you to specify key terms from the document and use them to conduct another search in the same or another source. A related search option is More Like Selected Text. This option allows you to select terms from a document to use as a search in the same or another source. An example of a search result screen displaying a document in Full format appears in Figure 10.6.

### 3. COST-EFFECTIVE SEARCHING IN WESTLAW AND LEXISNEXIS

If you conduct research in Westlaw or LexisNexis, advance planning will allow you to take advantage of strategies to make your research as cost-effective as possible:

- Construct word searches and plan your research path in advance.
- Use research assistance provided by Westlaw and LexisNexis.
- Execute your searches in a way that takes into account the way you are being billed.
- Determine charges for printing or downloading information.

The strategies discussed here can be applied to other fee-based services as well.

**FIGURE 10.6** LEXISNEXIS SEARCH RESULTS SCREEN

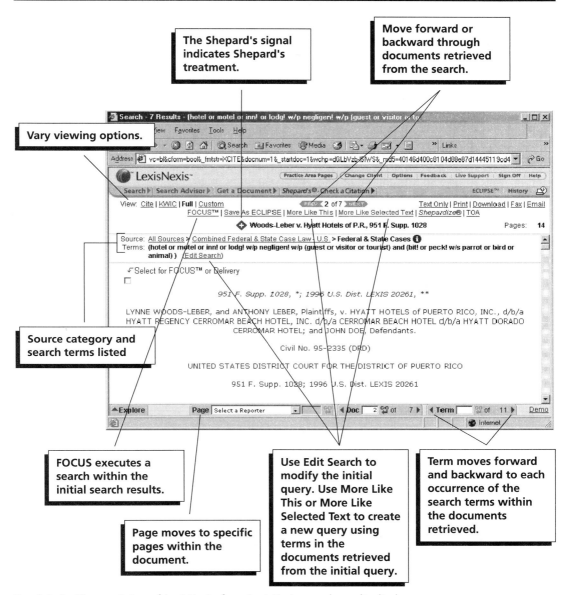

The Shepard's signal indicates Shepard's treatment.

Move forward or backward through documents retrieved from the search.

Vary viewing options.

Source category and search terms listed

FOCUS executes a search within the initial search results.

Page moves to specific pages within the document.

Use Edit Search to modify the initial query. Use More Like This or More Like Selected Text to create a new query using terms in the documents retrieved from the initial query.

Term moves forward and backward to each occurrence of the search terms within the documents retrieved.

Reprinted with permission of LexisNexis, from LexisNexis, search results display.

### a. Construct Word Searches and Plan Your Research Path in Advance

One of the best ways to cut costs is to draft your word searches and plan your research path before you get on-line. No matter how you are being billed, a thoughtful search strategy defined before you sign on is more likely to lead to useful results. This involves writing out your word searches and deciding which categories of information to consult in advance.

Writing out your word searches in advance allows you to generate a list of terms and refine your search before you start incurring charges. Deciding in advance which categories of information you plan to consult will also allow you to search quickly and efficiently. Recall that searching the narrowest category that meets your research needs makes evaluating your search results easier, which in turn reduces the amount of time you spend on-line. In addition, Westlaw and LexisNexis charge a premium for access to categories that contain multiple types of authority, such as those containing all federal or state cases. Deciding in advance which categories have the most appropriate information for your search, instead of automatically searching in the premium categories, will make your research more cost effective.

Advance planning also makes keeping notes of your search process easier. As noted in Chapter 11, on creating a research plan, it is important to keep track of your research process as you search for authority. If you have written out your word searches and intended research path, you will not have to keep as many notes while you are searching on-line. Of course, you may change your strategy based on what your searches retrieve, and you will need to keep notes of your revised searches as you execute them. At a minimum, however, you should begin with a search mapped out.

### b. Use Research Assistance

Another way to cut costs is to use the research assistance provided by Westlaw and LexisNexis. Both of these services employ research attorneys to provide assistance to users. You can obtain live help on-line or telephone assistance through their toll-free numbers. If you are unsure about whether your strategy is likely to be effective, you may want to contact the provider for assistance. The research attorneys will help you create word searches and select appropriate categories of information to search to maximize your search results.

### c. Execute Searches to Account for the Billing Structure

Once you have signed on to Westlaw or LexisNexis, some search options may be more cost effective than others. If you are being charged by the amount of time you spend on-line, you want to work as quickly as possible to minimize your costs. In that situation, it is especially important that you draft your planned word searches before you sign on because you do not want to spend time thinking up your search once you have started accruing charges. You also want to execute your searches quickly without spending a lot of time browsing documents. It is often more economical to print a list of the citations retrieved by your search so you can review the documents in hard copy off-line. If it turns out that your search was not effective, you can get back on-line to try again.

If you are being charged by the number of word searches you execute, you will often be able to modify your initial search at no additional cost. In that case, when you draft word searches in advance, you may want to devise relatively broad searches, along with potential narrowing modifications. You can then execute the broad searches, browse documents on-line, and execute modifications to narrow the results if necessary. This will allow you to maximize your search results at a lower cost than executing a series of new word searches.

### d. Determine Charges for Printing or Downloading Information

Regardless of the overall billing structure for use of Westlaw or Lexis-Nexis, it is often more cost efficient to photocopy materials from hard copy available in the library than it is to print or download information on-line. Even in law school, you may be charged for printing or downloading. Therefore, whether you are at work or at school, be sure to investigate printing and downloading costs before you get on-line.

## E. CITING ELECTRONIC LEGAL RESEARCH SERVICES

Much of the information you locate through electronic services will also be available in print format. Both the *ALWD Manual* and the *Bluebook* require that you cite the print format if possible. This is not as difficult as it might seem. Many electronic services provide all the information you need for a print citation, including page numbers. For cases, statutes, and other materials available only in electronic format, the following rules apply. This chapter does not contain complete explanations about citing cases, statutes, and other authorities. More information about citing each of these types of authority is included in the chapters devoted to those sources.

### 1. CASES

Citations to cases available only in Westlaw or LexisNexis are similar, but not identical, in *ALWD Manual* and *Bluebook* format. *ALWD Manual* Rule 12.12 provides that the citation must contain the following three components: (1) the case name; (2) the database identifier, including the year, the name of the database, and the unique document number; and (3) a parenthetical containing the jurisdiction and court abbreviations and the full date. A pinpoint reference can be provided with "at*" and the page number. Here is an example:

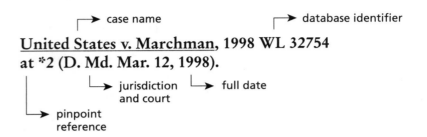

A *Bluebook* citation is the same, except that Rule 18.1 requires that the docket number for the case be included in the citation and that a comma appear before the pinpoint reference. Here is an example:

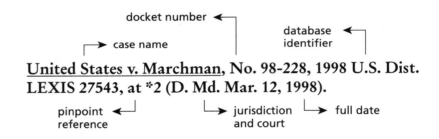

## 2. STATUTES

Statutory provisions retrieved from Westlaw or LexisNexis should be cited the same way print materials are cited, with additional information in the parenthetical indicating which electronic service was accessed and the date through which the service was updated. The examples in *Bluebook* Rule 18.1.2 show WESTLAW in all capital letters, whereas those in *ALWD Manual* Rule 14.5 show only the first letter capitalized. Otherwise, the citations are the same using either format. Here are two examples:

8 U.S.C.A. § 1423 (West, Westlaw through Pub. L. No. 105-220).

N.Y. Penal Law § 190.05 (McKinney, LEXIS through 1998 ch. 625).

### 3. MATERIALS AVAILABLE ON THE INTERNET

Both the *ALWD Manual* and the *Bluebook* discourage citations to information on the Internet if it is available in print form because of the transient nature of many Internet sites. If you are citing something available in both print and electronic form that you obtained from an electronic source, both the *ALWD Manual* and the *Bluebook* generally require that you provide the print citation, supplemented with additional information indicating the electronic source.

In the *ALWD Manual*, Rule 38 provides general guidance on citing electronic sources, and Rule 40 covers citations to information available only on the Internet. According to Rule 40, a citation to an authority available only via the Internet consists of up to five components: (1) the author of the item or owner of the web site; (2) the title of the item, underlined or italicized; (3) a pinpoint reference if one is available; (4) the URL; and (5) the date, which could be the date of the item, the date the site was updated, or the date you accessed the site, depending on the material you are citing. Here is an example of a citation to a news report in *ALWD Manual* format:

owner     title         URL

CNN, <u>Ukraine Mourns Airshow Dead</u>, http://www.cnn.com/
2002/WORLD/europe/07/28/ukraine.airshow/index.html
(July 28, 2002).

       full date of the news report

In the *Bluebook*, information on Internet citations appears in Rule 18.2. Rule 18.2.1 provides general guidance on citing information available on the Internet. The rest of Rule 18.2 (18.2.2-18.2.9) discusses how to cite specific forms of authority. To cite a source available only via the Internet in *Bluebook* format, you must combine the requirements of Rule 18.2.1 with those for the specific type of authority.

A citation to a news report in *Bluebook* format consists of the following five elements: (1) the name of the news organization; (2) the title of the item, underlined or italicized; (3) a parenthetical containing the full date of the report; (4) the notation "available at," underlined or italicized; and (5) the URL. Here is an example:

full date of
the news report

"available at"
notation

news organization      title

CNN, <u>Ukraine Mourns Airshow Dead</u> (July 28, 2002), <u>available
at</u> http://www.cnn.com/2002/WORLD/europe/07/28/
ukraine.airshow/index.html.      URL

The elements of *Bluebook* citations to other authorities available only on the Internet vary, depending on the information cited. For example, both the placement and the content of the date parenthetical vary in different types of citations. When you are citing information from the Internet, you should refer to the specific instructions in Rule 18.2.

## F. SAMPLE PAGES FOR ELECTRONIC LEGAL RESEARCH

Sample search screens for Westlaw and LexisNexis appear earlier in this chapter and throughout the text. Earlier chapters also contain sample search screens for several of the services outlined at the beginning of this chapter, including LegalTrac (Chapter 3), Thomas and LexisNexis Congressional (Chapter 7), and GPO Access (Chapter 8). Therefore, the sample pages in Figures 10.7 through 10.10 illustrate some of the services not highlighted elsewhere: FindLaw and Cornell Law School's Legal Information Institute.

**FindLaw organizes legal information by category.**

**FIGURE 10.7**   INTRODUCTORY SCREEN FOR FINDLAW

Reprinted with permission © 2002 FindLaw, Inc., from <http://www.findlaw.com>.

**Selecting the category for "Laws: Cases & Codes" brings up these options. You can choose a subcategory in which to execute a search.**

**FIGURE 10.8**   SEARCH OPTIONS IN FINDLAW

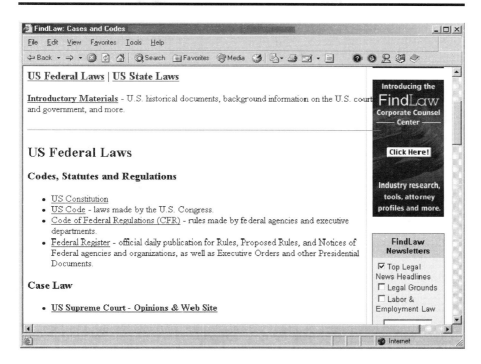

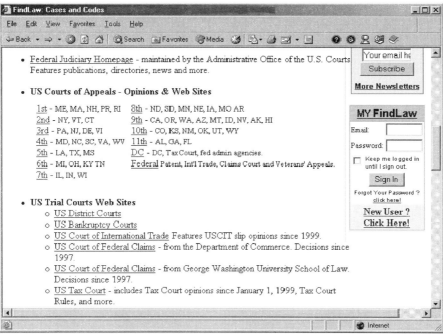

Reprinted with permission © 2002 FindLaw, Inc., from <http://www.findlaw.com/casecode>.

**Cornell Law School's Legal Information Institute contains a variety of legal information.**

**FIGURE 10.9**   INTRODUCTORY SCREEN, LEGAL INFORMATION INSTITUTE

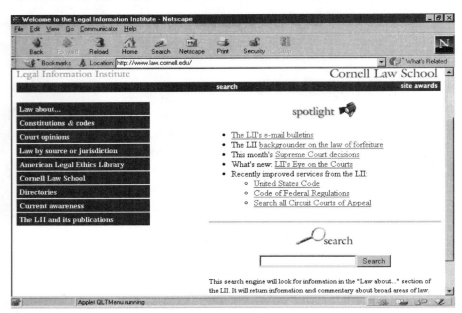

Reprinted with permission © 2002 Cornell Law School, from <http://www.law.cornell.edu>.

**The category for "Law by source or jurisdiction" will allow you to search for federal law. You can execute word searches in the subcategories of information.**

**FIGURE 10.10**   SEARCH OPTIONS IN LEGAL INFORMATION INSTITUTE

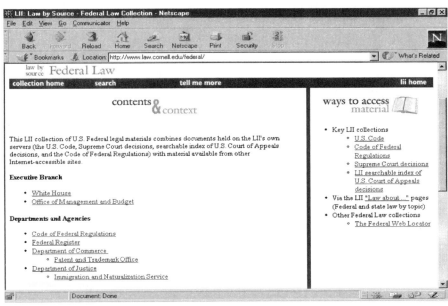

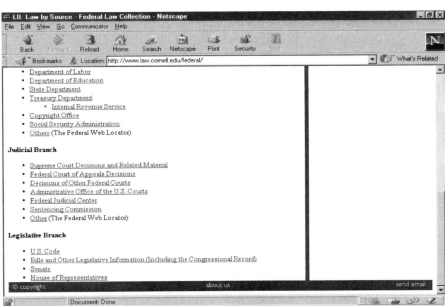

Reprinted with permission © 2002 Cornell Law School, from <http://www.law.cornell.edu>.

# G. CHECKLIST FOR ELECTRONIC LEGAL RESEARCH

### 1. SELECT AN ELECTRONIC RESEARCH SERVICE

❐ Consider the scope of coverage of the service.
❐ Consider the cost of the service.

### 2. SELECT A SEARCH TECHNIQUE

❐ Search techniques:

- Retrieving a document from its citation
- Browsing a publication's table of contents
- Searching by subject
- Conducting a word search

❐ For word searches, construct an effective Boolean search:

- Develop the initial search terms.
- Expand the breadth and depth of the search and add wildcard characters.
- Specify the relationships among the terms using connectors and parentheses.
- Use a field or segment restriction to target useful authorities.

❐ Natural language searching may also be available.

### 3. SELECT A CATEGORY OF INFORMATION TO SEARCH AND REVIEW THE RESULTS

❐ Search the narrowest category of information (database, library, file, or infobase) that contains the information you need.
❐ Browse documents or review a citation list to evaluate your search results.
❐ Refine word searches if necessary.

- Search in a narrower or broader category of information.
- Subtract or add terms.
- Make the proximity connectors more restrictive or less restrictive.
- Subtract or add wildcard characters.
- Subtract or add connectors that exclude terms.
- Subtract or add field or segment restrictions.

### 4. RESEARCH EFFECTIVELY IN WESTLAW AND LEXISNEXIS

❐ In Westlaw:

- Browse search results from the list of citations or using the Term function.

- Refine word searches by editing the search or using the Locate function.

☐ In LexisNexis:

- Browse documents in Full or KWIC using the Term function, or view a list of citations in Cite.
- Refine word searches by editing the query or using the FOCUS, More Like This, or More Like Selected Text functions.

☐ In both services, search cost effectively.

- Construct word searches and plan your research path in advance.
- Use research assistance provided by Westlaw and LexisNexis.
- Execute searches to account for the billing structure.
- Determine charges for printing or downloading information.

# CHAPTER 11

# Developing a Research Plan

A. Why create a research plan?

B. Creating a research plan

C. Finding help

D. Sample research plans

E. Research checklists

## A. WHY CREATE A RESEARCH PLAN?

When you get a research assignment, you might be tempted to begin the project by going directly to the library to see what authority you can find. In fact, searching for authority right away is not the best way to start. Thought and planning before you head for the library will help you in several ways. You will research more efficiently if you have a coherent research plan to follow. You will also research more accurately. Searching haphazardly can cause you to miss important authorities, and nothing is more disconcerting than feeling as though you came across relevant authority by accident. Following an organized plan will help ensure that you check all of the appropriate places for authority on your issue and will give you confidence that your research is correct and complete.

## B. CREATING A RESEARCH PLAN

Following a research plan requires three steps: (1) obtaining preliminary information about the problem; (2) writing out a plan to follow in the library; and (3) working effectively in the library. Each of these steps is discussed in turn.

### 1. PRELIMINARY STEPS

When you first receive a research assignment, you might feel like you do not know enough to ask very many questions about it. While this might be true as far as the substance of the problem is concerned, you need to determine the scope of your project by obtaining some preliminary information from the person making the assignment. Specifically:

### ■ HOW MUCH TIME DO I HAVE FOR THIS ASSIGNMENT?

The amount of time you have affects your overall approach, as well as your time management with other projects you have been assigned.

### ■ WHAT FINAL WORK PRODUCT SHOULD I PRODUCE?

You should determine whether you are expected to produce a memorandum, pleading, brief, or informal report of your research results. To a certain extent, this also will be a function of the amount of time you have for the project.

### ■ ARE THERE ANY LIMITS ON THE RESEARCH MATERIALS I AM PERMITTED TO USE?

As a matter of academic integrity, you want to make sure you use only authorized research tools in a law school assignment. In practice, some clients might be unable or unwilling to pay for research completed with tools requiring additional fees, such as LexisNexis or Westlaw research.

### ■ WHICH JURISDICTION'S LAW APPLIES?

This is a question the person giving you the assignment might not be able to answer. There will be times when the controlling jurisdiction will be known. In other cases, it will be up to you to determine whether an issue is controlled by federal or state law, and if it is a question of state law, which state's law applies.

### ■ SHOULD I RESEARCH PERSUASIVE AUTHORITY?

Again, the person making the assignment might not be able to answer this question. You could be asked to focus exclusively on the law of the controlling jurisdiction to answer your research question, or you could specifically be asked to research multiple jurisdictions. If either of those requirements applies to your research, you certainly want to know that before you go to the library. What is more likely, however, is that you will simply be asked to find the answer to a question. If the law of the controlling jurisdiction answers the question, you might not need to go further. If not, you will need to research persuasive authority. Understanding the scope of the assignment will help you focus your efforts appropriately.

In your research class, there will be many parts of the assignment that your professor will expect you to figure out on your own as part of learning about the process of research. In a practice setting, however, you might also ask the following questions:

### ■ DO YOU KNOW OF ANY SOURCES THAT ARE PARTICULARLY GOOD FOR RESEARCHING IN THIS AREA OF LAW?

Practitioners who are experienced in a particular field might know of research sources that are especially helpful for the type of research you are doing, including looseleaf or other subject-matter services.

### ■ WHAT BACKGROUND ON THE LAW OR TERMS OF ART SHOULD I KNOW AS I BEGIN MY RESEARCH?

In a law school assignment, you might be expected to identify terms of art on your own. In practice, however, the person giving you the research assignment might be able to give you some background on the area of law and important terms of art to help you get started on your research.

### ■ SHOULD I CONSULT ANY WRITTEN MATERIALS OR INDIVIDUALS WITHIN THE OFFICE BEFORE GOING TO THE LIBRARY?

Again, in law school, it would be inappropriate to use another person's research instead of completing the assignment on your own. In practice, however, reviewing briefs or memoranda on the same or a similar issue can give you a leg up on your research. In addition, another person within the office might be considered the "resident expert" on the subject and might be willing to act as a resource for you.

## 2. WRITING OUT A PLAN

Once you have preliminary information on your research project, you are ready to start writing out a plan to take you through the research process. The written plan should have the following components:

- an initial issue statement
- a list of potential search terms
- an outline of the sources you plan to consult, including the order in which you plan to consult them and whether you expect to use print or electronic tools for each source.

### a. Developing an Initial Issue Statement and Generating Search Terms

The starting points for your written plan are developing an initial issue statement and generating possible search terms. The issue statement does not need to be a formal statement like one that would appear at the beginning of a brief or memorandum. Rather, it should be a preliminary assessment of the problem that helps define the scope of your research. For example, an initial issue statement might say something like, "Can the plaintiff recover from the defendant for destroying her garden?" This issue statement would be incomplete in a brief or memorandum because it does not identify a specific legal question and might not contain enough information about the facts. At this point, however, you do not know which legal theory or theories might be successful, nor do you know for certain which facts are most important. What this question tells you is that you will need to research all possible claims that would support recovery.

Alternatively, you might be asked to research a narrower question such as, "Can the plaintiff recover from the defendant *in negligence* for destroying her garden?" This issue statement again might be insufficient in a brief or memorandum, but for purposes of your research plan, it gives you valuable information. Your research should be limited to liability in negligence; intentional torts or contract claims are beyond the scope of this project.

Although this might seem like an exercise in the obvious, the discipline of writing out a preliminary issue statement can help you focus your efforts in the right direction. If you are unable to write a preliminary issue statement, that is an indication that you are not sure about the scope of the assignment and may need to ask more questions about what you should be trying to accomplish.

Once you have written your initial issue statement, you are ready to generate a list of possible search terms. Chapter 2 discusses how to do this, and the techniques described in that chapter should be employed to develop search terms in your research plan.

## b. Identifying Research Sources

Once you have a preliminary view of the problem, the next step in creating an effective research plan is identifying potential research sources. First, you need to determine which research sources are likely to have relevant information. Then, you must determine the order in which you want to research those sources.

Chapter 1 discusses three general categories of authority: mandatory primary authority, persuasive primary authority, and secondary authority. You need to decide which of these categories of authority provides a good starting point for your research, and then, within each category, which specific authorities you should consult. The best way to do this is to begin with what you know, identify what you do not yet know, and determine the best ways to fill in the blanks.

For many research projects, your ultimate goal will be to produce a written document, such as a brief or memorandum, describing and applying primary mandatory authority relevant to the issue. If this type of authority does not exist or does not fully resolve the question, then you will also probably need to discuss primary persuasive authority, secondary authority, or both. Although this is not what you will be asked to do in every research project, this section will illustrate the process of writing a research plan based on this goal. As you will see, this process can be adapted for other types of research projects that you might be asked to complete.

The process of identifying what you know, identifying what you do not yet know, and determining how best to fill in the blanks can be applied to two components of the project: the search for primary mandatory authority, and the search for persuasive authority. You might not be able to write out a complete research plan for both components of the project before going to the library. At a minimum, however, you should try to map out your search for primary mandatory authority. If a search for persuasive authority becomes necessary, you can then rework your plan to include those sources.

### (1) Searching for primary mandatory authority

Beginning with the search for primary mandatory authority, the flow-chart in Figure 11.1 illustrates the process you might undertake.

As you can see from the flowchart, there are several places where you might consult secondary sources and several points at which you might make the jump into researching individual primary authorities, depending on how much information you have about your issue when you begin your research.

When you are ready to begin researching individual primary authori-ties, you need to decide the order in which to consult those sources. There are a couple of ways to do this. If you have consulted secondary sources, you should have a sense of whether the issue is a common-law issue governed by case law or an issue to which statutes, regulations, and other types of authority might apply. This information will help you determine the best starting point for researching individual primary authorities.

Once you have located some type of primary mandatory authority on the issue, whether through secondary sources or some other avenue, you can use that as a springboard to other primary authorities. As noted in the flowchart, for example, a case will contain headnotes that can lead you into the digest to locate other cases. The cases should also cite relevant statutory and regulatory provisions. Statutory annotations can lead you to legislative history, regulations, secondary sources, and cases. Of course, it is possible that the sources you consult initially will not lead you to other primary authorities. In that case, you might want to search independently in primary sources to make sure you have located all of the relevant authority.

### (2) Searching for persuasive authority

As you conduct your research, you might determine that you need to search for persuasive authority to analyze your research issue thoroughly.

**FIGURE 11.1**   FLOWCHART FOR DETERMINING YOUR RESEARCH PATH

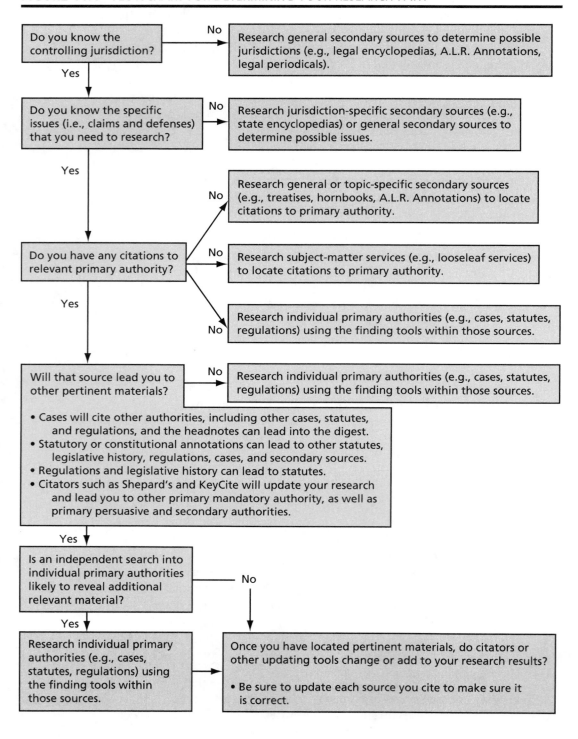

As in your search for primary mandatory authority, in your search for persuasive authority, you should begin with what you know, identify what you do not yet know, and determine the best ways to fill in the blanks.

The first thing you need to know is why you are searching for persuasive authority. Persuasive authority can serve a variety of purposes in your analysis of a research question. Here are four common reasons why you would want to research persuasive authority:

- When you want to buttress an analysis largely resolved by primary mandatory authority.
- When the applicable legal rules are clearly defined by primary mandatory authority, but the specific factual situation has not arisen in the jurisdiction. You might want to try to locate factually analogous cases from other jurisdictions.
- When the applicable rule is unclear and you want to make an analogy to another area of law to support your analysis.
- When the issue is one of first impression in the controlling jurisdiction for which no governing rule exists. In this case, you might want to find out how other jurisdictions have addressed the issue, or if no jurisdiction has faced the question, whether any commentators have analyzed the issue.

In each of these situations, you might want to research persuasive authority consisting of non-mandatory primary authority from within the controlling jurisdiction, such as cases or statutes in an analogous area of law; primary authority from other jurisdictions; or secondary authorities analyzing the law.

Once you have determined why you need to research persuasive authority, you should review the material you have already located. In your search for primary mandatory authority, you might already have identified some useful persuasive authority. Secondary sources consulted at the beginning of your research could contain persuasive analysis or useful citations to primary persuasive authority. Secondary sources often identify key or leading authorities in an area of law, and that might be enough to meet your needs. A citator might also have identified useful persuasive authority. If the authorities you have already located prove sufficient, you should update your research to make sure everything you cite remains authoritative and, if appropriate, end your search for persuasive authority.

On the other hand, you might review the results of your research and determine that you need to undertake a separate search for persuasive authority. When you first reviewed secondary sources and used citators, it might not have been with an eye toward locating persuasive authority. Therefore, you might want to take a second pass at these sources. In addition, the persuasive authority you ran across early in your research might not be the best material for you to cite; a more focused research effort could yield more pertinent material.

If you determine that you need to conduct a separate search for persuasive authority, your next step will be deciding the best research path to follow. The flowchart in Figure 11.2 illustrates several research avenues for locating persuasive authority. Your research path will vary according to a number of factors, including the amount of time you have, the resources available in your library, and the type of work product you are expected to produce. Therefore, the flowchart is intended simply to illustrate options that would be available to you, not to establish a definitive path for locating each type of authority.

One thing you might notice as you review the flowchart is that secondary sources play an important role in locating persuasive authority. Unless you know the precise jurisdiction from which you plan to cite persuasive authority, and the precise type of authority you need to locate (cases, statutes, etc.), beginning your search for persuasive authority in primary sources is not likely to be efficient in most cases. Secondary sources are key to determining which jurisdictions are likely to have relevant authority and which types of authority are likely to be helpful to you.

### c. Deciding Between Print and Electronic Sources

One additional decision you will need to make in formulating a research plan is whether to conduct your research using print research tools, electronic tools, or both. For many research projects, a combination of the two will be necessary for complete, accurate, and efficient research. Some sources can be accessed more easily in one format or the other. In addition, if an initial search for a particular type of authority is unfruitful, you might want to switch from print sources to electronic, or vice versa. For purposes of this discussion, electronic sources include LexisNexis and Westlaw, as well as CD-ROM and Internet resources that might be available in your library.

Generally speaking, you will want to use print research sources in the following circumstances:

■ **WHEN YOU ARE SEARCHING FOR MATERIAL NOT AVAILABLE ON-LINE.**
For example, although a number of secondary sources are available in electronic form, many others are not. Many treatises and hornbooks and a number of legal periodicals are not included in electronic research tools. LexisNexis and Westlaw in particular do not include all legal periodicals in their databases, and their coverage is limited to articles published after 1980.

■ **WHEN YOU NEED GENERAL INFORMATION ON A TOPIC ABOUT WHICH YOU ARE UNFAMILIAR.**
It is difficult to draft an effective word search if you have little or no information about your topic, and electronic subject searching is not

**FIGURE 11.2** FLOWCHART FOR RESEARCHING PERSUASIVE AUTHORITY

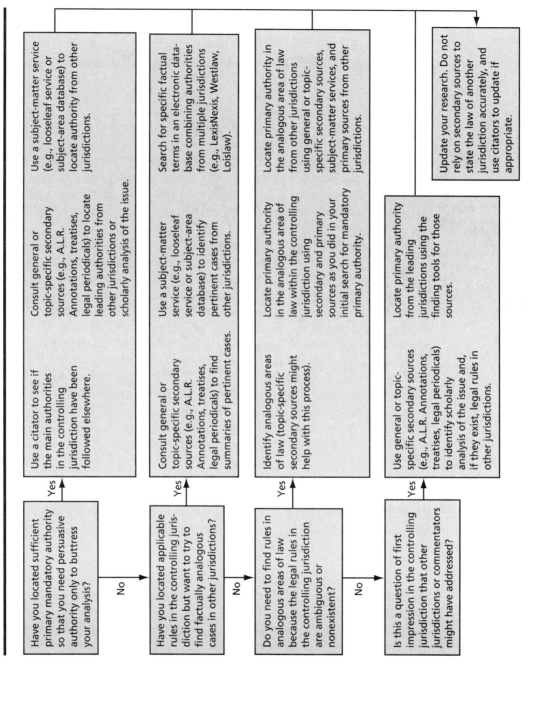

available in all services or for all types of authority. Searching by subject in print resources may be more effective in this situation.

■ **WHEN YOUR SEARCH TERMS ARE GENERAL OR THE SUBJECT OF YOUR RESEARCH INVOLVES BROAD CONCEPTS.**
A computer search for terms such as "negligence" or "equal protection" will probably retrieve too many documents to be useful because the computer will retrieve every document in the database that contains those terms. By contrast, these general topics could be useful search terms in a print index. The print index may subdivide these general topics into subtopics so that you can target pertinent authorities. It may also limit its references to key authorities under the topic, rather than referring you to every authority containing those terms.

■ **WHEN YOU ARE CONDUCTING STATUTORY OR REGULATORY RESEARCH.**
There are two reasons why researching statutes and regulations can be difficult to do on-line. First, an electronic word search will search only for the terms you specify. A word search that does not include the precise statutory or regulatory language will not be effective. A print index, by contrast, is organized by subject and will contain cross-references that can help direct you to the correct terms or concepts. Second, you will often need to review the complete statutory or regulatory scheme to analyze your research issue. This can be difficult to do through piecemeal research into individual code sections or regulations on the computer, although it has become easier to do through search functions that allow you to see outlines and tables of contents. Nevertheless, statutory and regulatory research is often easiest to accomplish in print.

■ **WHEN YOU NEED TO READ AUTHORITIES LOCATED THROUGH OTHER MEANS.**
It is difficult to read material on a computer screen. Although it is possible to print material retrieved from the computer, cost considerations could make that a poor choice, and the format of the computer printout might not be as easy to read as the print version.

By contrast, electronic sources can be a better option under some circumstances. As a general matter, many experienced researchers find electronic research most effective for locating one or two good "hits," or relevant authorities, which they can then use as an entry point into other research tools. Electronic research is most likely to be effective under the following circumstances:

■ **WHEN THE MATERIAL YOU NEED IS NOT AVAILABLE IN PRINT.**
The scope of the print collection will vary from library to library; thus, some material you need might only be available in electronic form. In addition, some subject-matter services are available only in CD-ROM

format or on the Internet. Even if material is available in print in your library, some material might be easier to access in electronic form. For example, legislative history research is often easier to conduct via the Internet using LexisNexis Congressional or Thomas than in the microfiche format available in many libraries.

■ **WHEN YOU HAVE UNIQUE SEARCH TERMS OR ARE SEARCHING FOR PROPER NAMES.**

If you have unique search terms, electronic sources can be a good search option because electronic word searches will search for the precise terms you need, whereas print sources organized by subject might not index those terms. Searches for proper names can also be accomplished effectively in electronic resources.

■ **WHEN YOU NEED TO UPDATE YOUR RESEARCH.**

Not all computer resources are more up to date than print resources, but many are. Updating your research can often be quickly and efficiently accomplished using electronic sources.

When these circumstances do not apply to your research, you will have a choice between print or electronic sources. The amount of time you have for your research, cost considerations, and your level of comfort with the tools you need to use will inform your choice about which research resources to use.

## 3. WORKING IN THE LIBRARY

### a. Keeping Track: Effective Note Taking

Once you have created your research plan, you are ready to go to the library to begin your search for authority. Keeping effective notes as you work in the library is important for several reasons. It will make your research more efficient. You will know where you have already looked, so you can avoid repeating research steps. This is especially critical if you will be working on the project for an extended period of time or if you are working with other people in completing the research. You will also have all of the information you need for proper citations. Moreover, if it happens that your project presents novel or complex issues for which there are no definitive answers, careful note taking will allow you to demonstrate that you undertook comprehensive research to try to resolve those issues.

Note taking is an individualized process, and there is no single right way to do it. Your personal preferences will largely dictate the method you use. Some people use a separate note card for each authority. Others use binders, folders, or pads of paper. Having said that, however, many people find their notes easiest to follow if the notes are organized around topics or issues, rather than by type of authority or individual source. Then within each topic or issue, specific information on each authority can be noted. Regardless of the method you use for keeping notes, you should try to keep each of the following items of information on each source you use:

| | |
|---|---|
| *Source or database* | |
| *Citation* | This does not need to be in proper citation form, but enough information for a proper citation should be included here. |
| *Method of locating the source* | This could include references to a secondary source that led you to this authority or the search terms you used in an index or electronic database. |
| *Summary of relevant information* | This might be a few sentences or a few pages, depending on the source and its relevance; specific page or section numbers should be noted, and all quotations should be marked clearly here to avoid inadvertent plagiarism later. |
| *Updating information* | Note whether the source has been updated and the method of updating, e.g., "updated w/'03 pocket part." |

This might not be the only information you need to note. For example, in case research, you might also want to note separately the topics and key numbers in the most important cases. At a minimum, however, you should keep track of these pieces of information. Once you find a method of note taking that is effective for you, you might be able to create a form or template that you use for each source while you are in the library.

As you work through your research plan, be sure to keep notes on computer research as well as print research. On the computer, it is easy to follow a series of links until you lose track of where you have gone. Although most computers have functions that will give you at least limited ability to retrace your steps during a research session, your computer might not save this information after you sign off. Therefore, it is important to keep notes on your electronic research while you are doing it.

There is a constant tension as you are working in the library between keeping written notes on the material you locate and photocopying or printing the material itself. Most people copy more than they need, and many students use copying as a procrastination technique, promising themselves that they will read the information later. Excessive printing or copying does not improve your research. Certainly, having copies of key authorities is important for accurate analysis, quotation, and citation. Facing a huge, disorganized stack of paper, however, can be demoralizing, especially because most of the information will probably prove to be irrelevant in the end if you have not made thoughtful choices about what to copy or print.

The fact is that you will not know for certain at the beginning of your research what should be copied and what should not. Only as you begin to understand the contours of the legal issue will the relevance (or irrelevance) of individual legal authorities become apparent to you. Therefore, you should conduct some research before you begin copying material, and as you delve into the research, you might find that you need to go back and copy material you bypassed originally. As you copy each item, make sure all of the necessary information for a proper citation is included, and make a note at the beginning indicating why you copied the item. You might also want to note directly on the copy the steps you took to update the source.

## b. Deciding When to Stop

Deciding when your research is complete can be difficult. The more research you do, the more comfortable you will be with the process, and the more you will develop an internal sense of when a project is complete. In your first few research assignments in law school, however, you will probably feel uncertain about when to stop because you will have little prior experience to draw upon in making that decision.

One issue that affects a person's sense of when to stop is personal work style. Some people are anxious to begin writing and therefore stop researching after they locate a few sources that seem relevant. Others put off writing by continuing to research and research, thinking that the answer will become apparent if they just keep looking a little bit more. Being aware of your work style will help you determine whether you have stopped too soon or are continuing your research beyond what is necessary for the assignment.

Of course, the amount of time you have and the work product you are expected to produce will affect the ending point for your research. If you are instructed to report back in half an hour with your research results, you know when you will need to stop. In general, however, you will know that you have come full circle in your research when, after following a comprehensive research path through a variety of sources, the authorities you locate start to refer back to each other and the new sources you consult fail to reveal significant new information.

The fact that a few of the sources you have located appear relevant does not mean it is time to stop researching. Until you have explored other potential research avenues, you should continue your work. It might be that the authorities you initially locate will turn out to be the most relevant, but you cannot have confidence in that result until you research additional authorities. On the other hand, you can always keep looking for one more case or one more article to support your analysis, but at some point, the benefit of continuing to research will be too small to justify the additional effort. It is unlikely that one magical source exists that is going to resolve your research issue. If the issue were clear, you probably would not have been asked to research it. If you developed a comprehensive research strategy and followed it until you came full circle in your research, it is probably time to stop.

## C. FINDING HELP

Even if you follow all of the steps outlined in this chapter, from time to time, you will not be able to find what you need. The two most common situations that arise are not being able to find any authority on an issue and finding an overwhelming amount of information.

### 1. WHAT TO DO IF YOU ARE UNABLE TO FIND ANYTHING

If you have researched several different sources and are unable to find anything, it is time to take a different approach. You should not expect the books to fall open to the material you need, and blind alleys are inevitable if you approach a problem creatively. Nevertheless, if you find that you really cannot locate any information on an issue, consider the following possibilities:

■ **MAKE SURE YOU UNDERSTAND THE PROBLEM.**
One possibility is that you have misunderstood a critical aspect of the problem. If diligent research truly yields nothing, you might want to go back to the person who gave you the assignment to make sure you correctly noted all of the factual information you need and have understood the assignment correctly.

■ **RETHINK YOUR SEARCH TERMS.**
Have you expanded the breadth and depth of your search terms? You might be researching the right concepts but not have expressed them in a way that yields information in print indices or computer databases. Expanding your search terms will allow you to look not only more widely for information, but also more narrowly. For example, if you have searched unsuccessfully under "moving vehicles" for authority

involving transportation equipment, you might need to move to more concrete terms, such as "automobiles" or "cars."

In addition, you might need to rethink search terms directed to applicable legal theories. If you have focused on a theory of recovery for which you have not been able to locate authority, you might need to think about other ways to approach the problem. Try not to become so wedded to a legal theory that you pursue it to the exclusion of other viable claims.

#### ■ GO BACK TO SECONDARY SOURCES.

If you did not consult secondary sources originally, you might want to take that route to find the information you need. The material on the issue might be scattered through many digest topics or statutory sections so that it is difficult to locate without secondary sources that compile the relevant information. In addition, the search terms that seemed applicable when you started your research might, in fact, not be helpful. Secondary sources can help point you in the right direction.

Another difficulty is that you might be looking for the wrong type of authority. Are you sure this is a question of state law? Might statutes as well as cases apply to the situation? Secondary sources can help you determine what type of primary authority is likely to be relevant to the situation.

Finally, secondary sources can help you determine whether you are facing a question of first impression. If the controlling jurisdiction simply has not faced this question yet, secondary sources should direct you to jurisdictions that have. If no jurisdiction has resolved the issue, legal periodicals might direct you to arguments and analogies that could be made.

## 2. What to Do if You Find an Overwhelming Amount of Material

The same research options that will help you if you are unable to find any material will also help you if you find an overwhelming amount of material. Making sure you understand the problem, of course, is critical. Rethinking your search terms to narrow your approach can also help. If you located information primarily using computer word searches, you might want to try searching by subject, using either print or electronic research tools, because searching by subject instead of by terms in the document might help you focus on relevant authority. Consulting secondary sources, however, is probably the most useful strategy. Synthesizing large amounts of authority is difficult. Secondary sources can help you identify the key authorities and otherwise limit the scope of the information on the issue.

Another consideration here is the scope of your research. If much of the authority you have located is secondary authority or primary persuasive authority, you might need to refocus on primary mandatory authority from the controlling jurisdiction. If the controlling jurisdiction has a sufficient amount of authority for thorough analysis of the issue, you might not need to cite persuasive authority. You might also need to narrow your scope by limiting the legal theories you are considering. If some are clearly more viable than others and you already have an overwhelming amount of authority, you might want to focus on the theories that seem to provide your client with the best chances of prevailing.

## D. SAMPLE RESEARCH PLANS

The research plans in Figures 11.3 through 11.6 are intended to help you develop a coherent research strategy in four of the common types of research problems: state common-law research, state statutory research, federal statutory research, and federal and state procedural research. These plans are representative samples of how you could approach the research process and may provide a useful starting point for your own research planning.

## 1. STATE COMMON-LAW RESEARCH

**FIGURE 11.3**   FLOWCHART FOR STATE COMMON-LAW RESEARCH

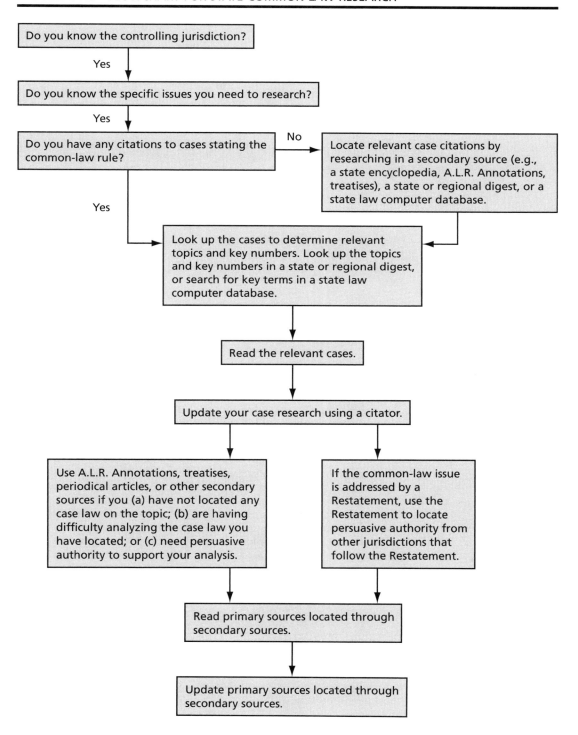

## 2. STATE STATUTORY RESEARCH

**FIGURE 11.4**   FLOWCHART FOR STATE STATUTORY RESEARCH

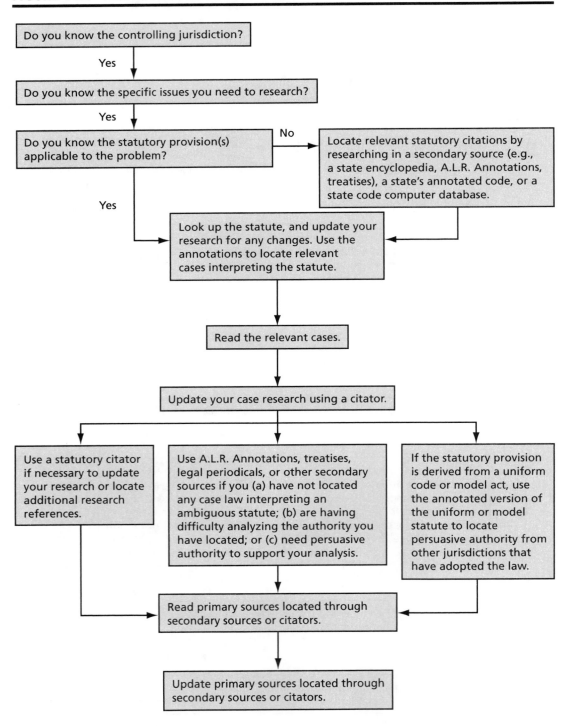

## 3. FEDERAL STATUTORY RESEARCH

**FIGURE 11.5** FLOWCHART FOR FEDERAL STATUTORY RESEARCH

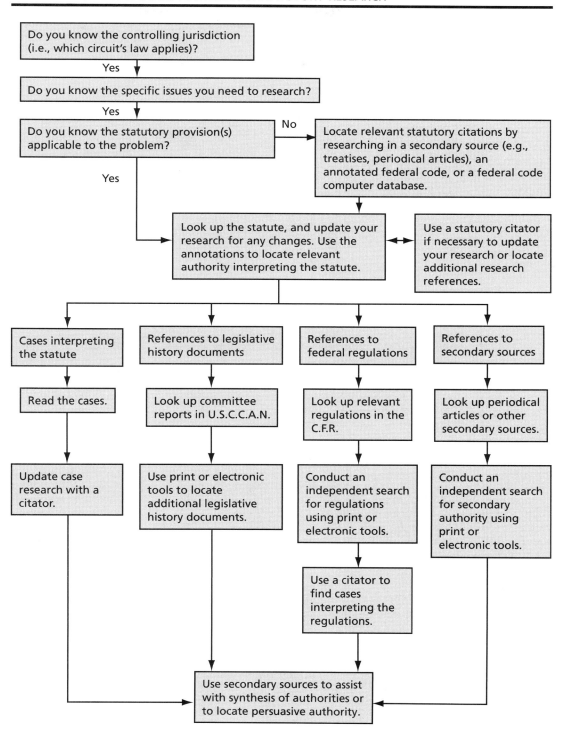

## 4. FEDERAL OR STATE PROCEDURAL RESEARCH

**FIGURE 11.6**   FLOWCHART FOR RESEARCHING RULES OF PROCEDURE

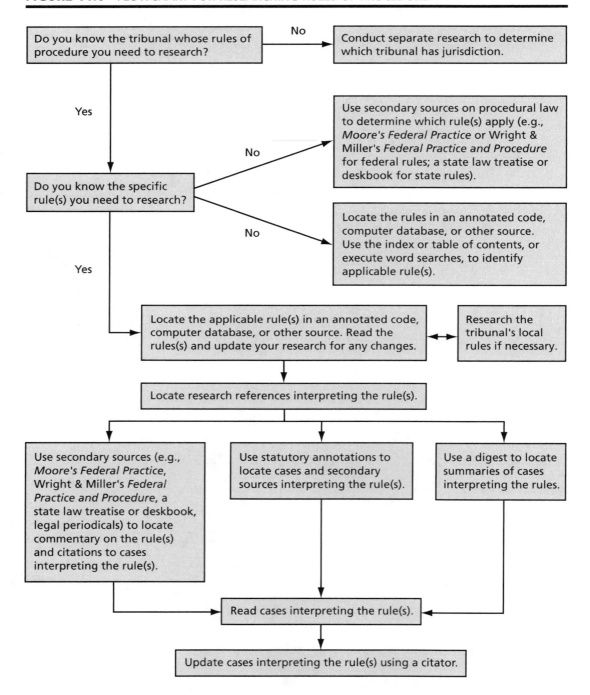

# E. RESEARCH CHECKLISTS

## 1. CHECKLIST FOR DEVELOPING AN EFFECTIVE RESEARCH PLAN

### 1. OBTAIN PRELIMINARY INFORMATION ON THE PROBLEM

❏ Determine the due date, work product expected, limits on research tools to be used, controlling jurisdiction (if known), and whether persuasive authority should be located (if known).

❏ If permitted, find out useful research tools, background on the law or terms of art, and whether other written materials or individuals with special expertise should be consulted.

### 2. WRITE OUT A PLAN

❏ Develop a preliminary issue statement.

❏ Generate a list of search terms.

❏ Identify the type and sequence of research sources to consult by identifying what you know, what you do not yet know, and how best to fill in the blanks.

- Locate primary mandatory authority first.
- Locate persuasive authority later, if necessary:

  - to buttress an analysis largely resolved by primary mandatory authority
  - to locate factually analogous cases from other jurisdictions
  - to make an analogy to another area of law when the applicable rule is unclear
  - to locate commentary or applicable rules from other jurisdictions on an issue of first impression.

- Determine the best mix of print and electronic research tools for your research project.

### 3. WORK EFFECTIVELY IN THE LIBRARY

❏ Keep effective notes.

❏ Stop researching when your research has come full circle.

❏ Find help if you need it.

- If you are unable to find anything or find too much material, make sure you understand the problem, rethink your search terms, consult secondary sources, and reevaluate the legal theories you are pursuing.

## 2. MASTER CHECKLIST OF RESEARCH SOURCES

The following is an abbreviated collection of the research checklists that appear at the end of the preceding chapters in this book. This master checklist may help you develop your research plan. It may also be useful to you while you are working in the library.

### Secondary Source Research

#### 1. LEGAL ENCYCLOPEDIAS

❐ Use for very general background information and limited citations to primary authority, but not for in-depth analysis of a topic.

❐ Locate information in print by using the subject index or table of contents, locating relevant sections in the main volumes, and updating with the pocket part.

❐ Use LexisNexis and Westlaw to access Am. Jur. 2d.; use Westlaw to access C.J.S.

#### 2. TREATISES

❐ Use for an in-depth discussion and some analysis of an area of law and for citations to primary authority.

❐ Locate treatises in print through the on-line catalog; locate information within a treatise by using the subject index or table of contents, locating material in the main volumes, and updating with the pocket part.

❐ Use LexisNexis and Westlaw to access selected treatises.

#### 3. LEGAL PERIODICALS

❐ Use for background information, citations to primary authority, in-depth analysis of a narrow topic, or information on a conflict in the law or an undeveloped area of the law.

❐ Locate citations to periodical articles by using the *Index to Legal Periodicals and Books* (ILP) and *Current Law Index* (CLI) print indices, or the LegalTrac and ILP electronic indices.

❐ Use LexisNexis and Westlaw to access periodical articles.

❐ Selected periodicals may be available on the Internet.

#### 4. *AMERICAN LAW REPORTS*

❐ Use A.L.R.3d, A.L.R.4th, A.L.R.5th, or A.L.R. Fed. for an overview of an area of law and citations to primary authority.

❏ Locate material in A.L.R. by using the A.L.R. Index, locating material in the main volumes, and updating with the pocket part.

❏ Use LexisNexis and Westlaw to locate A.L.R. Annotations.

### 5. RESTATEMENTS

❏ Use for research into common-law subjects and to locate mandatory and persuasive authority from jurisdictions that have adopted a Restatement.

❏ Locate information within a print Restatement by using the subject index or table of contents to find Restatement sections in the Restatement volumes, locating case summaries in the noncumulative Appendix volumes, and updating the Appendix volumes with the pocket part.

❏ Use LexisNexis and Westlaw to access selected Restatements.

### 6. UNIFORM LAWS AND MODEL ACTS

❏ Use to interpret a law adopted by a legislature and to locate persuasive authority from other jurisdictions that have adopted the law.

❏ Locate in print using *Uniform Laws Annotated, Master Edition* (ULA).

❏ Locate information in the ULA set by using the *Directory of Uniform Acts and Codes: Tables and Index*, locating relevant provisions in the main volumes, and updating with the pocket part.

❏ Use LexisNexis and Westlaw to access selected uniform laws and model acts.

## Case Research

### 1. SELECT A PRINT DIGEST

❏ Use federal, state, regional, or combined digests.

### 2. LOCATE TOPICS AND KEY NUMBERS IN A PRINT DIGEST

❏ Work from a case on point, the Descriptive-Word Index, or the topic entry.

### 3. READ THE CASE SUMMARIES IN THE PRINT DIGEST

❏ Use the court and date abbreviations to target appropriate cases.

### 4. UPDATE PRINT DIGEST RESEARCH

❏ Check the pocket part and any cumulative or noncumulative interim pamphlets.

❏ If necessary, check the closing table and mini-digests.

### 5. ELECTRONIC CASE RESEARCH

❏ Use Westlaw and LexisNexis to conduct word searches for cases.

❏ In Westlaw, use the Custom Digest function to search by digest topic and key number or the KeySearch function to search by subject.

❏ In LexisNexis, use the Search Advisor function to search by subject.

❏ Selected cases may be available on the Internet.

## Research with Shepard's Citations and Other Citators

### 1. LOCATE THE CORRECT SET OF SHEPARD'S IN PRINT

❏ Use a state or regional set of Shepard's for state cases.

❏ Use federal Shepard's for federal cases.

### 2. LOCATE THE CORRECT VOLUMES WITHIN THE PRINT SET

❏ Check the most recent supplement for the section "What Your Library Should Contain."

### 3. LOCATE THE ENTRIES FOR THE CASE WITHIN EACH VOLUME LOCATED IN STEP 2

### 4. INTERPRET THE ENTRIES

❏ Case history appears first, followed by citing sources.

❏ History and treatment codes signal how the history cases and citing sources treated the original case.

❏ Headnote references signal the proposition for which a citing source refers to the original case.

### 5. CHECK CASE CITATIONS ELECTRONICALLY

❏ To Shepardize a case in LexisNexis, enter the citation in Shepard's and interpret the entries as in Step 4.

❏ In Westlaw, use KeyCite by entering the citation.

## Statutory Research

### 1. LOCATE A STATUTE

❏ Use a subject index, popular name table, or for federal statutes, the conversion tables.

❏ Use LexisNexis and Westlaw to access state and federal statutes.

❒ On the Internet, locate statutes on government or general legal research web sites.

### 2. READ THE STATUTE AND ACCOMPANYING ANNOTATIONS

### 3. UPDATE PRINT RESEARCH

❒ Check the pocket part and any cumulative or noncumulative supplements.

### 4. SPECIAL NOTES

❒ In U.S.C.A., update entries to the popular name and conversion tables in the noncumulative supplements.

❒ In state codes, check for additional updating tools.

❒ In state or federal statutory research, update or find research references using Shepard's in print or in LexisNexis or KeyCite in Westlaw.

❒ In Internet research, check the date of the statute and update your research accordingly.

## Federal Legislative History Research

### 1. IDENTIFY THE SCOPE OF YOUR RESEARCH

❒ Determine whether you need to find the history of a particular statute or material on a general subject.

### 2. LOCATE A COMPILED LEGISLATIVE HISTORY

❒ Use the library's on-line catalog; Johnson, *Sources of Compiled Legislative Histories*; or Reams, *Federal Legislative Histories*.

### 3. LOCATE COMMITTEE REPORTS IN U.S.C.C.A.N.

❒ Use annotations in U.S.C.A. to locate cross-references to U.S.-C.C.A.N.

### 4. LOCATE COMPLETE LEGISLATIVE HISTORIES IN THE CIS MICROFICHE SET

❒ Use the Legislative Histories volumes or Index and Abstracts.

### 5. LOCATE FLOOR DEBATES IN THE *CONGRESSIONAL RECORD* USING PRINT SOURCES

❒ Locate references to floor debates using the CIS Legislative Histories volumes or reports reprinted in U.S.C.C.A.N.

❒ Use the *Congressional Record* index to search by subject or bill number.

### 6. SEARCH FOR LEGISLATIVE HISTORY ELECTRONICALLY

❑ Use LexisNexis Congressional, Thomas, GPO Access, Lexis-Nexis, and Westlaw to access a range of legislative history documents.

## Federal Administrative Law Research

### 1. LOCATE PERTINENT REGULATIONS

❑ Use statutory cross-references or a subject index to locate federal regulations in the C.F.R. in print.
❑ Use LexisNexis, Westlaw, GPO Access, or other Internet sites to access C.F.R. provisions electronically.

### 2. UPDATE PRINT OR INTERNET MATERIALS WITH THE LIST OF CFR SECTIONS AFFECTED (LSA) AND *FEDERAL REGISTER*

❑ Use the LSA in print to find *Federal Register* references affecting the regulation.
❑ Update in GPO Access using the electronic versions of the LSA and *Federal Register*.

### 3. UPDATE BEYOND THE LSA

❑ Use the *Federal Register*'s cumulative table of CFR Parts Affected to update from the LSA through the current issue of the *Federal Register*.
❑ Use GPO Access to search the *Federal Register* electronically to update beyond the LSA.
❑ Call the agency for more information.

### 4. USE SHEPARD'S IN PRINT OR IN LEXISNEXIS, OR KEYCITE IN WESTLAW, TO UPDATE YOUR RESEARCH OR LOCATE RESEARCH REFERENCES

## Subject-Matter Service Research

### 1. LOCATE A SUBJECT-MATTER SERVICE FOR YOUR RESEARCH ISSUE

❑ Use Table T.16 in the back of the *Bluebook*, a reference source such as *Legal Looseleafs in Print* or *Directory of Law-Related CD-ROMs*, or subject area databases in LexisNexis and Westlaw.

### 2. DETERMINE HOW TO USE THE SERVICE

❑ In print services, look for the "Overview" or "How to use this service" section.

❏ In CD-ROM services, follow the service's instructions or use Premise or Folio search commands.

❏ In LexisNexis and Westlaw, execute word searches.

### 3. USE THE INTERNET TO LOCATE INFORMATION ON THE SUBJECT

❏ Search subscription subject-matter services available on your library's computer network or publicly available web sites.

## Electronic Legal Research

### 1. SELECT AN ELECTRONIC RESEARCH SERVICE

❏ Consider the scope of coverage and cost.

### 2. SELECT A SEARCH TECHNIQUE

❏ Search techniques: retrieving a document from its citation; browsing a publication's table of contents; searching by subject; conducting a word search.

❏ For word searches, construct an effective Boolean search by developing the initial search, expanding the breadth and depth of the search, using connectors and parentheses, and using a field or segment restriction.

❏ Natural language searching may also be available.

### 3. SELECT A CATEGORY OF INFORMATION TO SEARCH AND REVIEW THE RESULTS

❏ Search the narrowest appropriate category of information.

❏ Browse documents or review a citation list to evaluate your search results.

❏ Refine the search if necessary.

### 4. RESEARCH EFFECTIVELY IN WESTLAW AND LEXISNEXIS

❏ In Westlaw, browse documents using the list of citations or Term function; refine word searches by editing the search or using the Locate function.

❏ In LexisNexis, browse documents in Full or KWIC using the Term function, or view a list of citations in Cite; refine word searches by editing the query or using the FOCUS, More Like This, or More Like Selected Text functions.

❏ In both services, use search strategies for cost effectiveness.

# Selected Internet Research Resources

## Federal Government Web Sites

FedWorld
*http://www.fedworld.gov*
> Provides access to a wide range of federal government information.

FirstGov
*http://www.firstgov.gov*
> The U.S. government's official portal to a wide range of government resources.

GPO Access
*http://www.access.gpo.gov*
> Contains Congressional bills, hearings, and reports, as well as a weekly compilation of Presidential documents. The *Code of Federal Regulations*, *Federal Register*, and *United States Code* are also included.

Library of Congress
*http://www.loc.gov*
> Search the on-line catalog of the Library of Congress, and locate a wealth of legal and general information.

Thomas
*http://thomas.loc.gov*
> The Library of Congress's on-line source for legislative information. This site contains committee reports, the *Congressional Record*, and other legislative history documents.

United States House of Representatives
*http://www.house.gov*
> The site for the House of Representatives.

United States Senate
*http://www.senate.gov*
    The site for the Senate.


United States Supreme Court
*http://www.supremecourtus.gov*
    The site for the U.S. Supreme Court.


The White House
*http://www.whitehouse.gov*
    The site for the White House.


## LAW LIBRARY WEB SITES

These sites can be used to search for a wide range of legal authorities, including state and federal cases and statutes, administrative materials, secondary sources, and legal news.


Cornell Law School's Legal Information Institute
*http://www.law.cornell.edu*


Emory Law Library Electronic Reference Desk
*http://www.law.emory.edu/erd/index.html*


The Indiana University School of Law WWW Virtual Law Library
*http://www.law.indiana.edu/v-lib/index.html*


Washburn University School of Law WashLaw WEB
*http://www.washlaw.edu*


## GENERAL LEGAL RESEARCH WEB SITES

Like the law library web sites, these sites provide access to a wide range of legal materials. Some can be accessed free of charge; others are fee-based services. Subscription services are not listed here. You should be able to access any services to which your library subscribes from the library's computer network.

## Free Services

All Law
*http://www.alllaw.com*

American Bar Association's LawLink Legal Research Jumpstation
*http://www.abanet.org/lawlink/home.html*

American Law Sources On-line
*http://www.lawsource.com*

CataLaw
*http://www.catalaw.com*

FindLaw
*http://www.findlaw.com*

Heiros Gamos
*http://www.hg.org*

LawGuru
*http://www.lawguru.com*

LRRX.com
*http://www.llrx.com*

Rominger Legal
*http://www.romingerlegal.com*


## Fee-based Services

Loislaw
*http://www.loislaw.com*

LexisNexis
*http://www.lexis.com*

VersusLaw
*http://www.versuslaw.com*

Westlaw
*http://www.westlaw.com*

## INTERNET SEARCH ENGINES

Search engines can be used to locate web sites on the Internet. You undoubtedly know of many general search engines. Those listed here search specifically for legal information, unless otherwise noted.

LawBot
*http://www.megalaw.com*

LawCrawler
*http://www.lawcrawler.com*

MetaCrawler
*http://www.metacrawler.com*
> Allows you to excute a search through multiple search engines simultaneously.

## OTHER WEB SITES OF INTEREST

Association of Legal Writing Directors (ALWD)
*http://www.alwd.org*
> Contains updates and information on the *ALWD Citation Manual*.

Introduction to Basic Legal Citation
*http://www.law.cornell.edu/citation*
> Provides tips on using the *Bluebook*.

Internet Archive Wayback Machine
*http://www.archive.org*
> Contains archived web pages. To see what a web site displayed on a date in the past, enter the URL for the site, and select the date.

Law.com
*http://www.law.com*
> Contains legal news, employment listings, and other legal information.

Lawyers Weekly USA
*http://www.lawyersweeklyusa.com*
> Contains legal news, classified advertisements, and selected court opinions. This site also has links to regional on-line newspapers.

Martindale-Hubbell
*http://www.martindale.com*
> Search for individual lawyers, firms, or government agencies employing attorneys.

University of Houston Law Center Law Library and Legal Research Guides
*http://www.lawlib.uh.edu/guides*
Explains legal citation. Also includes information on digest systems, Shepardizing, electronic research, and legal writing.

VeriSign, Inc.
*http://www.verisign.com*
Search for the person or entity that maintains a web site, using the domain name.

# INDEX

References to figures and tables are in **boldface**.